John McIntyre

The Holy Gospel according to St. John

John McIntyre

The Holy Gospel according to St. John

ISBN/EAN: 9783743329287

Manufactured in Europe, USA, Canada, Australia, Japa

Cover: Foto ©ninafisch / pixelio.de

Manufactured and distributed by brebook publishing software (www.brebook.com)

John McIntyre

The Holy Gospel according to St. John

PREFACE

ST. AUGUSTINE said of St. John's Gospel, "They are deep words that are spoken by him, not random words, nor such as may be easily understood." To speak clearly on such deep doctrine, especially to the young and with brevity, is no easy task; and even when one's best has been done, great attention is required on the part of the reader. If, when that attention has been given, much of what is here written still remains obscure, I will not join with the Saint in saying, "He that is not able to receive it, let him not charge it on me, but on his own dulness," but I do join with the Saint in saying, "If any one may not have understood because I have not declared it as I ought to have declared it, let him excuse the weakness of man."

To keep the volume within reasonable limits I have omitted all formal mention of many disputed points. For information on such I must refer the reader to fuller commentaries. Those most used in the present work were the commentaries of Knabenbauer and Meyer. The chief sources of the Introduction were Kaulen's *Einleitung*, Cornely's *Introductio*, Batiffol's *Six Leçons*, the 'Introductions' of Salmon and Davidson.

The grammatical hints will be made clear by a reference to Beelen's *Grammatica Græcitatis Novi Testamenti* and to Burton's *New Testament Moods and Tenses*.

JOHN McINTYRE.

ST. MARY'S COLLEGE, OSCOTT,
June, 1899.

CONTENTS

	PAGE
I. INTRODUCTION . . .	ix
§1. The Apostolic Ministry	ix
§2. Authorship of Fourth Gospel . . .	xiv
§3. The Author	xxvii
§4. The Fourth Gospel and the Synoptics .	xxxi
§5. Place and Time	xxxii
§6. Object and Plan	xxxiii
§7. Characteristics and Style . . .	xlvi
§8. The Text	xlvii
II. THE PROLOGUE (i. 1-18) .	1
III. FIRST MAIN DIVISION. THE MANIFESTATION OF CHRIST IN HIS LIFE (I. 19-xii. 50).	
1. The Testimony of the Baptist to the Deputation from Jerusalem (i. 19-28)	12
2. John's Testimony to the People (i. 29-34) . .	15
3. John's Testimony to his own Disciples (i. 35-42) .	16
4. Jesus, Philip, and Nathanael (i. 43-51) . .	18
5. The Sign at the Marriage-Feast (ii. 1-12) . .	23
6. The Festival at Jerusalem (ii. 13-22) . . .	26
7. Jesus and Nicodemus (iii. 1-21)	31
8. The Baptist again gives Testimony to Jesus (iii. 22-36)	37
9. Our Lord in Samaria (iv. 1-42)	40
10. Return to Galilee (iv. 43-54)	49
11. Our Lord at Jerusalem—Healing of an Infirm Man—Our Lord's Equality with the Father (v. 1-47)	52

CONTENTS.

		PAGE
12.	Another Manifestation in Galilee—The Bread of Life (vi. 1–72)	65
13.	Our Lord at the Feast of Tabernacles (vii. 1–39)	80
14.	The Results of Christ's Teaching vii. 40–53	89
15.	The Woman taken in Adultery (viii. 1–11)	91
16.	Christ the Source of Light and Truth (viii. 12–29)	95
17.	Discussion with the Jews (viii. 30–59)	100
18.	Jesus Cures the Man Born Blind (ix. 1–38)	106
19.	Jesus the Good Shepherd (x. 1–21)	113
20.	The Feast of Dedication (x. 22–42)	118
21.	The Raising of Lazarus (xi. 1–54)	122
22.	The Supper at Bethany (xii. 1–11)	133
23.	Our Lord's Triumphant Entry into Jerusalem (xii. 12–36)	136
24.	Retrospective Summary (xii. 37–50)	139

IV. SECOND MAIN DIVISION. THE MANIFESTATION OF CHRIST IN HIS DEATH AND RESURRECTION (xiii. 1–xxi. 23).

1.	The Washing of the Feet (xiii. 1–30)	142
2.	Our Lord's Manifestation to His Disciples (xiii. 31–xvi. 33	150
3.	Our Lord's Prayer for His Disciples (xvii. 1–26)	176
4.	The Betrayal and Capture (xviii. 1–12)	183
5.	St. Peter's Denials (xviii. 13–27	186
6.	Jesus and Pilate (xviii. 28–xix. 16)	189
7.	Death and Burial (xix. 17–42)	198
8.	The Triumph of the Resurrection (xx. 1–31)	207
9.	The Miraculous Draught of Fishes (xxi. 1–14)	215
10.	The Charge to Peter (xxi. 15–23)	220
	Epilogue (xxi. 24, 25)	223

MAPS.

THE HOLY LAND IN THE TIME OF OUR SAVIOUR	*Frontispiece*
PLAN OF JERUSALEM	*page* 1

INTRODUCTION

§ 1. THE APOSTOLIC MINISTRY.

WHEN the Apostles began their ministry they must have remembered that their Divine Master had written nothing. Instead of writing, Christ had done two things: He had preached the Gospel of the Kingdom, and He had founded the Church (Matt. iv. 23, ix. 35, xvi. 18, 19; Mark i. 14). The Apostles had been chosen and appointed to continue the work of Christ. In the discharge of that office two factors are prominent: the Apostles were commanded to "preach the gospel to every creature" and to be "witnesses unto Christ . . . even to the uttermost part of the earth" (Mark xvi. 15; Acts i. 8). The substance of the Apostolic preaching was therefore Christ—who He was, what He did, and what He taught. The warrant of their witness and testimony was the all-important fact that they had been eye-witnesses of what they narrated, and that they had lived and conversed familiarly with our Lord. Upon this fact, even apart from the Divine commission laid upon them, they solidly based their claim to be heard and believed (Luke i. 2; John i. 14, xix. 35, xxi. 24; Acts i. 3, 9; 2 Pet. i. 16; 1 John i. 1). They had seen and heard, and they spoke what they knew. How necessary it was that an Apostle should be an eye-witness is clearly marked in the narrative of the Acts, where Matthias is chosen to take the place left vacant in the Apostolic circle by the fall of Judas. St. Peter, in describing the qualities requisite in the candidate for the vacant post, lays down as an essential condition that he must be one "of these men who have companied with us, all the time that the Lord Jesus came in and went out among us, beginning from the baptism of John until the day wherein He was taken up from us" (Acts i. 21 ff.). It is this which gives point to the apology of St. Paul: "Am not I an Apostle? Have not I seen Christ Jesus our Lord?" (1 Cor. ix. 1); for St. Paul, who in this respect was at a disadvantage in comparison with the other Apostles, had in consequence to make frequent apologies (2 Cor. iii. 1 ff., xi. 22–xii. 13; Gal. i. 11–ii. 9).

The Apostles, then, were the chosen and authoritative witnesses of the life of Christ. Now, the events of that life were very numerous—so numerous, indeed, that only a selection from them was possible (John xxi. 25). Yet there were some events that could not possibly be omitted from any selection. Of these events the resurrection of Christ comes first; for, as St. Paul argued, unless the resurrection be true, all Christian teaching and all Christian faith are vain (1 Cor. xv. 12 ff.). The resurrection, therefore, was a subject constantly on the lips of the Apostles (Acts i. 22, ii. 32, iv. 33, x. 40, xiii. 30, 34, 37, xvii. 3, 18). But no clear knowledge of the resurrection is possible without a knowledge of our Lord's passion and death; the narrative of the death and burial consequently became as frequent as the narrative of the resurrection (Acts iii. 18, xvii. 3; Rom. v. 9; 1 Cor. i. 13, 23, ii 2, xv. 3; Heb. xiii. 12; 1. Pet. ii. 21, iii. 18, iv. 1). For this reason the preaching of the Apostles would be enclosed in the same broad outlines, and would show the same general features (Acts v. 42, viii. 5, ix. 20, xi. 20, xvii. 18, xix. 13; 1 Cor. i. 23, xv. 12). But outside main points such as these, the details selected from the great mass of material in our Lord's life would vary according to the purpose of the speaker and the needs of his hearers. The life of Christ would thus be cast into different forms, or viewed from different standpoints. Different selections would certainly be made at Jerusalem, Rome, and Antioch respectively. Of such selections one, like the Gospel of St. Matthew, would be intended mainly for Jewish converts; another, like the Gospel of St. Mark, mainly for Gentiles; and a third, like the Gospel of St. Luke, for such mixed communities as might be found throughout the whole field of St. Paul's missionary labours between Rome and Antioch (Acts ii. 22-44, x. 34-48, xi. 1-3).

The first centre of Apostolic activity was undoubtedly Jerusalem. The Holy City was a good centre, for, although the fixed population did not in all probability exceed sixty thousand souls, yet there was always there a large floating population of pilgrims from all the known quarters of the globe—from Mesopotamia and Syria, from Greece and Asia Minor, from Egypt and Rome (Acts ii. 9-11). The earliest group of Christian believers at Jerusalem consisted of unlettered Galileans (John vii. 48 f.; Acts i. 11, ii. 7). Shortly, however, many converts were made from among the Greek-speaking Jews. Many of these possessed a fair measure of Greek culture, and had something of the Greek keenness of intellect. The Hellenists—for so they were called—soon became a power in the Christian body. The names of all the seven deacons are Greek—Stephen, Philip, Prochorus, Nicanor, Timon, Parmenas, Nicolas (Acts vi. 5). The history of their appointment is in many ways important and interesting. We read, "In those days, the number of disciples increasing, there arose a murmuring of the Greeks against the Hebrews, for that their widows were neglected in the daily ministration. Then the twelve, calling together the multitude of the disciples, said: It is not reason that we should leave the word of God and serve tables. Wherefore, brethren, look ye out among you seven men of good reputation, full of the Holy Ghost and wisdom, whom we may appoint over this business. But we will give ourselves continually to prayer, and to the ministry of the Word" (Acts vi. 1-4). This phrase, "the ministry of the Word," is most significant. It does not mean mere preaching. The Seven also preached, although they had been appointed to serve tables and so to leave the Apostles free for the ministry of the Word. Philip preached and baptized in

Gaza; then "he was found in Azotus, and passing through he preached the Gospel to all the cities, till he came to Cæsarea" (Acts viii. 26-40). Nor did the Apostles consider such preaching as an encroachment upon their own appointed sphere of labour; on the contrary, when they heard of Philip's success in Samaria they sent Peter and John to crown the work and to confirm those whom Philip had converted and baptized (Acts viii. 5-17). Stephen, again, preached and argued so powerfully that his adversaries "were not able to resist the wisdom and the spirit that spoke" (Acts vi. 10). The Seven, like others, might preach, but the Apostles were ministers of the Word. The ministry of the Word, which the Apostles reserved to themselves, was not the mere preaching of doctrine, but the assured testimony of divinely appointed eye-witnesses. The peculiar Apostolic function was expressed by Peter and John before the council of the princes and ancients and scribes in Jerusalem: "For we cannot but speak the things which we have seen and heard" (Acts iv. 20). And St. Luke, who described the preaching of Stephen and Philip, called the preaching of the Apostles an attestation: "They testified and preached the Word of the Lord" (Acts viii. 25) —they testified, that is, to what they had seen and heard. This fact enables us to give a full and proper interpretation to that passage of St. Luke wherein he describes the sources of his information as those "who from the beginning were eye-witnesses and ministers of the Word" (Luke i. 2).

But while the original Apostles devoted themselves mainly to "testifying," the Hellenists drew inferences, and pointed out the necessary consequences that immediately flowed from the great facts of Christianity. We get an insight into the method of the Hellenists from the evidence given by the false witnesses against Stephen. They said, "This man ceaseth not to speak words against the holy place and the law. For we have heard him say that this Jesus of Nazareth shall destroy this place, and shall change the traditions which Moses delivered unto us" (Acts vi. 13 *seq.*). It is easy to surmise what was the line of argument which gave plausibility to such an accusation. St. Stephen doubtless argued, as St. Paul at a later date so forcibly argued, that by the redemption of Christ the works of the law were made void and of no effect (Gal. iii. 1–v. 4). Such a line of argument startled many even of the Jewish Christians, and it led to that hot controversy which necessitated the holding of the first Council by the Apostles at Jerusalem (Acts xv. 1–29). But the effect on Jewish non-Christians of the preaching of the Hellenists was twofold. On the one hand, many of the educated were deeply impressed and won over to the faith. "The word of the Lord increased, and the number of the disciples was multiplied in Jerusalem exceedingly: a great multitude also of the priests obeyed the faith" (Acts vi. 7). On the other hand, the anger of the Jewish leaders was furiously inflamed. Hitherto their attitude towards the disciples had been one of a somewhat mild, though envious, intolerance (Acts iv. 1–21, v. 17–40); but now their indignation passed all bounds. Not only was Stephen stoned to death (Acts vii. 56–59), but a general persecution was raised against the faithful at Jerusalem, and as far as Damascus (Acts viii. 1, ix. 1, 2, xii. 1–3). This persecution had, at any rate, one good result. It forced the active zeal of the Hellenists to occupy a wider field, and to spread abroad the method of studying more deeply the great facts and the great truths of Christianity (Acts viii. 1–5, 26, 40). It is to this deeper and more theological spirit that the Gospel of St. John appeals. This is why the selection of incidents from the life of our Lord contained in the fourth Gospel differs so much from the selections made in the other Gospels. "In the four Gospels," says St. Augustine, "or rather in the four books of the one Gospel, Saint John the Apostle, who on account of his spiritual understanding is compared not undeservedly to the eagle, has elevated his preaching higher and far more sublimely than the other three. . . . For the other three evangelists walked with the Lord on earth as with a man; concerning His divinity they have said but little; but this evangelist, as though disdaining to walk on earth, . . . soared not only above the earth and above the whole compass of air and sky, but even above the whole army of angels and the whole order of invisible powers, and reached to Him by whom all things were made; saying, 'In the beginning was the Word, and the Word was with God, and the Word was God.' . . . To this great sublimity of his opening words all the rest of his preaching well agrees; and he has spoken concerning the divinity of the Lord as none other has spoken" (In John Tract, xxxvi. c. 1).

§ 2. Authorship of Fourth Gospel.

The uniform tradition of the Church is that the fourth Gospel was written by St. John the Apostle. Even as early as the second century we find this fact attested throughout the Christian Church. It is expressly asserted by the Muratorian fragment, by Tertullian (c. Marc. iv. 2, 5), by Clement of Alexandria (apud Euseb. H. E. vi. 14), by St. Theophilus of Antioch (ad Autol. ii. 22), by St. Irenæus of Lyons (c. Haer. iii. 1)—that is to say, by representatives of the leading Churches of the world. Of these testimonies that of St. Irenæus is the most important. St. Irenæus tells us that he had studied in early youth under St. Polycarp, Bishop of Smyrna, who always taught the things which he had learned from the Apostles. But among the Apostles the only one actually named is St. John (c. Haer. iii. 3, 4). Now, St. Irenæus, doubtless repeating what he had learned from the disciple of St. John himself, says: "John, the disciple of the Lord, who also had leaned upon His breast did himself publish a gospel during his residence at Ephesus in Asia" (c. Haer. iii. 1, 1).

One or two simple remarks will show how impossible it is that the witnesses just quoted could have been mistaken.

(1) The witnesses belong to a period closely following upon that in which the fourth Gospel must have been written; they lived in widely severed parts of the world, and could not have been acting in collusion; they represent distinct lines of tradition and testimony. But they are

all found agreeing in the statement that St. John wrote the fourth Gospel. How came they to agree so perfectly in this matter? By the testimony of the fourth Gospel itself? This is unlikely; for the fourth Gospel, like the other three Gospels, is anonymous. Besides, the Fathers assign historical testimony as the ground of their belief. This testimony is the prime argument here. "How do we know that the works of Plato, Aristotle, Cicero, and Varro were written by these authors except by the continuous testimony of those who came after them? . . . How do we know the author of each book, except that each author declared it, at the time he wrote, to men who would hand it on? In this way the knowledge was transmitted from hand to hand; it took firm root in those that followed, and has thus come down even to our own times. But why speak of old books? Take the books now before us: should any one, after some years, deny that this book was written by m . . . where is the evidence for the fact to be found but in the information possessed by some at the present time, and transmitted by them through successive generations even to distant times" (St. Aug. c. Faust. Man. xxxiii. 6).

(2) Next, it must be borne in mind how first the Apostles and sacred writers themselves, and then the Church, took every precaution against falsification. The books of the New Testament were addressed to some Church or to some faithful of note and standing. They were kept and read in the particular Churches, were copied under supervision, and communicated to others in a duly attested form. When the Epistles were dictated the autograph signature of the author was attached as a proof of authenticity (2 Thess. iii. 17; Gal. vi. 11; 1 Cor. xvi. 21; Coloss. iv. 18). St. Paul not only sent his letters by special messengers, but also ordered them to be read to all the faithful, and then to be forwarded to another community (Rom. xvi. 1; 2 Cor. viii. 16-24; Ephes. vi. 21; Coloss. iv. 7-9; Philem. 10-12; 1 Thess. v. 27; Coloss. iv. 16).

The Church has always taken the like strict precautions. It has received only such writings as bore the names of Apostles or had been handed down as Apostolic. In case of doubt, the Church preferred incurring the risk of refusing recognition to genuine Scripture, to falsifying the Canon by a hasty acceptance of a book not fully accredited. St. Augustine expresses what has always been the mind of the rulers of the Church: "Holy Scripture was committed to posterity for the building up of our faith, not by unknown persons, but by the Apostles themselves. For this reason it has been invested with canonical authority, and therefore its truth must be made secure and indubitably certain on every side" (Ep. 82). The precautions taken in sending copies from place to place were very stringent. Special notes or letters commendatory, given to the bearers, were the chief of these safeguards. The Epistle of St. Polycarp proves that it was thought necessary to give such a note even with writings of less importance. For this purpose he sent a letter with the collection of the Epistles of St. Ignatius which he despatched to Philippi (cc. xiii. and xiv.) (see "Schanz's Apology," vol. ii. c. xii.)

We conclude, therefore, that it would have been impossible for a spurious Scripture to have secured at so early a date such a wide acceptance as was accorded to the fourth Gospel.

(3) The line of tradition can be traced back through still earlier writers, who, though not naming St. John, yet attest the existence and inspiration of the fourth Gospel.

(*a*) Tatian (d. about A.D. 180), once a disciple of St. Justin, but afterwards a heretic, wrote the Diatessaron, which is a harmony, or rather a digest, of the text of the four canonical Gospels, with the Prologue of St. John as an introduction. The freedom of the Diatessaron from all colouring of Tatian's later heretical notions seems to imply that it was composed while he was still orthodox. In any case, the contents of the Diatessaron prove conclusively that every word of the Gospels was then considered sacred, and that by the year A.D. 160 the fourth Gospel already possessed a fixed place on the Canon (see "Tatian's Diatessaron," by Rev. M. Maher, S.J.)

(*b*) St. Justin, the master of Tatian, carries us back a further stage. He frequently quotes both the Old Testament and the New; but his quotations are made freely, and are not always verbally exact. This is not surprising, for he wrote to non-Christians, and cites from memory the teaching of the Christian books. But there can be no doubt what were the Gospels St. Justin knew. The Diatessaron of his disciple would alone suffice to decide this point. But St. Justin himself affords direct evidence. He frequently speaks of the "Memoirs of the Apostles," written by the Apostles and their disciples (*i.e.*, Matthew, John, Mark, and Luke). He informs us that the "Memoirs" were called Gospels, and that they, as well as the writings of the prophets, were publicly read on Sundays in the Christian assemblies. He, moreover, repeatedly quotes from the "Memoirs" in terms distinctive of all four Gospels, and he reproduces all the characteristic features of St. John's doctrine of the Word. (St. Justin. 1 Apol. 5, 33, 52, 63, 64, 66, 67; 2 Apol. 6; Dialog. 48, 56, 58, 61, 62, 100, 103, 105, 107, 126, 128. See Dr. Ezra Abbot, "Authorship of Fourth Gospel.")

(*c*) Serapion (towards the close of the second century) and other ecclesiastical writers speak of a Gospel of Peter, which they condemn as heretical. In the winter of 1886–1887 a short fragment of this Gospel was found in a Christian tomb at Akhmim in Upper Egypt. The original work must have been composed before the time of Serapion. It may safely be dated at the middle of the second century or shortly after. The fragment gives the history of the Passion, from the scene where Pilate washes his hands, down to that where the disciples depart for Galilee, after the resurrection. A careful examination shows (1) that the Gospel belongs, by its particularities of language, to a period later than that of the canonical Gospels; (2) that it contains matter derived from all four Gospels, and, in the fragment, chiefly from the fourth; (3) that it depends on the four Gospels either immediately or through some form of Diatessaron (see Macpherson's "The Gospel of St. Peter," translated from Schubert).

(*d*) We must return for a moment to the testimony of St. Irenæus. His work against heresies was written between

A.D. 180-188. In that work he bears witness not only to the canonical authority of the *four* Gospels, but also to the fact that even then that authority had long been firmly established—so firmly, indeed, that he seeks everywhere for illustrative analogies to show that the fact *must* be so, and that it could not be otherwise. There are, he says, four zones of the world and four principal winds; and so, too, the Church spread throughout the world should rest on four Gospels, which breathe out immortality on every side. In the Apocalypse, again, the animals about the throne of God are four (Apoc. iv. 6, 7). Hence the Word of God, who sitteth upon the Cherubim and who was manifested to men, has four evangelists and a four-fold Gospel. These comparisons were, of course, not intended to be proofs, but only comparisons and analogies of what was already known to be immovably true (Haer. iii. 11, 8).

This testimony is of the greatest weight; for, on the one hand, St. Irenæus carries us back to St. Polycarp, and St. Polycarp to St. John, and, on the other, he is removed from St. Justin by only some twenty-five years, and even so, we can connect them by Tatian's Diatessaron. When, therefore, St. Justin informs us that the Gospels known to him had already secured a place in the Canon beside the Old Testament, and were read every Sunday in the Christian assemblies, it is quite evident that the Gospels known to him were the same that were known to St. Irenæus, and that both these writers had received them from a still earlier generation, that is, from the Apostolic Fathers.

(*c*) There are many causes which make it difficult to trace the Gospels in the writings of the Apostolic Fathers. (1) The writings that have come down to us from the Apostolic Fathers do not together make more than a few pages of print. (2) The labour of copying out the Scriptures by hand would necessarily have rendered the work of distribution somewhat slow. Even St. Irenæus spoke of many nations in his day who were Christians but still without written documents (Hær. iii. 4, 2). (3) Even when written documents were available the difficulty of reference was so great that many would be content with a substantial quotation from memory—there were no concordances, and manuscripts of Scripture were awkward in form, written without division into chapters and verses, and devoid of punctuation. (4) Those who had listened to the very voices of the Apostles would naturally mix much of what they had heard with what they had read. The safest guide, then, to the teaching of the Apostolic Fathers is found in the writings of those whom they taught, and who clung so tenaciously to what was handed down.

Now, in the immediately succeeding age we everywhere find evidence of four Gospels of a determinate form. These are known and received in every part of the Christian Church. They are contained in the ancient Latin and Syriac versions, and in the earliest Greek manuscripts. Can there be any doubt, therefore, that they have been handed down by the Apostolic Fathers?

Yet we are not without direct evidence from the Apostolic Fathers themselves. Papias certainly, and Polycarp almost certainly, knew the first Epistle of St. John. But as the fourth Gospel and the first Epistle were undoubtedly written by the same author, knowledge of the one is at least a confirmatory proof of the existence and authority of the other (Euseb. H. E. iii. 39). St. Ignatius's Epistle to the Romans has several marked coincidences with the fourth Gospel (see Rom. c. vii.), while the Epistle to the Philadelphians has clear allusions to it. St. Ignatius says, "The Spirit, being from God, is not deceived: for it knoweth whence it cometh and whither it goeth" (c. vii.; cf. John iii. 8); again, speaking of our Lord, he says, "He is the door of the Father, by which Abraham, and Isaac, and Jacob, and all the prophets enter in, as well as the Apostles and the Church" (c. ix.; cf. John x. 9). (See Cornely, vol. iii. p. 222.)

(4) Catholics did not stand alone in recognising the authority of the fourth Gospel. St. Irenæus informs us that the Valentinian heretics of the second century accepted this Gospel (Hær. iii. 11, 7). The theological vocabulary of Valentinus was derived from it; Heracleon the Valentinian wrote a commentary on it. Basilides (c. A.D. 125) the

predecessor of Valentinus (or, at least, the disciples of Basilides) agreed in this matter with Catholics and Valentinians. Celsus, a contemporary of Basilides, a pagan philosopher and a keen opponent of Christianity, by his attack on, amongst other things, some of the statements of the fourth Gospel, is a witness to Christian belief in it.

(5) Some of the objections urged against the Johannean authorship of the fourth Gospel are really an argument in its favour. It is objected that there are numerous points of apparent disagreement between the statements of the fourth Gospel and the statements of the other Gospels; between the style of the fourth Gospel and the style of the (Johannean) Apocalypse. We shall treat of these objections in the sequel; at present we insist upon them as an argument. Consider the facts of the case: an anonymous writing (for the fourth Gospel is anonymous) which seems seriously to differ from writings of acknowledged Apostolic authority, and from a work admittedly composed by St. John, is yet unanimously throughout the wide world attributed to him. What, in these circumstances, could have brought about such a consensus? Surely the weight of direct historical testimony for the Johannean authorship of the fourth Gospel must have been irresistible.

We have said that questions of authorship are properly decided by direct historical testimony, and we have shown that this testimony is absolutely in favour of the Johannean authorship of the fourth Gospel. But it will be interesting to search the Gospel itself for indications of authorship, and so to combine internal with external evidence.

The internal evidence of the fourth Gospel is in harmony with the external testimony already cited.

Although the internal indications of authorship vary in cogency, yet since they converge and strengthen each other they form a cumulative argument of great force.

(1) Not only is it claimed for the author that he was a witness of what he narrates (i. 14, xix. 26–35, xxi. 20–24), but the claim is put forward in language befitting the lips of an Apostle (see above, § i.), and perfectly agreeing with the undoubted language of St. John (1 John i. 1–3, iv. 14).

(2) The author is identified with "the disciple whom Jesus loved" (xiii. 23, xix. 26, xx. 2, xxi. 7, 20). Now, we know from the other Gospels that there were only three Apostles to whom this description could apply—Peter, James, and John. But when the fourth Gospel was written Peter and James were already dead (John xxi. 18, 19; Acts xii. 1, 2). Therefore the writer was St. John.

(3) The author is usually most careful to distinguish persons and mark them off clearly See his notes on Judas (vi. 72, xii. 4, xiii. 2, 26, xiv. 22), on Thomas (xi. 16, xx. 24, xxi. 2), on Caiphas (xi. 49, xviii. 13), on Nicodemus (xix. 39). Now, although the author narrates events in which St. John certainly appeared; although he describes many of St. John's distinctive traits of character; although he gives the names of other disciples—he yet not only fails to distinguish the Apostle from the Baptist, whom he calls simply "John," but he even suppresses altogether the name of the Apostle. This complete absence of St. John's name is a valid proof that the author is no other than St. John himself, who thus chose to veil his identity.

(4) A careful examination of the contents of the fourth Gospel discovers many points in every way confirmatory of the foregoing inference.

(*a*) Although the words of the Gospel are Greek, yet the author's sentences, the cast and form of his thought, his style, his ideas, and imagery are strongly Jewish. His mind is saturated with the history, the types, and prophecies of the Old Testament. This is, indeed, frequently quoted, and sometimes directly from the Hebrew. The author, moreover, shows a familiar and close acquaintance with all the varied elements of Jewish life—with Jewish feelings and habits of thought, with Jewish feasts and religious customs. Nor are all the matters with which he is familiar such as lie on the surface and easily offer themselves to the observation and descriptive power of a stranger; many of them belong to the inner circle of Jewish thought, and touch upon quaint points of Rabbinical scruple.

Thus, we notice the frequent use of Hebrew parallelism (iii. 11, v. 37, vi. 35, 56, xiii. 16, xv. 20, xvi. 20); of sentences imperfectly joined together, or altogether loose and in mere juxtaposition (i. 1–5, 10–12, ii. 9, iii. 19, vi. 22–24, x. 11, xv. 1–20, xvii. 2, 9, 11–25); the use of recurring clauses as in a psalm (iii. 15, 16, vi. 39, 40, 44, 46, 50, 51, 52–55, 59); the use of marked Hebrew idioms —Amen, Amen (twenty-five times), 'rejoiceth with joy' (iii. 29), "to go up" to a festal day (vii. 8, 10), the peculiar use of "cannot" (viii. 43), "$\dot{\epsilon}\kappa\ \tau o\tilde{v}\ a i\tilde{\omega} \nu o\varsigma$" = since the world began (ix. 32), $\tau\tilde{\eta}\ \dot{\epsilon}\iota\ \mu\iota\tilde{q}$ = on the *first* day (xx. 1), "son of perdition" (xvii. 12).

Again, Christ was typified in the paschal lamb (i. 36, xix. 36), the brazen serpent (iii. 14), the manna (vi. 31, 49), the water from the rock (vii. 37), the pillar of fire (viii. 12); of Christ Moses wrote, and David and the Prophets (i. 45, ii. 22, v. 46, xiii. 18, xvii. 12, xix. 24, 28, 36, 37, xii. 14, 15, 38, 40).

Further, the author is familiar with the details of Jewish life—baptism (i. 25), purifications (ii. 6, iii. 25, xi. 55), avoidance of legal defilement (xviii. 28, xix. 31), celebration of Pasch (ii. 13, 23), custom of selling at the Temple the animals for sacrifice (ii. 14), marriage customs (iii. 29); sentiments regarding Gentiles, Samaritans, and women (iv. 9, 27, vii. 35), regarding Abraham and the Prophets (viii. 52, 53), regarding the Messiah (i. 20, 25, 45, 49, iv. 25, vi. 14, 15, 30, vii. 27, 42, xii. 13, 34); the usages introduced by the Roman conquest (xviii. 29–31, xix. 1–12, 15, 19, 23), the power of the synagogue (vii. 32, ix. 22), the privilege of the people (xviii. 39), the feast of the dedication (x. 22), the proselytes (xii. 20), details regarding circumcision and the Sabbath (vii. 22, 23), details of the Pasch (xi. 55, xviii. 28, 39, vii. 37), the feast of Tabernacles (vii. 2), Rabbinical superstition and their contempt for the people (ix. 2, 34, vii. 49), the way of guarding flocks in Palestine (x. 1–5), the manner of embalming and of burying the dead (xi. 44, xix. 39, 40, xi. 38).

Even in these days of frequent and rapid travel such easy familiarity with the inner life of a foreign people is extremely rare; in the time of St. John it would have been practically impossible. It was far harder for a stranger to

INTRODUCTION.   xxiii

learn the spirit of Judaism than it is for a modern non-Catholic to learn the spirit and doctrines of Catholicity. Modern non-Catholic attempts to describe such common Catholic subjects as Purgatory, Indulgences, or the Infallibility of the Pope, give us an idea of the utter impossibility of a Gentile's doing what was done by the author of the fourth Gospel.

(*b*) The minute details of Jewish life familiar to the author of the fourth Gospel belong not to the Jewish life of the Dispersion, but to the life of Palestine itself. Thus, for instance, the Jews of the Dispersion would not have had that marked contempt for Galilee (i. 46, vii. 41, 52), nor have given the name of Jew exclusively to the inhabitants of southern Judæa (ii. 18, 20, iii. 25, vii. 1, xi. 7, 8). The topographical notices, no less than the details already given, mark the author of the fourth Gospel as a Palestinian Jew. He speaks of Palestine, not with the effort of a man describing a land which he had merely visited, or of which he had heard, but with the spontaneous and natural ease of a native. In this way he speaks of Cana of Galilee, a small town not mentioned by any earlier writer (ii. 1, 11, iv. 46, xxi. 2), of Capharnaum with its elevation lower than that of Cana (ii. 12), of Bethania beyond the Jordan (i. 28), and Bethania near Jerusalem (xi. 18), of Sichar (Sychar) in Samaria, and Jacob's well, which is deep (iv. 5, 6, 11), of the Sea of Galilee, "which is that of Tiberias," with its extent and bordering towns (vi. 1, 17, 19), of the pond called Probatica or Bethsaida (Bethesda), with its five porches (v. 2), of the treasury in the Temple (viii. 20), of Solomon's porch (x. 23), of the pool of Siloe (ix. 7), of the brook Cedron and the garden of Gethsemani (xviii. 1), of Golgotha (xix. 17), of Bethsaida in Galilee (xii. 21).

(*c*) Internal evidence further shows that the author lived in the first century. The religious and social circumstances, the controversies, the interests, the hopes and feelings amid which the author moves, all belong to the first century. His interest is fresh in Herod, Pilate, Cæsar, the Pharisees, the priests and the temple worship at Jerusalem, with its cycle of feasts. Some of the elements described may doubtless be found in other centuries; but they belong to the first century exclusively in their combination and in their freedom from the elements that appear at other periods of history. Thus, the author not only has no interest in, but he seems never to have even heard of, questions which had an important place in the religious life of the second century. His doctrine, it is true, overturns the teaching of the second century Gnostics, but it does so not controversially, but simply by the inherent antagonism that exists between truth and error.

(*d*) The author's claim to be one of the original eye-witnesses is corroborated by an examination of the Gospel itself. The writer shows a close familiarity with details which could have been known only to one most intimate with Christ and the Apostles, and which no one else would have even dreamed of. He knows the minutest particulars of time, of place, and of person. A marriage takes place in Cana of Galilee on the third day (ii. 1), the disciples go down to the sea in the evening (vi. 16), Jesus comes to Bethania six days before the Pasch (xii. 1), Pilate brings our Lord forth on the parasceve of the Pasch, about the sixth hour (xix. 14), Nicodemus comes to Jesus by night (iii. 2); one discourse is delivered in Bethania on the banks of the Jordan (i. 28), another at Jacob's well (iv. 6), another in the synagogue of Capharnaum just before the Pasch (vi. 4, 60), another on the last and great day of the festivity (vii. 37), another in Solomon's porch on the feast of the dedication in winter (x. 22, 23); see i. 29, 35–51, iv. 6, 43, 52, 54, vi. 5, 7, 8, viii. 20, ix. 2, 6, x. 23, xi. 30, 32, 35.

He knows the secret movements of the disciples and their quiet resorts (iv. 8, xi. 54, xviii. 2, xx. 19); he knows not only what the disciples said to Christ and to one another, but even what they thought (ii. 11, 17, 22, iv. 27, 33, vi. 7, 8, 69, ix. 2, xi. 8, 12, 13, 16, xii. 16, xiii. 6, 8, 9, 22–29, xvi. 17, xx. 9, 19–29, xxi. 3, 7); he knows not only the most secret and confidential sayings of our Lord to the disciples, but also His motives, feelings, emotions, and thoughts (i. 38-50, ii. 24-25, iv. 1-3, 6, 31-38, v. 6, vi. 5, 6, 15, 62, 71, vii. 1, ix. 2-5, xi. 15, 33, xiii. 1, 11, 21, xvi. 19, xviii. 4, xix. 28).

The contents of the fourth Gospel and its historical setting perfectly agree with the representation of the author himself and with the unanimous testimony of the Fathers and other ecclesiastical writers, that the fourth Gospel was composed by St. John the Apostle.

OBJECTIONS.

It has been urged against the Johannean authorship of the fourth Gospel—

(1) That in many particulars this Gospel is at variance with the others.

(2) That the portrait of our Lord and the character of His discourses are quite different from those given in the other Gospels.

(3) That St. John would scarcely have made himself so prominent, and almost boastfully, as "the disciple whom Jesus loved."

(4) That the style of the Gospel is very different from the style of the Apocalypse.

If we had no satisfactory answer to these objections they would remain as difficulties to be answered, but they would not overturn the clear historical testimony regarding the authorship. They would be only problems, like some of the problems about Shakespeare's plays. Still, there is an answer to all of them. The first will be answered in detail during the course of the Commentary; the second will be answered in § 4 and § 6 of this Introduction. There remain two, and to these we reply at once.

(*a*) That St. John should have called himself "the disciple whom Jesus loved," sprang not from self-complacency, but from a deep affection for our Lord, whose condescending love had filled the Apostle's heart with amazement, love, gratitude, and humility. St. John refers to it because he was filled with the thought of it. Besides, it was evidence that St. John, in writing the life of our

Lord, knew what he was writing about, and could give reliable testimony. He had lived on terms of familiar affection with our Lord, and knew His mind. (See below, § 6, where the importance of this is more fully explained.) Nor must we forget the authority that belongs to one who was an Apostle and an inspired writer. St. Paul, for instance, when it was necessary to confirm the faith of his readers, seems frequently to boast of his powers, graces, favours, labours, and dangers (2 Cor. xi. 21–xii. 6). Above all, he insists upon his knowledge and truthfulness. "I speak the truth in Christ, I lie not, my conscience bearing me witness in the Holy Ghost" (Rom. ix. 1. See 1 Cor. ii. 7–12, iii. 9, 10, iv. 1, 15, 20, 21, ix. 1, 19–27, xi. 1, 34, &c.). This is not boasting, but the necessary assertion of an important truth. Neither are the words of St. John a boast.

(*b*) There is great exaggeration in what is alleged about the differences of style between the Gospel and the Apocalypse. Really, there are no two books of the New Testament which have more in common. The current of ideas, the cast and form of thought, both doctrinal and literary, are substantially the same. The same characteristic doctrines and expressions abound in both, *e.g.*, the Word of God, the Lamb of God, life, light, glory, bridegroom and bride, manna, fount of water, true, truthful, to walk, to feed, to dwell, to enlighten, to hunger, to thirst, to do truth or falsehood, to overcome the world, to keep the word, to give testimony, to put into the heart, the hour cometh. Not the mere use of these expressions, but their peculiar application is what is so characteristic in St. John.

Of course there are differences between the Gospel and the Apocalypse; but these differences mainly spring from difference of subject. The Gospel belongs to the class of historical books, the Apocalypse to the class of prophetical books. Because the Gospel is a history, the writer, in accordance with ancient Jewish custom, to which the historical books of the Old Testament as well as the first three Gospels of the New Testament bear witness, does not give his name; but because the Apocalypse is a prophecy the writer, also in accordance with ancient Jewish custom, to which the prophetical books of the Old Testament bear witness, does give his name. Besides, the very difference of subject involved some change of style. Statements of historical fact are not made in the same style in which a prophet describes the mysterious symbols and imagery of prophecy. The few verbal, grammatical, and syntactical differences that remain are, in themselves, of very little weight, and may possibly be due to St. John's employment of different amanuenses, or to his own growing familiarity with Greek.

§ 3. THE AUTHOR.

St. John was a Galilean, son of Zebedee and Salome, and brother of St. James called the Greater (*i.e.* Elder). Zebedee was a fisherman of Bethsaida on Lake Tiberias (*i.e.* the Sea of Galilee), who, if we may judge from his employment of hired servants, and from his son's acquaintance with the high-priest (Mark i. 19, 20; John xviii. 15, 16), must have been in fairly prosperous circumstances. St. John followed his father's calling. Salome was one of that band of pious women who followed our Lord from Galilee, ministered to Him of their substance, attended upon Him, stood near His cross on Calvary, and brought the sweet spices to His sepulchre (Matt. xxvii. 55, 56; Mark. xv. 40, 41, xvi. 1). John and James followed their father's occupation, and were "Simon's partners." (Luke v. 10). These three, Peter, James, and John, were favoured by our Lord beyond all the other Apostles. They were chosen to be with Him at the Transfiguration (Matt. xvii. 1, 2); at the raising to life of Jairus's daughter (Mark v. 22, 23, 35–42); and during the Agony in the garden Matt. xxvi. 36–38). But St. John was distinguished by a more special intimacy with Christ and by peculiar tokens of His favour. He was emphatically "the disciple whom Jesus loved." Because he leaned on the breast of Christ at the Last Supper the Fathers gave him the name ὁ ἐπιστήθιος; because of his unsullied innocence and virginal life, they called him παρθένος. St. John had by nature a fervent temperament which, at times, made his zeal for our Lord's honour over-impetuous (Mark ix. 37–39, x. 35–37; Luke ix. 52–55). His brother James had the same characteristic; therefore Christ called them "Boanerges, which is the sons of thunder" (Mark iii. 17). In later life the impetuosity had disappeared; but the zeal for our Lord's honour remained (1 John ii. 22, iii. 8; 2 John 7–11). Christian tradition has preserved three stories about St. John which show his character at this later period.

(1) St. Irenæus, referring to St. Polycarp as the source of his information, relates that St. John went to bathe at Ephesus, but perceiving Cerinthus, who denied the doctrine of the Incarnation, he straightway rushed out of the bath-house, exclaiming, "Let us fly, lest even the bath-house fall down, because Cerinthus, the enemy of the truth, is within" (Hær. iii. 3, 4).

(2) Eusebius, quoting from Clement of Alexandria, relates that St. John had recommended a young man to the care of a certain bishop. The bishop instructed the youth and baptized him, but then relaxed in his oversight. The youth took to evil courses, joined a band of robbers, and became their chief. St. John, when revisiting the bishop, inquired after the young man, and learned the sad news. He immediately set out to find and reclaim him; allowed himself to be taken by the robbers, and was brought into the presence of the chief. The chief, recognising him, and being filled with shame, sought to fly. But St. John, tenderly embracing him, kissing his hands, and with many tears exhorting him, at length brought him back triumphantly to God and the Church (H. E. iii. 23).

(3) St. Jerome narrates that St. John, having grown old and very infirm, used to be carried to church, where he constantly repeated these words: "Little children, love one another." The faithful, growing weary of the repetition, at length said, "Master, why dost thou always say this?" St. John answered, "Because it is the commandment of the Lord, and if this is kept, it is enough (Commem. in Ep. ad Gal. vi. 10).

The fulness of detail regarding the Baptist in the fourth

Gospel (John i. 1-40, iii. 23 *seq.*, x. 41, 42) plainly suggests that St. John was that unnamed disciple of the Baptist who, together with Andrew the brother of Peter, left the Baptist to become a disciple of Christ (John i. 35-40). His call to be an Apostle came after the call of Peter and Andrew, and is told in Matthew iv. 18-22; Mark i. 14-20. He and Peter were sent by our Lord to prepare for the Last Supper (Luke xxii. 7, 8), during which he leaned on his Master's breast (John xiii. 23-26); he with Peter and James was taken apart by our Lord during the Agony in the garden (Matt. xxvi. 36-46); when Christ had been seized John followed Him into the hall of the highpriest, bringing Peter with him (John xviii. 15, 16); he stood by the Cross on Calvary, and received our Blessed Lady as a farewell charge (John xix. 26, 27); he and Peter hastened to the sepulchre when they had heard from Magdalen that Christ's body had been removed (John xx. 2-6). In obedience to our Lord's command, the disciples returned to Galilee, where they resumed their old occupation of fishing till He should manifest Himself (Matt. xxviii. 10, 11; John xxi. 3). On the occasion of Christ's showing Himself at the Sea of Tiberias, St. John was the first to recognise Him (John xxi. 1-7). When St. Peter had been confirmed in the Primacy he was curious, with curiosity of friendship, to know what St. John would receive; but he was bidden to lay his curiosity aside (John xxi. 15-22). St. John appears several times in the Acts, but always with St. Peter, and in subordination to him. After Pentecost he was with St. Peter when the latter healed the man born lame (iii. 1-8); together with Peter he was apprehended, and boldly confessed the name of Jesus before the Sanhedrin (iv. 1-21); he was doubtless with those Apostles who were cast into prison and scourged (v. 18-40); with Peter he went to Samaria to confirm the new converts there (viii. 14-17). After the return to Jerusalem (viii. 25) there is scarcely to be found in Scripture a trace of St. John's history. He seems not to have been at Jerusalem on the occasion of St. Paul's first visit (Gal. i. 18, 19), but he was there on occasion of another visit of St. Paul some fourteen years later (Gal. ii. 1–9). The only other direct notice in the New Testament occurs in the Apocalypse, where St. John tells us of his exile in the island of Patmos "for the word of God, and for the testimony of Jesus" (i. 9). But the striking coincidences of thought and language between St. John's writings and the first Epistle of St. Peter bear witness to the close connection of these two Apostles. (Cf. 1 Peter i. 7, 13 and Apoc. iii. 18, i. 1; 1 Peter i. 10 and John xii. 41; 1 Peter i. 22, 23, 25 and 1 John iii. 9, 11; 1 Peter ii. 5, 9 and Apoc. i. 5, 6; 1 Peter i. 18, 19 and Apoc. v. 6–10; 1 Peter v. 2 and 2 John i., 3 John i.; 1 Peter v. 13 and Apoc. xiv. 8, xvii. 5.)

It is impossible to say when St. John left Palestine; but it is certain that the later years of his long life were spent in Asia Minor. The opening chapters of the Apocalypse (ii. 1–iii. 22) are really an encyclical addressed to the leading Asiatic Churches—Ephesus, Smyrna, Pergamus, Thyatira, Sardis, Philadelphia, and Laodicea—and the letter shows the writer's intimate acquaintance with, and rule over, all seven. These facts imply a long sojourn in the country. But the centre of St. John's activity was Ephesus. Here many ecclesiastical traditions clustered round his memory; here he wrote his Gospel; here was his tomb. Direct historical testimony for St. John's Asiatic sojourn is weighty and abundant. (See Irenæus, ad Florin. fragm.; Hær. ii. 22; iii. 1, 3: ad Vict. fragm.; Polycrates apud Euseb. H. E. v. 24; Apollonius, apud Euseb. H. E. v. 18; Clement of Alexandria, apud Euseb. H. E. iii. 23.)

There is also a consensus of early ecclesiastical writers that St. John was banished to Patmos—by Nero (A.D. 54–68) according to some, by Domitian (A.D. 81–96), with far greater probability, according to others. After his release he returned to Ephesus, where he died, at an advanced age, during the reign of Trajan.

How the interval was filled up between the time of his leaving Palestine and the time of his arrival in Asia Minor, is unknown. All that is recorded is the tradition, mentioned by Tertullian, that St. John was cast into a cauldron of boiling oil at Rome without being harmed (de Præscr. 36).

§ 4. THE FOURTH GOSPEL AND THE SYNOPTICS.

The general purpose of St. Matthew's Gospel is to show that Jesus was the Messiah promised to the Jews, and that in Him the prophetic Scriptures received their interpretation and fulfilment; the general purpose of St. Mark's Gospel is to prove the divinity of Christ's mission from the greatness and majesty of His person, and from His wondrous power displayed in mighty works and miracles; the general purpose of St. Luke's Gospel is to set forth our Lord as the "salvation prepared before the face of all peoples. A Light to the revelation of the Gentiles, and the glory of Israel" (ii. 30); the general purpose of St. John's Gospel (see § 6) is clearly expressed in the Gospel itself: "These are written that you may believe that Jesus is the Christ the Son of God" (xx. 31).

To a certain extent there is overlapping; but St. John's purpose, and the manner in which he carried out that purpose, mark off his Gospel from the other three. At present we must be content with a broad review—

(1) The Synoptics are almost wholly occupied with the Galilean ministry, and so the central mass of material is substantially the same in all three—the same events and speeches, the same picture of our Lord. St. John is almost wholly occupied with the Judean ministry, and therefore the contents of the fourth Gospel are necessarily very different from those in the Synoptics, even in matters of importance. St. John generally avoids narrating what has already been narrated. Thus, in his account of the night before the Passion, he is silent regarding the institution of the Blessed Sacrament and regarding the Agony in the garden. Even in describing the same things, *e.g.*, the history of the Passion and of the Resurrection, many of the details are new, and the manner of treatment is quite different. (Cf. Matt. xxvii., Mark xv., Luke xxiii., John xix.)

(2) The discourses of Jesus recorded in the fourth Gospel present so remarkable a contrast in both matter and form with those recorded in the Synoptics, that they give us an almost entirely different picture of our Lord. This arises from the fact that St. John had a different purpose, and looked at the events of our Lord's life from a different point of view. The description of a man conducting a military campaign amid all the dangers of warfare would be very different from a description of the same man in the calm peace of his own home. In an analagous way the description of our Lord given by St. John differs from the description given by the other Evangelists. Hence St. Augustine says, "Two virtues have been proposed to the mind of man. Of these the one is active, the other contemplative. The one is occupied with precepts for the right exercise of this temporal life, the other deals with the doctrine of everlasting life. The one operates, the other rests. By this it is given us to understand, if one will only attend carefully to the matter, that those three Evangelists who, with pre-eminent fulness, have handled the account of the Lord's temporal doings and those of His sayings which were meant to bear chiefly upon the moulding of the manners of the present life, were conversant with that active virtue; and that John, on the other hand, who narrates fewer by far of the Lord's doings, but records with greater carefulness and with larger wealth of detail the words which He spoke, and most especially those discourses which were intended to introduce us to the knowledge of the unity of the Trinity and the blessedness of eternal life, formed his plan and framed his statement with a view to commend the contemplative virtue to our regard" (De Cons. Evang. i. 5, 8). (Further details in § 6.)

§ 5. Place and Time.

The fourth Gospel, which was certainly written in Greek, was composed, according to the earliest Ecclesiastical tradition, at Ephesus (Irenæus, Clement of Alexandria, Origen, Eusebius). This tradition seems practically certain. The interpretations and explanations that sometimes appear presuppose readers who are non-Palestinian (i. 38, 41, 42, iv. 25, v. 2, xix. 17); the internal characteristics of the Gospel, and especially the form of its ideas (see § 6), prove the author's remoteness from Palestine and from the current of Jewish life; the use of the past tense (*e.g.*, xi. 18, xviii. 1, xix. 41) is more naturally explained by the supposition that Jerusalem had already been destroyed and now lay in the background of history, than by the supposition that the Apostle was simply employing a form of historical narration—especially since in v. 2 he uses the present tense; the writer certainly knew the contents of the Synoptic Gospels, and wrote after their publication (see § 6); he wrote at a time when the prophecy foretelling the manner of St. Peter's death had already been fulfilled (xxi. 17-19), and when St. John himself had advanced so far in years that the brethren began to think he would never die (xxi. 20-23). The internal evidence therefore confirms the ancient tradition that the fourth Gospel was written at Ephesus towards the close of St. John's life, probably during the reign of Nerva (A.D. 96-98). The tradition that he wrote at Patmos did not arise till later, and was perhaps suggested by the fact that he there wrote the Apocalypse.

§ 6. OBJECT AND PLAN.

Ephesus, with a fine harbour opening on the Ægean Sea, was a busy centre of commerce. It was to Asia Minor what Alexandria was to Egypt, or Antioch to Syria, or Corinth to Greece. From numerous Mediterranean ports merchants thronged here to meet the caravans of the East. It was from Ephesus that St. John derived the elements of his description when, in the Apocalypse, he described the abounding wealth and ceaseless traffic of the great cities of the Roman Empire—"the merchants of the earth with their merchandise of gold, and silver, and precious stones; of pearls, and fine linen, and purple, and silk, and scarlet, and all thyine wood, and all manner of vessels of ivory, and all manner of vessels of precious stone, and of brass, and of iron, and of marble, and cinnamon, and odours, and ointment, and frankincense, and wine, and oil, and fine flour, and wheat, and beasts, and sheep, and horses, and chariots, and slaves; every shipmaster, and all that sail into the lake, and mariners, and as many as work in the sea" (Apoc. xviii. 11-13, 17). It was also a centre of sorcery and idolatry (Acts xix. 19, 27). Its temple of Diana Artemis was one of the seven wonders of the world. Here, too, were many Jews who had been attracted by the hope of gain. St. Paul, during the course of his second missionary journey, had made a short stay at Ephesus (Acts xviii. 19-21). On that occasion two convert Jews of Pontus accompanied him. These were Aquila and his wife Priscilla, who, like the Apostle, were tent-makers by trade, and who had been his hosts at Corinth. They remained at Ephesus after the Apostle had brought his short visit to a close (Acts xviii. 1-3, 18-22). About this time another Jew, a Hellenist named Apollo, came to Ephesus. Born at Alexandria, he had learned the science of the Scriptures in the schools of this famous city of learning. He was remarkable for eloquence and penetration of mind, and he explained the Scriptures according to the deeper method of the Hellenists (see § 1). He had been "instructed in the way of the Lord," but only imperfectly; for he knew "only the baptism of John" (Acts xviii. 24, 25). What he knew of Christianity he had learned from the scattered disciples of the Baptist. Being zealous for the truth, he began to speak boldly in the synagogue, and taught diligently the things that are of Jesus (Acts xviii. 26, 25). His knowledge was imperfect. He knew of our Lord only what the disciples of the Baptist had been able to teach. Therefore, when Priscilla and Aquila had heard him, "they took him to them, and expounded to him the way of the Lord more diligently" (Acts xviii. 26). Thereupon he went to Achaia, and with much vigour convinced the Jews openly, showing by the Scriptures that Jesus is the Christ (Acts xviii. 27, 28). But there were other disciples of John at Ephesus. Twelve of these were baptized and confirmed by St. Paul on his return, after about a year's absence, to Ephesus (Acts xix. 1-7). This second visit of the Apostle lasted some three years. It was one of the most trying periods of his life. Writing to the Corinthians, towards the close of his stay at Ephesus, he says, "We both hunger, and thirst, and are naked, and are buffeted, and have no fixed abode, and we labour working with our own hands; we are reviled, persecuted, blasphemed; we are made as the refuse of this world, the offscouring of all" (1 Cor. iv. 11-13). And in another letter, referring to this period, he says, "We would not have you ignorant, brethren, of our tribulation, which came to us in Asia, that we were pressed out of measure above our strength, so that we were weary even of life" (2 Cor. i. 8). "I fought with beasts at Ephesus. But I will tarry at Ephesus until pentecost. For a great door is opened unto me; and many adversaries" (1 Cor. xv. 32, xvi. 8, 9). In the end he was driven out of Ephesus by a popular tumult (Acts xix. 23, xx. 1). But his work had not been unsuccessful. There may have been exaggeration in the words of Demetrius, "that this Paul by persuasion hath drawn away a great multitude, not only of Ephesus, but almost of all Asia" (Acts xix. 26), but there was no exaggeration in the words of St. Luke that "all they who dwelt in Asia heard the word of the Lord, both Jews and gentiles," and that "the word of God grew mightily and was confirmed" (Acts xix. 10, 20). At this time, therefore, St. Paul probably laid the foundations of those seven Churches to which St. John wrote (Apoc. ii. 1, iii. 22).

But the faith planted by St. Paul was not destined to remain undisturbed. In his farewell address to the elders, or bishops, of Ephesus, he warned them to take heed to the whole flock. "I know that after my departure ravening wolves will enter in among you, not sparing the flock. And of your own selves shall arise men speaking perverse things, to draw away disciples after them" (Acts xx. 28-30). In his letters to his disciple Timothy, whom he left to take charge of the Ephesian Christians, he again refers to these false teachers who "give heed to fables and genealogies without end" (1 Tim. 1. 4), and who brought the work of the Apostle into grave peril. "Thou knowest this, that all they who are in Asia are turned away from me: of whom are Phigellus and Hermogenes" (2 Tim. i. 15).

St. Paul has described the leading characteristics of these heretics. They had gone astray, and had made shipwreck concerning the faith (1 Tim. i. 6, 19, vi. 21); with minds darkened by pride, they made boast of a special knowledge (1 Tim. vi. 4, 20); their teaching was vain babbling, consisting of fables and genealogies without end—mere old wives' fables (1 Tim. i. 4, iv. 7); they desire to be teachers of the law, although they do not understand its true meaning (1 Tim. i. 7); they make arbitrary commands of their own (1 Tim. iv. 3). In such errors we perceive the germs of that fantastic system which was developed into the Gnosticism of the second century. One of the first to cast this Judæo-Gnosticism into a system was Cerinthus. He was a contemporary of St. John, and came from Egypt into Asia Minor. He taught that the world was not made by God, but by a certain power far removed from God, and ignorant of Him. He represented Jesus as not having been born of a virgin, but as being the son of Joseph and Mary, but yet more holy, prudent, and wise than other men. Christ was distinct from Jesus, and descended upon Him after His baptism in the form of a dove; He then proclaimed the unknown Father, and performed miracles. At last Christ departed from Jesus, who then suffered and rose again, while Christ remained impassible, inasmuch as he was a spiritual being. Closely allied to the Cerinthians were the Ebionites. They agreed with Christians that the world was made by God; but they agreed with the Cerinthians in their opinions about our Lord. They practised circumcision, persevered in the observance of the Jewish law, and were so Judaic in their style of life, that they even adored Jerusalem as if it were the house of God (Iren., Haer. i. 26). They pursued an active propaganda in the Churches of Asia Minor. Under these circumstances was the fourth Gospel written at Ephesus.

We have seen that the fourth Gospel is very unlike the others. Mere accident will not account for that unlikeness. On the contrary, it seems to have been part of a settled plan with St. John not to repeat what had already been said by the other Evangelists, not to bear testimony to what had already been sufficiently attested, not to explain what could easily be explained by the reader's previous knowledge. Hence he omits so many matters of grave importance which are found in the Synoptics; hence he takes so much for granted, and leaves so much unexplained. He takes for granted that the reader is already acquainted with the main features of our Lord's life—with His birth at Bethlehem, and the ready solution it gives of Jewish difficulties (John i. 45, 46, vii. 41, 42, 52); with His baptism by John (John i. 32); with His ascension (vi. 63, xx. 17); with Simon Peter (John i. 40); with the Holy Family (i. 40, vi. 42); with the history of the Baptist (John iii. 24); with the call of the Twelve (John vi. 17); with the Christian doctrine of Baptism (John iii. 3–7), and of the Eucharist (John vi. 53). It has therefore been suggested that St. John wrote in order to complete the Synoptic accounts. This might have been a collateral purpose; but it could not have been a direct and substantial purpose. He chose, in working out his main purpose, matter not already given by the other Evangelists; but he did not intend, by supplementing them, to write a full life of our Lord. Rather, he plainly declares his belief in the hopelessness of such a task (xx. 30, xxi. 25).

St. John's method of treatment shows that his Gospel was written for a class of readers very different from those for whom the Synoptics were written. In St. John there are no simple narratives of our Lord's birth and infancy, no plain parables such as we find in the other Evangelists. But we meet with many profound discourses intended for readers already acquainted with the leading facts of our Lord's life, and with the main truths of Christian faith. Written after the destruction of Jerusalem, when the Mosaic law had received its death-blow, written among a community trained in Hellenistic culture and familiar with Gnostic speculations, the Gospel of St. John naturally differs much from the other Gospels. It was written for readers who had advanced in a knowledge of the deeper things of the Christian faith. The Fathers, indeed, tell us that one of its main purposes was polemical—to refute the heresies of Cerinthians, Ebionites, and Nicolaites (Iren., Haer. iii. 1, Jer., Prol. in Matt.). Such polemical purpose is most evident in St. John's Epistles. "There are become many Antichrists. They went out from us; but they were not of us. For if they had been of us, they would no doubt have remained with us . . . Who is a liar, but he who denieth that Jesus is the Christ? . . . Every spirit that confesseth that Jesus Christ is come in the flesh, is of God: and every spirit that dissolveth Jesus is not of God . . . Whosoever shall confess that Jesus is the Son of God, God abideth in him, and he in God . . . Many seducers are gone out into the world, who confess not that Jesus Christ is come in the flesh" (1 John ii. 18, 19, 22, iv. 2, 3, 14, 15, v. 5; 2 John 7. See Apoc. ii. 2, 6, 9, 15). In the Gospel, however, traces of such direct polemical purpose are not so clear. Still, the Gospel does bear marks of having been written after controversies had been started concerning our Lord's person. Even if it be allowed that St. John did not write his Gospel as a direct refutation of the Cerinthians and Ebionites, there is little doubt but that he had those heresies in mind. The very atmosphere of the time and place was filled with them; and there is an undeniable connection between the opening verses of the Gospel and the opening verses of the first Epistle (John i. 1–14 and 1 John i. 1–5). He wrote, in face of heresies then rampant, to strengthen the faith of Christians—to teach what we are to believe concerning the Divinity of Christ, His substantial union with the Father, and personal distinction, His real and true Incarnation, His office as Redeemer and Saviour of the world, and the union He wishes to establish between the faithful and Himself by grace.

St. John himself has told us very distinctly what was his purpose in writing: "These are written that you may believe that Jesus is the Christ the Son of God; and that believing you may have life in his name" (John xx. 31). The conception of our Lord as the Word, the Son of God, is the pervading idea of the Gospel. We at once feel its influence. In the prologue it is announced as the very theme of the Gospel (i. 1-5); and the Evangelist immediately adds, "and we saw his glory, the glory as it were of the only-begotten of the Father," *i.e.* glory altogether such as that of an only-begotten Son (i. 14. See Commentary). Then come testimonies of the truth: first, the testimony of the Baptist that "this is the Son of God" (i. 34); then the testimony of the first disciples that Christ is "the Messias, of whom Moses and the prophets did write, the Son of God, the King of Israel" (i. 41, 45, 49). By His first miracle, in Cana of Galilee, Jesus "manifested his glory" (ii. 11), and when He had cast the buyers and sellers out of "his Father's house," He foretold His resurrection from the dead as a sign of His Divine mission (ii. 16, 18-22). To Nicodemus He revealed Himself as "the only-begotten Son, sent into the world from the Father, that whosoever believeth in him may not perish, but may have life everlasting" (iii. 15-17). This declaration is confirmed by the further testimony of the Baptist that Christ "came from above, and is above all" (iii. 31). Our Lord, then, turning to the Samaritans, not only declared most plainly that He was the Messias, but also manifested His glory so clearly that the Samaritans confessed that "this is indeed the Saviour of the world" (iv. 25, 26, 42). On His return to Jerusalem the Jews brought against Him the charge that He said "God was his Father, making himself equal to God" (v. 18). Our Lord did not deny the charge; on the contrary, He asserted that He was indeed the Son of God, and therefore the author of life and the supreme judge of mankind. In proof of His assertion He appealed to the testimony of John, and to a testimony "greater than that of John"—to the testimony of the works which the Father had given Him to perfect, and to the testimony of the Father Himself (v. 21-37). But this may suffice to show how carefully St. John works out the main idea of his Gospel.

When St. John wrote, the burden of the Mosaic law had been completely taken away, and the exclusive privileges of the Jewish people had departed. Mount Garizim of Samaria had been the schismatical rival of Mount Sion. But when the Samaritan woman asked our Lord which were right, the Jews or the Samaritans, He replied, "Believe me, that the hour cometh, when you shall neither on this mountain, nor in Jerusalem adore the Father . . . But the hour cometh, and now is, when the true adorers shall adore the Father in spirit and in truth" (John iv. 21, 23). And to those Jews who believed Him He said, "You shall know the truth, and the truth shall make you free . . . If therefore the son shall make you free, you shall be free indeed" (John viii. 32, 36). Again, speaking to the Jews, He said, "I am the door of the sheep . . . By me, if any man enter in, he shall be saved . . . And other sheep I have, that are not of this fold; them also I must bring, and they shall hear my voice, and there shall be one fold" (rather, one flock) "and one shepherd" (John x. 7, 9, 16).

Next, the Jews, at the time of St. John's writing, had had a period of gracious probation, but had grown hard in stubborn unbelief. "The light shineth in darkness, and the darkness did not comprehend it . . . [Christ] came unto his own, and his own received him not" (John i. 5, 11). With sadness the Apostle records how miracle and Scripture had alike failed to break down the barrier of Jewish prejudice. "Whereas he had done so many miracles before them, they believed not in him" (John xii. 37); [you] "search the scriptures, for you think in them to have life everlasting; and the same are they that give testimony of me" (John v. 39). "How can you believe, who receive glory one from another; and the glory which is from God alone, you do not seek?" (John v. 44.)

From this it follows that St. John wrote his Gospel in the very centre of Asiatic culture, for those mixed Christian communities of Jewish and Gentile origin, among whom he lived and laboured, and whose faith was endangered by heresies which combined elements of Judaism with Gnostic speculation. To the boasted false knowledge of the heretics St. John opposed the true Christian Gnosis. He explained what doctrine had indeed been taught by Christ and by those best qualified to teach — by those who had lived with Christ and had received their doctrine from Christ Himself. Therefore the Gospel of St. John is emphatically a Gospel of testimony — the testimony of the Baptist and of Christ's early disciples, the testimony of the Father, the testimony of Christ's miracles, but most of all the testimony of Christ's own discourses, of which the disciple whom Jesus loved would naturally be, to say nothing of the power of inspiration, a perfect witness and most reliable exponent. It is not necessary, however, to believe that all the discourses of our Lord are reported in our Lord's very words. It seems evident that, for the most part, St. John gives us what our Lord said, not the very words in which He said it, *i.e.* we have the substance of our Lord's discourses in St. John's Greek. Sometimes, indeed, we probably get the very words merely translated into Greek; but it is impossible to say how often, and where, this is the case. But what we are sure of is, that our Lord really said what St. John ascribes to Him. Another writer would have reported in a different style the same speeches. But St. John had his own style, and used it. This is one explanation why the discourses of our Lord have one style in St. John, and another style in the Synoptics. St. John has also chosen a deeper side of Christ's teaching. For our Lord had two methods of teaching. He himself said to the disciples, "These things I have spoken to you in proverbs. The hour cometh when I will no more speak to you in proverbs, but will show you plainly of the Father" (John xvi. 25). "These things have I spoken to you, abiding with you. But the Paraclete, the Holy Ghost, whom the Father will send in my name, he will teach you all things, and bring all things to your mind, whatsoever I shall have said to you (John xiv. 25, 26). "I have yet many things to say to you: but you cannot bear them now. But when he, the Spirit of truth, is come, he will teach you all truth. For he shall not speak of himself:

but what things so ever he shall hear, he shall speak; and the things that are to come he shall show you. He shall glorify me; because he shall receive of mine, and shall shew it to you" (John xvi. 12-14). May we not say that in the Gospel of St. John we have a fulfilment of that promise?

The contents of the Gospel admirably correspond to the design.

The Prologue (i. 1-18) announces the general theme. It declares what the Word has been from all eternity, what He chose to become in time, and what has been the result of His coming as man into this world. From all eternity he was God—distinct in Person from the Father, but possessing the self-same Divine nature, and so equal to the Father in all things. Essentially light and life in Himself, becoming man He brought supernatural light and life to all mankind. That light is accepted by some and rejected by others. Mankind is thus divided into two classes—the children of light and the children of darkness, the children of God and the children of the world. Thus there is a conflict, which the Gospel sets forth in a series of contrasts—light and darkness, life and death, truth and error, spirit and flesh, heaven and earth, love and hatred, the Church and the world, Christ and Satan. The whole Gospel is a development of these ideas. There is a clear connection of every part with the announcement of the Prologue. The events and discourses are selected to show a progressive manifestation of the Word made flesh, and of the struggle between light and darkness. The progressive revelation of Christ is naturally made by Christ Himself, and it is confirmed and symbolised by the works which the Father had given Him to perfect. Our Lord claims to be the Christ (iv. 25, 26); He asserts that He is the giver of living water to mankind (iv. 10), the living bread, the bread of life (vi. 35, 41, 48, 51), the light of the world (viii. 12), the way and the truth (xiv. 6), the resurrection and the life (xi. 25); that He came from above (viii. 23); that He and the Father are one (x. 30); that He is the Son of God (x. 36); that He is in the Father, and the Father in Him (xiv. 10); and that He came into the world to give testimony to the truth (xviii. 37). Christ reads the hearts and consciences of men (i. 48, iv. 16-19); He knows that Judas will betray Him (xiii. 11); He has no need to be told that Lazarus is dead (xi. 11-14). By facts such as these He shows that He is the truth, and, as St. Peter confessed, knows all things (John xxi. 17). All the events recounted by St. John, all the miracles selected by him, are in harmony with these ideas—they symbolize the ideas, give them point and a concrete manifestation. The change of water into wine manifested the glory of Christ, the transforming power of His grace, and the change from the law of Moses into the grace and truth of the Gospel (John i. 17, ii. 1-11); the cure of the man so long infirm represents Christ's power of giving spiritual life and strength (v. 1-21), the miraculous feeding of the multitude represents the bread from heaven by which Christ nourishes our souls to everlasting life (vi. 1-14, 32-60), the healing of the man born blind represents to us our Lord as the light of the world (ix. 1-7, 39-41); the raising of Lazarus from the dead represents our Lord as the resurrection and the life, and His word as the principle of life to all that believe (xi. 1-27). Thus the miracles and other events in Christ's life are indissolubly interwoven with the discourses and lead to the same conclusion. But even in themselves the miracles are admirably chosen for manifesting the glory of the only-begotten Son of God. The ruler's son at Capharnaum was healed at a distance (iv. 45-53); the infirm man had been lying helpless eight and thirty years (v. 1-9); the blind man had been so from his birth (ix. 1-7); Lazarus had been dead four days, and was already believed to be in a state of putrefaction (xi. 39).

Side by side with this revelation of the Word made flesh there is a progressive manifestation of the struggle between light and darkness. The struggle is announced in the Prologue (i. 5, 10-12), and the elements of the struggle immediately begin to gather. We have the first group of true believers whose faith is confirmed by the miracle at Cana (i. 35-51, ii. 11), then we have those who are altogether deficient, and those who are merely imperfect in faith (ii. 13-iii. 12). Next we have the effect of Christ's preaching amongst those who were outside the Jewish polity (iv. 28, 29, 40–42). This preaching to those outside was occasioned by the opposition of the Jewish leaders (iv. 1–4). In Galilee, again, the ruler and his whole house believed (iv. 53), but at Jerusalem the Jews sought to kill Jesus (v. 18). After the multiplication of the loaves we get another contrast—on the one hand, the action of many disciples who went back, and walked no more with Christ, but on the other hand, the confession of St. Peter, "Thou hast the words of eternal life. . . . Thou art the Christ, the Son of God" (vi. 67–70). Thus we follow the tumult of opinions and the growing opposition of the Jews (vii. 1, 30–32, 40–53, viii. 12–59, ix. 13–34, x. 19–42). At length the rulers decide to put Christ to death (xi. 45–50). They carry out their purpose and crucify Him; but their apparent victory is really the triumph of faith. Christ rising gloriously from the tomb has established the faith of His followers upon an immovable foundation (xiii. 31–33, xiv. 1–3, 11–14, 18–20, 27, 28, xvi. 32, 33, xvii. 1–5, xx. 30, 31).

While developing his argument, St. John seems to have arranged his materials in the order of time, which he is careful to indicate. The first events are assigned to their several days till the history of a week is completed by the marriage-feast at Cana (i. 29, 35, 43, ii. 1). Our Lord then went down to Capharnaum, where He remained "not many days" (ii. 12). All subsequent events are arranged according to the Jewish feasts—the Pasch (ii. 13), a festival day—either Pentecost or Pasch (v. 1), the Pasch (vi. 4), Feast of Tabernacles (vii. 2, 14), Feast of the Dedication (x. 22), the Pasch (xi. 55, xii. 1). Thus the events described by St. John are distributed between three or four Passovers.

The main outlines of the plan are as follows:—

I. *The Prologue* (i. 1–18).

(1) The Word in His own absolute, eternal Being (i. 1–5).

(2) The Word in relation to the enlightenment and sanctification of mankind (i. 6–13).

(3) The Word made flesh, and the fruits of the Incarnation (i. 14–18).

II. *First Main Division. The Manifestation of Christ in His Life* (i. 19–xii. 50).

(1) The manifestation, as yet without opposition of unbelief (i. 19–ii. 12).

(*a*) The testimony of the Baptist (i. 19–39).
(*b*) The testimony of the first disciples (i. 40-51).
(*c*) The testimony of the first miracle (ii. 1-12).

(2) The manifestation of the First Pasch—the varying results (ii. 13 iv. 54).

(*a*) The Jews at Jerusalem (ii. 13–25).
(*b*) Nicodemus the Pharisee (iii. 1–21).
(*c*) The Jews, St. John, and the disciples of St. John (iii. 22–36).
(*d*) First signs of opposition—Christ and the Samaritans (iv. 1–42).
(*e*) The testimony of the second miracle in Galilee (iv. 43–54).

(3) Fresh miracles, discourses, and testimonies—the opposition deepening (v.–xi. 56).

(*a*) The miracle at the pond during the feast, the anger of the Jews; our Lord's manifestation of Himself (v. 1–47).
(*b*) The feeding of the multitude; the discourse occasioned thereby; the apostasy of many of Christ's disciples (vi. 1–72).
(*c*) Unbelief among the brethren of Jesus. The self-revelation of Christ advances by words and deeds till it culminates in the testimony of the great miracle of the raising of the dead. But this miracle leads the Jews to the determination of putting Christ to death (vii. 1–xi. 56).

(4) Concluding testimonies of the Public Life (xii. 1–50).

(*a*) The testimony of the multitude (xii. 1–36).
(*b*) The testimony of the Evangelist (xii. 37–43).
(*c*) The testimony of Jesus Himself (xii. 44–50).

III. *Second Main Division. The Manifestation of Christ in His Death and Resurrection* (xiii. 1–xxi. 23).

(1) The manifestation of Christ in His last discourses to the disciples (xiii. 1–xvii. 26). The disciples make an

act of faith in the revelation of their Divine Master (xvi. 29–31).

(2) The manifestation of Christ in His Passion and Death (xviii. 1–xix. 37). The glory of Christ is manifested before the soldiers and servants in the garden (xviii. 6), is solemnly declared before the High-priest and before Pilate (xviii. 19–23, 36, 37, xix. 8–14), and is attested by miracle and the fulfilment of prophecy in our Lord's death (xix. 28–37).

(3) The triumph of Christ in His burial and resurrection (xix. 38–xxi. 23).

(*a*) The body of our Lord is embalmed at great cost and buried in a new sepulchre by men of wealth and distinction (xix. 38–42; see Matt. xxvii. 57–60; Mark xv. 42–46).

(*b*) Our Lord rising gloriously from the tomb sets the Divine seal upon His mission and firmly establishes the faith of His disciples (xx.)

(*c*) Our Lord by the miraculous draught of fishes foreshadows the fecundity of His Church, and then solemnly confirms St. Peter in the Primacy over the whole flock (xxi. 1–23).

Epilogue attesting the truth of the whole history (xxi. 24, 25).

§ 7. CHARACTERISTICS AND STYLE.

The fourth Gospel is characterised by loftiness and penetration of thought, sublime mysticism and a deeply spiritual tone. St. John seems to throw open the very gates of heaven, and to set before our eyes the wondrous nature of the Son of God in its overpowering splendour. In St. John, as St. Augustine well says, "You perceive one who has passed beyond the cloud in which the whole earth is wrapped, and who has reached the liquid heaven, from which, with clearest and steadiest mental eye, he is able to look upon God the Word. Hence from the earliest times the Gospel of St. John has been called the "Spiritual Gospel." Conformably with his main purpose, St. John has given us a careful selection of our Lord's symbolical miracles and of His most spiritual discourses.

INTRODUCTION. xlvii

This abundance of spiritual ideas has entailed the use of many characteristic words and phrases in a deeply spiritual meaning. Such for instance, are ὁ λόγος, ὁ μονογενὴς υἱός, παράκλητος, τὸ πνεῦμα τῆς ἀληθείας, ἐξελθεῖν ἐκ τοῦ θεοῦ, γεννηθῆναι ἄνωθεν, or, ἐκ τοῦ πνεύματος, or, ἐκ θεοῦ, τέκνα τοῦ θεοῦ, μένειν ἐν Χριστῷ, or, ἐν τῷ λόγῳ, εἶναι ἐκ and εἶναι ἐν, δόξα, φῶς, ἀλήθεια, ἀγάπη, κόσμος, σάρξ, σκοτία, περιπατεῖν ἐν τῇ ἡμέρᾳ, ἐν τῇ νυκτί, ἐν τῇ σκοτίᾳ, &c., &c.

St. John's command of Greek words appears to have been somewhat limited; the words are well chosen, but their number is not large. The construction of the sentences is very simple, successive ideas being often set in mere juxtaposition or loosely connected by the conjunctions καί, οὖν, and δέ. This gives to the language a strongly Hebraic tone, which is intensified by constant repetitions and by a frequent use of that parallelism which is so common in Hebrew poetry. (For other characteristics see § 2.)

§ 8. THE TEXT.

The fourth Gospel was written in Greek. Of the Greek MSS. still extant the following are the most important:—

Codex Vaticanus (B), 4th century. In the library of the Vatican. Perhaps the weightiest single document we possess. The whole Gospel.

Codex Sinaiticus (א). At St. Petersburg. The whole Gospel. In much the same style as the Codex Vaticanus, and possibly quite as old.

Codex Alexandrinus (A). 5th century. In the British Museum. Wants vi. 50–viii. 52.

Codex Ephraemi Rescriptus (C), 5th century. In the National Library at Paris. The works of St. Ephraem were written over it in the twelfth century. Eight fragments; i. 1–41; iii. 33–v. 16; vi. 38–vii. 3; viii. 34–ix. 11; xi. 8–46; xiii. 8–xiv. 7; xvi. 21–xviii. 36; xx. 26–xxi. 25.

Codex Bezae (D). Perhaps 6th century. In Cambridge University Library. Has Latin text as well as Greek. Wants i. 16–iii. 26, and xviii. 13–xx. 13 is by a later hand.

Codex Regius Parisiensis (L), 8th or 9th century. In the Royal Library at Paris. Wants xxx. 15–25. Has a strong resemblance to B—less, however, in St. John's Gospel than elsewhere.

The fourth Gospel was very early translated into various languages. Thus we possess it in the following versions:—

The Latin.

The Old Latin (Vetus Latina (Itala?)), 2nd century. Whole Gospel.

The Vulgate Latin. 4th century. St. Jerome's revision, at the request of Pope Damasus, of the Vetus Latina. Whole Gospel.

The Syriac.

(*a*). *Curetonian or Old Syriac.* Frequently, though not decisively, attributed to 2nd century. Mere fragments; i. 1–42; iii. 5–vii. 37; xiv. 10–12; 15–19; 21–23; 26–29. Another MS. containing a text of the same type as the Curetonian, has recently been discovered by Mrs. Lewis in the Convent on Mount Sinai—"The Sinaitic Palimpsest." The following passages, besides many words and clauses, are missing: i. 1–24; i. 47–ii. 15; iv. 38–v. 5; v. 26–45; xviii. 32–xix. 39. Of these five passages three may be supplied from the Curetonian.

(*b*). *The Peshitto Syriac*—the Syrian Vulgate. Perhaps the oldest Syriac version. The whole Gospel.

(*c*). *The Philoxenian*, made by Philoxenus about A.D. 508. This was revised by Thomas of Harkel in the 7th century (Harkleian, Harclean, or Harklensian). The whole Gospel.

The Egyptian Versions (possibly made at close of 2nd century) are (1) the Bohairic (also called Memphitic and Coptic) (2) the Sahidic (also called Thebaic). The whole Gospel.

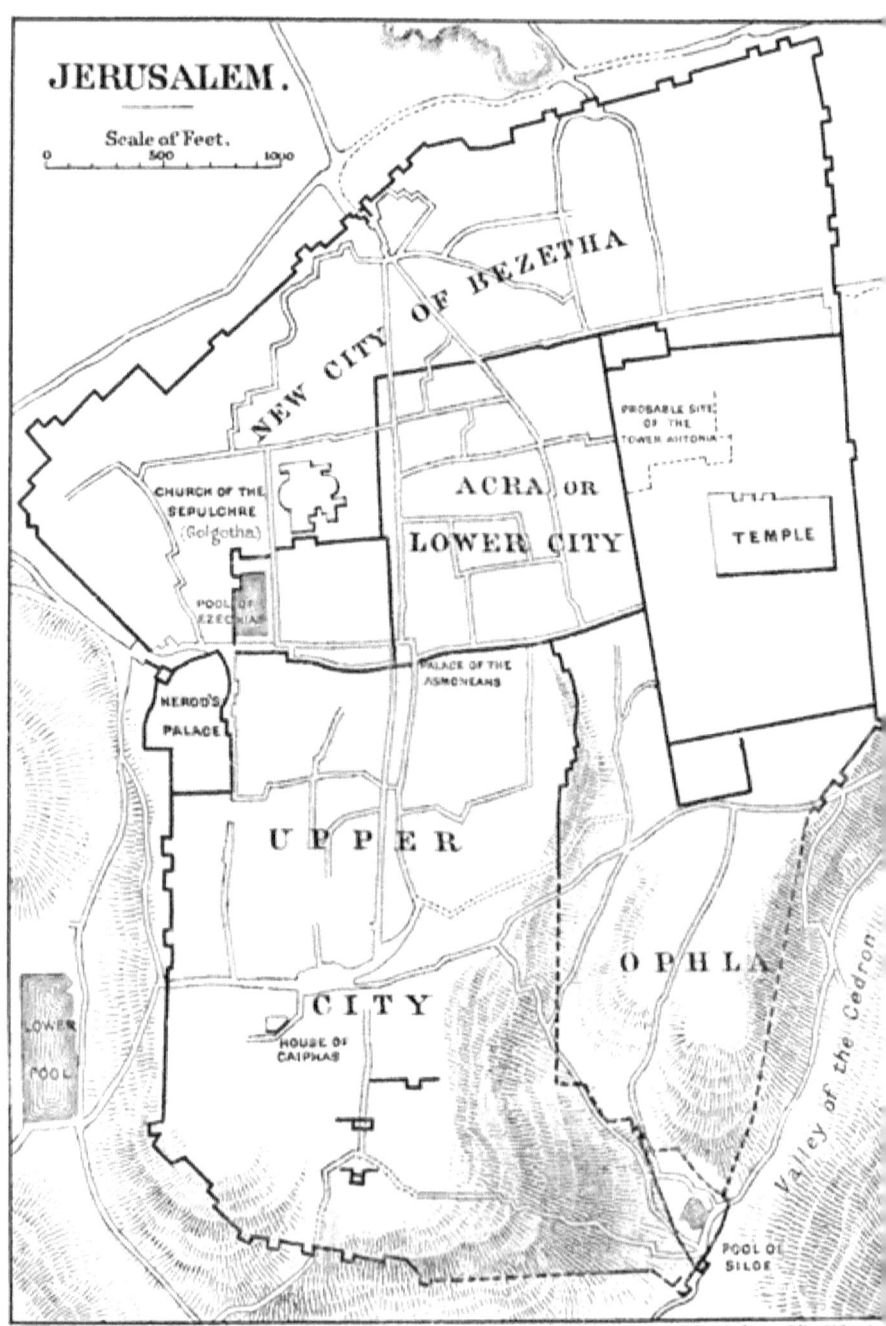

ND ACCORDING
THE HOLY GOSPEL ACCORDING TO SAINT JOHN.

CHAPTER I.

Prologue.

(VERS. 1–18.)

IN the beginning was the Word, and the Word was with God, and the Word was God. The same was in the

In the Prologue St. John announces the general theme of his Gospel. He teaches that the Word existed before anything created had begun to be; that He was a real concrete Person, distinct indeed from the Father, but consubstantial (*i.e.*, having essential unity) with Him; that He created all things; that He is the source of life and light to mankind; that He became truly man; that the Baptist had given testimony to Him, and the Apostles had been witnesses of His glory; that in Him alone is the fulness of grace and revelation.

1. *In the beginning.* The sense of the term 'beginning' must always be determined by the context. Here the parallelism between the opening words of the Gospel and the opening words of Genesis —a parallelism that can hardly be accidental—as well as the subsequent consideration of the Word in relation to the creation of all things (*v.* 3) gives to the phrase the meaning, 'in the beginning of creation.' The sense is, before creation began, before anything created had come into existence, the Word already was, *i.e.*, He is eternal and uncreated.

was (ἦν, not ἐγένετο). The context carefully distinguishes these verbs. When anything begins to be only at the point of time specified, the latter verb is used (*vv.* 3, 6, 14); but if it does not then begin to be, being already in existence, the former verb is used (*vv.* 1, 2, 4, 9). St. John does not say, 'In the beginning of creation the Word began to be' (ἐγένετο), but the Word already was (ἦν). Compare our Lord's own saying: "Glorify thou me, O Father, with thyself, with the glory which I had, *before the world was*, with thee" (John xvii. 5); and the

³ beginning with God. All things were made by him:

words of St. Paul in reference to Christ, "He is before all, and by him all things consist" (*i.e.*, are created and preserved in being) (Col. i. 17).

the Word (ὁ λόγος). St. John assumes that his readers will readily understand this profound and highly technical term. A long preparation had been made by God for a full revelation of its meaning. In Genesis the act of creation is effected by God speaking—by the word of God. This creative word is frequently personified in the Old Testament Scriptures, especially in poetic passages. (See Ps. xxxii. 6, cvi. 11, cxlvii. 15 ; Isa. lv. 10 *seq.*) But there is a clearer revelation of a personal or hypostatic character in what was said of God's eternal and uncreated Wisdom. It is said to be the eternal possession of God, conceived and brought forth before the beginning of creation ; and being set up from eternity, it was with God forming all things (Prov. viii. 22-31). Moreover it is said to be holy, omnipotent, omniscient, omnipresent ; a pure emanation of the glory of the Almighty God, the brightness of eternal light, and the unspotted mirror of God's majesty, and the image of His goodness (Wisd. vii. 21-27). There is more in this language than a mere poetic personification of the Divine attributes. But it was only in the New Testament that God clearly revealed to us the full meaning of the words which He had inspired in the Old Testament. Taking up the language of the Old Testament, St. Paul says of the Son of God that, "being the brightness of [God's] glory, and the figure of his substance . . . [He] sitteth on the right hand of the majesty on high" (Heb. i. 3).

When God speaks to man He uses words that man understands ; but He frequently invests those words with a richness and depth of meaning which they never before possessed. How intensive is the force in the New Testament of the common terms 'grace,' 'salvation,' 'redemption,' 'baptism,' 'call,' 'election,' 'apostle,' &c. ! The primary meaning of these terms is in no wise commensurate with their Christian significance. So is it with the term 'Word.' It bears a technical sense in the writings of Plato and of the Alexandrian Jew Philo, as well as in the Targums, or Aramaic paraphrases of the Old Testament ; but even this technical sense is very different from the sense which the term bears in the writings of St. John.

St. John is the only New Testament writer who calls the Son of God 'the Word.' From this it may be inferred that he chose this name (receiving it perhaps by direct revelation—see Apocalypse xix. 13, and gave it its true meaning in opposition to the Gnostics, who abused it, as they also abused the terms ἀρχή, ζωή, χάρις, ἀλήθεια, μονογενής— terms which St. John has also set in their true meaning.

God is a pure spirit ; and the term λόγος is very appropriate for expressing the spiritual nature of the Son and the spiritual manner of His procession from the Father : for, as St. Augustine says, "Thou canst have a word in thy heart, as it were a design born in thy mind, so that thy mind brings forth the design ; and the design is, so to

and without him was made nothing that was made. In
speak, the offspring of thy mind, the child of thy heart." The Son,
then, is the substantial image and perfect expression of the Father.
Invisible in Himself, He became visible in our human nature through
the Incarnation, as the hidden word of our heart becomes audible in
spoken language.

and the Word was with God (πρὸς τὸν Θεόν). The term πρός does
not here mean motion towards, but social union with, God. It is
equivalent to the saying, "a friend is with me." St. John, in v. 18,
expresses the same idea in a more emphatic way, saying, "the only-
begotten Son, who is in the bosom of the Father." This shows the
Son's real subsistence and personal distinction from the Father. See
1 John i. 2.

and the Word was God (Θεὸς ἦν ὁ λόγος). The predicate Θεός is
placed first for emphasis. Compare iv. 24 (πνεῦμα ὁ Θεός = God is a
spirit). Nouns used as predicates are usually without the article, but
here the omission of the article was necessary; for the insertion of the
article would have implied *identity of person* between the Word and
ὁ Θεός of v. 2 (πρὸς τὸν Θεόν), i.e., the Father. The Son is not the
Father; but the Son is God, possessing the same Divine nature with
the Father. St. John therefore teaches unity of Essence and distinction
of Person.

The doctrine of the Trinity is, of course, a great mystery, which
some inaccurate thinkers turn into a plain contradiction. Knowing, as
we all know, that God is a personal God, they first think of Him
vaguely as one infinite personal being and then as three infinite personal
beings, as one person and at the same time as three persons. But
there is no such contradiction in Catholic teaching. According to the
Catholic faith God is not first one person and then three persons, but
the Divine nature, essence, substance, or being is the three Persons,
and the three Persons are that one infinite nature or substance. By
experience we learn that the finite nature of man in each individual is
only one person; by God's revelation of Himself we learn that the
Divine nature is three Persons—Father, Son, and Holy Ghost. Now
because the three Persons are one and the self-same God, the term
God may be used indifferently of all and each of them. It is used of
all, as in 1 Cor. viii. 4, "There is no God, but one"; it is used of the
Father, as in John xx. 17, "I ascend to my Father and to your Father,
to my God and your God"; it is used of the Son, as in John xx. 28,
where the Apostle Thomas says to Christ, "My Lord, and my God;"
it is used of the Holy Ghost, as in Acts v. 3, 4, "Why hath satan
tempted thy heart, that thou shouldst lie to the Holy Ghost? . . . Thou
hast not lied to men, but to God."

2. *The same was in the beginning with God.* An emphatic combination and re-assertion of the clauses of v. 1. 'The same' (οὗτος) = he,
this = with emphasis (vii. 18).

After declaring the nature of the Word in Himself, St. John declares
His relations to the world in general, and to mankind in particular.

⁵ him was life, and the life was the light of men: And the

3. *All things were made by him* (δι' αὐτοῦ). Literally, 'through Him.' The one God, Father, Son, and Holy Ghost, is the Creator of all things, and therefore the three Persons are one and the same principle of creation. But since the Son proceeds from the Father and is the Word of the Father, the Father is said by appropriation to create through the Son. It must be noted, however, that the term διά is used in reference to the Father also (1 Cor. i. 9; Rom. xi. 36). Hence it implies nothing of inferiority, nothing of mere instrumentality.

and without him was made nothing (οὐδὲ ἕν, more emphatic than οὐδέν) *that was made* (ὃ γέγονεν: perf. = that has been made, and now is). This clause asserts by antithetic parallelism, common enough in Hebrew, what had been asserted in the first clause. "All things were made by Him, and without Him hath been made not even one thing."

4. *In him was life*, &c. St. John himself points out the interpretation of this verse. "This is the testimony, that God hath given to us eternal life. And this life is in his Son. He that hath the Son, hath life" (1 John v. 11 *seq.*). As the life of the whole plant is found in the seed, so the whole supernatural life of man is found in the grace and gift of the Word. "Whosoever is born of God, committeth not sin: for his seed abideth in him" (1 John iii. 9). This grace, this life, is also an illumination of mind in respect of Divine truths. "Now this is eternal life: that they may *know thee*, the only true God, and Jesus Christ, whom thou hast sent" (xvii. 3). It is said, "In him *was* life," because it was destined for mankind from the beginning. Hence St. John speaks of our Lord as "the Lamb, which was slain from the beginning of the world" (Apoc. xiii. 8).

Some understand this verse of the natural gifts of existence, life, and the light of intelligence, so that the meaning would almost coincide with St. Paul's, "for in him we live, and move, and be" (Acts xvii. 28). Such an interpretation yields a certain truth; but it is not what St. John says here. All natural gifts are included in "all things" of *v.* 3. Besides, the light of which St. John speaks is the light which men "did not receive" (*v.* 5), and to which the Baptist bore witness (*v.* 7). But that is not the natural light of reason.

Some of the oldest MSS., and many ancient writers, give a different punctuation for *vv.* 3 and 4. They read thus: "Without Him was made nothing. What was made in Him was life." From this reading three interpretations are drawn. (*a*) What was made in (*i.e.*, by, or through) Him, was life (*i.e.*, living). This meaning is obviously false; for life is not found in all things. (*b*) What was made was life in Him, *i.e.*, as before a house is built its idea is in the mind of the architect, so before the world was created its plan was in the mind of the living God. This is true, but not to the purpose of St. John's argument. (*c*) "What was made, in *it* was the life," *i.e.*, the Word, who is life, is in the world which He made, "upholding all things by the word of his power" (Heb. i. 3). This also is true; but it is not St. John's statement. For, to pass over the unwarranted insertion of

light shineth in darkness, and the darkness did not
comprehend it. There was a man sent from God, whose 6
name was John. This man came for a witness, to give 7
testimony of the light, that all men might believe through
him. He was not the light, but was to give testimony of 8

the definite article before "life," the perfect γέγονεν (that which has
been made, and now is) would require ἐστί (in it *is* life) instead of ἦν
(in it *was* life); or, if the historical ἦν be retained, then γέγονεν would
require to be changed into ἐγένετο.

5. *The light shineth in darkness*. More accurately, 'in the
darkness.' By the darkness is meant the mass of men who, since the
Fall, have had their minds morally darkened by sin and ignorance.
"You were heretofore darkness, but now light in the Lord" (Eph. v.
8). The light *shineth*, *i.e.*, has continued to shine uninterruptedly
even until now. (This is the only present tense in the section.) In
v. 9 it is said that the light "enlighteneth every man that cometh
into this world." But not all are willing to receive the light.

and the darkness did not comprehend it. The Revised Version
translates "*apprehended* it not." This is a better translation of the
verb κατέλαβεν. It means that men made no energetic effort, did not
strive to possess the light. (See on this meaning of the verb, 1 Cor. ix.
24; Phil. iii. 12, 13.)

The Revised Version has in the margin [1] the alternative rendering
"overcame it not." The verb may be so translated, and it is appropriately so translated in xii. 35; but this meaning is inappropriate
here. (See *vv.* 9, 11, 12.)

St. John has just touched upon that antithesis between light and
darkness, between those who receive and those who do not receive
the light, which antithesis, as was said in the Introduction, pervades
the Gospel. In the following verses he speaks of it more at length,
after declaring, by way of historical preface, what had been the mission
and testimony of the Baptist. The Introduction has explained the
importance of the Baptist's testimony in St. John's argument.

6. *There was* (ἐγένετο = appeared, came, arose) *a man*. The Greek
verb is used to denote historical manifestation. (See Mark i. 4;
Luke i. 5.)

sent from God. This phrase is descriptive of the prophetical office.
There appeared a God-sent man. St. John's mission was so important
that he was "more than a prophet," and his work had itself been foretold in prophecy. (See Mal. iii. 1; Luke iii. 2; vii. 27.)

7. *This man came for a witness* (εἰς μαρτυρίαν), *i.e.*, to give testimony of what had been prophetically made known to him about the
light (περὶ τοῦ φωτός).

8. *He was not the light*. John, indeed, was not only a light, but a
bright light (v. 35); yet he was not The Light: but [he came] in

---

[1] Future references will be expressed by the letters R.V. and R.V.M.

9 the light. That was the true light, which enlighteneth
10 every man that cometh into this world. He was in the
world, and the world was made by him, and the world
11 knew him not. He came unto his own, and his own
12 received him not. But as many as received him, he

order to give testimony about the light (ἀλλ' ἵνα μαρτυρήσῃ: ἦλθεν is supplied before ἵνα from v. 7).

9. *That was the true light* (ἦν τὸ φῶς: R.V., "There was the true light"). The verb is emphatic from position, and τὸ φῶς is the subject, not the predicate. The meaning is, John was not the light; but the very light, light itself (τὸ ἀληθινόν), was then existing.

which enlighteneth every man that cometh (ἐρχόμενον) *into this world* (εἰς τὸν κόσμον) (R.V., "There was the true light, even the light which lighteth," &c. R.V.M., "The true light, which lighteth every man, was coming," &c., or, "lighteth every man as he cometh). The participle may be taken as nominative neuter in agreement with φῶς, or as accusative masculine agreeing with ἄνθρωπον. The first would mean that the light coming (*i.e.*, at its coming) into the world enlighteneth every man; but this is excluded by v. 4, where it is said that the Word was the light of men from the very beginning. Besides, ἦν is emphatic, and too remote from ἐρχόμενον. The second means that every man born is enlightened by the Word. This meaning we adopt.

10. *He was in the world.* How? Upholding all things, and showing forth His wisdom, power, and divinity in the wonderful beauty and harmony of nature, in the appointments of His providence, and in the law of conscience written in man's heart (see Heb. i. 3; Wisd. xiii. 1-5; Acts xiv. 16, xvii. 26-28; Rom. i. 19, 20, ii. 14, 15).

the world knew him not. The term 'world' here passes into a narrower sense. It has four meanings in the New Testament—(1) the universe; (2) the earth; (3) the inhabitants of the earth; (4) worldlings. The meaning must in each particular case be determined by the context. St. John generally uses it to denote those who are deceived and blinded by love of earthly things.

knew him not. That is, with a *practical* recognition. Although men knew Him they 'did not glorify him as God'; 'they liked not to have God in their knowledge' (Rom. i. 21, 28).

11. *He came unto his own* (τὰ ἴδια), *and his own* (οἱ ἴδιοι) *received him not.* The neuter might be translated 'His own home' (xix. 27). In any case, it certainly means Israel, God's own inheritance and possession (Exod. xv. 17). God frequently visited His people, but their stiffnecked resistance (Acts vii. 51-53) culminated in the awful drama of the crucifixion. In v. 14 St. John begins the description of the *manner* of the Word's coming. This transition from the world at large to the chosen people deepens the antithesis.

12. *But as many as received him.* Not all were hardened in unbelief; some received Him, that is, as the parallelism of the verse shows, "believed in His name." The phrase to believe in (πιστεύειν

gave them power to be made the sons of God, to them that believe in his name. Who are born, not of blood, nor of the will of the flesh, nor of the will of man, but of God. And the Word was made flesh, and dwelt among us

εἰς), is very frequent in St. John. Some take as synonymous πιστ· τινί and πιστ· with ἐν, εἰς or ἐπί. But since St. John uses verbs of motion with particles of state or rest (v. 4), and verbs of state or rest with particles of motion [comp. Matt. x. 16; Mark ii. 1], and thus elliptically connects both ideas together, we naturally take the phrase πιστεύειν εἰς as denoting a movement of soul towards God and rest in Him by faith.

he gave them power (ἐξουσίαν) *to be made* (γενέσθαι = to be born, to become) *the sons of God.* The power is not an abstract possibility, but a true and real power (v. 27, x. 18). Hence the Council of Trent defined that faith is "the beginning, the foundation and root of all justification." By sanctifying grace, which is given only to those that believe, we are not only cleansed from sin but are "made partakers of the Divine nature" (2 Pet. i. 4); we are spiritually created, being made "a new creature" (2 Cor. v. 17), and truly "born of God" (John iii. 3, 6, 7), and thus are made 'the sons of God' (cf. Rom. viii. 16). Moreover, since sanctifying grace is the living root of eternal life, now planted in our souls, we are "sons of God and joint-heirs with Christ" (Rom. viii. 17). We, by grace, are adopted sons; Christ, by nature, is the μονογενής, the only-begotten Son.

13. *Who are born.* Better, 'who were born' (ἐγεννήθησαν). This cannot refer to "them that believe," for these are said to receive *power to become* the sons of God; it explains what is meant by sons of God. The sons of God are those who were born, not by a natural human generation, but by a spiritual and supernatural generation. That is to say, "not of blood" (αἱμάτων: plural used for singular), for blood was considered to be the basis of life (Lev. xvii. 11), and man was said to be "compacted in blood" (Wisd. vii. 2), (which statement is expanded into two further parallel statements—"nor of the will of the flesh, nor of the will of man"), but of grace and the Holy Spirit.

The previous verses have in general terms described the Word in His eternity, in the work of creation, in the past history of mankind, in the history of the Chosen People; the narrative now passes to a fuller history of the Incarnation.

14. *And the Word was made* (ἐγένετο = became) *flesh, and dwelt* (ἐσκήνωσεν = tabernacled) *among us.*

The first "and" has only its ordinary conjunctive force, continuing the narrative. St. John says that He who had done so much from the beginning, now became flesh (*i.e.*, man—cf. xvii. 2). The Son of God, eternal and infinite, while remaining perfectly unaltered in Himself, in His Divine nature, took to Himself a perfect human nature like ours, and became what He was not before. He took that human

us (and we saw his glory, the glory as it were of the only-
nature to Himself, not in that mere external way in which a man may
take money in his hand, but by a substantial union so true and close
that the assumed human nature became as really His as our bodies and
souls are ours. The depths of this mystery we cannot fathom, but we
can gain some idea of it from an illustration. We know that death
separates soul from body. After that separation the soul still lives and
thinks, but the body is lifeless. At the resurrection the lifeless and
separated body will again be taken up by the soul and thereafter
claimed by it as its own. In a somewhat similar way the Word
assumed a human nature (*i.e.*, both body and soul) into substantial
union with Himself, and truly claims that nature as His own. This is
called the Incarnation, and it now means, not an action, but a state of
continuous personal possession. Whatever of action there was in the
act of incarnation was common to the three Persons of the Blessed
Trinity, just as the act of clothing would be common to three men
engaged in clothing one of themselves. Because man has body and
soul, contradictory predicates are applied to him, *e.g.*, he is at once
mortal (body) and immortal (soul). So because Christ has two natures
He is the subject of contradictory predicates. In His Divine nature
He "thought it not robbery to be equal with God" (Phil. ii. 6), in His
human nature He "was made a little lower than the angels" (Heb.
ii. 9); as God He said, "I and the Father are one" (John x.
30), but as man, "The Father is greater than I" (John xiv. 28);
as God, "what things soever the Father doth, these the Son also
doth ὁμοίως" (= equally, in same manner) John v. 19; as man,
"Father, not my will, but thine be done" (Luke xxii. 42).
The verb '*tabernacled*' is most significantly chosen. During the
desert-wanderings of the Israelites the cloud that rested on the tabernacle was the symbol of God's presence, and therefore was called the
glory of the Lord (Num. ix. 15; Exod. xl. 32). But the Incarnation
was the fulfilment of what the ancient tabernacle, with its glory, dimly
foreshadowed, and of what God had expressly promised, "I will set
my tabernacle (τὴν σκηνήν μου—LXX.) in the midst of you" (Lev.
xxvi. 11).

and we saw his glory. St. John continues the idea just expressed.
The Apostles had witnessed the manifestation of Christ's Divine power
and majesty shining through the tabernacle of His human nature.
"That which was from the beginning, which we have heard, which we
have seen with our eyes, which we have looked upon, and our hands
have handled, of the word of life: for the life was manifested: and we
have seen, and do bear witness, and declare unto you the life eternal,
which was with the Father, and hath appeared to us" (1 John i. 1, 2).

"*the glory as it were* (ὡς) *of the only-begotten of the Father.* The particle ὡς does not mean 'as if,' but 'such as belongs to.' The whole
phrase is qualitative, and declares that the glory really corresponded to
the nature and dignity of God's Son. In the same way St. Paul says
of our Lord that He was "in habit found as (ὡς) a man," *i.e.*, the real

begotten of the Father) full of grace and truth. John 15 beareth witness of him, and crieth out, saying: This was he of whom I spoke: He that shall come after me, is preferred before me: because he was before me. And of 16 his fulness we all have received, and grace for grace. For the law was given by Moses, grace and truth came 17

nature that truly belongs to man (Phil. ii. 7). Comp. Matt. vii. 29; Rom. vi. 13. In Greek the article is absent before 'glory' and before 'only-begotten.' This makes the clause parenthetical. We saw His glory (glory such as was natural in an only-begotten Son).

"*full* (πλήρης) *of grace and truth.* The word πλήρης, though in the nominative, is in apposition with αὐτοῦ (comp. Apoc. ii. 20, ix. 14, &c.) "Full of grace and truth" = full of life and light; for grace is life, and truth is light (comp. *vv.* 4, 9, 12). See note after *v.* 18.

15. *John beareth witness.* Present tense, as if the testimony of John still endured.

and crieth out (κέκραγε, perfect in its classical use for present). This cry is the solemn announcement made by a divinely-sent herald (see vii. 28; Rom. ix. 27; and comp. Matt. iii. 1–3; Mark i. 2–4; Luke iii. 1–4).

This was he of whom I spoke (R.V., "said"), ὃν εἶπον. St. John Baptist, supposed to be speaking in the present, looks back historically to his testimony, and therefore says, 'This *was* he' whom I meant when I said, &c.

He that shall come after me (ἐρχόμενος), *is preferred before me* (ἔμπροσθέν μου γέγονεν): *because he was before me* (πρῶτός μου). This testimony to our Lord was given before He began His public ministry by coming to the baptism of John (Matt. iii. 11–13). We must therefore think of John as speaking before our Lord had begun His public ministry, and as saying, 'There is one who will come after me (ὁ ἐρχόμενος = the Coming One = the Appointed and Expected One), but He has already been appointed to a greater office than mine ("is mightier than I," Matt. iii. 11), because He existed (from eternity) before I was born.' Touching the language, ἔμπροσθεν may certainly be used for priority in dignity (see Gen. xlviii. 20, LXX.); πρῶτος has also the meaning of the comparative (see Acts i. 1).

16. *And* (ὅτι = because) *of his fulness* (πληρώματος, referring to πλήρης of *v.* 14)[1] *we all have received, and grace for grace* (χάριν ἀντὶ χάριτος). These are the words, not of the Baptist, but of the Evangelist, who confirms what the Baptist had said. Christ is shown to be greater than John, to be the life and light of mankind, because all have received, from His fulness, grace and truth. Not once only; but truly grace following upon grace in unceasing flow. The 'and' before 'grace' is emphatic = and indeed.

17. *For* (ὅτι) *the law was given by Moses, grace and truth came by*

---

[1] See note at end of this section, *i.e.*, after *v.* 18.

18 by Jesus Christ. No man hath seen God at any time:

Jesus Christ. This verse gives the reason why all receive grace from the fulness of Christ alone. The Law declared to man his duty, yet did not enable him to fulfil it (Rom. iii. 20, v. 20; 2 Cor. iii. 6). Grace, it is true, was given also under the Law, but not by the Law; it was given through the merits of the Redeemer that was to be, and only in comparatively limited measure (Acts iv. 12; Joel ii. 28; Acts ii. 16-18; Heb. ix. 15, x. 1). Truth, again, was certainly revealed in the Old Law, but only partially and with comparative imperfection (Heb. i. 1, 2; Gal. iii. 23-25; 1 Cor. ii. 7-10). Thus it is true that "grace and truth came by (or through) Jesus Christ." He was, and is, the universal source of both. By referring all to "Jesus Christ" the Apostle identifies Him with the Eternal Word, of whom it had just been written that He was the life and light of mankind.

18. *No man hath seen God at any time* ($\pi\acute{\omega}\pi o\tau\epsilon$ = ever yet). It no man, therefore not even Moses, of whom it is said, "The Lord spoke to Moses face to face, as a man is wont to speak to his friend" (Exod. xxxiii. 11). Moses and the prophets were favoured with visions and revelations, but they had not been admitted to a direct vision of God as in Himself He really is, to a clear intuition of God's unveiled essence.

the only-begotten Son (or, as many ancient authorities read, God only-begotten) *who is in the bosom* ($\epsilon\iota\varsigma$ $\tau\grave{o}\nu$ $\kappa\acute{o}\lambda\pi o\nu$) *of the Father, he hath declared him* (Greek omits 'Him'). "What signifieth 'in the bosom of the Father'? In the secret of the Father. For God has not a bosom, as we have; . . . but because our bosom is within, the secret of the Father is called the bosom of the Father" (St. Aug., Tract iii. c. 17). The Apostle here points out the supreme warrant for the sublime doctrine just set before us—a doctrine surpassing all other teaching. No man has ever yet seen God in Himself, so as to declare the deep things of God; the only-begotten Son, who is intimately united with the Father, He ($\epsilon\kappa\epsilon\tilde{\iota}\nu o\varsigma$—emphatic from position) hath brought forward and expounded ($\epsilon\xi\eta\gamma\acute{\eta}\sigma a\tau o$) the doctrine we teach. (comp. iii. 13, xiv. 11, xv. 15, xvii. 6-8). Hence St. Paul speaks of Christ as "the power of God and the wisdom of God" (1 Cor. i. 24).

NOTE.—From the statement of *v.* 18 we infer that our Lord, who came as man to teach us, also possessed as man the privilege of a direct and intuitive vision of the Divine essence. If our Lord, as man, had no such direct vision of God, but, like Moses and the prophets, had received His doctrine by simple revelation, the point of the contrast made by St. John would be broken. "No man hath ever yet seen God," and "the only-begotten Son who is in the bosom of the Father he hath declared." The contrast is not merely between doctrine and doctrine, but also between the sources of each doctrine. The prophets taught, but they had never seen God; Christ is therefore preferred before them as Teacher, because He had seen God. But Christ taught as man. Therefore as man also He had seen God. This conclusion is perfectly obvious. Now, Christ's intuitive vision of God is part of

the only-begotten Son who is in the bosom of the Father, he hath declared him.

the πλήρωμα spoken of in v. 14 and v. 16. That term seems to have secured its place as a technical term of Christian doctrine years before St. John wrote. It denotes Christ's perfect fulness of grace, wisdom, power, and spiritual gift of every kind. Our Lord as man is a very ocean of life and light. The source of that fulness is the Hypostatic Union itself. Because the Sacred Humanity was assumed into the unity of the Word, the soul of Christ was filled to its utmost capacity with all grace and spiritual perfection. From the fulness of Christ the Church derives her life, her gifts, her doctrine, her holiness, her infallibility, her sacraments, and all her means of life and light to mankind; through the Church every child of God is enlightened and nourished. This doctrine is nowhere more clearly expressed than in St. Paul's Epistle to the Colossians. Of the Hypostatic Union he says that in Christ "dwelleth all the fulness of the Godhead corporally" (ii. 9); of the Pleroma he says that in Christ "are hid all the treasures of wisdom and knowledge," and that in Him "it hath well pleased the Father, that all fulness should dwell" (ii. 3, i. 19). Of the consequent life of the Church he says that we "are filled in him, who is the head of all principality and power." "For in him were all things created. And he is before all, and by him all things consist. And he is the head of the body, the church" (ii. 10, i. 16–18). We must therefore reject what is sometimes said about the limitations, imperfections, and defects of Christ's knowledge. All are excluded by the clear doctrine of the Pleroma. In becoming man at all He "emptied himself" (Phil. ii. 7), but that does not mean that He assumed an *empty* human nature. Rather, in that nature were hid from the beginning "all the treasures of wisdom and knowledge," but those treasures were unfolded only gradually before the eyes of men (Luke ii. 40–52).

At the time St. John wrote his Gospel he could appeal to well-known facts in the history of the Church to confirm the statement, "and of his fulness we have all received." The descent of the promised Spirit at Pentecost, and His outpouring of grace; the charismata so bountifully given to the early Christians—the gift of tongues, of healing, of prophecy, of spiritual illumination; the ministry of angels, the miracles, the numberless signs and tokens of God's presence in the Church; the supernatural charity which moved the hearts of the faithful so potently that, as St. Paul argued, "the Spirit himself giveth testimony to our spirit, that we are the sons of God" (Rom. viii. 16)—all these things were a cumulative proof clearly present to the minds of St. John's readers.

In the Introduction we said that the fourth Gospel might be called the Gospel of Testimony. Everything in the Gospel is arranged to show what testimonies were given to our Lord, and what manifestations He made of Himself; how those testimonies and manifestations were received; how some men believed, some wavered, and some grew

The Testimony of the Baptist to the Deputation from Jerusalem.

(VERS. 19–28.)

19 And this is the testimony of John, when the Jews sent from Jerusalem priests and Levites to him, to ask him:
20 Who art thou? And he confessed, and did not deny:

hard in unbelief: in a word, we have a record of the Light shining in darkness, and being rejected by some, but received by others, who are filled with grace and made sons of God.

The Jewish expectation of the Messiah had never died out. We know from history that about the time of our Lord's birth that expectation had grown most intense. There was a widespread and deep impression that the long-deferred hope of Israel was now about to be satisfied. When John therefore appeared "in the spirit and power of Elias," clad, as the ancient prophets were sometimes clad, in poor raiment with a leathern girdle, and began to preach penance because the kingdom of heaven was at hand, his words and the sanctity of his life drew great multitudes to him. St. John knew what his mission meant. Zachary, his father, being filled with the Holy Ghost, had prophesied, saying: "Thou, child, shalt be called the prophet of the highest: for thou shalt go before the face of the Lord to prepare his ways" (Luke i. 67, 76). St. John, therefore, had announced not only the kingdom, but also the King. He had said, "He that shall come after me, is preferred before me" (i. 15). Yet St. John had never, probably, met our Lord; hence when our Lord came to be baptized St. John did not at first recognise Him (i. 31). But as soon as John had learned by sign from heaven and by Divine illumination that the King whom he had been announcing was no other than Jesus, he began to bear witness to that fact. The evangelist records some of John's testimonies. And first that to the deputation from Jerusalem. The sending of such a deputation of priests and levites shows how strongly the souls of the people had been stirred, and how great was the perplexity of the religious leaders; the public character of the deputation gives great solemnity to the testimony of the Baptist.

19. *And this is the testimony.* These words look back to *v.* 15 ("John beareth witness"). 'And now this is what John testified.'

the Jews. St. John uses this term more than sixty times, and generally in the spirit of one who now looks upon them as an alien race, and who is writing for those to whom the Jews are strangers both in faith and in blood. As the deputation consisted of priests and levites, it came probably from the Sanhedrin or Great Council. The Sanhedrin, which was the supreme tribunal of the Jews, consisted of 71 members (some passages of the Mishna mention 72). These members belonged to three orders. The leading order was that of the ἀρχιερεῖς—the Chief Priests past and present, with whom were

and he confessed: I am not the Christ. And they asked 21
him: What then? Art thou Elias? And he said: I am
not. Art thou the prophet? And he answered: No.
They said therefore unto him: Who art thou, that we 22
may give an answer to them that sent us? what sayest

joined the chief of the twenty-four priestly families. The next order
was that of the γραμματεῖς—professional lawyers and theologians.
The third order was that of the πρεσβύτεροι and ἄρχοντες—leading
men, either priests or laymen, whose qualifications marked them out for
public duties (see Matt. xxvii. 41; Mark xi. 27, xiv. 53; Luke
xxiii. 13, xxiv. 20). To this supreme court it belonged to pass judgment on false prophets and false teachers. But the deputation may
not have been a formal one from the whole tribunal. John belonged
to a priestly family; and those who came were priests and levites—
those who perhaps felt a special interest in the Baptist, and had therefore arranged with the rulers for a deputation to interrogate him. The
levites, who accompanied the priests, were official teachers of the
people (2 Paral. xxxv. 3; 2 Esdr. viii. 7-9). Whether, then, the
deputation was formal or no, its coming was a solemn and important
event. It was a means for making John's testimony to Jesus more
widely known. Even before the baptism of our Lord the people had
begun to think that John was perhaps the Christ—the Anointed and
Promised One (Luke iii. 15). Hence, when asked "Who art thou?"
his first thought turned to the common suspicion, and he at once
replied, "I am not the Christ" (v. 20). From the order of the
words the emphasis falls on the pronoun "I," as though John said,
'You are now seeking the Christ; but I am not He': thus implying
that he knew of another who was the Christ. John, however, had
made too deep an impression on the conscience of the nation for men
to be satisfied with a bare denial of what he was not. The priests,
therefore, continue, not without anger—

21. *What then? Art thou Elias?* The scribes taught that
Elias would usher in the Messianic kingdom (see Matt. xvii. 10;
Mark ix. 10). But this opinion arose from a false interpretation of
Malachias iv. 5, in which passage the prophet speaks of the Second
Advent. The question runs thus: "You say you are not the Christ:
what, then, is the meaning of your conduct? Are you Elias?" They
were thinking of the literal Elias; and St. John could answer, 'I am
not'; though in a figurative sense he was Elias (Matt. xi. 14,
xvii. 12; Luke i. 17).

Art thou the prophet? The article marks some well-known but
unnamed prophet. This can only be the unnamed prophet who was
promised by Moses (Deut. xviii. 15), and who was really identical with
the Messiah (John i. 45, vi. 14; Acts iii. 22). After these denials,
which have been growing in abruptness, the priests demand a positive
answer.

22. *Who art thou?* St. John, quoting the words of Isaias (xl. 3), in

²³ thou of thyself? He said: *I am the voice of one crying in the wilderness, Make straight the way of the Lord*, as said ²⁴ the prophet Isaias. And they that were sent were of the ²⁵ Pharisees. And they asked him, and said to him: Why then dost thou baptize, if thou be not Christ, nor Elias, ²⁶ nor the prophet? John answered them, saying: I baptize with water; but there hath stood one in the midst of you, ²⁷ whom you know not. The same is he that shall come after me, who is preferred before me: the latchet of whose

which reference is made to the coming of the Redeemer (words, too, which are applied to John by the first three evangelists), says that he is only a herald who runs before the King to announce His coming. "I am a voice," &c.

24. *And they that were sent were of the Pharisees.* St. John had clearly testified that he was the forerunner of the Christ. His questioners, however, could not, or would not, understand; but being "of the Pharisees" they proceeded to put to him a further question characteristically Pharisaic. The words 'and they that were sent, were of the Pharisees,' point forward, and explain why the question which follows was put.

25. *Why then dost thou baptize, if thou be not Christ, nor Elias, nor the prophet?* The Jewish custom of baptizing proselytes seems not to have arisen till after the destruction of Jerusalem. John's innovation, therefore, accompanied as it was by the preaching of repentance and by the confession of sins (Matt. iii. 2, 5, 6), appeared to the Pharisees an unwarranted step of gravest moment. It was, indeed, of gravest moment; but not unwarranted. According to the prophets, repentance was the preparation for the Messianic kingdom (Ezech. xvi. 61-63; Mich. vii. 9), and in the days of the Messiah there was to be a true baptism (Ezech. xxxvi. 25; Zach. xiii. 1), of which John's baptism was the preparation. Hence it was by command of God Himself that John baptized (v. 33). His baptism, therefore, had a Messianic import; and to this John refers in his reply.

26. *I baptize with water* (ἐν ὕδατι), *i.e.*, my baptism is only a baptism of water, a symbolic action pointing to a greater reality (see v. 33 and Matt. iii. 11).

but there hath stood (στήκει = "standeth," R.V.) *one in the midst of you, whom you know not.* There is a double emphasis; the one on 'I,' and the other on 'water.' Christ is the antithesis.

27. [*The same is*] *he that shall come after me* (ἐρχόμενος: as in v. 15) [*who is preferred before me*]. The words in brackets are omitted in the oldest MSS. They have probably slipped in from v. 15.

The latchet of whose shoe I am not worthy to loose. This, then, is the sense: My baptism is only a preparation for the true baptism of Him who is already in your midst—of Him who cometh after me; whose slave I am not worthy to be.

shoe I am not worthy to loose. These things were done 28 in Bethania beyond the Jordan, where John was baptizing.

John's Testimony to the People.
(Vers. 29-34.)

The next day John saw Jesus coming to him, and he 29 saith: Behold the lamb of God, behold him who taketh away the sin of the world. This is he of whom I said: 30 After me there cometh a man, who is preferred before me: because he was before me. And I knew him not, but 31

28. *These things were done in Bethania beyond the Jordan.* Testimony so important as that given by John to the deputation demanded a definite statement of the place where it had been given. The evangelist therefore tells us that it was given in "Bethania beyond the Jordan," *i.e.*, to the east of the river, in Peræa. There was another Bethania near Jerusalem (xi. 18). Many ancient authorities read Bethabara or Betharabah. Currency was given to this mistake by Origen, who thought that the Bethabara of his day marked the site of Bethania. The site, however, has not yet been identified; and the derivation of the name is altogether doubtful.

29. *The next day.* Our Lord had gone, as the Evangelist supposes his readers to know, immediately after His baptism into the desert for forty days; and now, on the day after that on which John had given testimony, He returns. John saw Him, and pointing Him out to the multitude, said: *Behold (ἴδε) the lamb of God.* The words ἴδε, ἄγε, &c., are used in the singular, even by classical writers, as interjections. The article denotes some well-known, some appointed and expected lamb. We are thus referred to the well-known passage of Isaias in which the Messiah is described as a lamb before His shearers, and bearing the sins of many (Isa. liii.; comp. Matt. viii. 17; Luke xxii. 37; Acts viii. 32; Apoc. v. 6, 12, 13, xiv. 1-4, xxii. 1-3). He is the lamb of God (genitive of possession), *i.e.*, God's own lamb, and appointed by God: "The Lord hath laid on Him the iniquity of us all" (Isa. liii. 6).

who taketh away (ὁ αἴρων) *the sin of the world.* Αἴρων might mean "who taketh on Himself," or "who taketh away." The latter meaning seems to be that determined by the evangelist himself (1 John iii. 5). 'The sin,' *i.e.*, all the sins, as a collective whole, of all mankind. According to St. Paul, "almost all things, according to the law, are cleansed with blood; and without shedding of blood there is no remission" (Heb. ix. 22). The reference, therefore, is to our Lord's offering of Himself to death for all mankind.

30. *This is he of whom I said*, &c. The Baptist refers to testimony already given. This testimony is that of *v.* 15.

31. *And I knew him not* (see introductory remarks of previous § 1), *i.e.*, His features were unknown to me. This prepares the way for what follows.

that he may be made manifest in Israel, therefore am I
32 come baptizing with water. And John gave testimony,
saying: I saw the Spirit coming down as a dove from
33 heaven, and he remained upon him. And I knew him
not: but he, who sent me to baptize with water, said to
me: He upon whom thou shalt see the Spirit descending
and remaining upon him, he it is that baptizeth with the
34 Holy Ghost. And I saw; and I gave testimony, that this
is the Son of God.

John's Testimony to his Own Disciples.
(Vers. 35–42.)

35 The next day again John stood, and two of his disciples.

but that he may, &c. The past tense is preferable: 'That He should be made manifest in Israel (or, to Israel) I came baptizing with water.' John's baptism was a manifestation of Christ, (1) for the reason given in *v.* 25; (2) because the Father had designed to give testimony to Christ on occasion of His baptism by John (Matt. iii. 13–17).

32. *And John gave testimony.* These words mark either the continuation of the preceding testimony, or the beginning of a distinct act of testimony. John testifies to what he had witnessed at Christ's baptism—the descent of the Holy Ghost upon Christ (Luke iii. 22). The Holy Ghost "remained upon him"; not by a continuation of the bodily shape (dove), but by manifesting His presence in our Lord's public life. St. Luke expresses it thus: "Jesus *being full of* the Holy Ghost, returned from the Jordan, and was led by the Spirit into the desert" (iv. 1).

33. *He upon whom thou shalt see the Spirit descending.* This descent of the Holy Ghost had been promised to John as a sign whereby he might recognise the Son of God (see *v.* 31).

34. *And I saw; and I gave testimony, that this is the Son of God.* In this verse the verbs are in the perfect tense. St. John repeats the words which he had heard from heaven: "Thou art ('this is') my beloved Son" (Matt. iii. 17; Mark i. 11). By those words the Father pointed out Christ as the Eternal Son, the promised Messiah-King foretold in Psa. ii. Whether John's audience understood the full import of these words may be doubted; but that John himself understood, there can be no doubt. The purpose of the evangelist in quoting John's testimony is a decisive proof of this. Now John has testified to three things concerning Christ: (1) that He is the lamb of God, who taketh away all sin; (2) that He baptizes in the Holy Ghost, *i.e.*, gives life and light to all; (3) that He is the Son of God.

35. *Two of his disciples.* One of these was the Apostle Andrew

And beholding Jesus walking, he saith: Behold the lamb 36
of God. And the two disciples heard him speak, and 37
they followed Jesus. And Jesus turning, and seeing 38
them following him, said to them: What seek you? Who
said to him: Rabbi (which is to say, being interpreted,
Master), where dwellest thou? He saith to them: Come 39
and see. They came, and saw where he abode, and they
staid with him that day: now it was about the tenth
hour. And Andrew the brother of Simon Peter was one 40
of the two who had heard of John, and followed him.
He findeth first his brother Simon, and saith to him: We 41
have found the Messias, which is, being interpreted, the

(*v*. 40); the other, whose name is not given, was the evangelist himself. The incidents here recorded took place before these disciples were called to be apostles of Christ (see iii. 11).

39. *The tenth hour.* According to the Jewish mode of reckoning this would be about two hours before sunset—for they divided the time between sunrise and sunset into twelve hours. The length of the hour consequently varied considerably, being longer in summer and shorter in winter. According to our method of reckoning it would be about 10 a.m. The words, "and they staid with him that day," are favourable to this second interpretation. But against this must be set the fact that in so interpreting we make the evangelist's language quite abnormal. Throughout the rest of the New Testament the Jewish method is observed, as it is also observed in the writings of Josephus. See note on xix. 14.

40. *Andrew, the brother of Simon Peter.* This designation of Andrew shows how very much more prominent Peter was in the eyes of the Church.

41. *He findeth first his brother Simon.* This implies that the evangelist had also sought *his* brother, though, with his usual reticence about himself, he does not mention the fact; but Andrew was *the first* to be successful in the search. As Peter was near at hand, although a Galilean, it may be inferred that he was a disciple of the Baptist.

We have found the Messias. There is an indication of overabounding joy in Andrew's eager words. The Baptist's testimony had been powerfully confirmed by our Lord during the time that Andrew "staid with him."

which is, being interpreted, the Christ. The article should be omitted; it is not in the Greek. The words 'Messiah' and 'Christ,' the one Hebrew and the other Greek, mean 'anointed' (see Psa. ii. 2; Dan. ix. 24, 25). The name implies that Christ was emphatically the Anointed One—King and Priest and Prophet (see Acts iv. 27, x. 38; cf. 1 Sam. x. 1; Num. iii. 3; Isa. lxi. 1).

Christ. And he brought him to Jesus. And Jesus
looking upon him said: Thou art Simon the son of Jona:
thou shalt be called Cephas, which is interpreted Peter.

Jesus, Philip, and Nathanael.

(VERS. 43–51.)

⁴³ On the following day he would go forth into Galilee,
and he findeth Philip. And Jesus saith to him: Follow
⁴⁴ me. Now Philip was of Bethsaida, the city of Andrew

42. *And Jesus looking upon him* (ἐμβλέψας αὐτῷ). It denotes
a fixed look of close attention. Jesus, who read men's hearts and
"knew what was in man" (ii. 25), immediately shows what that glance
of interest portended.

Thou art Simon the son of Jona. The true reading here, as in
xxi. 15-17 and Matt. xvi. 17, is 'John.' Where 'Jona' appears in the
MSS. it is an apocopated form of Johanan (John).

thou shalt be called Cephas, which is interpreted Peter (*i.e.*, Rock).
The term πέτρος is common enough among classical writers (not, however, in Homer) in the sense of 'a rock,' not merely 'a stone' as in
A.V. (R.V.M. has "rock" or "stone"). Hence in Matt. xvi. 18,
where it is a question rather of the thing signified than of the name,
the form used is πέτρα, which only means Rock. The name Peter is
here only promised to Simon, its actual bestowal came later (Mark
iii. 16), and its explanation later still (Matt. xvi. 18). Like Abraham,
Sarah, and Israel, Peter really became what his name signified
(John xxi. 15-17). Our Lord at His first meeting with Nathanael
(i. 47-49) and with the Samaritan woman (iv. 16-19) gave them a
sign of His Divine mission by a display of superhuman knowledge.
We may, therefore, conclude that our Lord intended to give a similar
sign by an immediate indication of Simon's name and parentage—
"Thou art Simon, son of John."

43. *On the following day*, *i.e.*, the fourth from the beginning of
John's testimony. The days are (1) *v*. 19; (2) *v*. 29; (3) *v*. 35;
(4) *v*. 43.

he would go forth (ἠθέλησεν = He was just intending to go forth)
into Galilee, and he findeth Philip. Peter and Andrew may have
communicated with Philip (see *v*. 45). In any case, the finding was
not accidental (xvii. 6).

Jesus saith to him: Follow me. This was only a general call to
become a disciple—a follower of Christ (see Matt. viii. 22). The
formal call to the Apostolate came later.

44. *Philip was of Bethsaida.* In xii. 21 he is said to be of Beth-

and Peter. Philip findeth Nathanael, and saith to him: 45
We have found him of whom Moses in the law, and the
prophets did write, Jesus the son of Joseph of Nazareth.

saida *in Galilee*. Is this addition to be taken as implying that there
was another Bethsaida? We think so. There was a town named
Bethsaida (= House of Fishing) on the left bank of the Jordan and
near the river's mouth; it was named Julias (also Julias of Peræa), in
honour of the daughter of Augustus. Near it lay the desert place
where our Lord fed the five thousand (Luke ix. 10 *seq.*; John vi. 1–10;
Matt. xiv. 13–21; Mark vi. 31–45). Now, although the miracle is
expressly stated to have occurred at Bethsaida, our Lord told the disciples to take ship from the place and to go over the water to Bethsaida
(Mark vi. 45). This Bethsaida was "in the land of Genezareth"
(Mark vi. 53), and was near Capharnaum (John vi. 17), with which
place it is joined in our Lord's denunciations (Matt. xi. 21; Luke
x. 13). Thus there were two Bethsaidas: Bethsaida Julias on the
north-east of Lake Tiberias, and Bethsaida on the west in Galilee.

But an ingenious plea is put forward for the opinion that there was
only one Bethsaida, viz., Bethsaida Julias. It is urged (1) that the
province of Galilee ran round the Lake of Galilee so as to include
most of the level coast-land on the east. (2) The phrase 'to go over
(or across) the water' does not necessarily imply a passage from east
to west. Josephus speaks of sailing over from Tiberias to Tarichea—
towns on the same side of the lake. (3) If we suppose the miracle to
have taken place some distance down the eastern coast, all the require-
ments of the narrative will be met.

This theory is very plausible; but it must assume that 'the land of
Genezareth' stretched across to the east of the Jordan.

the city of Andrew and Peter. Since Peter and Andrew had their
home at Capharnaum (Matt. viii. 5–14; Mark i. 29), it follows that
Bethsaida was their birthplace.

45. *Philip findeth Nathanael* (= Theodore, 'Gift of God'). It is
not said *when* and *where;* perhaps Nathanael, too, was a disciple of
John; for he belonged to Cana of Galilee (xxi. 2). Nathanael is
identical with the Apostle Bartholomew; for (1) in the lists of the
Apostles (Matt. x. 3; Luke vi. 14) we find the names 'Philip and
Bartholomew' joined together, as Philip and Nathanael are themselves
connected here; (2) St. John never mentions Bartholomew, but he
does mention Nathanael, and that, too, amongst the Apostles to whom
Christ appeared (xxi. 2), while the other evangelists never mention
Nathanael; (3) all the others, whose call is here recorded by St.
John, afterwards became Apostles, and St. John is evidently narrating
how our Lord drew the first Apostles to His service; (4) the name
Bartholomew is only a patronymic like Barjona, and = son of Tolmai.
All the disciples so far called by our Lord were Galileans. "From
first to last, the Galileans were a chivalrous and a gallant race. 'The
country,' says Josephus proudly, 'hath never been destitute of men of

46 And Nathanael said to him: Can anything of good come from Nazareth? Philip saith to him: Come and see.
47 Jesus saw Nathanael coming to him, and he saith of him:

courage.' Their fidelity, often unreasoning and ill-tempered, was always sincere. 'The Galileans,' according to the Talmud, 'were more anxious for honour than for money; the contrary was true of Judæa.' For this cause also our Lord chose His friends from the people; and it was not a Galilean who betrayed him" (Dr. G. A. Smith, 'Historical Geography of the Holy Land,' p. 422). The population of Galilee was very numerous, but mixed. It was "Galilee of the gentiles," and the gentiles were most strong in the coast-towns. The names Andrew and Philip are both Greek.

Jesus, the son of Joseph of Nazareth. These are the words, not of the evangelist, but of Philip, who spoke then according to the common estimation; Jesus "being, as it was supposed, the son of Joseph" (Luke iii. 23).

Nazareth. "The position of Nazareth is familiar to all. The village lies on the most southern of the ranges of Lower Galilee, and on the edge of this just above the Plain of Esdraelon. You cannot see from Nazareth the surrounding country, for Nazareth rests in a basin among hills; but the moment you climb to the edge of this basin, which is everywhere within the limit of the village boys' playground, what a view you have! Esdraelon lies before you, with its twenty battle-fields —the scenes of Barak's and of Gideon's victories, the scenes of Saul's and Josiah's defeats, the scenes of the struggles for freedom in the glorious days of the Maccabees. There is Naboth's vineyard and the place of Jehu's revenge upon Jezebel; there Shunem and the house of Elisha; there Carmel and the place of Elijah's sacrifice. To the east the Valley of Jordan, with the long range of Gilead; to the west the radiance of the Great Sea, with the ships of Tarshish and the promise of the Isles. You see thirty miles in three directions. It is a map of Old Testament history" (Smith, l.c., p. 432).

46. *Can anything of good come from Nazareth?* This expression of contempt must not be confounded with the Judean expressions of contempt for all Galilee; "search the scriptures, and see that out of Galilee a prophet riseth not" (vii. 52). Nathanael, himself a Galilean, could not have so spoken. But Nazareth had a bad moral repute amongst its neighbours; and we find strong indications, in the Gospels, of its ungrateful hardness of heart (Matt. xiii. 57, 58; Luke iv. 15–29). Such a saying would have been current only in the vicinity, for Nazareth itself was a village so obscure, though in a busy and populous district, that it is nowhere mentioned except in the New Testament— not even in Josephus.

Come and see. For experience is the true corrector of prejudice.

47. *Jesus saw Nathanael coming to him, and he saith of him* (περὶ αὐτοῦ). These words were addressed to the disciples as Nathanael approached in company with Philip.

Behold an Israelite indeed, in whom there is no guile. Nathanael saith to him: Whence knowest thou me? ⁴⁸ Jesus answered and said to him: Before that Philip called thee, when thou wast under the fig-tree, I saw thee. Nathanael answered him, and said: Rabbi, thou art the ⁴⁹ Son of God, thou art the king of Israel. Jesus answered, ⁵⁰ and said to him: Because I said unto thee, I saw thee under the fig-tree, thou believest: greater things than these shalt thou see. And he saith to him: Amen, amen, ⁵¹

Behold an Israelite indeed (ἀληθῶς), *i.e.*, not merely by descent and in outward show, but inwardly and by moral character reflects the uprightness, simplicity, and sincerity of Jacob. "For all are not Israelites that are of Israel" (Rom. ix. 6). The words that follow explain what is meant, and give the secret of Nathanael's character: "In whom there is no guile."

48. *Whence knowest thou me?* Although the words had not been addressed to Nathanael, he had heard them as he approached, and being filled with astonishment at our Lord's unaccountable knowledge of him, said: "Whence knowest thou me?" In answer to this question our Lord gave Nathanael an example of heart-searching still more surprising: "Before that Philip called thee, when thou wast under the fig-tree, I saw thee." Verse 50 shows that the order of the words is, I saw thee under the fig-tree, before Philip called thee. The use of the definite article implies that the fig-tree in question had some prominence in the thoughts of Nathanael. John's preaching had probably come home to Nathanael with unusual force as he sat thinking alone under the fig-tree, and he had then wondered when He that was greater than John would come. The words of our Lord gave the answer to Nathanael's self-questioning, and Nathanael understood the sign given him in the revelation of his secret thoughts.

49. *Rabbi, thou art the Son of God, thou art the king of Israel.* If we remember how tardy were the Apostles in rising to the sublime doctrine of our Lord's true Godhead, and how Peter's confession of that doctrine, at a later time, was so magnificently rewarded (Matt. xvi. 16-19), we cannot for a moment suppose that Nathanael meant more than that our Lord was the Messiah-king for whom all Israel was looking. Peter and Nathanael used the same words, but with a wide difference of meaning; Peter used them in the sense which had been revealed to him by the Father; Nathanael used them in the sense in which the Jews generally spoke of the Messiah as the Son of God. The words that follow tacitly promise to Nathanael a higher knowledge of Christ through signs still greater of Christ's dignity and power.

50. *Greater things than these* (plural of class) *shalt thou see.* What they are is stated :—

51. *Amen, amen, I say to you* (all the disciples), *you shall see the heaven opened, and the Angels of God ascending and descending upon the*

I say to you, you shall see the heaven opened, and the Angels of God ascending and descending upon the son of man.

son of man. The double 'amen' is peculiar to St. John, and is also very frequently used by him (about 25 times). The verse evidently promises some great and wondrous sign, but in what the sign should consist is only obscurely hinted. Amid a variety of interpretations, into which it is unnecessary to enter, the following one may be given as highly probable. The Apostles are promised a sign which will lead to a firmer and more perfect faith in Christ. Therefore it was to be given while they were with Him on earth, not, as some suppose, at the day of judgment. The promise is made in terms which recall Jacob's vision (Gen. xxviii. 12), and which come most appropriately after the words, 'Behold an Israelite indeed.' Besides, as our Lord had not long started from the fords of the Jordan for Galilee, it is not unlikely that He was now in the vicinity of Bethel, where Jacob had the vision. Further, the Jews had a keen sense of the angelic ministry in the Theocracy. They had "received the law by the disposition of angels" (Acts vii. 53; comp. Heb. i. 14; Matt. xviii. 10), and angelic manifestations had been so frequent in their history that their faith was firm in a constant invisible ministry. Our Lord therefore promised that the Apostles would see such continuous signs in His ministry that they would feel in constant touch with heaven and constantly behold the opened heaven (ἀνεῳγότα : perfect participle) and the continuous ministry of angels (comp. Eph. iii. 8-10.)

upon the son of man. Not counting the parallel passages, the phrase "Son of man" is applied to Himself by our Lord about 50 times. The most obvious meaning of the phrase is found in the well-known prophecy of Daniel (vii. 13, 14), beginning, "I beheld therefore in the vision of the night, and lo, one like the Son of man came with the clouds of heaven." What is in itself most obvious seems to be absolutely determined by our Lord's own references (see Matt. xvi. 27, xix. 28, xxv. 31), *e.g.*, "You shall see the son of man sitting on the right hand of the power of God, and coming in the clouds of heaven" (Matt. xxvi. 64). From this we learn that the phrase denotes our Lord's claim to universal authority, and to supreme power of judgment over all mankind. Hence the significant words, the Father "hath given him power to do judgment *because* he is the son of man" (v. 27).

CHAPTER II.

The Sign at the Marriage-Feast.

(VERS. 1-12.)

AND the third day there was a marriage in Cana of Galilee: and the mother of Jesus was there. And Jesus also was invited, and his disciples, to the marriage.

1. *And the third day*, i.e., from the date last given (i. 43), thus making a week in all.

there was a marriage. "It must be borne in mind that marriage conveyed to the Jews much higher thoughts than merely those of festivity and merriment. The pious fasted before it, confessing their sins. It was regarded almost as a sacrament. Here it ought to be specially noticed, as a striking evidence that the writer of the fourth Gospel was not only a Hebrew, but intimately acquainted with the varying customs prevailing in Galilee and in Judea, that at the marriage of Cana no 'friend of the bridegroom' is mentioned, while he is referred to in iii. 29, where the words are spoken outside the boundaries of Galilee. For among the simpler Galileans the practice of having 'friends of the bridegroom' did not obtain" (Edersheim, 'Jesus the Messiah,' p. 71).

in Cana of Galilee. In Josue (xix. 28) mention is made of a Cana in Aser, and therefore also in Galilee, but the indications of the text preclude our thinking of that Cana. The Cana mentioned by St. John was somewhere in the neighbourhood of Nazareth, and has been identified with Kana-el-Jelil, about six miles north. Jelil is an exact Arabic reproduction of Galil (= Galilee), and Kana-el-Jelil = Cana of Galilee. The Hebrew name Kana (= the place of reeds) suits this site, where are ruins overlooking a marshy plain covered with reeds. Cana of Galilee may have been its full name, like our Newcastle-on-Tyne, or Weston-super-Mare. The identification with Kefr Kenna is very improbable.

and the mother of Jesus was there. The prominence here given to our Lady prepares us for the important part she will play in the subsequent narrative of the miracle. She was apparently a friend or relative of the family. That St. Joseph was not there leads to the supposition that he was now dead.

2. *And Jesus also was invited, and his disciples.* "All connected

3 And the wine failing, the mother of Jesus saith to him:
4 They have no wine. And Jesus saith to her: Woman, what is it to me and to thee? my hour is not yet come.

with the account of it is strictly Jewish—the feast, the guests, the invitation of the stranger Rabbi, and its acceptance by Jesus. There is not any difficulty in understanding that on His arrival Jesus would hear of this 'marriage,' of the presence of His Mother in what seems to have been the house of a friend, if not a relative; and that He and His disciples would be bidden to the feast" (Edersheim, l.c., pp. 71, 72). The mention of the disciples shows that St. John here intends to give one of those scenes in which the Apostles "saw his glory" (i. 14), and therefore it is said that, by this miracle Jesus "manifested his glory, and his disciples believed in him" (v. 11). In this opening narrative, therefore, "we behold Him now as freely mingling with humanity, entering into its family life, sanctioning and hallowing all by His presence and blessing; then as transforming the 'water of legal purification' into the wine of the new dispensation; and, lastly, as having absolute power" (Eders., l.c., p. 69).

3. *And the wine failing* (having failed), *the mother of Jesus saith to him; They have no wine*. These words are an evident appeal to our Lord for help; and they are a proof at once of our Lady's tender sympathy with the distressed host, and of her absolute confidence that her Son could provide, and that at her request He would provide.

4. *Woman* (γύναι = 'Lady': a solemn term of affection or respect. xix. 26), *what is it to me and to thee* (τί ἐμοὶ καὶ σοί)? A rebuke has been seen in these words. But our Lady did not so understand them. She understood them as implying a favourable answer to her request (v. 5), and our Lord by His action shows that He had so meant them (vv. 7-9). "He reproved not His Mother by what He said, who honoured her by what He did." The whole context cries out against every supposition of rebuke. Whatever the words mean, then, they cannot mean *that*. The phrase was frequently used, not only by Jews, but also by Greeks and Romans, and was in itself an expression of surprise and (generally) remonstrance or expostulation (Jud. xi. 12; 4 Kings iii. 13), or simply of surprise and appeal (3 Kings xvii. 18; Luke viii. 28). The context must always determine the sense in which the phrase is employed; and the context here shows that it means, 'Why not leave me alone?'

my hour is not yet come. This 'hour' is the hour of manifesting His glory and dignity by the public performance of miracles (v. 11). Taking the sentence as a whole it may first be interpreted in the light of other Scriptural passages. Because Daniel was a man of desires the time of the Messiah's coming was shortened, *i.e.*, hastened (Dan. ix. 20-24); because Moses prayed God yielded, and spared the Jews: yet He had said, "Let me alone, that I may destroy them" (Exod. xxxii. 10). Prayer altered what would have been; and seems almost to have constrained God. So at the prayer of our Lady, Jesus anticipated His hour:

His mother saith to the waiters: Whatsoever he shall say ⁵ to you, do ye. Now there were set there six waterpots of ⁶ stone, according to the manner of the purifying of the Jews, containing two or three measures a-piece. Jesus ⁷ saith to them: Fill the waterpots with water. And they filled them up to the brim. And Jesus saith to them: ⁸ Draw out now, and carry to the chief steward of the feast. And they carried it. And when the chief steward had ⁹ tasted the water made wine, and knew not whence it was, but the waiters knew who had drawn the water; the chief steward calleth the bridegroom, and saith to him: ¹⁰ Every man at first setteth forth good wine, and when men have well drank, then that which is worse. But thou hast kept the good wine until now. This beginning of ¹¹

but spoke as God spoke to Moses, and as if loath to anticipate that hour. But there is a second interpretation. On critical grounds, solidly probable, the last clause may be taken interrogatively: "Hath not my hour come?" (see Knabenbauer, p. 118). That is, our Lord knowing all things (xxi. 17) had, in His foreknowledge, fixed upon the occasion of the marriage-feast to manifest His power. When, therefore, the Blessed Virgin appealed to Him, He replied, 'Let Me alone; why make unnecessary requests? Hath not My hour come?'

5. *His mother saith to the waiters: Whatsoever he shall say to you, do ye.* Our Lady had understood her Son, and at once told the servants to obey Him.

6. *Now there were set there* (probably in the vestibule) *six waterpots of stone, according to the manner of* (κατά = for the sake of) *the purifying of the Jews.* Such purification was an element in legal sanctity. The waterpots were used for washing the hands before and after meals, and for cleansing the vessels.

containing two or three measures (μετρητάς) *a-piece.* The metretes was nearly nine gallons (8¾). Therefore in all from about 100 to 160 gallons. "For such an occasion the family would produce or borrow the largest and handsomest stone-vessels that could be procured" (Eders., l.c., p. 72).

8. *Draw out now.* This would be done with the vessel from which the drinking-cups were filled.

and carry to the chief steward of the feast (ἀρχιτρίκλινος, *i.e.*, table-master, the manager of the feast, who also was taster of what had to go to table).

10. *Every man at first setteth forth good wine.* When the steward had tasted the wine and found it unusually good, he expressed his surprise in words of jocular exaggeration—words which, of course, were not intended to apply literally to the guests at Cana.

11. *This beginning of miracles did Jesus in Cana of Galilee.*

miracles did Jesus in Cana of Galilee: and manifested
12 his glory, and his disciples believed in him. After this he
went down to Capharnaum, he and his mother, and his
brethren, and his disciples: and they remained there not
many days.

The Festival at Jerusalem.
(VERS. 13–22.)

13   And the pasch of the Jews was at hand, and Jesus went

According to the Greek (ταύτην ἐποίησεν ἀρχὴν τῶν κ.τ.λ.) = this
He did as a beginning of His miracles. This was His first miracle
absolutely, not merely the first at Cana.
and manifested his glory (see i. 14), *and his disciples believed in
him*, i.e., with deeper, firmer faith.
  12. *After this he went down to Capharnaum.* (A.V., Capernaum.
The Douay form is undoubtedly the more correct.) Capharnaum was
Kephar Nahum (= the village of Nahum). It was situated on the sea-
coast (Matt. iv. 13), i.e., the coast of the Lake of Galilee. There is
thus a delicate touch of authenticity in the words "he went down" to
Capharnaum. It was a large and busy town, though of recent growth.
Here was Peter's house; here the good centurion was stationed (Matt.
viii. 5, 14); here Matthew sat at the receipt of custom (Mark ii. 1, 13, 14),
and here our Lord lived so long that it was called His own city (Matt.
ix. 1; Mark ii. 1-12). Opinion is divided regarding its exact site. Two
places are named—Tell-Hum, on the north-western shore, about three
miles from where the Jordan falls into the sea, and Khan Minyeh,
some two miles further south. Against the identification of Tell-Hum
with Capharnaum it is urged that Tell-Hum is an impossible contrac-
tion from Kephar Nahum; that there is no Tell (= hillock) at the
place; that the name is derived from Tanhum, a Jewish Rabbi there
buried; that it is a waterless site, with no such fountain as Josephus
describes in Capharnaum; and that it it is not near enough to Gen-
nesareth to suit Josephus' description. On the other hand, Khan
Minyeh corresponds to the Gospel references to Capharnaum, and suits
generally the description of Josephus (Smith, l.c., p. 456).
  he and his mother, and his brethren, and his disciples. "Whence
had the Lord brethren? For surely Mary did not give birth a second
time? God forbid: with her begins the dignity of virgins. Then,
whence the brethren? The kinsmen of Mary, of whatever degree, are
the brethren of the Lord. How do you prove this? From Scripture
itself. Lot is called Abraham's brother; he was his brother's son.
Yet they are called brethren. Why, but because they were kinsmen?
When thou hast known this rule, thou wilt find that all the blood
relations of Mary are the brethren of Christ" (St. Aug., Tract x. c. 2).
  13. *And the pasch of the Jews was at hand.* Some take 'and' in

up to Jerusalem. And he found in the temple them that 14
sold oxen and sheep and doves, and the changers of money
sitting. And when he had made as it were a scourge of 15

the sense of 'for,' as though explaining why our Lord remained not many days at Capharnaum (*v.* 12). But it is simply continuative. The phrase 'not many days' marks a contrast with the subsequent longer stay. St. John calls the feast 'the Pasch of the Jews,' because he writes from a Christian standpoint.

All male adults were bound to go up to the Temple at the three great annual festivals of Pasch, Pentecost, and Tabernacles (Deut. xvi. 16). The first and the greatest was the Pasch, or Passover (also called Phase). It was celebrated in the first month of the religious year, the month Nisan or Abib (between March and April), from the 14th to the 21st of the month. A characteristic feature in its celebration was the eating of unleavened bread during the seven days of the festival, and the sacrifice of the Paschal Lamb (Deut. xvi. 1–8; Exod. xii. 1–28). Hence it was also called the feast of the Azymes, or Unleavened Bread. It was primarily intended as a memorial of the deliverance from Egypt, and derives its name from the passing over (Hebrew 'pasch' = to pass over) of the Jewish houses when the angel destroyed all the first-born of Egypt (Exod. xii. 21–27). But secondarily, it was an agricultural festival marking the beginning of the harvest—"the month of new corn" (Deut. xvi. 1). It was prophetic of our Lord, the true Lamb of God (John xix. 36; Exod. xii. 46). Hence St. Paul's "Purge out the old leaven, that you may be a new paste, as you are unleavened. For Christ our pasch is sacrificed" (1 Cor. v. 7).

14. *And he found in the temple them that sold oxen and sheep and doves, and the changers of money sitting.* All this noisy traffic was carried on in the Court of the Gentiles. Here were set up the stalls where animals, oil, wine, incense, and other requisites for sacrifice could be bought. All Jews and proselytes, except priests, women, slaves, and minors, had to pay, under pain of distraint of their goods, the annual Temple-tribute of half a shekel (= 1s. 2d.). This Temple-tribute had to be paid in exact half-shekels of the Sanctuary. When it is remembered that, besides strictly Palestinian coin, Persian, Tyrian, Syrian, Egyptian, Grecian, and Roman money circulated in the country, it will be understood what work fell to the money-changers. We can picture to ourselves the scene around the table of an Eastern money-changer—the weighing of the coins, deductions for loss of weight, arguing, disputing, bargaining—and we can realise the terrible truthfulness of our Lord's charge (ver. 16) (Eders., l.c., p. 76).

15. *And when he had made as it were* ('as it were' omitted in Greek) *a scourge of little cords, he drove them all out of the temple, the sheep also and the oxen.* As is evident from the next verse, the 'all' does not refer to the sellers and money-changers, but only to the animals. The Greek = 'He drove all out of the temple, both the sheep and the oxen.'

little cords, he drove them all out of the temple, the sheep also and the oxen, and the money of the changers he
16 poured out, and the tables he overthrew. And to them that sold doves he said: Take these things hence, and
17 make not the house of my father a house of traffic. And his disciples remembered that it was written: *The zeal of
18 thy house hath eaten me up.* The Jews therefore answered, and said to him: What sign dost thou show unto us, seeing
19 thou dost these things? Jesus answered and said to them:

16. *And to them that sold doves he said*, &c. Some see here a sign of greater leniency, because the doves were the offerings of the poor. But this is imaginary. The simpler explanation is that doves in cages could not be driven out like sheep and oxen (comp. Matt. xxi. 12, on which occasion such supposed leniency was absent).

the house of my Father. Our Lord here implies that he is the Son of God, and He assumes authority in the temple (see *v.* 18). We thus see a fulfilment of the prophecy: " And presently the Lord, whom you seek, and the Angel of the testament, whom you desire, shall come to his temple" (Mal. iii. 1). 'Presently,' *i.e.*, suddenly, unexpectedly, although the Precursor had announced His coming (Mal. iii. 1; Matt. xi. 10). A second cleansing, with a few differences of detail, took place in Passion-week (Matt. xxi. 12, 13; Mark xi. 15-17; Luke xix. 45, 46). Abuses, particularly public and legally tolerated abuses, die hard. Repetition of the abuse naturally called for a repetition of the cleansing.

17. *And his disciples remembered that it was* [better, is] *written: The zeal of thy house hath eaten* [will eat] *me up.* The words remembered are in Psa. lxviii. 10. This psalm is certainly Messianic, and is one of the two psalms (the other is Psa. xxi.) most frequently quoted in the New Testament (see xv. 25, xix. 28; Acts i. 20; Rom. xv. 3, xi. 9).

18. *The Jews* (*i.e.*, the leaders, or Temple-officials) *therefore answered and said to him: What sign dost thou show unto us, seeing thou dost these things?* The very majesty of Christ's presence had overawed them; their own consciences, too, made cowards of them: they dared not resist. They did not venture even to condemn what He had done; but they craftily sought to turn away attention from their own evil-doing, by putting our Lord upon the defensive. They asked our Lord for a sign, *i.e.*, miracle, to justify His assumption of authority over them. This move would attract the attention, and probably enlist the sympathy, of the crowd.

19. *Destroy this temple, and in three days I will raise it up.* Their question was deceitful and captious; but they were caught in their own deceit. Our Lord utters a prophecy which reads like a challenge. The words are enigmatic. Our Lord's sacred humanity in

Destroy this temple, and in three days I will raise it up.
The Jews then said: Six and forty years was this temple ²⁰
in building, and wilt thou raise it up in three days? But ²¹
he spoke of the temple of his body. When therefore he ²²

which dwelt the fulness of the Godhead was truly the very shrine of a temple (ναός, not the more comprehensive term ἱερόν of *v*. 14). By His reply, therefore, our Lord foretold His resurrection from the dead (*v*. 21). It was a prophecy with which He afterwards met similar requests during the subsequent course of His ministry. "An evil and adulterous generation seeketh a sign: and a sign shall not be given it, but the sign of Jonas the prophet" (Matt. xii. 39, xvi. 4). If the Jewish leaders had been acting in good faith they might have learned, as the disciples learned, what our Lord's language meant; but in their malicious eagerness they jumped at conclusions, and in so jumping they landed themselves in a dilemma. Taking our Lord's words literally, they understood them to be a challenge. Let the Jews pull down the temple, and the sign they had asked for would be given in the raising of it up in three days. But they were afraid to pull the temple down; and so they themselves stood in the way of the sign for which they had asked, and dared not take up their own challenge. In their confusion, therefore, they could only put a futile and evasive question.

20. *Six and forty years was this temple in building, and wilt thou raise it up in three days?* The rebuilding of Zorobabel's temple was begun by Herod the Great in the eighteenth year of his reign (A.U.C. 734 or 735), and the work was not finished till the year A.D. 64, in the reign of Agrippa II. It was therefore not completed at the time referred to in St. John's narrative.

22. *When therefore he was risen again from the dead, his disciples remembered that he had said this.* Words that seemed dead, incidents that had been forgotten, spring into life again and are clearly remembered when the mind receives an unusual stimulus.

and they believed the scripture, and the word that Jesus had said. We read in St. Luke (xxiv. 44-45) that our Lord, after His resurrection, said to the Apostles, "These are the words which I spoke to you while I was yet with you, that all things must needs be fulfilled, which are written in the law of Moses, and in the prophets, and in the psalms, concerning me. Then he opened their understanding, that they might understand the scriptures." After our Lord's resurrection, then, the minds of the Apostles were flooded with fresh light; they saw more clearly than before the meaning of the Old Testament Scriptures concerning the Messiah, and our Lord's own words came back to their memory with redoubled force. Therefore did the Apostles believe with a faith that had grown in clearness and intensity.

The narrative is continued of what resulted from our Lord's manifestation of Himself at the first Pasch in Jerusalem. Two groups have been set before us—the one of unbelieving Jews who

was risen again from the dead, his disciples remembered
that he had said this, and they believed the scripture, and
23 the word that Jesus had said. Now when he was at
Jerusalem at the pasch, upon the festival day, many
24 believed in his name, seeing his signs which he did. But
Jesus did not trust himself unto them, for that he knew all
25 men. And because he needed not that any should give
testimony of man: for he knew what was in man.

resist the light of evidence, the other of disciples who believe, and are
rewarded by a clearer and more abundant knowledge. In the narrative
that immediately follows we get first a group of another kind, and
then an important typical instance. The sections are clearly marked
by the language. The first transition in ii. 23 (ὡς δὲ ἦν ἐν
Ἱεροσολύμοις) and the second in iii. 1 (ἦν δὲ ἄνθρωπος). In each
case δέ introduces the special matter.

23. *Now when he was at Jerusalem at the pasch, upon the festival
day* (ἐν τῇ ἑορτῇ), Better, When He was in Jerusalem at the time of
the Pasch, keeping the festival (εἶναι ἐν τῇ ἑορτῇ = to be engaged in).

many believed in his name, seeing his signs which he did. That is,
they saw in His miracles a sign that He was the Greater One of whom
the Baptist had spoken. For, "John indeed did no sign" (x. 41, 42).

24. *But Jesus did not trust himself unto them.* In the Greek the
same verb is used as for 'believe' in the preceding verse. Thus an
antithesis is made: they believed in Him, but He did not believe in
them so as to trust Himself to them, *i.e.*, in the way in which He
trusted Himself familiarly and unreservedly to the disciples.

for that he knew all men. Because He knew all things, He knew
the thoughts and feelings of the crowd. He knew that they were
looking for a temporal kingdom, and hoped to find in Him a conquering
leader, but that when they were undeceived in this matter they would
abandon Him.

25. *And because he needed not that any should give testimony of
man: for he knew what was in man.* The same thought expanded
and expressed in a more popular way. 'He had no need to be told or
warned: because He could read the hearts of all.'

CHAPTER III.

Jesus and Nicodemus.

(VERS. 1–21.)

AND there was a man of the Pharisees, named Nicodemus, a ruler of the Jews. This man came to Jesus by night, and said to him: Rabbi, we know that thou art come a teacher from God: for no man can do these signs which thou dost, unless God be with him. Jesus answered

1. *And* (δὲ = now) *there was a man of the Pharisees, named Nicodemus, a ruler* (ἄρχων) *of the Jews, i.e.*, a member of the Sanhedrin (comp. vii. 50, and note on i. 19).

2. *This man came to Jesus by night.* We learn from Nicodemus' measures of concealment that the opposition of the Pharisees to our Lord had already begun; but we also learn how deep an impression had been made on the mind of Nicodemus. "If from xix. 27 we might infer that St. John had 'a home' in Jerusalem itself, the scene about to be described would have taken place under his roof. Up in the simply-furnished Aliyah—the guest-chamber on the roof—the lamp was still burning. There was no need for Nicodemus to pass through the house, for an outside stair led to the upper room. It was night, when Jewish superstition would keep men at home; a wild, gusty spring night, when loiterers would not be in the streets; and no one would see him as at that hour he ascended the outside steps that led up to the Aliyah." (Eders., l.c., p. 81).

we know that thou art come a teacher from God: for no man can do these signs (ταῦτα τὰ σημεῖα = these so great signs) *which thou dost, unless God be with him.* Nicodemus confesses that Christ is a prophet; he does not yet believe that Christ is *the* prophet. His language implies that others—possibly, like him, members of the Sanhedrin—shared his belief ('*we* know').

3. *Jesus answered and said to him.* The Baptist had preached saying: "The kingdom of heaven is at hand" (Matt. iii. 2). Our

and said to him: Amen, amen I say to thee, unless a man
4 be born again, he cannot see the kingdom of God. Nicodemus saith to him: How can a man be born when he is old? can he enter a second time into his mother's womb,
5 and be born again? Jesus answered: Amen, amen, I say to thee, unless a man be born again of water and the Holy
6 Ghost, he cannot enter into the kingdom of God. That which is born of the flesh, is flesh: and that which is born
7 of the Spirit, is spirit. Wonder not, that I said to thee,
8 you must be born again. The Spirit breatheth where he

Lord's miracles would be taken as connecting Him with that kingdom; and so the object of Nicodemus' coming would be to inquire about that kingdom. But before he has had time to speak a word our Lord reads his thoughts and "answers" his unexpressed question.

Amen, amen, I say to thee, unless a man be born again, he cannot see the kingdom of God. These words are not merely an answer to the thoughts of Nicodemus; they are also a warning against the deeply-rooted persuasion of the Jews that all blessing was to be found in their descent from Abraham (comp. Matt. iii. 9, viii. 11, 12). The word ἄνωθεν (translated '*again*') may mean (1) 'from the beginning' (Luke i. 3); (2) 'again' (Gal. iv. 9); (3) 'from above' (iii. 31, xix. 11). The context decides in favour of 'again' (*v.* 4). "He cannot see," *i.e.*, become partaker of (viii. 51); in the parallel passage we find 'he cannot enter into' (*v.* 5). St. John takes for granted that his readers will understand, from their knowledge of Christian baptism, what to Nicodemus is a puzzle.

5. *Unless a man be born again of water and the Holy Ghost* (Greek = 'the Spirit'). These words explain that 'to be born again' is to be born of (ἐκ) water and the Spirit. The particle ἐκ retains here the causal force which it always has with verbs of origin, of begetting, &c. (see i. 13). The Holy Ghost is the principal, and water (*i.e.*, the external rite) the instrumental, cause of our being born again. Wherefore the rite of baptism is truly said to "wash away sins" (Acts xxii. 16), and to be "the laver of regeneration, and renovation of the Holy Ghost" (Tit. iii. 5). Its necessity is thus evident. But our Lord still further points out why this regeneration is necessary for entrance into the kingdom of God.

6. *That which is born of the flesh, is flesh* (*i.e.*, merely human): *and that which is born of the Spirit, is spirit* (*i.e.*, the child of God, and partaker of the Divine nature (see i. 12, 13, 16; 2 Pet. i. 4). Like begets like.

7. *Wonder not, that I said to thee, you must be born again.* Possibly, just as He was speaking, the night wind was heard as it went murmuring and blowing along. The very sound would enhance the appositeness of the comparison, which was immediately drawn.

8. *The Spirit* (τὸ πνεῦμα) *breatheth* (πνεῖ) *where he will* (θέλει):

will: and thou hearest his voice, but thou knowest not whence he cometh and whither he goeth: so is every one that is born of the Spirit. Nicodemus answered, and said to him: How can these things be done? Jesus answered, and said to him: Art thou a master in Israel, and knowest

and thou hearest his voice (φωνήν = articulate voice), *but thou knowest not whence he cometh and whither he goeth: so is every one that is born of the Spirit.* The word πνεῦμα, which occurs more than twenty times in St. John's Gospel, and about 350 times in the New Testament, uniformly means 'Spirit,' the term ἄνεμος being used for 'wind.' With this agrees the use, in the present verse, of 'will' and 'voice' in connection with πνεῦμα.

On the other hand, the verb πνεῖ cannot, according to New Testament usage, mean 'breatheth,' but 'bloweth.' Thus there are linguistic difficulties in the way of clear interpretation. The context, under these circumstances, should decide. Now, in the context the first part of the verse clearly is given as a comparison to what is stated in the second part. But we cannot compare a thing to itself. Therefore the reference in the first part is not to the Spirit, but to the wind, to which the action of the Spirit is compared. The very comparison makes the wind be considered almost as a person, and explains the use of 'will' and 'voice.' 'As the wind bloweth where it listeth [A.V.], but no one can see its movements or tell where it began to blow or or where its course will end,' "so (οὕτως) is every one that is born of the Spirit," *i.e.*, a similar thing happens when one is born of the Spirit. The grace of the Spirit is free, and mysterious in its action; but though unseen it is none the less real, and men must believe in its reality. It comes from the unseen God, and leads to things unseen; yet its presence may be inferred from its fruit in the soul of man—charity, joy, peace, patience, benignity, goodness, longanimity, mildness, faith, modesty, continency, chastity (Gal. v. 22, 23).

9. *How can these things be done?* Nicodemus had gained a dim perception of what our Lord meant—he saw that our Lord spoke of a spiritual regeneration very different from the mere outward correctness and precise formalism of the Pharisees; and, astonished at the wonder of it, he asked, perhaps in simple amazement, 'how can these things be done?' Nicodemus ought to have learned better than this from the prophets (*e.g.*, Ezech. xxxvi. 25, 26); he would have learned better had he not put a 'veil upon his heart' (2 Cor. iii. 14-16).

10. *Jesus answered and said to him: Art thou a master* (ὁ διδάσκαλος, *i.e.*, the teacher), *in* (of) *Israel, and knowest not these things?* The teacher of Israel (*i.e.*, a member of the great teaching council) not to know these things! With solemn emphasis, therefore, and with impressive use of the plural of majesty and authority, our Lord continues as in the following verse.

not these things? Amen, amen I say to thee, that we speak what we know, and we testify what we have seen, and you receive not our testimony. If I have spoken to you earthly things, and you believe not: how will you believe if I shall speak to you heavenly things? And no man hath ascended into heaven, but he that descended from heaven, the son of man who is in heaven. And as Moses lifted up the serpent in the desert, so must the son

11. *Amen, amen I say to thee, that we speak what we know, and we testify what we have seen*, ἑωράκαμεν = have seen, and now behold: cf. ix. 37; 1 John iv. 20.

and you receive not our testimony: see on i. 18.

12. *If I have spoken to you earthly things, and you believe not: how will you believe if I shall speak to you heavenly things?* Our Lord had spoken only of the mystery of grace which is wrought in the soul of man here upon earth; but if that mystery is hard to believe, how will Nicodemus believe all the deep things to be revealed concerning God Himself in heaven?

13. *And no man hath ascended into heaven, but he that descended from heaven, the son of man.* Christ, the God-man, is our supreme and absolute authority for all supernatural truth; in Him are hid all the treasures of wisdom and knowledge. If we refuse to accept His testimony, we can find no other teacher. Christ is both God and man. As God He has been with the Father from all eternity; but He became flesh and dwelt among us. He is thus said to have *descended* from heaven; and, in His human form, He revealed what man alone could never have known. For "no man hath seen God at any time." Our Lord is said to have *ascended*, because His eternal presence in heaven is more than equivalent to an ascent into heaven, and includes all the knowledge that any ascent, with its subsequent vision of God, could give. Besides, even the Sacred Humanity of our Lord can be said, by reason of the hypostatic union, and the consequent pleroma, to have ascended into heaven at the Incarnation.

who is in heaven. The Son of God, being true God, is always in heaven. Some ancient (ℵ B) and other (later) MSS. omit this last clause. It is, however, too well attested to be made doubtful by an anomalous omission (see Miller's edition (4th) of Scrivener's 'Introduction,' vol. ii. p. 360).

14. St. Paul, after speaking of some events in the history of Israel, added, "Now all these things happened to them in figure" (τυπικῶς) (1 Cor. x. 1–11). In these words the Apostle touched upon a general principle of God's revealing providence; for God uttered prophecies not only by the lips of the prophets, but also by many things in the history of the chosen people. Shadows of the good things to come (Heb. x. 1) were thrown along the path of Israel's life and history. Persons, things, and events in that history were chosen by God to be

of man be lifted up: That whosoever believeth in him, 15
may not perish, but may have life everlasting. For God 16
so loved the world, as to give his only begotten Son; that
whosoever believeth in him, may not perish, but may have
life everlasting. For God sent not his Son, into the world, 17
to judge the world, but that the world may be saved by
him. He that believeth in him is not judged. But he 18

types and figures of greater things in the Christian dispensation. Not
all connected with Israel was intended by God to be a mute prophecy
silently pointing to Christianity; but much was so intended. How
much, we can learn only from God, upon whose free choice such mute
prophesying depended. Without light there is no shadow. We therefore need the light of Christian revelation shining across the history of
the past to show what things in the Old Testament were really types
and shadows of the New Testament. Our Lord here tells Nicodemus
of one type.

And as Moses lifted up the serpent in the desert (see Num. xxi.
4-9), *so must* (*i.e.*, in the disposition of Divine providence (Acts iii.
23, iv. 12; Heb. ii. 9) *the son of man be lifted up* (*i.e.*, on the cross,
viii. 28, xii. 32, 33): *That whosoever believeth in him, may not perish,
but may have life everlasting* (*v.* 15). The clause 'may not
perish,' is not genuine: it has slipped in from the next verse. The
Greek is clearer: "that every one who believeth may in Him (*i.e.*,
through union with Him: εἰς αὐτόν) have eternal life."

16. It is disputed whether the discourse with Nicodemus ends here,
and what follows is the evangelist's fuller explanation of Christ's words.
But *v.* 22 seems clearly to indicate that all was spoken by our Lord
Himself. There is, it is true, a close parallel between what follows
and St. John's prologue; but the resemblance may be due to St. John's
close adherence to his Master's words (see 1 John i. 1-3). The
doctrine, again, may appear too sublime and difficult to have been
proposed to Nicodemus; but, on the other hand, the doctrine quite
accords with the promise in *v.* 12.

For God so loved the world (*i.e.*, mankind), *as to give* [that He
gave] *his only begotten Son: that whosoever believeth in him, may not
perish* (therefore he who does not believe, will perish), *but may have
life everlasting.* This explains what was said in the preceding verse,
and declares *how* eternal life was brought to mankind. The same
thought is developed in the verses that immediately follow.

17, 18. *For God sent not his Son into the world, to judge the world*
(*i.e.*, by the judgment of condemnation; cf. viii. 15, xii. 47), *but
that the world may be saved by Him. He that believeth in Him is
not judged* (for he receives power to be made the son of God and heir
of eternal life, i. 12). *But he that doth not believe, is already judged.*
All have sinned; and need the glory of God (Rom. iii. 23; 1 John
i. 8-10); all, through Adam's fall, are void of grace, and so by nature

that doth not believe is already judged: because he believeth not in the name of the only begotten Son of
19 God. And this is the judgment: because the light is come into the world, and men loved darkness rather than
20 the light: for their works were evil. For every one that doth evil hateth the light, and cometh not to the light,
21 that his works may not be reproved. But he that doth truth, cometh to the light, that his works may be made manifest, because they are done in God.

children of wrath (Eph. ii. 3). Christ came to redeem mankind from that sentence of death. If, therefore, a man refuses to accept what Christ offers, that man remains under sentence still, and "the wrath of God abideth on him" (v. 36). "So far, then, as it lies in the physician, He is come to heal the sick. He that will not observe the orders of the physician destroys himself" (St. Aug., Tract. xii. c. 12).

because he believeth not ὅτι μή = the charge; ὅτι οὐ would express only the fact.

19. *And this is the judgment* (*i.e.*, by which a man condemns and destroys himself): *because the light is come into the world, and men loved darkness rather than the light.* "Whose works does the Lord find to be good? The works of none: He finds the works of all evil (v. 18). How is it, then, that some have done the truth, and are come to the light? (v. 21). But 'they loved,' saith He, 'darkness rather than the light.' There He laid the emphasis: for many loved their sins; many confessed their sins; and he who confesses his sins doth now work with God. God accuses thy sins; and if thou also accusest, thou art united to God. The confession of evil works is the beginning of good works. Thou doest the truth and comest to the light" (St. Aug. l. c., c. 13). This verse, then, explains more minutely what was said in the preceding, viz., "is already judged."

20. *For every one that doth evil hateth the light.* This is a general law of conduct, explanatory of what had just been said. Every one doing (πράσσων) evil (φαῦλα = mean, worthless deeds) shuns the light.

and cometh not to the light, that his works may not be reproved: ἵνα μή ἐλεγχθῇ = in order that he may not have to face inevitable censure.

21. *But he that doth truth* (ὁ ποιῶν: *the* truth) *cometh to the light, that* (ἵνα = in order that) *his works may be made manifest, because they are done* (εἰργασμένα = have been done) *in God* (*i.e.*, in accordance with the will of God. Comp. i. 9, Rom. ii. 14, 15). When a man has followed the light of God's illuminating grace and kept the law of conscience written in his heart, he is led on easily and even gladly to greater light and to the fuller law of the Gospel.

Our Lord's discourse with Nicodemus is deserving of repeated study. It teaches us some of the most important truths—the Blessed Trinity; the Divinity of our Lord; the Incarnation; the necessity of faith for

The Baptist again gives Testimony to Jesus.
(Vers. 22–36.)

After these things Jesus and his disciples came into the 22
land of Judea; and there he abode with them and baptized.
And John also was baptizing in Ennon near Salim; because 23
there was much water there, and they came, and were
baptized. For John was not yet cast into prison. And 24
there arose a question between some of John's disciples 25
and the Jews concerning purification: and they came to 26

salvation; the universality of redemption; the impediments which
man, by closing his eyes to the light of faith, may put in the way of
God's mercy; the necessity of a new birth by grace; the existence of a
sacramental system in which the Holy Spirit operates through an
external rite; Christ's sacrifice the meritorious, and God's love for
mankind the determining, cause of grace and salvation.

22. *After these things* (*i.e.*, the events in Jerusalem) *Jesus and his disciples came into the land of Judea* (*i.e.*, into the country which formed the province); *and there he abode with them and baptized* (ἐβάπτιζεν. Imperf. = during His stay). This baptism was administered not by Christ Himself, but by His disciples (iv. 2¹). As this rite was observed only during a short stay in the land of Judea, and was not administered in Galilee, it was only a baptism like John's, and not the Christian sacrament. If Christian baptism had been administered at this time St. Paul could hardly have argued that "all we, who are baptized in Christ Jesus, are baptized in his death. For we are buried together with him by baptism into death" (Rom. vi. 3-5). Therefore the use of Christian baptism was introduced after our Lord's resurrection.

23. *Ennon* (Αἰνών = Aenon) *near Salim*. The only clue which the text gives concerning the site of these places is, that Ennon was not on the Jordan. In that case the statement "there was much water there" (ὕδατα πολλά = many waters) would be superfluous. Our Lord was certainly in Judea; but it does not follow that John also was in Judea. The identification of Salim is uncertain; but probably it was situated in the district between Jezreel and Scythopolis (Bethsan). The word Αἰνών = 'springs.' St. John had come into the neighbourhood of Herod's territory, who soon imprisoned him (*v.* 24. Cf. Matt. iv. 12) and put him to death. St. John had continued his work of preparation because our Lord had not yet publicly declared Himself; and our Lord by baptizing marked the transition from John's mission to His own.

25. *And* (οὖν = therefore, *i.e.*, because Jesus was baptizing) *there arose a question between some of John's disciples and the Jews* (rather, a Jew) *concerning purification* (*i.e.*, baptism). Some inhabitant of Judea

John, and said to him: Rabbi, he that was with thee beyond the Jordan, to whom thou gavest testimony, behold ²⁷ he baptizeth, and all men come to him. John answered and said: A man cannot receive anything, unless it be ²⁸ given him from heaven. You yourselves do bear me witness, that I said, I am not Christ, but that I am sent before him. ²⁹ He that hath the bride, is the bridegroom: but the friend of the bridegroom, who standeth and heareth him, rejoiceth with joy because of the bridegroom's voice. This my joy ³⁰ therefore is fulfilled. He must increase but I must decrease. ³¹ He that cometh from above, is above all. He that is of the earth, of the earth he is, and of the earth he speaketh.

had probably been speaking of Christ's baptism. This had evidently fired the zeal of John's disciples for his honour. They therefore came to John, and, not without exaggeration, complained (*v.* 26).

27. *John answered and said: A man cannot receive anything, unless it be given him from heaven.* This is a general statement with, of course, an intended application to Christ. The providence of God rules all things; therefore Christ's success came from God. Next, John insists, as he had before insisted, on his own subordinate position.

28. *You yourselves do bear me witness, that I said, I am not Christ* (ὁ Χριστός = the Christ), *but that I am sent before him* (see i. 20, 30). In the Greek there is great emphasis in John's assertion of his own inferiority (εἶπον ἐγώ, οὐκ εἰμὶ ἐγὼ ὁ Χριστός).

29. *He that hath the bride,* &c. St. John further declares, by an illustration drawn from Jewish marriage customs, his relation to Jesus. The illustration is symbolical. The bride is the chosen people (Isa. liv. 1-6; Jer. ii. 2; Osea ii. 16-20); the bridegroom is Christ (Eph. v. 23-32; Apoc. xix. 7, xxi. 9); the marriage, which is now at hand, is the setting up of the kingdom of heaven; the attendant friend of the bridegroom is John - he who stands waiting attentively to do the bridegroom's bidding (ὁ ἑστηκὼς καὶ ἀκούων αὐτοῦ). In hearing, therefore, that "all men come to Jesus," John understands that the work he came to do is being accomplished, and so his "joy is fulfilled." The Greek is very expressive: "*This* joy, therefore, which is mine, has been fulfilled" (πεπλήρωται).

30. *He must increase, but I must decrease.* As the herald gives place to the king, as the light of the stars melts away before the face of the sun, so must John's mission yield to the more excellent mission of Jesus.

31. *He that cometh from above* (*i.e.*, is of heavenly origin) *is above all. He that is of the earth* (*i.e.*, of earthly origin), *of the earth he is* (*i.e.*, has all the limitation of his human origin), *and of the earth he speaketh* (*i.e.*, his knowledge is only of things pervious to human reason). *He that cometh from heaven is above all.*

He that cometh from heaven, is above all. And what he 32
hath seen, and heard, that he testifieth: and no man
receiveth his testimony. He that hath received his testi- 33
mony, hath set to his seal that God is true. For he whom 34
God hath sent, speaketh the words of God: for God doth
not give the spirit by measure. The Father loveth the 35
Son: and he hath given all things into his hand. He that 36
believeth in the Son, hath life everlasting: but he that
believeth not the Son, shall not see life, but the wrath of
God abideth on him.

32. *And what he hath seen, and heard* (*i.e.*, seen in God, and heard from God) *that he testifieth: and no man receiveth his testimony.* The true cause of complaint is just the opposite of that alleged by John's disciples. Too few, rather than too many, believe in Christ.

33. *He that hath received* (ὁ λαβών = he that receiveth) *his* (*i.e.*, Christ's) *testimony hath set to his seal* (ἐσφράγισεν = hath affixed his seal to his declaration) *that God is true* (truthful).

34. *For he whom God hath sent, speaketh the words of God.* Therefore, to accept the word of Christ is to believe in the truthfulness of God: to reject the word of Christ is to treat God as if He were a liar. Nor should they be surprised if Christ should teach truths never before revealed, even to John himself.

for God doth not give the Spirit by measure (ἐκ μέτρου), *i.e.*, God is not tied by any confining and restricting law in the distribution of His gifts.

35. *The Father loveth the Son: and he hath given all things into his hand i.e.*, all fulness of the Spirit, and unlimited power.

36. *He that believeth in the Son, hath life everlasting* (see i. 12, 16): *but he that believeth not* (ἀπειθῶν = is disobedient: compare the "obedience of faith." Rom. i. 18) *the Son, shall not see life* (cf. *vv*. 3, 5, *but the wrath of God abideth on him*, cf. v. 18.

St. John's prophetic life had been a life of testimony to our Lord.

(*a*) Before our Lord's baptism John had foretold the nearness of the Messiah (Matt. iii. 11, 12; Mark i. 7, 8; Luke iii. 15, 16); he afterwards refers to this testimony (John i. 15, 30).

(*b*) After the baptism John's testimony was almost continuous (John i. 34). But testimonies of a more solemn character are recorded by St. John.

(*c*) The testimony to the deputation (i. 19-28).
(*d*) The testimony to the people (i. 29-34).
(*e*) The testimony to John's disciples who became apostles (i. 35, 36).
(*f*) The last public testimony to John's followers (iii. 25-36).

CHAPTER IV.

Our Lord in Samaria.

(Vers. 1-42.)

WHEN Jesus therefore understood that the Pharisees had heard that Jesus maketh more disciples, and

The country of Samaria ran, on the north, along the southern edge of Esdraelon, from the Mediterranean to the Jordan; on the east and west it was bounded by the Jordan and the edge of Sharon; on the south its limits had varied much during the course of its history, but in the time of Christ they ran from Wady esh Shair to Wady Farah—that is, about 23 miles by 35 in all.

Samaria, the capital of the country, and giving its name to the whole, fell before the Assyrian army after a siege of three years (B.C. 722). Sargon, who had just ascended the Assyrian throne, in an inscription on the walls of his great palace at Khorsabad says, "The city Samaria I besieged, and 27,290 people, inhabitants of it, I took away captive; but the rest I allowed to retain their possessions (cf. 2 Paral. xxx. and xxxi.). But a gradual process of deportation and recolonization, lasting perhaps a century (Esdr. iv. 10) soon began. The Book of Kings (4 Kings xvii. 6, xviii. 11) seems to imply that there were three great bodies of exiles, sent respectively to Hala, Habor, and Media. The same book names the various places whence new colonists were drawn (4 Kings xvii. 24). The country thus contained a mixed population of ancient inhabitants and of new settlers. The latter were idolaters, but they adopted a mongrel kind of Judaism (4 Kings xvii. 25-41). On the return of the Jews from Babylon, Esdras and Nehemias not only refused all offers of help from the Samaritans, but ordered a strict religious separation between Jews and them. In revenge the Samaritans afterwards built a rival temple on Mount Gerizim, and the enmity of the two peoples became constant.

Although the religion of the Samaritans was at first a gross mixture of Judaism and heathenism, the Jewish element gradually obtained a marked preponderance. The Samaritans were never treated as

baptizeth *more* than John, (though Jesus *himself* did not 2
baptize, but his disciples,) he left Judea, and went again 3
into Galilee. And he was of necessity to pass through 4
Samaria. He cometh therefore to a city of Samaria which 5
is called Sichar; near the land which Jacob gave to his son

idolaters, but decidedly distinguished from them. They believed in the unity of God; they acknowledged the authority of Moses as the greatest of the prophets; they accepted the Pentateuch as having Divine authority, but rejected all injunctions that went beyond the Pentateuch; they observed the Jewish rite of circumcision on the eighth day, the sanctification of the Sabbath, and the Jewish annual festivals; they looked for the Messiah promised by Moses [see Schürer, "The Jewish People," § 22].

1. *When Jesus therefore understood that the Pharisees had heard that Jesus maketh more disciples, and baptizeth more than John.* This is a direct narration and verbatim report: hence the repetition of the name and the use of present tenses.

3. *He left Judea and went again into Galilee.* The powerful Pharisees hated John and plotted against him (see Matt. xi. 18, xvii. 12). Naturally their hatred of our Lord was still keener. He therefore withdrew for a time from Judea, the headquarters of the hierarchy, and retired to Galilee.

4. *And he was of necessity to pass through Samaria.* That is, on the supposition that He desired to take the shorter route generally taken by Galileans. The stricter Jews, desirous of avoiding contact with the Samaritans, went round by the east of the Jordan, through Peræa.

5. *A city of Samaria which is called Sichar* (Sychar). The site is marked by two notes: it was "near the land which Jacob gave to Joseph," and "Jacob's well was there." The well is called both a fountain (πηγή, *v.* 5) and a pit (φρέαρ, *vv.* 11, 12). Now the land bought by Jacob was near Sichem—(Shechem, now Nablus = Neapolis)—(Gen. xxxiii. 18, 19; xlviii. 22). Is Sichar, then, identical with Sichem? St. Jerome, who is followed by many, thought so; he suggested that Sichar was a copyist's error for Sichem. Others have thought that Sichar was either a nickname (drunkard, or liar), or a descriptive appellation (commercial). Both suggestions are quite groundless. As early as the fourth century Eusebius and the Bordeaux Pilgrim mention a Sichar distinct from Sichem. In the Samaritan Chronicle (fourteenth century) it is spelt Ischar; but the Samaritans themselves, in translating their chronicle into Arabic, call Ischar 'Askar.' This name still attaches to a few ruins at the foot of Mount Ebal, about one mile and three quarters east-north-east from Nablus, and little over half a mile north from Jacob's well. The well is nearly two miles from Sichem (Nablus).

But granted that Sichar is either Nablus or 'Askar,' is it likely that any one seeking water should have come past streams in their im-

6 Joseph. Now Jacob's well was there. Jesus therefore being wearied with his journey, sat thus on the well. It was about 7 the sixth hour. There cometh a woman of Samaria to draw 8 water. Jesus saith to her: Give me to drink. For his 9 disciples were gone into the city to buy meats. Then that Samaritan woman saith to him: How dost thou, being a Jew, ask of me to drink, who am a Samaritan woman? For the Jews do not communicate with the Samaritans. 10 Jesus answered, and said to her: If thou didst know the gift of God, and who he is that saith to thee, Give me to

mediate neighbourhood to the more distant, the deep and scanty well of Jacob? There are eighty springs of water in and around Sichem; there is a copious fountain in 'Askar.'
But the real difficulty is not why the woman should have come to the well, but why a well should have been dug so deep in the neighbourhood of so many springs. Its existence is a proof that the woman would have a reason for using it. Perhaps in those far away summers the surface streams ran dry; perhaps the waters of the well were more suitable. It is not uncommon in the East to send to a great distance for a supply of drinking water. The springs at Nablus are, as the natives express it, very 'heavy.' They not unjustly attribute many of their complaints to this cause. The fountain at 'Askar' is of particularly 'heavy' water. Now, Jacob's well has a reputation among them of containing good water, free from the deleterious qualities of their other supplies. The woman, therefore, would gladly have come to get a supply. (Dr. Smith, l.c., 367-375, 676.)
6. *Jesus therefore being wearied with his journey, sat thus* (οὕτως) *on the well.* The οὕτως is very obscure. It cannot mean "tired as He was," because in that case the οὕτως would have been placed before the verb (Acts xx. 11; xxvii. 17). Most probably it means, 'just as He was, without any preparation.'
the sixth hour, i.e., mid-day (see on i. 39).
7. *A woman of Samaria.* One designation = a Samaritaness. She came from Sichar (see vv. 9, 28, 39).
8. *Into the city, i.e.*, the only city so far mentioned – Sichar.
to buy meats (τροφάς) = simply 'food.' The disciples would have asked if they had been present—
9. *How dost thou, being a Jew.* The woman would have recognised our Lord's nationality not only by His speech and appearance, but also by His phylactery and by the white fringes on the border of His garment. The Samaritan fringe is blue.
10. *If thou didst know the gift of God.* Our Lord takes occasion from the woman's question to speak to her of spiritual things. The 'gift of God' means the opportunity now given of obtaining the means of salvation. (Cf. "If thou hadst known the things that are to thy peace"—Luke xix. 42.) The words that follow explain what the

drink; thou perhaps wouldst have asked of him, and he would have given thee living water. The woman saith to 11
him: Sir, thou hast nothing wherein to draw, and the well is deep: from whence then hast thou living water? Art 12
thou greater than our father Jacob, who gave us the well, and drank thereof himself, and his children, and his cattle? Jesus answered, and said to her: Whosoever drinketh of 13
this water, shall thirst again: but he that shall drink of the

opportunity is, the καί being exegetical. "If thou didst know thy opportunity, and who I am."
thou perhaps wouldst have asked of him. 'Perhaps' is not genuine.
living water. By living water our Lord meant Divine grace, which is so frequently compared in Scripture to living water—the water of life; but the Samaritaness took the words literally of spring-water, as contrasted with water accumulated in pools or cisterns. She is therefore surprised. Our Lord had not wherein to draw from the well: whence then the living water? (*v.* 11.)

12. Since our Lord had not wherein (ἄντλημα = rope and bucket) to draw from Jacob's well, He must be able to provide other living water. She therefore asks, *Art thou greater* (μὴ σὺ μείζων = thou surely thou art not able to provide better) *than our father Jacob?* Her tone of respect had deepened (*v.* 11, Κύριε = sir), but still there was a great difference between an unknown Jew and Jacob. We need not inquire whether Jacob *was* father of the Samaritans.
who gave us the well. It is nowhere said in Scripture of Jacob that he dug a well; but it is said of Abraham and Isaac, and is possibly true of Jacob also.
and his cattle (θρέμματα = things that are fed). Perhaps better = sheep and goats. The word is sometimes used of slaves and of children.

13. *Whosoever drinketh of this water shall thirst again: but he that shall drink of the water that I will give him, shall not thirst for ever.* Our Lord implies that He *is* greater than Jacob, and can bestow a better gift—water by which a man is for ever set free from thirst (vi. 35). Divine grace is the root of immortality; it makes a man the child of God, and heir of heaven. Hence, as by grace a man obtains the right of citizenship in heaven, it is truly called eternal life. In that life man's longing for happiness is perfectly satisfied. "They shall not hunger, nor thirst, neither shall the heat nor the sun strike them" (Isa. xlix. 10). Since, then, eternal life is looked upon as an actual possession, and grace is its title; grace is described in language that belongs to eternal life itself. In this lies the force of our Lord's contrast. On the one side, there is earthly water with its "fleeting bodily refreshment," and on the other side, grace with its fruit in the perfect and enduring joys of heaven.

water that I will give him, shall not thirst for ever. But
the water that I will give him, shall become in him a
fountain of water springing up into life everlasting. The
woman saith to him : Sir, give me this water, that I may
not thirst, nor come hither to draw. Jesus saith to her :
Go, call thy husband, and come hither. The woman
answered, and said : I have no husband. Jesus said to
her : Thou hast said well, I have no husband : for thou
hast had five husbands : and he whom thou now hast, is
not thy husband. This thou hast said truly. The woman
saith to him : Sir, I perceive that thou art a prophet. Our

14. *The water that I will give him, shall become in him a fountain
of water springing up into life everlasting.* He in whom the Holy
Spirit dwells (iii. 5, 6) has within himself an overflowing fountain of
grace, springing up with full impulsive force until it reaches heaven
(cf. i. 16, vi. 27). As water seeks its level, so grace, which comes
from heaven, tends heavenward.

15. *Sir, give me this water.* The woman has not yet guessed the
deeper meaning of our Lord's words. Even the significant phrase
'into life everlasting' has suggested no more than a vague length of
time (cf. "O king, live for ever," Neh. ii. 3).

16. *Go, call thy husband, and come* (ἐλθὲ=come back) *hither.* The
sequel shows that our Lord is now touching the plague-spot of the
woman's life. By thus bringing her suddenly face to face with her sin,
He prepares her for repentance, and gives proof of His superhuman
knowledge.

17. *I have no husband.* She seeks to cover her fault by evading
the request.

Thou hast said well (καλῶς=rightly), *I have no husband.* There is
a marked emphasis in the Greek on 'husband'—'thou hast said rightly,
husband I have not.' This emphasis is a warning to the woman that
her subterfuge has been detected.

18. *For thou hast had five husbands.* This unexpected revelation
of her past now makes clear to the woman that our Lord is possessed
of supernatural knowledge.

19. *Sir, I perceive that thou art a prophet.* Not yet Messiah, but
still a prophet.

20. *Our Fathers adored* (i.e., offered public sacrifice) *on this
mountain* (Gerizim). The temple on Gerizim had been destroyed by
John Hyrcanus ; but the site was held sacred.

The stages in the woman's mental change are clearly marked :
(1) flippancy and aloofness (v. 9) ; (2) dawning respect for our Lord's
impressive seriousness (v. 11) ; (3) readiness to accept His words,
although not understood by her (v. 15) ; (4) belief in Him as a
prophet of God (v. 19) ; (5) anxiety to learn the truth from Him (v. 20).

fathers adored on this mountain, and you say, that at Jerusalem is the place where men must adore. Jesus saith 21 to her: Woman, believe me, that the hour cometh, when you shall neither on this mountain, nor in Jerusalem adore the Father. You adore that which you know not: we 22 adore that which we know; for salvation is of the Jews. But the hour cometh, and now is, when the true adorers 23

She, remembering the warning of our Lord, "if thou didst know who it is that speaketh to thee" (v. 10), and now being convinced that He is a prophet, at once desires to know by which worship—that of the Jews or that of the Samaritans—God is most pleased. A prophet, although a Jew, will faithfully tell her the truth. Her question is the question of one anxious to be guided aright, not the evasion (for how would our Lord have consented to such evasion?) of one desirous of putting off the hour of repentance.

21. *Woman, believe me, that the hour cometh* ("and now is," v. 23). The phrase 'believe me,' occurs but once; the usual form is, 'I say unto thee.' Our Lord's first reply is that the question between Jerusalem and Gerizim is over; it has now lost all meaning. In the new dispensation both are on the same footing; for the Mosaic law is dead.

you shall . . . adore the Father. This is spoken from the standpoint of the new dispensation. This first reply marks the fulfilment of the ancient prophecy, "I will not receive a gift of your hand. For from the rising of the sun even to the going down (*i.e.*, from east to west = over the whole world) my name is great among the Gentiles, and in every place there is sacrifice (*i.e.*, the sacrifice of the Mass), and there is offered to my name a clean (*i.e.*, unbloody) oblation" (Mal. i. 10, 11).

22. *You adore that which you know not.* In this second reply our Lord says that, although the question raised by the woman has lost all significance, yet in a deeper matter the truth belongs to the Jews. Theirs are "the glory, and the testament, and the giving of the law, and the promises" (Rom. ix. 4). "The law shall come forth from Sion, and the word of the Lord from Jerusalem" (Isa. ii. 3). With the Jews will be found a true idea of God and of His worship; and the reason is because, by the Divine appointment and promise, "salvation is of the Jews."

23. *But the hour cometh.* Although the true idea of God could not be altogether destroyed from amongst the Jews, nevertheless a fuller knowledge and more perfect worship were at hand.

the true (ἀληθινοί: see i. 9) *adorers shall adore the Father in spirit and in truth.* The phrase 'in spirit and truth' characterises Christian worship as contrasted with Jewish; but since the Jewish was true, the phrase must mean more truly spiritual and real. The knowledge of God shall be deeper and clearer; He shall be known as Father: and in agreement with that knowledge the adoration shall be more perfect

shall adore the Father in spirit and in truth. For the Father
24 also seeketh such to adore him. God is a spirit, and they
25 that adore him, must adore him in spirit and in truth. The
woman saith to him: I know that the Messias cometh
(who is called Christ), therefore when he is come, he will
26 tell us all things. Jesus saith to her: I am he who am
27 speaking with thee. And immediately his disciples came:
and they wondered that he talked with the woman. Yet
no man said: What seekest thou, or why talkest thou with
28 her? The woman therefore left her waterpot, and went

(in spirit) and more real (in truth). Christians are the true adorers, because their reverence springs from more abundant grace, and from a clearer revelation. But the perfect excellence of Christian worship is found in the sacrifice of the Mass, wherein God's own true Son offers Himself as a sacrifice to the Father. What sacrifice so real and perfect as this? What adoration so true? What love so intense and spiritual? But Christ is offered for all; and in uniting ourselves to Him, we also, in Him and through Him, become true adorers in spirit and in truth.

24. *God is a spirit.* Therefore [καὶ is illative] the worship He accepts must be spiritual, *i.e.*, from an inward principle of grace and reverence. Outward ceremony is little worth without faith and inward fervour. Both should enter into our worship. "These things you ought to have done, and not to leave those undone" (Matt. xxiii. 23).

25. *I know that the Messias cometh.* Messiah (without the article here) is used as a proper name by the woman. 'Cometh'—either, 'is at hand,' or 'is sure to come.' The Samaritans could not have been ignorant of an expectation which was known, about this time, even to Romans. The Samaritan name for the Messiah was the Returner, or the Restorer. Speaking to a Jew she used the Jewish name.

26. *I am he.* Her expression of unreserved obedience to the Messiah was rewarded by this revelation. Such revelation to the Samaritans was not likely to cause the dangers which would have attended a similar revelation to the Jews generally, and on account of which our Lord's language amongst the Jews was more reserved (see Matt. xvi. 20, xvii. 9).

27. *And they wondered.* It was contrary to all Jewish notions that a Rabbi should talk with a woman, even his own wife, in the street. Hence the disciples wondered that "He was talking with *a* woman" (Greek), and she, moreover, a Samaritan. Yet, in their reverence, they asked not the reason of Christ's condescension.

28. *The woman therefore, i.e.*, because the coming of the disciples interrupted the colloquy. But, with her mind excited, she forgot her errand and hurried to the city.

her way into the city, and saith to the men there: Come, 29
and see a man who has told me all things whatsoever I
have done. Is not he the Christ? They went therefore 30
out of the city, and came unto him. In the meantime the 31
disciples prayed him, saying: Rabbi, eat. But he said to 32
them: I have meat to eat which you know not. The 33
disciples therefore said one to another: Hath any man
brought him to eat? Jesus saith to them: My meat is to 34
do the will of him that sent me, that I may perfect his
work. Do not you say, there are yet four months, and 35

29. *Who has told me all things* (πάντα ἅ or ὅσα). What had been disclosed was sufficient proof that everything in her life could have easily been disclosed.

Is not he the Christ? (μήτι οὗτος). In form this expects a negative answer—'Is it possible that he is the Christ?' But the apparent doubt comes from mere wonderment at the greatness of the discovery.

30. *And came unto him* (ἤρχοντο: imperfect = and were coming). It is the language of an eye-witness.

31. *In the meantime*, i.e., after the departure of the woman and before the arrival of the Samaritans (their arrival is noted in v. 40).

34. *My meat is to do* (ἵνα ποιήσω). This expression may be simply equivalent to the infinitive, or it may express desire, i.e., my delight is in doing.

35. *There are yet four months* (ἔτι τετράμηνός ἐστιν), *and then* ('then' omitted in Greek and Vulg.) *the harvest* (ὁ θερισμός) *cometh*. Many take this as a proverbial saying; and although the saying has not elsewhere been found, parallels have been found. But in matters of this kind, to argue from parallels is precarious. On the other hand, absence of evidence is not always a proof of non-existence: the saying might have been current, although no extant writing contains it. The simplest explanation sees in the words a plain statement of fact which is adopted as the ground of a spiritual comparison (see iii. 8, 29; iv. 10): "You say the harvest is yet four months off, but I say that the countries are white for the harvest *even now*" (ἤδη). What kind of harvest is meant the next verse shows: "fruit unto life everlasting." The word τετράμηνος is an adjective masculine in agreement with χρόνος understood. But we may not improbably supply σῖτος instead of χρόνος = "The crop is already four months old and the harvest is coming" (See *Dublin Review* April, 1890). This explains better the comparison drawn by our Lord.

Harvest began in the middle of Nisan, 'the month of new corn.' The words were, therefore, spoken about the middle of December, when the seed, sown at the beginning of November, was beginning to appear above ground. Consequently our Lord had made a stay of about eight months in Judea (ii. 13, 23; iii. 22; iv. 3, 4). This

then the harvest cometh? Behold I say to you, lift up your eyes, and see the countries, for they are white already
36 to harvest. And he that reapeth receiveth wages, and gathereth fruit unto life everlasting: that both he that
37 soweth, and he that reapeth, may rejoice together. For in this is the saying true: that it is one man that soweth,
38 and it is another that reapeth. I have sent you to reap that in which you did not labour: others have laboured,
39 and you have entered into their labours. Now of that city many of the Samaritans believed in him, for the word of the woman giving testimony: He told me all things
40 whatsoever I have done. So when the Samaritans were come to him, they desired him that he would tarry there.
41 And he abode there two days. And many more believed
42 in him because of his own word. And they said to the

is the common opinion; but in the second opinion just mentioned the time was near Pentecost.

36. *He that reapeth receiveth wages* (*i.e.*, a reward for himself), *and gathereth fruit unto life everlasting* (συνάγει καρπὸν εἰς = stores up as in a granary), *i.e.*, brings souls to heaven.

that both he that soweth (*i.e.*, Christ Himself, who was then sowing the seed of faith), *and he that reapeth* (*i.e.*, every apostle of Christ), *may rejoice together.*

37. *For in this* (*i.e.*, in this instance at least) *is the saying true* (ἀληθινός = genuine—true indeed). The saying follows: 'It is one man that soweth,' &c. The saying is verified, but yet so that sower and reaper rejoice together.

38. *I have sent you to reap* (ἀπέσταλκα = I sent. All the other verbs are in the perfect). I sent you to reap that which you have not laboured. The mission of the Apostles had already been practically determined, and, in an informal way, even begun (iii. 22, 26; iv. 2).

others have laboured. Moses, the Prophets, and John had been preparing the ground for the seed of Christ's sowing. But chiefly Christ Himself (i. 4, 9).

40. *They desired him:* ἠρώτων = kept beseeching Him.

42. *We now believe, not for thy saying* (λαλιάν). A Hebraism = not so much for thy saying. λαλιά = speech, *utterance*, as distinct from the thought uttered (λόγος). In classical Greek used for mere talk, chatter; but this connotation of contempt had disappeared in later Greek, in which it means simply 'discourse,' 'speech' (cf. viii. 43).

this is indeed the Saviour of the world (A.V. 'the Christ, the Saviour': but the words 'the Christ' are not genuine). Therefore our Lord must have revealed Himself as Saviour of the world. This truth underlies vv. 21-24.

woman: We now believe, not for thy saying: for we ourselves have heard him, and know that this is indeed the Saviour of the world.

Return to Galilee.
(Vers. 43–54).

Now after two days he departed thence; and went into Galilee. For Jesus himself gave testimony that a prophet hath no honour in his own country. And when he was come into Galilee, the Galileans received him, having seen

43. *After two days he departed.* The stay was short, in accordance with our Lord's plan of first evangelizing the house of Israel (Matt. x. 6; xv. 24). The narrative is resumed from v. 3, as it had been interrupted by the episode in Samaria. Hence it begins μετὰ δὲ τὰς δύο ἡμέρας, *i.e.*, 'but after *the* two days' (v. 40), marking the conclusion of the episode.

44. *For Jesus himself gave testimony.* An obscure verse. 'He went into Galilee. For He Himself gave testimony that a prophet hath no honour in his own country' (ἐν τῇ ἰδίᾳ πατρίδι). The opposition is between Judea and Galilee. Therefore the meaning cannot be that He avoided Nazareth, where His home was, and went to Capharnaum (Matt. iv. 12, 13). Both places were in Galilee, and there is no contrast with Judea. Some, therefore, take πατρίς in the strict sense of native country. Our Lord, then, having been born in Bethlehem of Juda, left His own country and went into Galilee. But this is excluded by the fact that our Lord applies the same proverb to Nazareth, which He calls His πατρίς (Matt. xiii. 54; Mark vi. 4; Luke iv. 16–24). Others take πατρίς in a higher sense, as signifying the home or native land of the prophets. They appeal to the Jewish saying, "Search the scriptures, and see that out of Galilee a prophet riseth not" (vii. 52). But, again, this is opposed to our Lord's own use of the word; it is not true to fact; for, "behind the exile, Galilee had traditions, a prophetic succession, and a history almost as splendid as Judah's own. These utterances were due to the spitfire pride of Judea" (Smith, l.c., p. 423). See on vii. 52. Perhaps the most satisfactory explanation is that which supplies the ellipsis suggested by the context. Our Lord had left Galilee for Judea, from which, however, He withdrew, owing to the opposition of the Pharisees (iv. 1–3), and so returned to Galilee, *to which He would not otherwise have returned*, "for Jesus Himself gave testimony that a prophet hath no honour in his own country."

Like all proverbs, this proverb expresses not an absolute, but a general, truth—a truth with exceptions and subject to modification.

all the things he had done at Jerusalem on the festival
46 day: for they also went to the festival day. He came
again therefore into Cana of Galilee, where he made the
water wine. And there was a certain ruler whose son
47 was sick at Capharnaum. He having heard that Jesus was
come from Judea into Galilee, went to him, and prayed
him to come down and heal his son: for he was at the
48 point of death. Jesus therefore said to him: Unless you
49 see signs and wonders, you believe not. The ruler saith
50 to him: Lord, come down before that my son die. Jesus
saith to him: Go thy way, thy son liveth. The man
believed the word which Jesus said to him, and went his
51 way. And as he was going down, his servants met him:
2 and they brought word, saying, that his son lived. He
asked therefore of them the hour, wherein he grew better.
And they said to him: Yesterday at the seventh hour the
53 fever left him. The father therefore knew that it was at

46. *A certain ruler* (τις βασιλικός). This means a royal officer, either civil or military (A.V. 'nobleman,' R.V.M. 'king's officer'). He would be attached to the service of the tetrarch Herod Antipas, who was popularly called king (comp. Matt. xiv. i.; Mark vi. 14).

whose son (ὁ υἱὸς: in verse 49 παιδίον, therefore still young). The article probably implies that he was an only son.

was sick at Capharnaum. Better, 'there was a ruler in Capharnaum, whose son was sick.'

47. *And prayed him to come down*, because Capharnaum was on the coast (see ii. 1, 12).

48. *Unless you see signs.* This reproach is addressed to the Galileans generally, and, of course, to the ruler (see v. 45). Instead of accepting the authority of Christ and His testimony, for which sufficient warrant had already been given, they were thirsty, in their mental feverishness, for fresh and fresh wonders. How different the whole-hearted faith of the disciples and of the simple Samaritans! So, too, it sometimes happens that one accepts in a half-hearted way the Divine authority of the Church, yet shows a feverish eagerness for proofs that what has been revealed, and should therefore be accepted on authority, is really true. The fault is just the same, though its action lies in a different direction.

52. *Yesterday at the seventh hour.* Either the ruler did not reach home the same day, or he reached home after sunset, and the description follows the Jewish manner of reckoning the day from sunset to sunset, and speaks of yesterday where we should speak of 'this morning.' The seventh hour is one o'clock in the afternoon.

the same hour, that Jesus said to him, 'Thy son liveth; and himself believed and his whole house. This *is* again 54 the second miracle that Jesus did, when he was come out of Judea into Galilee.

54. *The second miracle.* Not the second absolutely, but the second in Galilee (ii. 11). It was done after the return from Judea to Galilee.

The miracle here recorded must be distinguished from that recorded in Matt. viii. and Luke vii. Many points of difference are to be noted. (1) One was done in Cana, the other in Capharnaum; (2) the one healed a son, the other a servant; (3) the one for a ruler, the other for a centurion; (4) the ruler was blamed for the imperfection of his faith, the centurion was praised for its perfection; (5) our Lord refused to go to the ruler's house; He went unasked to the centurion's, for He wished thus to correct the wrong idea which the ruler had formed of Him. Since our Lord was the author of life He could restore life at a distance by a word as easily as by His bodily presence. This truth the ruler learned to understand; (6) the son was on the point of death from fever, the servant was tormented with paralysis.

CHAPTER V.

The Healing of an Infirm Man.

(VERS. 1-15.)

AFTER these things was a festival day of the Jews, and Jesus went up to Jerusalem. Now there is at

In this second visit of our Lord to Jerusalem, we see Him display His power by healing a man that had been eight and thirty years under infirmity (*v.* 5); we see the opposition of the Jewish leaders, which had already shown itself against our Lord (ii. 18, iii. 2, iv. 1), now growing in violence; but we also see our Lord more plainly revealing His equality with the Father.

1. *A festival day of the Jews.* This seems to be the true reading; but many ancient authorities read 'the festival day.' It is scarcely possible to say what feast is referred to. When our Lord was in Samaria, the time was probably December (iv. 35); but the next feast mentioned, after this unnamed festival-day, is the Pasch (vi. 4). The only feast between December and the Pasch was the Feast of Purim, or of Lots. Now, in favour of the opinion that Purim is intended, it may be urged (1) that St. John on the three other occasions names the Pasch (ii. 13, vi. 4, xi. 55); (2) if this feast is the Pasch, then St. John goes at once (vi. 3) to a third Pasch, thus passing over the events of a whole year. In favour of the opinion that the Pasch is intended, it may be urged (1) that the events which the text implies cannot have occurred between Purim and the Pasch. If our Lord went up alone at the Feast of Purim, His disciples must have returned to their homes. But when the Pasch was at hand, which would have been less than a month afterwards, our Lord is not only back in Galilee, but He has again gathered His disciples together, and He is followed by a great multitude that had been attracted by His miracles (vi. 2-4); (2) the narrative of St. Luke seems to require that we should understand the words 'a feast' of the Pasch. The miracle of the feeding of five thousand occurred between the unnamed feast and the nearest Pasch (vi. 4-13). Now, St. Luke in describing the same miracle (ix. 11-17)

Jerusalem a pond, *called* Probatica, which in Hebrew is named Bethsaida, having five porches. In these lay a great multitude of sick, of blind, of lame, of withered,

places its occurrence not only after our Lord's return to Galilee in the winter following the first Pasch (Luke iv. 14 *seq.*, cf. John iv. 35, 43), but also after a second Pasch. He describes the disciples as plucking ears of corn, and rubbing them in their hands (vi. 1). But before the Pasch it was unlawful to eat the new corn (Lev. xxiii. 10–14), even if it were ripe enough, which is most unlikely, to be rubbed out of the ear. This, therefore, implies that the miracle occurred after the second Pasch, and that the Pasch in vi. 4 was the third Pasch of our Lord's public life. St. John, then, either omits all mention of one Pasch, or refers to it in *v.* 1.

A third opinion, perhaps most probable, takes the feast to be Pentecost. This opinion explains why the feast is not named (for the Pasch would have been named), and it may be made to agree with St. Luke's narrative by supposing that the events of John v. 1 *seq.* occurred immediately after those narrated in Luke vii. 11–50. Indeed, John v. 21, "As the Father raiseth up the dead, and giveth life: so the Son also giveth life to whom he will," is most appropriate after the raising of the widow's son, as told in Luke vii. 11–16. The silence of St. John regarding the second Pasch may be explained by the supposition that our Lord did not go up to Jerusalem on that occasion, as He also seems not to have gone up for the third Pasch—"because the Jews sought to kill him" (John vii. 1).

2. *A pond, called Probatica, which in Hebrew is named Bethsaida* (ἐπὶ τῇ προβατικῇ κολυμβήθρα ... Βηθσαϊά), A.V. "by the sheep market a pool"; R.V. "by the sheep gate a pool." The Vulgate simply gives the Greek word—Probatica. This word is an adjective, leaving the noun to be supplied. Now, since reference is elsewhere made to a sheep gate, or flock gate (Neh. iii. 1, 31; xii. 38), it is most natural to supply here the word 'gate.' The sense is, 'there is at the sheep gate a pool named Bethsaida.' A more common form of the name is Bethesda. The meaning of the name cannot be determined. Many suggestions have been made, of which three appear sufficiently probable. 'The House of Porches,' or 'The House of Mercy,' or 'The House of the Stream.' Each is also appropriate: the first on account of the five porches, the second on account of the healings, the third on account of the ever-flowing waters. The sheep gate was north of the Temple, at the north-west angle of Antonia.

3. *Waiting for the moving of the water.* These words, and the whole of the next verse, raise a grave textual difficulty as to their genuineness. The passage is expunged by Tischendorf, Tregelles, Alford, Westcott and Hort, but retained by Scholz and Lachmann. Of the five old Uncials only three omit all the words (אBC), and the second corrector of C replaces them in that manuscript. D retains the last clause of *v.* 3, but omits *v.* 4, while A retains *v.* 4, but

4 waiting for the moving of the water. And an Angel of
the Lord descended at certain times into the pond; and
the water was moved. And he that went down first
into the pond after the motion of the water, was made
5 whole of whatsoever infirmity he lay under. And there
was a certain man there, that had been eight and thirty
6 years under his infirmity. Him when Jesus had seen
lying, and knew that he had been now a long time, he
7 saith to him: Wilt thou be made whole? The infirm
man answered him: Sir, I have no man, when the water
is troubled, to put me into the pond. For whilst I am

omits the last clause of v. 3. On the other hand, the rest of the
Uncials, the preponderating mass of the cursives, the Peshitto and
Jerusalem Syriac, most of the Old Latin MSS., as well as the Vulgate,
with Tertullian, St. Ephraem, St. Ambrose, St. Chrysostom, St.
Jerome, St. Cyril of Alexandria, St. Augustine, contain the reading.
(See Scrivener, vol. ii. p. 361; Burgon, 'The Traditional Text,'
p. 82). It must always be borne in mind (1) that the versions as a class
go much further back than the oldest extant Greek manuscripts;
(2) that the writings of the early Fathers are also older than the
Greek manuscripts; (3) that St. Jerome (A.D. 385), who gave us the
Latin Vulgate, revised the old Latin of the New Testament by the aid
of Greek MSS. that were old even at that early date. ("Codicum
Græcorum emendata collatione, sed veterum," Præf. ad Damasum);
(4) that the cursives may represent the older text. Besides, the statement of v. 7, 'I have no man, when the water is troubled (ταραχθῇ)
—a passage about which there is no textual difficulty—presupposes the
statement of v. 4, 'An angel descended . . . and the water was
moved' (ἐτάρασσε τὸ ὕδωρ = and troubled the water).

4. *He that went down first.* The description of the cure effected
by the water shows that the action was miraculous.

5. *Eight and thirty years.* "In him, as a typical case, could the
Saviour best do and teach that for which He had come. This man,
for thirty-eight years a hopeless sufferer, without attendant or friend
among those whom misery had made so intensely selfish, seemed the
fittest object for power and grace. It is idle to speak either of faith
or of receptiveness on the man's part. The essence of the whole
history lies in the utter absence of both; in Christ's raising, as it were,
the dead, and calling the things that are not as though they were"
(Eders. l. c., p. iii.).

6. *Him when Jesus had seen lying, and knew* (ἰδών καὶ γνούς = saw,
and knew that). We take this as another instance of supernatural and
intuitive knowledge (cf. 14, i. 42, 47, 48, ii. 24, 25, iv. 18).

7. *Another goeth down before me.* Only the first to enter was
healed (v. 4).

coming, another goeth down before me. Jesus saith to 8
him: Arise, take up thy bed, and walk. And imme- 9
diately the man was made whole: and he took up his bed
and walked. And it was the sabbath that day. The 10
Jews therefore said to him that was healed: It is the
sabbath, it is not lawful for thee to take up thy bed. He 11
answered them: He that made me whole, he said to me:
Take up thy bed, and walk. They asked him, therefore: 12
Who is that man who said to thee: Take up thy bed, and
walk? But he who was healed, knew not who it was. 13
For Jesus went aside from the multitude standing in the
place. Afterwards Jesus findeth him in the temple, and 14

8. *Take up* (ἆρον: aor. imperat. = single action) *thy bed, and walk* (περιπάτει: pres. imper. = continuous action) cf. v. 9 (ἦρε καὶ περιπάτει).

9. *And it was the sabbath.* This note prepares the ground for the opposition that follows—the opposition of men so blinded by the bare letter of Scripture and the law that they failed to see the Divine authority in our Lord's miracles. A similar thing is observable now in the case of those who appeal, as the Jews appealed, to bits of the letter, and so fail to recognise the authority of the Church, as the Jews failed to recognise the authority of Christ. Yet "to the Catholic Church alone belong all those many and admirable tokens which have been divinely established for the evident credibility of the Christian faith. Nay, more, the Church by itself, by reason of its marvellous extension, its eminent holiness, and its inexhaustible fruitfulness in every good thing, its catholic unity and its invincible stability, is a great and perpetual motive of credibility, and an irrefutable witness of its own Divine mission" (Vat. Concil. Constit. 'Dei Filius,' chap. iii.).

10. *It is not lawful.* It was certainly opposed to the letter of the law (cf. Jer. xvii. 21, 22).

11. *He that made me whole.* On the fact of the miracle the man bases his justification for having obeyed Christ, and the miracle was certainly a sufficient reason for trusting Christ.

12. *Who is that man?* (ὁ ἄνθρωπος) said with perhaps a tone of angry contempt.

13. *Jesus went aside* (ἐξένευσεν, from ἐκνεύω; if from ἐκνέω = he escaped) *from the multitude* (rather, "a multitude being in the place"). It may mean either that He escaped, being lost in the crowd, or that He withdrew because of the crowd. The verb is in the aorist, and naturally means that, as soon as the controversy began, our Lord withdrew; but it may be taken in the sense of the pluperfect = "for He had withdrawn."

14. *Sin no more.* Therefore our Lord knew that the man's in-

saith to him: Behold thou art made whole: sin no more,
15 lest some worse thing happen to thee. And the man went
his way, and told the Jews that it was Jesus who had made
him whole.

Our Lord's Discourse.

(Vers. 16–47.)

16 Therefore did the Jews persecute Jesus, because he did
17 these things on the sabbath. But Jesus answered them:
18 My Father worketh until now; and I work. Hereupon
therefore the Jews sought the more to kill him, because

firmity had been caused by his sin; and the man's outward cure was intended to prepare his soul for an inward healing, the temporal gift to prepare for an eternal blessing.

lest some worse thing. Not bodily infirmity merely, but spiritual death.

15. *And told the Jews.* Filled with grateful joy, he returned to answer the question that had been put to him (*v.* 12), and to proclaim that it was Christ who had healed him.

The miracle just described was symbolical. In the discourse that follows our Lord explains at length the deep truths of which the miracle was but a dim reflection or symbol.

16. *Therefore did the Jews persecute* (ἐδίωκον) *Jesus, because he did* (ἐποίει) *these things on the sabbath.* 'Therefore' is not St. John's usual particle, but the more emphatic διὰ τοῦτο ὅτι. In this phrase the διὰ τοῦτο (= for this cause) refers to what precedes, and ὅτι introduces a more precise explanation. The full meaning is: "For this cause, therefore, were the Jews persecuting Jesus, because, namely, He was doing these things on the Sabbath" (cf. *v.* 18, vi. 65, viii. 47, ix. 22, x. 17, xii. 39, xiii. 11, xv. 19, xvi. 15). Both verbs are in the imperfect, and so denote a continued course of action on the part both of the Jews and of our Lord.

17. *My Father worketh until now; and I work.* A profound answer to the charge of Sabbath-breaking. From the beginning of creation God has never ceased doing good—conserving, governing, and providing for all; in this He knows no Sabbath-rest. But Christ is also God. Therefore He, too, like the Father, knows no Sabbath. The miracles performed on the Sabbath are but acts of that unceasing, ever-active power. Moreover, Christ, as God, is Lord also of the Sabbath, and can dispense whom He pleases from its observance.

18. *Hereupon therefore.* More exactly, "For this cause, therefore [cf. *v.* 16], the Jews were seeking still more to kill Him, because He was not only loosening (ἔλυε) the Sabbath, but was also saying God

he did not only break the sabbath, but also said God was his Father, making himself equal to God.

(*a*) OUR LORD'S OWN TESTIMONY (vers. 19–30).

Then Jesus answered, and said to them: Amen, amen, 19 I say unto you: the Son cannot do anything of himself,

was His own Father (πατέρα ἴδιον = uniquely His own), making Himself equal to God." The imperfect tenses of this verse and of *v.* 16 show that a contention had been progressing, during which the Jews had come to see, perhaps somewhat indistinctly as to the consequences involved, but at any rate distinctly enough, that our Lord was putting Himself on the same level with God. Our Lord, so far from repudiating such interpretation of His words, proceeds to give it greater definiteness by asserting His unity of nature and essence with the Father. But in the course of the explanation, which regards the person of Christ Himself, who is both God and man, some things are said in reference to Christ as God, and some are said in reference to Him as the God-man (cf. on i. 14).

The discourse may be divided into four sections; (*a*) Our Lord's own testimony (19–30); (*b*) the testimony of John (31–35); (*c*) the testimony of miracle (36); (*d*) the testimony of the Father (37–47).

19. *The Son cannot do anything of himself, but what he seeth the Father doing.* We say, God cannot lie, cannot die, &c. Such expressions do not mean that there is any imperfection in God; on the contrary, they mean that God is so perfect by an inner necessity of His very nature that no failing or imperfection can touch Him. In the same way our Lord says of Himself, that by the inner necessity of His own perfection He cannot do anything alone, *i.e.*, apart from the Father. That inner necessity lies in the unity of the Divine nature. There is only one God, one Divine nature, power, omnipotence, intellect, and will. What God does is done by the three Persons equally; for they are the one God, the one Divine power, the selfsame principle of all creation. Therefore, whatever the Father does, the Son does equally; whatever the Son does, the Father does equally. And as their action is common, so is their knowledge common. They see and know in common what they do in common. But since the Son proceeds from the Father, it is said: 'The Son cannot do anything, but only what He seeth the Father doing,' thus connoting the relation of origin. The limiting clause ('*but what he seeth*') applies to the principal thought (*do anything*), and not to the addition (*of himself*); for the Son cannot do *of himself* even what He seeth the Father doing (cf. xv. 4).

in like manner (ὁμοίως = equally). Because Father and Son act with the same identical power, not with similar powers. These things are said of Christ in His Divine nature; and they are ex-

but what he seeth the Father doing : for what things soever
20 he doth, these the Son also doth in like manner. For the
Father loveth the Son, and sheweth him all things which
himself doth : and greater works than these will he shew
21 him, that you may wonder. For as the Father raiseth up
the dead, and giveth life · so the Son also giveth life to
22 whom he will. For neither doth the Father judge any
23 man : but hath given all judgment to the Son. That all

pressed to the Jews in language borrowed from a simple and familiar fact—the fact that children observe with attention what their father does.

20. *The Father loveth the Son.* Our Lord continues the illustration drawn from our human life. Since the illustration is drawn from human things, it cannot perfectly illustrate Divine things, but it gives us something to go upon. As men enrich their sons whom they love, so the Father has withheld nothing from His well-beloved Son. The miracles already performed are not the only signs of the infinite power and knowledge communicated by the Father to the Son.

greater works than these will he show him (this is said in reference to their temporal manifestation), *that you may wonder* (ἵνα θαυμάζητε). In many cases ἵνα with the subjunctive has practically lost its original idea of purpose. The verse here may mean, 'He will do such great things that you will wonder at His Divine power, whom now you accuse of blasphemy'; or the verse may express the purpose of God 'in order that you may wonder, and so be led to believe.' What those 'greater works' will be our Lord explains.

21. *As the Father raiseth up the dead, and giveth life.* The Father is the 'Life-giver' in the most complete and absolute sense. All life, temporal and eternal, natural and supernatural, comes from Him. He raises the dead body from the grave, He raises the soul dead in sin. "So the Son also" has the same universal, life-giving power—a power supreme and unconstrained : He "giveth life to whom he will" (cf. i. 4 ; Acts iii. 14, 15).

22. *For neither* (οὐδὲ γάρ = for not even) *doth the Father judge any man.* The Son came as man to offer grace and life to mankind. The gift is the gift of both Father and Son ; but the Son became flesh and appeared before the eyes of men in order to bear that gift to mankind. Therefore, in the judgment of those who refuse or abuse the gift, the sentence, though coming from Father and Son, will be passed by the Word made flesh. The reason follows.

23. *That* (ἵνα = in order that) *all men may honour the Son, as* (καθὼς = equally, 'even as,' A.V.) *they honour the Father.* Since the Father sent His own co-equal Son into the world, those who do not honour the Son with that full Divine worship which is His due dishonour the Father. As the nature of Father and Son is one, so is their honour one (cf. iii. 33, 34).

men may honour the Son, as they honour the Father. He who honoureth not the Son, honoureth not the Father who hath sent him. Amen, amen, I say unto you, that he 24 who heareth my word, and believeth him that sent me, hath life everlasting; and cometh not into judgment, but is passed from death to life. Amen, amen, I say unto you, 25 that the hour cometh, and now is, when the dead shall hear the voice of the Son of God, and they that hear shall live. For as the Father hath life in himself; so he hath 26 given to the Son also to have life in himself: and he hath 27 given him power to do judgment, because he is the son of man. Wonder not at this, for the hour cometh wherein 28

24. *He who heareth my word.* In verse 21 our Lord had declared that He was the Giver of life; then he declared (*vv.* 22, 23) what was indeed a corollary of the foregoing, that to Him belonged the judgment both of life and of death. In the verses that immediately follow He explains how each judgment is carried out. And first the judgment of supernatural life.

he who heareth . . . *and believeth* . . . *hath life everlasting.* For the sense in which the just have life everlasting, even here on earth, see on i. 12, 13, 16; iii. 16-18.

and cometh not into judgment, i.e., of condemnation (cf. iii. 18). *but is passed* (μεταβέβηκεν : perf., denoting abiding results) *from death to life* (i. 12, 13, 16).

25. *The hour* (an hour) *cometh, and now is.* The judgment of supernatural resurrection had already begun. Christ's word of power was even then being heard, His grace was busy amongst men, raising them to life from the darkness and death of error and sin (cf. Matt. iv. 12-16).

26. *As the Father hath life in himself* (*i.e.*, is essential life, life itself); *so* (οὕτως καί = thus also, *i.e.*, in the same way) *he hath given* (*i.e.*, by eternal generation) *to the Son also to have life in himself* (cf. i. 4, 9, 14, 16).

27. *Power to do judgment, because he is the son of man* (υἱὸς ἀνθρώπου). The article may be omitted in a grammatical predicate; we may therefore take this as said of the Incarnate Word in the same way as in *v.* 22, and especially in i. 51. But we may also consider the omission of the article as strictly defining the predicate—'because He is a son of man.' The sense will then be, God exalted Him because He became man (cf. "He humbled himself. . . . For which cause God also hath exalted him," Phil. ii. 6-11).

28. As He spoke, wonder was depicted on the faces of His audience. He therefore said: *Wonder not at this, for the hour* (an hour) *cometh* (He does not add 'and now is,' as in *v.* 25) *wherein all that are in*

all that are in the graves shall hear the voice of the Son of
29 God. And they that have done good things, shall come
forth unto the resurrection of life ; but they that have done
30 evil, unto the resurrection of judgment. I cannot of
myself do anything. As I hear, so I judge : and my judgment is just : because I seek not my own will, but the will
of him that sent me.

the graves shall hear the voice of the Son of God (αὐτοῦ = His voice). These words manifestly refer to the bodily resurrection (cf. 1 Thess. iv. 15).

29. *And they that have done good things.* There is a different punctuation which yields the same sense, but makes a different connection of thought. 'They shall hear His voice, and shall come forth (*i.e.*, from the grave) ; they that have done good, unto the resurrection of life ; and they that have done evil (τὰ φαῦλα. Cf. iii. 20), unto the resurrection of judgment' (A.V.).

30. *I cannot of myself.* A change from the third to the first person. Our Lord returns upon what He had already said (see v. 19), and summing it up applies it directly to Himself. As God, He has the same identical knowledge, power, and will as the Father (see on v. 19) ; as the God-man, He possesses even in His human nature, by reason of the hypostatic union, the fulness of grace and life, and all the treasures of wisdom and knowledge (see note on the Pleroma after i. 18). We must therefore give the widest meaning to these concluding words : "I cannot of myself do anything. As I hear, so I judge," &c. On the whole section, compare, "All things are delivered to me by my Father. And no one knoweth the Son, but the Father : neither doth any one know the Father, but the Son, and he to whom it shall please the Son to reveal him" (Matt xi. 27).

"This that displeased the Jews, pleased the Father. This, without doubt, pleases them too that honour the Son as they honour the Father ; for if it does not please them, they will not be pleasing. For God will not be greater because it pleases thee, but thou wilt be less if it displeases thee. Now, against this calumny of theirs, coming either of ignorance or of malice, the Lord speaks not at all what they can understand, but that whereby they may be agitated and troubled, and, on being troubled, it may be, seek the Physician. And He uttered what should be written, that it might afterwards be read even by us. Now, we have seen what happened in the hearts of the Jews when they heard these words ; what happens in ourselves when we hear them, let us more fully consider. For heresies, and certain tenets of perversity, ensnaring souls and hurling them into the deep, have not sprung up except when good Scriptures are not rightly understood, and when that in them which is not rightly understood is rashly and boldly asserted. And so, dearly beloved, ought we very cautiously to hear those things for the understanding of which we are but little ones, and that, too, with pious heart and with trembling, holding this rule of soundness,

(b) THE TESTIMONY OF JOHN (vers. 31–35).

If I bear witness of myself, my witness is not true. 31
There is another that beareth witness of me: and I know 32
that the witness which he witnesseth of me is true. You 33
sent to John: and he gave testimony to the truth. But I 34

that we rejoice in what we have been able to understand, according to the faith with which we are embued; and in what we have not yet been able to understand, that we lay aside doubting, and defer the understanding of it for a time, yet so as we doubt not in the least that it is good and true" (St. Aug., Tract xviii. c. 1).

"'The hour cometh,' He does not add, 'and now is': therefore He means to make known to us a certain hour in the end of the world. The hour is now that the dead rise, the hour will be in the end of the world that the dead rise: but that they rise now in the mind, then in the flesh. It will not be the Father Himself that will come to judgment, notwithstanding the Father doth not withdraw Himself from the Son. How, then, is it that the Father Himself will not come? In that He will not *be seen* in the judgment. That form which stood before the judge, will be Judge: that form will judge which was judged; for it was judged unjustly, it will judge justly. There will come the form of a servant, and that same will be apparent. For how could the form of God be made apparent to the just and to the unjust, since it is not permitted to the wicked to see God? Such a Judge will appear as may be seen by those whom He is about to crown, and by those whom He is about to condemn. Hence the form of a servant will be seen, the form of God will be hid " (St. Aug., Tract xix. c. 16).

31. *If I bear witness of myself* ($\pi\epsilon\rho i\ \dot{\epsilon}\mu\alpha\nu\tau o\tilde{\upsilon}$ = regarding myself), *my witness is not true.* Our Lord here refers to what was passing through the minds of His hearers, and what, on another occasion, they plainly expressed (see viii. 13). The meaning is, you will say that if I bring forward only My own personal testimony regarding Myself, My testimony is not trustworthy. Such an argument, if applied to our Lord, is utterly false (comp. viii. 16); nor is it universally true even of mankind. There are many things of our own personal experience of which we ourselves are the sole authentic witnesses (cf. viii. 14). But for the present our Lord waives all this. He replies more directly to the objection.

32. *There is another that beareth* ($\dot{o}\ \mu\alpha\rho\tau\upsilon\rho\tilde{\omega}\nu$) *witness of me* = 'another is My witness.' This other is the Father, as the context shows (vv. 34, 36, 37). But before appealing to the testimony of the Father, He shows that the Jews had already heard the testimony of a trustworthy witness.

33. *You sent to John* (thereby showing that you thought him worthy of credence): *and he gave testimony to the truth.* The verbs are in the perfect tense, and so bring the force of John's testimony nearer.

34. *But I* ($\dot{\epsilon}\gamma\dot{\omega}\ \delta\dot{\epsilon}$) *receive not testimony from man.* You ask for testimony. Well, your own witness has given it. But I, for My part,

receive not testimony from man: but I say these things
35 that you may be saved. He was a burning and a shining
light. And you were willing for a time to rejoice in his light.

(c) THE TESTIMONY OF MIRACLE (ver. 36).
36 But I have a greater testimony than that of John. For
the works which the Father hath given me to perfect: the
works themselves, which I do, give testimony of me, that
the Father hath sent me.

(d) THE TESTIMONY OF THE FATHER (vers. 37–47).
37 And the Father himself who hath sent me, hath given
testimony of me: neither have you heard his voice at any

do not stand in need of any human testimony; and therefore I do not
here insist on John's testimony.
but I say these things that you may be saved, i.e., be led by your
belief in John to believe in Me.
   35. *He was a burning and a shining light* (ὁ λύχνος). The article
denotes that John was the *appointed* "lamp" provided by God to show
men the way to the Messiah (see Luke i. 76, 77). John had now been
cast into prison; and so it is said that, he *was* the lamp. Λύχνος is a
lamp placed on a stand.
   And you were willing for a time to rejoice in his light. When John
began to preach the advent of the kingdom, the hearts of the Jews
bounded with joy at the thought of a mighty empire; but when John
demanded fruit worthy of penance, their ardour cooled, and they
turned from him with the fickleness of children (cf. Matt. iii. 5–12,
xi. 16–19).
   36. *But I have a greater testimony than that of John* (μείζω τοῦ
Ἰωάννου: Brachylogy, the full form being μείζω τῆς τοῦ Ἰωάννου).
The words run literally, I have the witness greater than John.
   For the works (i.e., the works indicative of the Messiah, see Matt.
xi. 3–5) *which the Father hath given me to perfect* (ἵνα τελειώσω = in
order that I may fully accomplish them): *the works themselves* (αὐτὰ τὰ
ἔργα = those very works, highly emphatic) *which I do* (= which I am
doing), *give testimony of me, that the Father hath sent me* (cf. iii.
2, x. 37, 38).
   37. *And the Father himself.* There is reference now to a direct
testimony of the Father, a testimony distinct from the Father's indirect
testimony through Christ's works.
   hath given testimony of me. The verb is in the perfect tense, and so
implies something more than a mere historic testimony, for which the
aorist would have been used. The context shows that this testimony is
God's word in the Old Testament Scriptures (vv. 39, 45, 46).
   neither have you heard his voice. The Father has, in truth,
spoken, and has manifested His will, but you are deaf and blind.

time, nor seen his shape. And you have not his word 38
abiding in you: for whom he hath sent, him you believe
not. Search the scriptures, for you think in them to have 39
life everlasting: and the same are they that give testimony
of me: And you will not come to me that you may have 40
life. I receive not glory from men. But I know you, that 41
you have not the love of God in you. I am come in the 42,43
name of my Father, and you receive me not: if another
shall come in his own name, him you will receive. How 44
can you believe, who receive glory one from another: and
the glory which is from God alone, you do not seek?
Think not that I will accuse you to the Father. There is 45

How great that blindness! for God had, as it were, presented to them
His very shape (εἶδος).

38. *And you have not his word abiding in you.* No! it is only in
their books; it is not in them, for they do not understand it.

for whom he hath sent, him you believe not. If they did rightly
understand they would certainly receive Christ, of whom the Scriptures
clearly speak.

39. *Search the scriptures.* The verb (ἐρευνᾶτε) may, according to
its form, be either in the imperative or in the indicative. But since all
the other verbs are in the indicative, even the correlative verb (καὶ οὐ
θέλετε) the most obvious inference is, that this also is in the indicative.
The context, too, seems to require the indicative. Our Lord, then,
continues His reproach of the Jews. "You search the Scriptures,
because you fancy that by your searching you will find eternal life;
but although these very Scriptures are witnesses bearing testimony to
Me, yet you do not wish to come to Me that you may indeed have life"
(v. 40). If ἐρευνᾶτε were in the imperative, the address would have
run thus: 'Search the Scriptures, because in them you will find eternal
life, and come ye to Me.' As a matter of fact, they were only too
ready to search the Scriptures, but against our Lord (cf. vii. 52;
2 Cor. iii. 14, 15).

41. *I receive not glory from men.* That is, not from any desire of
human glory do I bring this charge against you; but because I know
that you have not the love of God in you (v. 42). If they really loved
God, they would receive Christ (viii. 42).

43. *I am come in the name of my Father:* see v. 36.

44. *How can you believe?* Not only, as a fact, do they refuse to
believe (v. 40), but by their earthly ambition, their absorption in
things of earth, their intellectual pride, they make belief in Christ a
moral impossibility (comp. 2 Cor. x. 4, 5; Matt. xxiii. 5-7; Luke xi.
43). 'You seek glory from one another, and *the* glory from God, you
do not seek.'

45. *Think not that I will accuse you,* for such accusation would be

46 one that accuseth you, Moses, in whom you trust. For if you did believe Moses, you would perhaps believe me also.
47 For he wrote of me. But if you do not believe his writings: how will you believe my words?

quite needless; "another is (already) your accuser, Moses, in whom you have placed your trust." Thus the Greek, more emphatically.

46. *For if you did believe Moses, you would perhaps* ('perhaps' is a wrong rendering: ἐπιστεύετε ἄν = you would indeed) *believe me also. For he wrote of me* (comp. iv. 10, xix. 7). This is a most important principle for the interpretation of the Pentateuch (cf. iii. 14).

47. *But if you do not believe his writings.* The antithesis is not between 'writings' and 'word,' but 'if you do not believe Moses, in whom you already trust, how will you believe Me, in whom you do not trust?'

and said: Amen, amen, I say to you, you seek me, not because you have seen miracles, but because you did eat of the loaves, and were filled. Labour not for the meat 27 which perisheth, but for that which endureth unto life everlasting, which the Son of Man will give you. For him hath God, the Father, sealed. They said therefore unto 28 him: What shall we do that we may work the works of

had thought of proclaiming Christ king (vv. 14, 15), for they were thinking not of the true kingdom of God, but of a kingdom "with miraculous wilderness-banquets to Israel, and coarse miraculous triumphs over the Gentiles. Every figure in which prophets had clothed the brightness of those days was first literalised, and then exaggerated, till the most glorious poetic descriptions became incongruous caricatures of spiritual Messianic expectancy. The fruit trees were every day, or at least every week or two, to yield their riches, the fields their harvests; the grain was to stand like palm trees, and to be reaped and winnowed without labour. Similar blessings were to visit the vine; ordinary trees would bear like fruit trees, and every produce of every clime would be found in Palestine in such abundance and luxuriance as only the wildest imagination could conceive" (Eders. l.c., p. 235). It was with thoughts like these that they had followed our Lord, who now explains to them the higher meaning of the wonders they had seen. The discourse which follows contains the very highest teaching. Its circumstances, therefore, must be carefully considered. It was delivered in the city which had been the centre of Christ's teaching and of many great miracles: it was delivered after two high points had been reached by the people—that Jesus was the Messiah-King; by the ship's company (Matt. xiv. 33), that He was the Son of God. However imperfectly these truths may have been apprehended, yet the teaching of Christ must start from them, and then point onwards (Eders., l.c., p. 234).

27. *Labour* (work) *not for the meat* (food) *which perisheth*. Christ knew what was in their thoughts, and wishes to give their eagerness a higher object (cf. Matt. vi. 25-33, 'Seek first the kingdom of God'). As on previous occasions, our Lord speaks of the spiritual after the analogy of the material thing that was then actually in question (see iv. 13, 14, 32, 35, v. 14). Here the material thing was food, and our Lord says, 'Work not for perishable food, but for food spiritual and imperishable.' This food the Son of Man can give.

For him hath God, the Father, sealed. The word 'sealed' is very significant. It was a well-known Jewish expression, according to which 'the seal of God was Truth.' It meant therefore that the Father's testimony had already sealed and authenticated Christ as the Messiah, and therefore as the giver of spiritual food (see on iii. 33).

28. *What shall we do?* Better, what must we do? They had a dim perception of what was meant, but, with their minds accustomed to

29 God? Jesus answered, and said to them: This is the work of God, that you believe in him whom he hath sent. 30 They said therefore to him: What sign therefore dost thou shew that we may see, and may believe thee? what 31 dost thou work? Our fathers did eat manna in the desert as it is written, *He gave them bread from heaven to eat.* 32 Then Jesus said to them: Amen, amen, I say to you: Moses gave you not bread from heaven, but my Father 33 giveth you the true bread from heaven. For the bread of God is that which cometh down from heaven, and giveth

legal observances, they inquire what special observances they must now undertake that, 'working the works of God,' they may please Him, and so secure that food.

29. *This is the work of God* (i.e., this is what God commands) *that you believe.* Faith in Christ is an essential condition of spiritual life (see on i. 12). Now that the duty they asked for is put plainly before them, they hesitate, and demand a clearer sign that the Father has sealed Christ.

30. *What sign therefore dost thou shew* (ποιεῖς) *that we may see* (i.e., see that thou hast been sent by God) *and may believe thee?* This is their request after all Christ's miracles! Yet another sign! for they were insatiable. The sign given only the previous day had been held sufficient (v. 14); but to-day more is required. This change of mind had perhaps been brought about by the insidiousness of the leaders, who were now mingled with the crowd in the synagogue (vv. 41, 60). The kind of sign which is asked for implies a suggestion on the part of the scribes. They argued that the prophet foretold by Moses, a prophet like to Moses himself, ought to show a sign similar to that of Moses. Yesterday's miracle was not sufficient.

31. *Our fathers did eat manna . . . bread from heaven.* Our Lord replies by denying that the manna was, in the strictest sense, bread from heaven. On the other hand, if they will believe in Him they will secure bread really from heaven.

32. *My Father giveth* (present tense—Christ is the gift, and is now before them) *you the true bread from heaven.* In the Greek τὸν ἀληθινόν is placed emphatically at the end. 'My Father giveth you the bread from heaven which is the real bread.' The proof of this statement lies in the very definition of what constitutes the real bread from heaven, the bread of God. That only can be called bread of God.

33. *Which cometh down from heaven* (i.e., is of heavenly origin), *and giveth life to the world* (i.e., to all mankind). In these words our Lord expresses in veiled language the great truth which is immediately set forth in plainer terms and at greater length (vv. 35, 41, 48, 51, 52, 54, 59). The Jews understood, so far, that the Father giveth through Christ a heavenly bread superior to the manna.

life to the world. They said therefore unto him: Lord, 34
give us always this bread. And Jesus said to them: I am 35
the bread of life: he that cometh to me shall not hunger;
and he that believeth in me, shall never thirst. But I 36
said unto you, that you also have seen me, and you
believe not. All that the Father giveth me shall come 37
to me; and him that cometh to me, I will not cast out.
Because I came down from heaven, not to do my own will, 38
but the will of him that sent me. Now this is the will of 39
the Father who sent me; that of all that he hath given me,
I should lose nothing, but should raise it up again in the
last day. And this is the will of my Father that sent me; 40

34. *Lord* (i.e., Sir), *give us always this bread.* Rather, "Always give us this bread" (πάντοτε emphatically leads). This they would accept as the sign asked for (v. 30).

35. *I am the bread of life*, i.e., the bread from heaven, the bread that giveth life to the world (vv. 32, 33). For the rest of the verse cf. iv. 13, 14. Notice that according to the parallelism, "cometh to me" = "believeth in me" (see vv. 37, 44, 45).

36. *But I said unto you, that you also* (καὶ) *have seen me* (i.e., have seen the miracles by which I have been sealed, v. 26) *and* (καὶ) *you believe not.* The double καὶ has here the force of 'although'—'yet.' Although you have seen, yet you have not believed. Therefore they put an insuperable obstacle in the way, so that they cannot receive the spiritual food which gives eternal life (vv. 27, 29, 33, 35).

37. *All that* (neuter, denoting mankind impersonally and universally) *the Father giveth me.* Therefore it is by the grace of the Father that all are efficaciously brought to Christ. Without that grace none can believe (v. 44); that grace is offered to all (i. 4, 5, 9), but not all obey it (i. 11, 12). It is a double mercy, therefore, to receive a grace which secures its effect and efficaciously brings us to Christ. The recipients of this grace are indeed *given* to Christ by the Father, and *shall come* to Christ, that is, shall certainly believe in Him.

I will not (οὐ μὴ) = I certainly will not) *cast out* (cf. xv. 6; Matt. xxii. 13). The reason why Christ will certainly not cast out from His kingdom the true believer is immediately given in the verses that follow.

38. *Because I came down* (καταβέβηκα = I have come down); cf. iv. 34.

39. *In the last day.* A phrase peculiar to St. John, and used by him seven times. The raising up in the last day of course refers to the 'resurrection of life' (v. 29).

40. *And* (γάρ = for) *this is.* An explanation of the preceding verse. In the Greek it runs, 'For this is the will of my Father, that every one,' &c. The clause 'that sent Me' is not in the Greek.

that every one who seeth the Son, and believeth in him, may have life everlasting, and I will raise him up in the
41 last day. The Jews therefore murmured at him, because he had said, I am the living bread which came down
42 from heaven. And they said: Is not this Jesus the son of Joseph, whose father and mother we know? How then
43 saith he, I came down from heaven? Jesus therefore answered and said to them: Murmur not among your-
44 selves. No man can come to me, except the Father, who hath sent me, draw him, and I will raise him up in the last
45 day. It is written in the prophets: *And they shall all be taught of God.* Every one that hath heard of the Father
46 and hath learned, cometh to me. Not that any man hath

every one who seeth . . . and believeth. This is said in reference to those who saw our Lord in the flesh. For many saw, and did not believe (*v*. 36).

41. *Murmured at him* (ἐγόγγυζον περὶ αὐτοῦ). Rather, 'were murmuring or muttering' (the verb is used of the cooing of doves) amongst themselves (*v*. 43) concerning Him. In this verse we have the first mention of "the Jews": hitherto in this chapter it has been "the multitude." Hence we are to understand the leaders—the hostile faction.

I am the bread which came down from heaven (cf. *vv*. 33, 35, 38). The word 'living' is not in the Greek.

42. *The son of Joseph.* They speak according to what they thought.

44. *No man can come:* see on *v*. 37.

except the Father . . . draw him. Without grace it is impossible to believe, even though sufficient miracles have been wrought. What was needed was not more miracles, but obedience to the call and attractions of grace. That grace had been drawing them, but, owing to their obstinacy, drawing them in vain. These severe words, and the deep language which follows, were addressed not so much to the crowd as to 'the Jews'—the educated leaders (*v*. 53). Two great truths stand side by side: 'all that are given by the Father will come,' and, 'no one can come except the Father draw him.' Let them, therefore, seek the gift of the Father, and learn how to come. This is the lesson already given by the prophets.

45. *And they shall all be taught of God.* That is, since the prophets foretold that in the Messianic kingdom all should obey the teaching of God, it follows that the Jews who have not been drawn by the Father, are excluded from that kingdom. "The appeal to their own prophets was the more telling, that Jewish tradition also applied these two prophecies (Isa. liv. 13; Jer. xxxi. 33, 34) to the teaching by God in the Messianic age" (Eders. l. c., p. 239).

46. *Not that any man.* That is, "I do not say that any man has,

seen the Father, but he who is of God, he hath seen the
Father. Amen, amen, I say unto you: He that believeth 47
in me, hath everlasting life. I am the bread of life. 48
Your fathers did eat manna in the desert, and are dead. 49
This is the bread which cometh down from heaven: that if 50
any man eat of it, he may not die. I am the living bread, 51
which came down from heaven. If any man eat of this 52
bread, he shall live for ever: and the bread that I will
give, is my flesh for the life of the world. The Jews there- 53

with his eyes, seen the Father, but "*he who is of God*" (and therefore
believes in Me) "*he hath*" (through Me and in Me) "*seen the Father*"
(cf. i. 18).

47. *Hath everlasting life:* see on i. 12.

48. *I am the bread of life.* Our Lord resumes in one personal
application, to be afterwards more fully developed, the main idea of
the previous statements (*vv.* 27, 32, 33, 35). The manna had not
been the bread of life—it had not preserved for ever even bodily life.
Those who had eaten it had died, and their carcases had fallen in the
wilderness. But those who eat the true bread shall live for ever.

52. *The bread that I will give, is my flesh* (σάρξ). This gift has
not yet been given; it is held out in promise. Moreover, the gift is
Christ's 'flesh': most literally the very flesh of Christ—not a generic
gift as in *v.* 27 (βρῶσιν = food) but that specific flesh which the Word
had become, "The Word was made flesh" (i. 14). Therefore, not the
flesh exclusively, but the whole body of Christ (Matt. xxvi. 26; Luke
xxii. 19).

my flesh for the life of the world (ὑπὲρ τῆς τοῦ κόσμου ζωῆς). This is
the full declaration to which the whole discourse has been gradually leading—from the food which perisheth, to the food which endureth to life
everlasting; from the food which endureth, to the bread of God, which
cometh down from heaven and giveth life to the world; from the
bread of God, to Christ Himself personally; from Christ personally, to
His flesh for the life of the world. From the outset the general idea
has been deepening and growing in definiteness. The giving for the
life of the world points to Christ's coming sacrifice (iii. 14-17); the
giving of Christ's flesh as bread points to the manner of our nourishment by the saving flesh of Christ. (In the A.V. there is an inauthentic
addition, 'the bread that I will give is My flesh, *which I will give* for
the life of the world.' This addition is removed from the text in R.V.).
These words must have sounded mysterious to the Jews; none the less
did they fail to perceive the substantial idea that Christ was promising
to give His flesh as food.

53. *The Jews therefore strove among themselves* (πρὸς ἀλλήλους):
cf. *v.* 41.

How can this man (οὗτος = this fellow) *give us His flesh to eat?*
Instead of believing, on the strength of Christ's word, that it could be

fore strove among themselves, saying: How can this man
54 give us his flesh to eat? Then Jesus said to them:
Amen, amen, I say unto you: Except you eat the flesh of
the son of man, and drink his blood, you shall not have
55 life in you. He that eateth my flesh, and drinketh my
blood, hath everlasting life: and I will raise him up in the
56 last day. For my flesh is meat indeed: and my blood is
57 drink indeed: He that eateth my flesh, and drinketh my

done, and that the manner of its doing should be left to Christ's
omnipotent wisdom, their souls are lost in vain conjectures about its
possibility and the manner of its accomplishment. But faith is the
essential condition of life (vv. 29, 35, 36, 40), therefore our Lord
insists on belief in the truth, which He at once sets forth in more
definite terms (cf. iii. 3-5).

54. *Except you eat the flesh of the son of man, and drink his blood,
you shall not have life in you.* These words were said in their literal
meaning. Even the exuberant and florid imagery of the Oriental
imagination has never expressed the simple idea of accepting a teacher's
doctrine by the metaphor of eating and drinking the teacher's flesh and
blood. The words 'eat my flesh, drink my blood,' cannot therefore
mean 'believe in me,' 'accept my doctrine.' Whenever the phrase
'eating a man's flesh' was used, not in its literal, but in a metaphorical
sense, it meant to destroy or to injure him (Job xix. 22; Psa. xxvi. 2;
James v. 3). It only remains, therefore, to take the words in their
obvious meaning, as the Christian Church has always taken them, and
not to "make a riddle what Christ made so plain." St. Paul in
speaking of the heinousness of an unworthy communion says, "Whosoever shall eat this bread, *or* drink the chalice of the Lord unworthily,
shall be guilty of the body and of the blood of the Lord" (1 Cor. xi. 27).
In these words we see that our Lord is received whole and entire under
each form, so that it is not necessary to receive both forms. Christ is
not divided; hence, although by force of the words of consecration the
bread is changed only into the body of Christ, and the wine only into
His blood, yet, by force of union and concomitance, the whole Christ,
body, blood, soul, and Divinity, is under each species.

55. *He that eateth* (ὁ τρώγων). The idea of the previous verse
emphatically repeated affirmatively. The verb used is most expressive.
Its primary meaning is 'to crunch,' 'to chew.' It is again employed in
vv. 57, 58, 59.

56. *For* (γάρ, assigning reason of the statement) *my flesh is meat
indeed* (ἀληθὴς βρῶσις), *i.e.*, is true and real food: and My blood true
and real drink (ἀληθὴς πόσις); not by metaphor, but in truth and in
deed My flesh is food.

57. *Abideth in me* (cf. xv. 4-6). It means the closest and most
intimate union. The phrase is characteristic in St. John. For the
doctrine cf. i. 16. The closeness of this union is shown by the

blood, abideth in me, and I in him. As the living Father hath sent me, and I live by the Father: so he that eateth me, the same also shall live by me. This is the bread that came down from heaven. Not as your fathers did eat manna, and are dead. He that eateth this bread shall live for ever. These things he said teaching in the synagogue, in Capharnaum.

(e) THE EFFECTS OF THE DISCOURSE (vers. 61–72).

Many therefore of his disciples hearing it, said: This saying is hard, and who can hear it? But Jesus knowing in himself, that his disciples murmured at this, said to them: Doth this scandalize you? If then you shall see

fact that our Lord compares it to the union between Himself and the Father.

58. *As the living Father hath sent me, and I live by the Father* (διὰ τὸν πατέρα). Διά with the accusative usually denotes the reason for which, or on account of which, anything is done; but it may also denote the efficient reason, as here (cf. v. 26).

59. *This is the bread.* That is, 'and now the description of the bread from heaven is completed;' 'such is the bread of which I began to speak.'

60. *In the synagogue.* Had those who came across the Lake of Galilee seeking our Lord, found Him in the synagogue? (v. 25). Certainly no real break can be found in the discourse (vv. 26-59). We must therefore take it that by the words, 'these things he said,' St. John means the whole discourse, and that the whole was delivered in the synagogue. The article is absent: 'In synagogue.' Compare the phrase 'in church.'

61. *This saying is hard* (offensive, intolerable). There were many things in the discourse too hard for them to receive; but what was most offensive was the command to eat Christ's flesh, and to drink His blood. This command they understood, not only in a literal sense, as it ought to be understood, but also in a gross, material sense.

62. *But Jesus knowing in himself*, i.e., without communication, and therefore in a superhuman way.

63. *If then you shall see the son of man ascend up.* (ἐὰν οὖν θεωρῆτε). This verse is obscure both in itself, and in its connection with the preceding verse. First of all, the sentence, breaking off abruptly (what rhetoricians call aposiopesis), leaves something to be mentally supplied. The meaning depends on what is supposed to be understood. Next, is οὖν to be taken in an illative sense = 'therefore,' or in the sense of 'but what if?' If οὖν be taken in the former sense, the passage will run thus: 'Doth *this* scandalize you? What therefore will your scandal be, if,' &c.; but if οὖν be taken in the latter sense,

64 the son of man ascend up where he was before? It is the
spirit that quickeneth: the flesh profiteth nothing. The
65 words that I have spoken to you, are spirit and life. But
there are some of you that believe not. For Jesus knew
from the beginning who they were that did not believe,
66 and who he was that would betray him. And he said:
Therefore did I say to you, that no man can come to me,
67 unless it be given him by my Father. After this many of
his disciples went back; and walked no more with him.

the passage will run, 'Doth this *scandalize* you? But what if, &c.
Will you be scandalized even then?' The first interpretation supposes
that our Lord intensified the trial to which the faith of his hearers was
to be subjected. If what I have just said about My flesh as being the
source of life, scandalizes you, how will you believe when that flesh
has been taken up to heaven, and you are told that it must still be
eaten on earth? The second interpretation supposes that our Lord
wished to remove a difficulty raised in the way of belief by a gross,
material interpretation of His words, 'Doth this scandalize you? But
what if you see My flesh glorified and spiritualized, as it will be at My
ascension? Will you still find my words offensive and incredible?'
This second interpretation seems preferable (cf. i. 50, 51; iii. 7,
8, 12, 13).

It must be noted that the verb θεωρέω does not mean only 'to gaze
upon,' 'to behold,' but also 'to perceive mentally,' 'to get knowledge
of,' 'to consider' (iv. 19, xii. 19; Acts xvii. 22; Heb. vii. 4).

64. *It is the spirit that quickeneth* (giveth life). Our Lord still
further lessens the difficulty. As in every man the body without a soul
is dead and incapable of any living action, so in Christ the flesh has its
life-giving power not because it is flesh, but because it is the living flesh
of the God-man, and is hypostatically united to the Word, who became
flesh. Because of that union it is that the flesh of Christ is living
bread, giving life to the world (vv. 48-52).

The words that I have spoken. If you choose to accept what My
words offer, you will indeed find spirit and life.

65. *But there are some of you that believe not.* Obstinate unbelief
was the true source of their scandal. If they had accepted the Father's
testimony to Christ they would never have been scandalized at what
Christ taught.

For Jesus knew from the beginning (cf. v. 62). This is a
parenthesis. The phrase ἐξ ἀρχῆς ('from the beginning': only here
and in xvi. 5) means from the beginning, when He began to gather
disciples around Him.

66. *Therefore did I say to you* (v. 44): cf. v. 16 and see note
on vv. 37, 44.

67. *After this* (ἐκ τούτου). The phrase occurs only here and in
xix. 12. It may mean either 'on this account' or 'thenceforth.'

Then Jesus said to the twelve: Will you also go away? 68
And Simon Peter answered him: Lord, to whom shall we 69
go? thou hast the words of eternal life. And we have 70
believed and have known that thou art the Christ the Son
of God. Jesus answered them: Have not I chosen you 71
twelve; and one of you is a devil? Now he meant Judas 72
Iscariot, the son of Simon: for this same was about to
betray him, whereas he was one of the twelve.

68. *To the twelve.* These have not before been mentioned. The synoptic account of their call is supposed to be known. Pilate and Mary Magdalen are introduced with like abruptness (xviii. 29, xix. 25).

Will you also? (μὴ καὶ ὑμεῖς θέλετε) = "Surely you also are not like-minded?"

70. *We have believed* (for some time now) *and have known* (have learned to know – are convinced) *that thou art the Christ the Son of God.* The true reading seems to be, 'the Holy One of God,' *i.e.* (most probably), the Messiah. Peter's clear confession of our Lord's Divinity came later (Matt. xvi. 16).

71. *Have not I chosen you twelve?* The Greek is more forcible, 'Did not I choose you out for Myself, the Twelve?' But not even all the Twelve believed.

and one of you is a devil: cf. viii. 44, xiii. 2; 1 John iii. 8.

72. *Judas Iscariot, the son of Simon.* Better, 'Judas, the son of Simon Iscariot.' Iscariot = the man from Carioth (Kerioth), a town in the possession of the tribe of Juda (Jos. xv. 25). The other Apostles were Galileans.

CHAPTER VII.

Our Lord at the Feast.

(VERS. 1-39.)

AFTER these things Jesus walked in Galilee, for he would not walk in Judea, because the Jews sought

The opposition to our Lord on the part of the leaders had been growing in violence and intensity. To avoid provoking them still more, at a time when they were already exasperated against Him, He refrained from attending the Pasch that year in Jerusalem (vi. 4, vii. 1), and did not go up till the Feast of Tabernacles in November. Thus He had been absent from Jerusalem for many months (see on v. 1), that is, from the Pasch or Pentecost of one year till the Feast of Tabernacles in the next year. And even now He goes up, "as it were in secret" (vii. 10).

It is easy to follow the different stages of our Lord's manifestation. First, He goes up in secret (vii. 2-13); next He speaks openly in the Temple, justifies His acts of healing on the Sabbath, and meets the doubts suggested regarding His Messianic dignity (vii. 14-36); then He claims to possess the fulness of Messianic power and grace—a life-giving stream for all that believe (vii. 37-39). In reply to all our Lord's testimony, the Jews can only bring forward the absurdly false argument that He cannot be the Messiah because He was of Galilee, whereas the Messiah must spring from David and be of Bethlehem, David's town (vii. 40-44). The Pharisees reprove their officers for not apprehending Jesus, and reprove Nicodemus for taking His part (vii. 45-53). The history of the woman taken in adultery unmasks the hypocrisy of the Pharisees, and gives occasion to a retort upon them for their charges against Himself (viii. 1-11). The succeeding discourses represent our Lord as the Light of the World, who came from the Father, and goes to Him—a testimony which is borne by two witnesses, and is therefore valid even according to the Mosaic law (viii. 12-18). But those who do not know the Father cannot accept this testimony; and, since they know Him not, they are not His children, but the to kill him. Now the Jews' feast of tabernacles was at 2

children of the devil. They boast that Abraham is their father; but this boast is a vain assumption, because Abraham rejoiced in the day of Christ's manifestation, and will not acknowledge as children the unbelieving Jews (viii. 19-59). By giving sight to the man born blind, our Lord shows forth His power as the Light-giver. The Jews again disregard the miracle, and fasten on the circumstance that it was performed on the Sabbath. Our Lord accuses them of wilful blindness. Those who wish may see the truth; unbelief therefore is self-condemned (ix. 1-41). The idea of our Lord as Light of the World, guiding all men securely, is further developed under a fresh figure. He is the Good Shepherd who leads and tends the sheep, and is ready even to die for them. The Pharisees, on the contrary, are hirelings, nothing better than thieves and robbers who abandon the sheep when danger threatens (x. 1-21). (Davidson, 'Introduction,' vol. ii. pp. 283-285).

1. *After these things* (vi. 1-72) *Jesus walked* ($\pi\epsilon\rho\iota\pi\acute{a}\tau\epsilon\iota$ = went about as a teacher) *in Galilee*. In these few words St. John sums up the labours of several months.

2. *Feast of tabernacles.* This feast is several times alluded to in the Old Testament (3 Kings viii. 2, xii. 32; 2 Paral. v. 3, vii. 8-10; Esdr. iii. 4; Neh. viii. 14-18; Zach. xiv. 16); but it is prescribed, and its specific object indicated, in Exod. xxiii. 16, xxxiv. 22; Lev. xxiii. 34-36, 39-44; Num. xxix. 12-39; Deut. xvi. 13-16, xxxi. 10-13. It was celebrated from the 15th to the 22nd of the seventh month (Tisri) of the Jewish sacred year, and followed closely on the Day of Atonement (the 10th of the month). It marked the completion of the harvest of fruit, oil, and wine, and historically commemorated the wanderings in the wilderness. This was pre-eminently the feast for foreign pilgrims coming from the farthest distance, whose temple contributions were then received and counted. The sacrifices were far more numerous at this feast than at any other. On each of the seven days one kid was offered as a sin-offering, and two rams and fourteen lambs as a burnt-offering. Also seventy bullocks were offered on the seven days, beginning with thirteen on the first day, and diminishing by one each day until on the seventh day seven were offered. After the seven days came the great day of the Feast (*v.* 37). On this day one bullock, one ram, and seven lambs were offered as a burnt-offering, and one goat for a sin-offering. (Hastings, 'Bible Dict.,' vol. i. p. 861).

" All day long the smoke of the burning sacrifices rose in slowly-widening column, and hung between the Mount of Olives and Zion; the chant of the Levites and the solemn responses of the Hallel (Psa. cxii.-cxvii.) were borne on the breeze, or the clear blast of the priests' silver trumpets seemed to waken the echoes far away. And then, at night, how all these vast temple-buildings stood out, illuminated by the great candelabras that burned in the court of the women, and by the glare of torches, when strange sound of mystic hymns and dances came floating over the intervening darkness !

3 hand. And his brethren said to him: Pass from hence and go into Judea: that thy disciples also may see thy
4 works which thou dost. For there is no man that doth anything in secret, and he himself seeketh to be known openly. If thou do these things, manifest thyself to the
5 world. For neither did his brethren believe in him.
6 Then Jesus said to them: My time is not yet come;

"Early on the 14th all the festive pilgrims had arrived. Then it was indeed a scene of bustle and activity. Hospitality had to be sought and found; guests to be welcomed and entertained; all things required for the Feast to be got ready. Booths must be erected everywhere—in court and on housetop, in street and square, for the lodgment and entertainment of that vast multitude; leafy dwellings everywhere, to remind of the wilderness-journey, and now of the goodly land.

"The whole symbolism of the Feast, beginning with the completed harvest, pointed to the future. The Rabbis themselves admitted this. The strange number of sacrificial bullocks—seventy in all—they regarded as referring to 'the seventy nations' of heathendom. The ceremony of the outpouring of water, which was considered of such vital importance as to give to the whole festival the name of 'House of Outpouring,' was symbolical of the outpouring of the Holy Spirit: the Temple-illumination, of the light which was to shine from out the Temple into the dark night of heathendom. It must have been a stirring scene, when from out the mass of Levites, with their musical instruments, who crowded the fifteen steps that led from the court of Israel to that of the Women, stepped two priests with their silver trumpets. As the first cock-crowing intimated the dawn of morn, they blew a threefold blast, another on the tenth step, and yet another threefold blast as they entered the Court of the Women. And, still sounding their trumpets, they marched through the Court of the Women to the Beautiful Gate. Here, turning round and facing westwards to the Holy Place, they uttered solemn protest against heathenism, and made solemn confession of Jehovah" (Eders., l.c., pp. 309–311).

3. *And his brethren*, that is, some of His kinsfolk (cf. ii. 12). We have seen that many of His disciples had been shaken from their belief in Christ, because of His reply to the challenge for a sign from heaven (vi. 67). His kinsfolk shared in that doubt and unbelief (*v.* 5), and therefore they propose to Him that He should recover lost ground by some striking public manifestation. A great feast was at hand; let Him go up to Jerusalem and manifest Himself to the assembled multitudes. Surely it is only reasonable that, if He can do great works, He should do them where they could be tested and, if genuine, prove most effective.

6. *My time is not yet come.* His 'time,' or His 'hour,' most frequently means the time, or hour, of His Passion (Matt. xxvi. 18, 45; John xii. 27, xiii. 1). But it is also used to mark the time for the doing

but your time is always ready. The world cannot hate you; but me it hateth: because I give testimony of it, that the works thereof are evil. Go you up to this festival day, but I go not up to this festival day: because my time is not accomplished. When he had said these things, he himself staid in Galilee. But after his brethren were gone up, then he also went up to the feast, not openly, but as it were in secret. The Jews therefore sought him on the festival day, and said: Where is he? And there was much murmuring among the multitude concerning him. For some said: He is a good man. And others said: No, but he seduceth the people. Yet no man spoke openly of him, for fear of the Jews. Now about the midst of the feast, Jesus

of some specified action mentioned in the context (ii. 4). In the present instance it would refer to the suggested manifestation of Himself in Jerusalem. But both may be combined here. In reply to the suggestion of His brethren our Lord, knowing that the Jews sought to kill Him (*v.* 1), and knowing also that His work was not yet accomplished (*v.* 8), and that the hour of His death was, consequently, not yet come (*v.* 6), refused to do what was suggested, because it would have hastened His death.

your time is always ready. The brethren expected, and asked for, a manifestation in harmony with Jewish hopes and aspirations. The time for that is always ready, for the multitude is always willing to accept what is in accordance with its own spirit. But the manifestation contemplated by our Lord was opposed to the views of the Jewish world, and would necessarily provoke their enmity. The brethren would be safe; but Christ would not be safe.

7. *The world cannot hate you; but me it hateth.*" This was the reason for what follows.

8. *I go not up to this festival day* to do what you are urging Me to do. Consequently, He tarried behind while they went up. But when the danger of publicity was over, He also went up, not publicly, as they had desired, but privately (*vv.* 9, 10). Some ancient authorities read, 'I do not *yet* (οὔπω instead of οὐκ) go up.'

11. *The Jews therefore sought him.* During the first days of the festival our Lord did not appear (*v.* 14). But all were looking out for Him. The Jews, that is, the leaders, in order to seize Him; the crowds with divided feelings (*v.* 12).

12. *There was much murmuring* (*i.e.*, secret debate) *among the multitude* (ἐν τοῖς ὄχλοις = among the different crowds). They spoke in whispers, for the leaders had set their face against any discussion of His claims and merits (*v.* 13).

14. *About the midst of the feast* (*i.e.*, suddenly, on one of the half

15 went up into the temple, and taught. And the Jews wondered, saying: How doth this man know letters, 16 having never learned? Jesus answered them and said: 17 My doctrine is not mine, but his that sent me. If any man will do the will of him: he shall know of the doctrine, whether it be of God, or whether I speak of 18 myself. He that speaketh of himself, seeketh his own glory: but he that seeketh the glory of him that sent 19 him, he is true, and there is no injustice in him. Did not Moses give you the law, and *yet* none of you

holy-days) *Jesus went up into the temple and taught.* "All along the inside of the great wall which formed the Temple-enclosure ran a double colonnade—each column a monolith of white marble, twenty-five cubits high, covered with cedar-beams. These colonnades, which from their ample space formed alike places for quiet walk and for larger gatherings, had benches in them; and, from the liberty of speaking and teaching in Israel, Jesus might here address the people in the very face of His enemies" (Eders. l.c., p. 312).

15. *And the Jews wondered.* St. John does not record the subject of our Lord's teaching, but he marks its effect—the very leaders of the people were filled with amazement. The only known means of acquiring a knowledge of theology ("letters," γράμματα, included the whole circle of rabbinical training) was through the schools of the Rabbis. How did Jesus, who had never attended those schools, learn His doctrine? Our Lord tells the source of His doctrine.

16. *My doctrine is not mine* (i.e., My own invention), *but his that sent me* (cf. v. 30). But how shall they know this? Our Lord offers them two tests—one of personal, the other of general, experience. First, then, He gives a test of personal experience.

17. *If any man will do the will of him.* One of the greatest impediments to faith is a sinful life. If any man wishes to know the truths of faith, let him first do the will of God as clearly manifested by Moses and the Prophets, and he will be led on to the fuller faith of Christ (cf. 1 Cor. iii. 1-3; Heb. v. 11-14). Let the Jews, therefore, refrain from sin, and make experiment of Christ's teaching. But there is another test.

18. *He that speaketh of himself* (i.e., propounds his own doctrine) *seeketh his own glory*. This is a fact of common observation. Self-inspired teachers speak for their own ends. With Christ it was otherwise. He sought not the glory of men, but only to do the will of the Father (v. 41, vi. 38). Therefore, *he is true.*

With the Jews both tests are condemnatory. They seek their own glory (v. 44) and they do not seek the will of God—*none of you keepeth the law* (v. 19). Our Lord at once gives an instance in point—their fierce desire to kill Him. In v. 19 the note of interrogation should come after the first 'law'; none after the second.

keepeth the law? Why seek you to kill me? The 20
multitude answered and said: Thou hast a devil; who
seeketh to kill thee? Jesus answered and said to them: 21
One work I have done; and you all wonder: therefore 22
Moses gave you circumcision (not because it is of Moses,
but of the fathers;) and on the sabbath-day you circum-
cise a man. If a man receive circumcision on the sabbath- 23
day, that the law of Moses may not be broken; are you
angry at me because I have healed the whole man on the
sabbath-day? Judge not according to the appearance, but 24

20. *Why seek you to kill me?* They attempt to repel the charge by pretending that it is either an illusion or a wicked invention.

Thou hast a devil. Wickedness and madness were both attributed to Satan's influence (x. 20, 21; Luke vii. 33). This was the reply, not of the leaders, whom conscious guilt made silent, but of the ignorant multitude. Disregarding the interruption, our Lord proceeds.

21. *Jesus . . . said: One work I have done* (did); *and you all wonder*. This work was the healing of the man on the Sabbath (v. 9, 16). On account of that miracle the Jews began to persecute Jesus, who thus points to the very deed which started their desire to kill Him.

22. *Therefore* (διὰ τοῦτο). This may be connected with the preceding verse: "And you all wonder at it." They wondered, because our Lord seemed to violate the Sabbath. He repels the charge by retorting the argument. According to the Rabbis a positive law superseded a negative one. The positive law, in this argument, was that a child should be circumcised on the eighth day; the negative law forbade work on the Sabbath. But if the eighth day, the day for circumcision, happened to be a Sabbath, the Jews disregarded the negative law, and circumcised on that day, in order that the (positive) law of Moses might not be broken. Why then be angry at our Lord because He healed the whole man (*i.e.*, made him sound both in body and soul) on the Sabbath-day? Every argument for a postponement of the healing would have been equally valid for a postponement of circumcision. Besides, Christ did (aorist) *one* work, which scandalised them, but Moses gave (perfect = continuing action) an ordinance *regularly* setting aside the Sabbath law. Hence their scandal was an affectation.

24. *Judge not according to the appearance* (κατ' ὄψιν). This is a general principle to be applied in the particular case in question. 'Judge not according to mere outward appearance, but according to the true merits of the case—do not condemn Me as violating the law of God, simply because My action may seem a breach of that law.' The phrase is not the same as, 'take no account of persons, be not a respecter of persons'; for this the Greek expression is βλέπειν εἰς πρόσωπον, λαμβάνειν πρόσωπον.

⁲⁵ judge just judgment. Some therefore of Jerusalem said:
²⁶ Is not this he whom they seek to kill? And behold he speaketh openly, and they say nothing to him. Have the
²⁷ rulers known for a truth that this is the Christ? But we know this man whence he is: but when the Christ cometh
²⁸ no man knoweth whence he is. Jesus therefore cried out in the temple, teaching and saying: You both know me, and know whence I am, and I am not come of myself; but
²⁹ he that sent me is true, whom you know not. I know him, because I am from him, and he hath sent me.
³⁰ They sought therefore to apprehend him: and no man laid hands on him, because his hour was not yet come.
³¹ But of the people many believed in him, and said: When the Christ cometh, shall he do more miracles than these
³² which this man doth? The Pharisees heard the people murmuring these things concerning him: and the rulers
³³ and Pharisees sent ministers to apprehend him. Jesus

26. *Some therefore of Jerusalem* (Jerusalemites). The inhabitants of the metropolis knew better than the crowd of strangers what were the feelings of the Sanhedrin.

27. *But we know this man.* The tolerance of the rulers succeeding their avowed hostility would seem to imply a change of idea about Christ. This at first perplexed the Jerusalemites; but they solve the question with the rough-and-ready methods of ignorance. It was a settled belief that the Messiah would come suddenly and mysteriously (Mal. iii. 1).

no man knoweth whence he is. The 'whence' does not denote birthplace (*v.* 42), nor Davidic descent (*v.* 42), both of which were well known, but the immediate parentage (cf. vi. 42). An argument perfectly frivolous; yet it suffices for a denial of Christ's claim, although that claim was based on undeniable testimonies. In reply, our Lord partly grants their argument, and then turns it against them. He grants that they know Him as the carpenter of Nazareth, but His true descent they are ignorant of.

28. *You both know me.* They would, indeed, have known both Him and whence He came if He had come of Himself. But *I am not come of myself* (cf. viii. 42). *He that sent me is true* (real), *whom you know not.* Thus their alleged argument recoils upon them (cf. v. 37, 38). Their test holds good in His case.

30. *His hour was not yet come:* see *v.* 6.

31. *And said.* Better, 'Kept saying,' *i.e.*, to objectors. They discussed Christ's claim.

32. *The rulers.* The chief priests. These were Sadducees. Hence both parties had now combined.

33. *Jesus therefore said to them.* The phrase 'to them' should be

therefore said to them: Yet a little while I am with you: and *then* I go to him that sent me. You shall seek me, 34 and shall not find me: and where I am, *thither* you cannot come. The Jews therefore said among themselves: Whither 35 will he go, that we shall not find him? will he go unto the dispersed among the gentiles, and teach the gentiles? What is this saying that he hath said: You shall seek me, 36 and shall not find me; and where I am, you cannot come? And on the last *and* great day of the festivity, Jesus stood 37 and cried, saying: If any man thirst, let him come to me,

omitted. Because the officers were on the watch to apprehend him, *therefore* He said. Said to whom? Not to the crowd, for the crowd had been dispersing, and discussing as they went (*vv.* 31, 32), but to the leaders (*v.* 35). In the words that follow, our Lord reasserts His dignity as Messiah, and couples a threat with the assertion.

Yet a little while I am with you. That is, 'Your design against My life is premature; for I shall still be with you a little while; and then I certainly go (ὑπάγω: the present tense is frequently used by St. John of what will soon and certainly come to pass) to Him that sent Me.'

34. *You shall seek me.* This is a threat. The day would come when they would desire the exercise of His protecting Messianic power. We know from Josephus' account of the siege and fall of Jerusalem how truly the threat was fulfilled; they desired the Messiah, but found Him not.

and where I am (*i.e.*, where I shall be), *thither you cannot come*. These words are said simply of their physical incapability to ascend up to heaven; they are not a declaration that true repentance would be vain (cf. xiii. 33).

35. *Whither will he go, that* (ὅτι = seeing that, as He said) *we shall not find him?* There is a tone of contempt in their language. 'Whither will the man go?'

unto the dispersed among the gentiles? (τὴν διασποράν τῶν Ἑλλήνων). The abstract 'dispersion' is used for 'the dispersed,' just as 'the circumcision' is used for 'the circumcised.' (As to the use of the genitive, cf. Matt. i. 11, 12, x. 5). The meaning is, Will He go to the Jews of the Dispersion and teach them and the gentiles among whom they lived? They speak contemptuously. But their contemptuous language cannot remove the anxiety of their heart. They still repeat and ponder the words of His threat (*v.* 36).

37. *And on the last and great day.* Better, 'Now on the last, the great day of the Feast.' This was the eighth day (*v.* 2), or, perhaps more probably, the seventh.

Jesus stood and cried, i.e., cried out (cf. i. 15, vii. 28). A most solemn introduction.

If any man thirst (cf. on iv. 10, 13, 14). "To the sound of

38 and drink. He that believeth in me, as the scripture saith,
39 *Out of his belly shall flow rivers of living water.* Now this
he said of the spirit which they should receive who believed
in him: for as yet the spirit was not given, because Jesus
was not yet glorified.

music a procession started from the Temple. It followed a Priest who
bore a golden pitcher, capable of holding about two pints. Onwards it
passed down the edge of the Tyropœon Valley, where it merges into
that of the Kedron. When the Temple-procession had reached the
Pool of Siloam, the Priest filled his golden pitcher from its waters.
Then they went back to the Temple, so timing it that they should
arrive just as the pieces of the sacrifice were being laid on the great
Altar of Burnt-offering towards the close of the ordinary Morning-
Sacrifice service. A threefold blast of the Priests' trumpets welcomed
the arrival of the Priest, as he entered through the 'Water-gate,' and
passed straight into the Court of the Priests. Here he was joined by
another Priest, who carried the wine for the drink-offering. The two
Priests ascended 'the rise' of the altar, and turned to the left. There
were two silver funnels here, with narrow openings, leading down to
the base of the altar. Into that at the east, which was somewhat wider,
the wine was poured, and, at the same time, the water into the western
and narrower opening.

"Immediately after 'the pouring of water,' the great 'Hallel' was
chanted antiphonally, or rather with responses, to the accompaniment
of the flute. . . . The public services closed with a procession round
the altar by the Priests. . . . But on 'the last, the great day of the
Feast,' this procession of Priests made the circuit of the altar, not only
once but seven times, as if they were again compassing, but now with
prayer, the Gentile Jericho which barred their possession of the
promised land. Hence the seventh or last day of the Feast was also
called that of 'the Great Hosannah.'

"When Jesus stood and cried, it must have been with special
reference to the ceremony of the outpouring of the water, which was
considered the central part of the service. Moreover, all would understand that His words must refer to the Holy Spirit, since the rite was
universally regarded as symbolical of His outpouring" (Eders. l.c.,
pp. 317-319). Therefore our Lord insinuated that in Him the Messianic
prophecies were fulfilled (Isa. xii. 3, xli. 18, xliv. 3, xlix. 10, lxv. 13;
Joel ii. 28, iii. 18; Zach. xiii. 1).

38. *Out of his belly* (ἐκ τῆς κοιλίας = the soul, the heart, the innermost part, whence thought and feeling). The words are a sum of the
sense of many passages of Scripture (v. 37). Thus Isaias says, 'Thou
shalt be like a watered garden, and like a fountain of water whose
waters shall not fail' (lviii. 11).

39. *As yet the spirit was not given, i.e.*, in the abundant and manifest way in which He was about to be poured out upon the apostles and
disciples. This giving could be made only after Christ's resurrection

The Results of Christ's Teaching.

(VERS. 40–53.)

40. Of that multitude therefore, when they had heard these words of his, some said: This is the prophet indeed.
41. Others said: This is the Christ.
42. But some said: Doth the Christ come out of Galilee? Doth not the scripture say: That Christ cometh out of the seed of David, and from Bethlehem, the town where David was?
43. So there arose a dissension among the people because of him.
44. And some of them would have apprehended him: but no man laid hands upon him.
45. The ministers therefore came to the chief priests and the Pharisees. And they said to them: Why have you not brought him?
46. The ministers answered: Never did man speak like this man.
47. The Pharisees therefore answered

and triumphant return to the Father (cf. xvi. 7). By "glorified" is meant the entire process of glorification, beginning with and including Christ's death (xii. 23, 31–33).

40. *This is the prophet indeed.* Of course they mean the great prophet foretold by Moses.

41. *This is the Christ, i.e.,* the Messiah. They seem to have thought that 'the prophet' was only a forerunner of the Messiah (cf. i. 20, 21).

42. *Doth not the scripture say?* St. John supposes that the reader can answer this futile objection (cf. iii. 4, vi. 53).

of the seed of David (Isa. xi. 1; Jer. xxiii. 5; Ezech. xxxiv. 23, 24).

from Bethlehem (Mich. v. 2. Cf. Matt. ii. 1–6).

the town (village) *where David was* (1 Sam. xvi. 4, 13, xvii. 12).

But while this heated discussion was agitating the crowd to such an extent that some even thought of seizing our Lord and dragging Him before the Sanhedrin, He receives a striking testimony from a most unexpected quarter—from the officers who had been sent (v. 32) to apprehend Him. They returned, overawed by the majesty of His person and impressed by the truth of His words, of which words St. John has given us only a brief outline.

47. *Are you also seduced?* (μὴ καὶ ὑμεῖς = surely you also are not seduced). A harsh sneer. They appeal to a very specious argument against our Lord—all who have authority, and learning, and reputation for holiness (rulers and Pharisees) are against Him. Only the ignorant multitude, who are accursed for their ignorance, believe in Him (v. 48). In the midst of this violent outburst, one of their own number, Nicodemus, defends our Lord by calling upon the Sanhedrin to observe in

⁴⁸ them: Are you also seduced? Hath any one of the
⁴⁹ rulers believed in him, or of the Pharisees? But this
multitude that knoweth not the law, are accursed.
⁵⁰ Nicodemus said to them, he that came to him by night,
⁵¹ who was one of them: Doth our law judge any man,
⁵² unless it first hear him, and know what he doth? They
answered and said to him: Art thou also a Galilean?
Search the scriptures, and see that out of Galilee a
⁵³ prophet riseth not. And every man returned to his own
house.

His regard those forms of trial which the law itself prescribed in the case of even the most criminal.

50. *He that came to him by night* ($\pi\rho\acute{o}\tau\epsilon\rho\sigma\nu$ = before: see iii. 1, 2).

51. *Unless it first hear him.* Such an elementary principle of justice was repeatedly prescribed by the law (Exod. xxiii. 1, 2; Lev. xix. 15; Deut. i. 16, xiii. 14, xvi. 19, xvii. 4, xix. 18). They who condemned the multitude for not knowing the law were therefore self-condemned. But in their blind anger they turn upon Nicodemus with contemptuous reproach.

52. *Art thou also a Galilean?* ($\dot{\epsilon}\kappa$ $\tau\tilde{\eta}\varsigma$ $\Gamma\alpha\lambda\iota\lambda\alpha\acute{\iota}\alpha\varsigma$ = from Galilee). We know what they thought of Galilee, but they were as much deceived in their ideas about Galilee as they were in their ideas about our Lord.

out of Galilee a prophet riseth not (hath not arisen: perfect tense). A denial as a matter of history, but used as presumptive that no prophet would arise out of Galilee. The presumption was based on an error. Jonas certainly was a Galilean (4 Kings xiv. 25); so may some of the other prophets, whose birthplaces are either unknown or cannot be identified, have been Galileans—Nahum the Elcesite (Elkoshite), Osee, Eliseus.

53. *And every man returned to his own house.* Nothing was then decided upon against our Lord. The words of Nicodemus were so far effective that they weakened the resolve of the Sanhedrin.

CHAPTER VIII.

The Woman taken in Adultery.

(VERS. 1–11.)

AND Jesus went unto mount Olivet. And early in the morning he came again into the temple, and

A very serious question is raised touching the authenticity of the passage vii. 53-viii. 11. But in this question three points must be kept distinct: (1) Is the passage part of the inspired Scripture? (2) is it in its proper place, as it now lies in the fourth Gospel? (3) is it the composition of St. John?

With regard to the first question it must be borne in mind that inspiration is a hidden act of God which can be known only from God's own assertion, that is, from revelation. Therefore we can learn what books have been inspired from that authority alone from which we learn all that God has revealed. That authority is the Church. "For what man knoweth the things of a man, but the spirit of a man that is in him? So the things also that are of God no man knoweth, but the Spirit of God" (1 Cor. ii. 11). The Spirit of God abiding in the Church, and leading her to the knowledge of all revealed truth, so that she becomes in very deed and infallibly "the pillar and ground of the truth" (1 Tim. iii. 15)—that Spirit guides the Church to an infallible judgment as to what books "are of God." The Spirit knows what writings He has Himself inspired, and imparts that knowledge to the Church. Now, according to the Acts of the Council of Trent, published by Theiner, there is little room for doubting that the Council expressly intended to define the inspiration of, amongst other parts, this part of St. John. We therefore accept it as inspired Scripture.

The answer to the other two questions is not so easy. The questions are critical rather than theological, and the critical evidence is very complicated. First, then, is the passage in its proper place as it now lies in the fourth Gospel? In answer to this question Dr. Scrivener writes, "On all intelligent principles of mere criticism the passage must needs be abandoned: and such is the conclusion arrived at by all the

all the people came to him, and sitting down he taught

critical editors" (Introduction vol. ii. p. 364). The passage is wanting in the oldest Uncials ℵ, B, C, A, in four other Uncials L (8th cent.), T (5th cent.), X (9th or 10th cent.), Δ (9th or 10th cent.). But LΔ leave a space void, as if conscious of an omission; and X is a commentary on the Gospel, *as the Gospel used to be read in public*. It is wanting in more than sixty cursives, and in some thirty evangelistaries (lectionaries, public service-books). Speaking generally, copies which contain a commentary omit the paragraph.

Of the versions, the passage is entirely omitted in the Peshitto, the Curetonian, the Harkleian, and the Lewisian Syriac; in some of the best MSS. of the Old Latin (though its reception by the Latin Fathers shows that it was in their old version); in the Sahidic; in some Bohairic MSS.; in the Gothic; in some ancient MSS. of the Armenian.

Of the Greek writers, Euthymius (12th cent.) is the first to mention the paragraph in its proper place—but considers it an interpolation. It must be remembered, however, that St. Chrysostom does not give a continuous commentary. He gives no comment on the whole of vii. 46-viii. 21, parts of which are certainly genuine and in their proper place. Later Greek commentators depend on St. Chrysostom, and omit what he passed over. Of others, only fragments of their writings have survived. They are silent, but not adverse.

On the other hand, the passage is found in seven Uncials—D (6th cent.), F (8th to 10th cent.), G (10th cent.), H (9th cent.), K (middle of 9th cent. at latest), U (about 10th cent.), Γ (9th cent.); it is found in 331 cursives, and six evangelistaries. Moreover, St. Jerome is a witness that in his time it was found in many codices both Greek and Latin. St. Augustine complains that some omitted it for fear of giving scandal, and St. Nicon (10th cent.) brings a similar charge against the Armenians. It is found in the Vulgate, in the Jerusalem Syriac, and in more recent versions (Arabic, Persian, Ethiopic, &c.), whose authority is not very great.

Thirteen cursives place the whole passage at the end of the Gospel; four place part of it (viii. 3-11) at the end; five give the whole at the end of Luke xxi. Further, four Uncials—E (7th or 8th cent.), S (amongst the earliest dated manuscripts of the Greek Testament, A.D. 949), M (9th cent.), Λ (8th or 9th cent.)—and more than forty cursives contain the passage, but marked with an obelus or similar sign of doubt.

The internal evidence, like the external, is ambiguous. On the one side it is alleged that the text runs more smoothly without the passage, and on the other side it is contended that viii. 20 pre-supposes the passage.

It is easy to explain how the passage was omitted—at least to a very great extent (thus in codex *b* of the Old Latin, a codex of 4th or 5th cent., the whole passage has been wilfully erased); but it is not easy to explain how a passage which has raised so many scruples against it could have been inserted and so widely accepted. "The arguments in

them. And the scribes and Pharisees bring unto him 3
a woman taken in adultery; and they set her in the
midst, and said to him: Master, this woman was even 4
now taken in adultery. Now Moses in the law com- 5
manded us to stone such a one. But what sayest thou?

its favour, internal even more than external, are so powerful, that we
can scarcely be brought to think it an unauthorized appendage to the
writings of one who in another of his inspired books (Apoc. xxii. 18,
19) deprecated so solemnly the adding to or taking away from the
blessed testimony he was commissioned to bear" (Scrivener, l.c.,
p. 364¹.

The answer just given to the second question is to a great extent an
answer to the third—Is the passage the composition of St. John? This
is a question of style, and includes a variety of minute details in literary
criticism. The narrative in its present form seems more in the style of
the Synoptics, and especially of St. Luke's Gospel. But the various
readings are so numerous (eighty in 183 words) that there does not
seem to be sufficient ground for a sure judgment in a matter of such
literary nicety. But see commentary on passage. On the whole
question, see Scrivener, vol. ii. pp. 364-368; Cornely, pp. 193-199;
Burgon, 'Causes of Corruption in Traditional Text,' pp. 232-265.

1. *Jesus went unto* (ἐπορεύθη εἰς) *mount Olivet*. The phrase for
'went unto' occurs also in vii. 35. But the introduction of Mount
Olivet, without a descriptive note, is hardly Johannean (comp. i. 44,
iv. 5, v. 2, vi. 1, xix. 13, 17). The mount lay less than a mile to the
east of Jerusalem (a Sabbath day's journey off, Acts i. 12), from which
it was separated by the Cedron valley (see xviii. 1). Later on, our
Lord used to pass the night on the mount (Luke xxi. 37).

2. *And early in the morning* (ὄρθρου) *he came again* (παρεγένετο)
into the temple, and all the people (πᾶς ὁ λαός) *came to him, and sitting
down he taught them*. The word for early in the morning is used only
by St. Luke, and by him only twice (Luke xxiv. 1; Acts v. 21). St.
John uses πρωΐ (xviii. 28, xx. 1) or πρωΐα (xxi. 4). The verb for 'he
came' is Johannean (iii. 23). The phrase for "all the people" is used
nearly twenty times by St. Luke, but nowhere by St. John, who uses
instead ὁ ὄχλος, and that twenty times.

3. *And the scribes and Pharisees*. This is the usual Synoptic
designation for the opponents of our Lord. St. Luke uses it thrice.
St. John never mentions the scribes, and his usual designation for our
Lord's opponents is 'the Jews.'

4. *This woman was even now taken*. Ἐπ' αὐτοφώρῳ = in the very act.

5. *Now Moses in the law*. Stoning to death was the penalty for
one not actually married, but only espoused (Deut. xxii. 23, 24). In
the case of a wife the manner of death was not specified (Lev. xx. 10;
Deut. xxii. 22). When death simply was spoken of, strangling was
understood.

6 And this they said, tempting him, that they might accuse him. But Jesus bowing himself down, wrote with his
7 finger on the ground. When therefore they continued asking him, he lifted up himself and said to them: He that is without sin among you, let him first cast a stone at
8 her. And again stooping down, he wrote on the ground.
9 But they hearing *this* went out one by one, beginning at

6. *This they said, tempting him.* This design connects the narrative with what St. John has said of their hatred against our Lord. They thought that our Lord in His mercifulness would be led to violate the law here, as He seemed to violate the law of Sabbath observance. Perhaps, too, they thought that if He pronounced against the woman, some of the crowd, who held Him for Messiah (vii. 12, 31, 40, 41), would hurry away the woman to instant death, and thus bring our Lord into conflict with the Roman authorities. It has been said that the verb for 'tempting' is Synoptic, but not Johannean. The assertion is groundless. Only one case of tempting is narrated by St. John, but the Synoptics narrate several; hence they had occasion to use the verb, while he had not. (But cf. vi. 6.)

Wrote (ἔγραφεν: descriptive imperfect). The action was a sign that He declined to answer. A.V. adds a gloss, 'as though He heard them not.'

7. *They continued asking him* (ἐπέμενον ἐρωτῶντες). The verb for 'continued' (= remained) occurs nowhere else in the Gospels, but is frequent in Acts and in St. Paul. On the other hand, the verb for 'to ask' is strongly Johannean, occurring twenty-nine times.

He that is without sin (ἀναμάρτητος = sinless). A classical word used nowhere else in N. T. Our Lord does not refer to absolute sinlessness, but to sinlessness in the very matter in which they accused the woman.

let him first cast a stone. According to the more probable reading, 'let him first cast *the* stone,' *i.e.*, let him be the first among you scribes and Pharisees to cast the stone required for the legal stoning. The first stone absolutely was cast by the witnesses (Deut. xvii. 7; Acts vii. 57, 58).

9. *But they hearing.* Codices E, G, H, K, S, add 'and convicted by their conscience.' The A.V. also gives the clause, which is most probably a gloss.

went out (ἐξήρχοντο: descriptive imperfect).

at the eldest. Literally, 'at the elders.' The word may be either an adjective or a substantive. But the context seems to require the sense given in the English.

And Jesus alone remained (κατελείφθη = was left). The verb does not elsewhere occur in St. John, but is usual enough in the Synoptics. Only those concerned in the accusation went off; the disciples and others remained,

the eldest. And Jesus alone remained, and the woman standing in the midst. Then Jesus lifting up himself, ¹⁰ said to her: Woman, where are they that accused thee? Hath no man condemned thee? Who said: No man, ¹¹ Lord. And Jesus said: Neither will I condemn thee. Go, and now sin no more.

Christ the Source of Light and Truth.

(VERS. 12-29.)

Again therefore Jesus spoke to them, saying: I am the ¹² light of the world: he that followeth me, walketh not in

10. *Jesus lifting up himself.* A.V. adds, 'and saw none (seeing none) but the woman'; but in R.V. these words are removed from the text to the margin. By 'lifting up himself' is meant 'lifting up His head' after bending down to write.

Hath no man condemned thee (κατέκρινέν = did no one condemn thee)? St. John nowhere uses this compound verb; but he uses the simple verb nineteen times in the Gospel and nine times in the Apocalypse.

11. *No man, Lord* (= Sir).

now sin no more (μηκέτι ἁμάρτανε). Quite Johannean (v. 14). Nowhere else in N. T.

To the linguistic peculiarities already noted it may be added that the clause 'and sitting down he taught them' is Synoptical rather than Johannean, and that St. John's favourite conjunction οὖν occurs but once (v. 5), being replaced by δέ (eleven times). The general literary impression certainly seems at first sight adverse. But there are considerations on the other side: (1) Some of the MSS. give variants of which the language is quite Johannean; (2) in a longer passage (ii. 1-17) the conjunction οὖν does not even once appear, but is replaced by καί and δέ (about ten times), or no conjunction is used where we should expect οὖν (cf. vii. 37-44). (3) Other passages in St. John have peculiarities of diction. Thus in chap. ix. we find ἡλικίαν ἔχειν (21, 23), which occurs nowhere else in N. T.; the verb συντίθεμαι (22), nowhere else in St. John, but only in St. Luke; the verb λοιδορέω (28), nowhere else in St. John, and only thrice besides in all the N.T. The literary argument, therefore, is not conclusive; but, although not absolutely conclusive, it makes one dubious about the Johannean (not the divine) authorship of the passage. Nor does the Council of Trent, which defines the divine inspiration of the passage, clearly define its Johannean authorship.

12. *Again, therefore.* This is a fresh discourse, delivered 'in the treasury' (v. 20), and perhaps on the following day—the octave day of the Feast. The octave was kept as a Sabbath, and the Temple would be again thronged with worshippers.

13 darkness, but shall have the light of life. The Pharisees therefore said to him: Thou givest testimony of thyself: 14 thy testimony is not true. Jesus answered, and said to them: Although I give testimony of myself, my testimony

"The Treasury would be within 'the Court of the Women,' the common meeting place of the worshippers. Here, in the hearing of the leaders of the people, took place the first dialogue between Christ and the Pharisees. It opened with what probably was an allusion alike to one of the great ceremonies of the Feast of Tabernacles, to its symbolic meaning, and to an express Messianic expectation of the Rabbis. As the Mishnah states: On the first, or, as the Talmud would have it, on every night of the festive week, the Court of the Women was brilliantly illuminated, and the night spent in the demonstrations already described (vii. 2). This was called 'the joy of the feast.' This 'festive joy,' of which the origin is obscure, was no doubt connected with the hope of earth's great harvest-joy in the conversion of the heathen world, and so pointed to 'the days of the Messiah.' The Messiah is also designated as the 'Enlightener,' the words 'The light is with him' (Dan. ii. 22), being applied to Him. The Pharisees, then, could not have mistaken the Messianic meaning in the words of Jesus, in their reference to the past festivity: 'I am the Light of the world'" (Eders. l.c., p. 322).

the light of the world (cf. i. 4, 9, iii. 19; Isa. xlii. 6; Luke ii. 32). Since the Feast of Tabernacles commemorated the wanderings in the wilderness, the outpouring of water will naturally be referred to the stream from the rock, and the illumination at night to 'the pillar of fire.' The ceremonies, therefore, applied to Christ, both in what they commemorated and in what they foreshadowed (cf. vii. 37).

he that followeth me, walketh not (shall in no wise walk) *in darkness*. The negative (οὐ μή) is very strong. By darkness is meant moral evil. A like antithesis occurs in i. 4, 5. To follow is to believe and obey. To walk is to live. Hence, he—

shall have the light of life (cf. i. 12, xii. 36, 46). The light is the permanent gift of faith, which guides a man safely to eternal life. It is, of itself, permanent—never withdrawn, unless we cast it away—and brings to us grace upon grace (see on iii. 15, 16, i. 16).

13. *Thy testimony is not true* (cf. v. 31). The Pharisees raise the merely formal objection that the testimony of one witness does not suffice. Our Lord had already answered that objection at some length (v. 32-47); but He now gives a fresh answer.

14. *Although I give testimony.* (κἂν ἐγώ = even if.) That is, even if I do give testimony of Myself, I am competent to give it, and My testimony is true, because I know "whence I came," *i.e.*, that I came from God, and cannot lie. You do not take that testimony, because *you know not whence I come.* Observe the change of tense: "whence I came"—referring back to the historical point of the Incarnation,

is true: for I know whence I came, and whither I go: but you know not whence I come, or whither I go. You judge according to the flesh: I judge not any man. And if I do judge, my judgment is true: because I am not alone, but I and the Father that sent me. And in your law it is written, that the testimony of two men is true. I am one that give testimony of myself: and the Father that sent me, giveth testimony of me. They said therefore to him:

"whence I come"—of His continuous coming forward in the work He was accomplishing. The root of their error lay in their obstinate refusal to judge otherwise than "according to the appearance" (vii. 24).

15. *You judge* (and condemn me and My testimony) *according to the flesh*. "They saw the flesh, the God they knew not; they observed the habitation, of the inhabitant they were ignorant. That flesh was a temple, within it dwelt God" (St. Aug., Tract xviii. c. 2). Moreover, they judged according to carnal, worldly ideas, not according to the Spirit of truth (Rom. viii. 4-7). Therefore they erred concerning Christ. But how different is His conduct!

I judge not (do not condemn) *any man* (cf. iii. 17).

16. *And if I do judge.* That is, if ever I do judge (ἐὰν κρίνω); *my judgment is true, i.e.*, real.

because I am not alone (cf. iii. 30-34, v. 17, 19, 30, xiv. 10). Mention of the Father marks a transition to another argument—even their own demand for two witnesses is satisfied in the case of Christ. His witness to Himself is quite in accordance with Jewish law (v. 18).

17. *And in your law.* More emphatic in the Greek, 'Now in the law also, your law, it is written.'

18. *I am one.* The Rabbinic canon laid it down that a man's witness in his own case was only then not admissible, when it stood alone; but if it were corroborated by the testimony of even one slave, male or female—and slaves were ordinarily unfit for testimony—it would be admissible.

the Father that sent me, giveth testimony (in Christ's miracles, and in Holy Scripture; see on v. 36-39). According to the Jewish standpoint, the argument was unanswerable. The two witnesses required by law had really given their evidence. But the Pharisees, shutting their eyes to all the evidence that had been offered, in mockery ask our Lord to produce His second witness.

19. *Where is thy Father?* This question enables our Lord to return to the main subject of the discourse. The question had been put from mere cavilling; for they knew where the Father was (v. 17, 18, 36). Their blindness was wilful. Hence our Lord's answer.

Neither me do you know, nor my Father. Their wilful ignorance of Him was the reason they did not know the Father (cf. v. 37, 38).

Where is thy Father? Jesus answered: Neither me do you know, nor my Father: If you did know me, perhaps 20 you would know my Father also. These words Jesus spoke in the treasury, teaching in the temple: and no man laid hands on him, because his hour was not yet 21 come. Again therefore Jesus said to them: I go, and you shall seek me, and you shall die in your sin. 22 Whither I go, you cannot come. The Jews therefore said: Will he kill himself, because he said: Whither I 23 go, you cannot come? And he said to them: You are from beneath, I am from above. You are of this world,

If you did know me, perhaps (rather 'without doubt,' cf. iv. 10, xiv. 7, 28) *you would know my Father also*. Belief in Christ would bring true knowledge of the Father (see vi. 45, 46).

20. *Because his hour was not yet come* (see on vii. 6).

21. *Again therefore*. These words seem to mark the beginning of another discourse (cf. *v*. 12), of which the conclusion is noted in *v*. 30, 'When he spoke these things, many believed in him,' as the conclusion of the previous discourse was noted in *v*. 20, 'No man laid hands on him.' In all probability, the discourse was delivered in one of the 'porches' enclosing the Court of the Gentiles. Here discussions might take place freely, in which the people could join, for the porches were not strictly a part of the Sanctuary. Stones might be picked up in the Court of the Gentiles, but not in any part of the Sanctuary, and our Lord could easily escape, by entering the crowd moving through the porches to the outer gate (*v*. 59).

Again therefore Jesus said (εἶπεν οὖν πάλιν), *i.e.*, repeated what He had before said (contrast *v*. 12. "Again Jesus *spoke*" πάλιν ἐλάλησεν). The same threat was uttered in vii. 34; but a fresh element is now introduced which intensifies the meaning.

you shall die in your sin. The singular is used of the state of sin. Moreover 'sin' is highly emphatic: 'In your sin you shall die.' The sin, of course, is their sin of obstinate unbelief (cf. i. 5, 9, 11, iii. 18, 19, 36). If, then, they desired to escape eternal death, they must abandon their unbelief (*v*. 24); otherwise, they will never see God (vii. 33, 34).

22. *Will he kill himself!* When our Lord had before so spoken, His words had been treated with scorn (vii. 35); but now the scorn is far more offensive and malicious, for, according to Pharasaic belief, the lot of suicides was in the lowest hell. They professed to believe that He was capable of committing what was held to be one of the most heinous of crimes.

23. *You are from beneath. You are of this world.* "Without further noticing their venomous scorn, Jesus simply holds up before them, with more firm and elevated calmness, their own low nature,

I am not of this world. Therefore I said to you, that you 24
shall die in your sins. For if you believe not that I am
he, ye shall die in your sin. They said therefore to him: 25
Who art thou? Jesus said to them: The beginning, who
also speak unto you. Many things I have to speak and to 26
judge of you. But he that sent me is true: and the things

which made them capable of thus mocking Him, because they did not
understand Him, the Heavenly One" (Meyer). For the force of the
antithesis, see on i. 10, iii. 6, 31. Not because of His committing
suicide would He be separated from them; but because they were of the
earth, and earthy, while He was of heaven, and heavenly, therefore
it was that an impassable gulf was set between them. Faith was
the necessary condition of bridging the gulf.

24. *Ye shall die.* Here the emphasis falls, not on 'sin,' as in
v. 21, but on 'die.'

if you believe not that I am he. 'He' is not found either in the
Vulgate, or in the Greek. The meaning is, 'that I am the Messiah.'
This would have been at once understood, without explanation, by all.
It was the thought that had been most prominent all through the discussions with the Jews (cf. v. 28, iv. 25, 26, v. 17 19, xiii. 19). Our
Lord did not utter the name, but left them to supply it mentally,
because He did not then wish to say anything upon which they could
bring against Him a legal charge of blasphemy.

25. *Who art thou?* Better, '*Thou*, who art thou?' They pretended
not to see what our Lord had implied, and were desirous of forcing
Him to make a clearer confession. He had said simply, 'I am'; they
retort, 'Thou, who art thou?'

The beginning (τὴν ἀρχήν: adverbial accusative: cf. Mark vi. 19;
1 Tim. vi. 5; Jude 7, &c.) *who* (ὅ τι = that which) *also speak
unto you* (R.V., "even that which I have also spoken unto you from
the beginning"). Their own question condemned them. Not know
who He was! Why, He was, what all along, from the beginning, He
had been telling them. But this interpretation gives to λαλῶ (speak)
the sense of λέγω (say).

But τὴν ἀρχήν may be taken in the sense of 'indeed,' 'certainly,'
and ὅ τι as an interrogative—'why.' Thus, in answer to their malicious
question, our Lord, instead of giving a direct reply, pointed out how
unworthy they were of His addressing them at all. 'Indeed, why do
I even speak to you?' Yet since I do speak—

26. *Many things* (emphatic from position) *I have to speak.* After
the interruption (v. 25) our Lord resumes from v. 24. Besides the
sin of their unbelief, He had many other things for which to condemn
them.

But (ἀλλά) *he that sent me is true.* 'ἀλλά' is adversative, and the
sentence is elliptical. 'You may say My accusations are untrue. But
I speak only what I have heard from Him who sent Me; and He is

I have heard of him, these same I speak in the world.
27 And they understood not that he called God his father.
28 Jesus therefore said to them: When you shall have lifted up the son of man, then shall you know that I am he, and that I do nothing of myself, but as the Father hath
29 taught me, these things I speak: and he that sent me is with me, and he hath not left me alone: for I do always the things that please him.

Discussion with the Jews.

(VERS. 30-59.)

30 When he spoke these things, many believed in him.
31 Then Jesus said to those Jews who believed him: If you

true.' (For the ellipsis cf. v. 31; for the general thought cf. v. 30.) He insinuates, as the reference (v. 30) shows, that He is the Son of God.

27. *And they understood not.* Better, 'They perceived not that He was speaking to them of the Father.' These words show how strong was the angry tumult of their minds. Our Lord's meaning was perfectly plain (*v.* 18); but passion often blinds one to the meaning of even the simplest language. Since they would not now stop to understand, our Lord warns them that the time would come when they could not help understanding.

28. *When you shall have lifted up* (iii. 14) *the son of man, then shall you know that I am he* (*v.* 24). The very Cross would be His path to glory and triumph (xii. 32). Their eyes would be opened, partly because the Jews would afterwards be willing to believe (Acts ii. 36-41, iv. 4, vi. 7; Rom. xi. 11-27), partly against their will, and too late (Luke xiii. 24-30). For mighty manifestations would follow the death of Christ—the outpouring of the Spirit; the miraculous works of the Apostles; the expansion and building up of the Church; the destruction of Jerusalem and punishment of the Jews; the second coming of Christ to judgment (see Meyer in h.l.).

I do nothing of myself. For explanation see on v. 19, 20, 30, 36.

29. *He hath not left me alone.* They will also see that the Father was always working with Christ (see on v. 17). Our Lord here passes to His visible mission, to His work in the world as man; and He explains the meritorious cause why the Father was always with Him.

for I do always. The words 'I' and 'always' are very emphatic. 'Because I do His will at all times' (cf. the thought in xv. 10).

30. *Many believed in him.* A similar statement was made in reference to the result of our Lord's preaching at the first Pasch, but with the addition that "He did not trust himself unto them" (ii. 23,

continue in my word, you shall be my disciples indeed, 32
And you shall know the truth, and the truth shall make
you free. They answered him: We are the seed of Abra- 33
ham, and we have never been slaves to any man: how
sayest thou: You shall be free? Jesus answered them: 34
Amen, amen, I say unto you, that whosoever committeth
sin, is the servant of sin. Now the servant abideth not in 35
the house for ever: but the son abideth for ever. If there- 36
fore the son shall make you free, you shall be free indeed.
I know that you are the children of Abraham: but you 37
seek to kill me, because my word hath no place in you.

24). Nor will He now trust Himself unto them until their faith has been tried. He tries it; and it breaks down in the testing.

32. *You shall know the truth.* The reward of faith is greater enlightenment and a growing knowledge of God and of things spiritual (see on i. 14, 16, 17).

and the truth shall make you free. What slavery and what freedom is explained in *v.* 34. As usual, the Jews manifest their perversity of understanding, in their reply.

33. *We have never been slaves to any man.* "I am moved, brethren, by the hollow pride of men, because even of that very freedom of theirs, which they understood carnally, they lied when they said, 'We have never been slaves to any man'" (St. Aug. xli. 2). The words were evidently intended to be taken in a moral sense—in a sense, too, quite familiar to the Jews, for their own Rabbinic tradition taught that he only was free who laboured in the study of the law. But they take the words literally and profess to be indignant at being called slaves. They deny in their anger the plainest historical facts. How often had they been reminded by God that He had delivered them from the house of bondage! And at the very time they spoke they were paying tribute to Cæsar. But our Lord was not concerned with their historical falsehoods. He proceeds to force on their notice the idea of a spiritual bondage to which they were shutting their eyes—the bondage and servitude of sin (*v.* 34). They were in sin—were servants of sin. Therefore our Lord, by a familiar example of domestic life—for a slave may at any time be dismissed or sold—gives them warning that they will not be allowed to stay in the house of God for ever, unless He, the Son and Heir, make them free indeed (see on i. 12, 18, iii. 13).

37. *I know that you are the children of Abraham, i.e.*, by mere natural descent. But there was a more important moral descent (cf. Rom. ix. 8), and in that they were not the children of Abraham, but the children of the devil.

you seek to kill me, because my word hath no place (οὐ χωρεῖ = doth not advance, striketh no root) *in you.* They had already lost their

38 I speak that which I have seen with my Father: and you
39 do the things that you have seen with your father. They
answered, and said to him: Abraham is our father.
Jesus saith to them: If you be the children of Abraham,
40 do the works of Abraham. But now you seek to kill me,
a man who have spoken the truth to you, which I have
41 heard of God. This Abraham did not. You do the
works of your father. They said therefore to him: We
are not born of fornication: we have one Father *even* God.
42 Jesus therefore said to them: If God were your father, you
would indeed love me. For from God I proceeded, and

feeble faith (*v.* 30) under the test, and therefore returned to their previous state of animosity.

38. *I speak that which I have seen* (perfect: expressive of continuous action = have seen and still see) *with my Father*: cf. v. 19, 20, 30.

and you do (= are doing) *the things that you have seen* (ἠκούσατε = that you heard) *with your father*. On the principle, 'Like father, like son,' our Lord implies that the Jews could not claim descent spiritually from Abraham. They repudiate the insinuation (*v.* 39). Our Lord replies :—

39. *If you be* (*i.e.*, 'If you are indeed) *the children of Abraham, do the works* (*i.e.*, the faith and obedience) *of Abraham*.' But they show quite other morals (*v.* 40). Instead of Abraham's ready faith in God, they show a desire to kill God's own messenger.

41. *You do* (= are doing) *the works* (not of Abraham, but) *of your father*. The Jews now perceive the deeply moral tone and application of our Lord's words; and they claim a true moral descent from God, and therefore from Abraham.

We are not born of fornication. In Scriptural language idolatry was called fornication (Exod. xxxiv. 16; Judg. ii. 17; Jer. ii. 20, iii. 9; Osee ii. 4). 'We are not idolaters, or the children of idolaters.'

we have one Father. Better, One Father we have (not many gods like the heathens)—*even God* (τὸν θεόν) = the true God. This answer serves them nothing.

42. *If God were your father, you would indeed love me. For from God I proceeded.* More emphatic in Greek, 'For I came forth from God and am here' (ἥκω), *i.e.*, on this visible stage of earth. The reference is to the Incarnation. For the argument, cf. vi. 37, 44, 45. Because Christ had not come of Himself, but had been sent by God, the Jews would have received Him if they had been children of God. But they did not receive Him; they would not even understand Him. Therefore He plainly declares to them the moral cause of their spiritual blindness. They were morally incapable of His doctrine (*v.* 43), because of the sinfulness of their nature (*v.* 44).

came: for I came not of myself, but he sent me. Why
do you not know my speech? Because you cannot hear
my word. You are of *your* father the devil, and the
desires of your father you will do. He was a murderer
from the beginning, and he stood not in the truth; because
truth is not in him. When he speaketh a lie, he speaketh
of his own: for he is a liar, and the father thereof. But
if I say the truth, you believe me not. Which of you
shall convince me of sin? If I say the truth to you, why

43. *Why do you not know my speech* (λαλιάν)? That is, 'Why do you not recognise My Divine accent?' (cf. 'Thou also art one of them: for even thy *speech* doth discover thee,' Matt. xxvi. 73). Christ's accent was truly that of a Divine messenger (cf. Matt. vii. 28, 29).

Because you cannot hear my word (λόγον = doctrine, meaning). It is not now a case of mere unwillingness; they were really, in their malice and blind anger, stopping up the very avenues of intelligence and destroying the possibility of faith (cf. vi. 44, 45). And now our Lord says plainly what He had before implied (vv. 38, 41).

44. *You are of your father the devil, and the desires of your father you will* (θέλετε = you are wishing) *do*. What those desires are, is immediately explained.

He was a murderer from the beginning of man's history, for by causing the Fall he brought death upon all mankind (cf. 1 John iii. 12; Wisd. ii. 24).

and he stood not (standeth not) *in the truth, i.e.*, his life and conduct are alien from the truth (cf. Psa. i. 1).

because truth is not in him. Compare the phrase, 'It is not in him to speak the truth.'

When he speaketh a lie, he speaketh of his own (ἐκ τῶν ἰδίων), *i.e.*, he bringeth out of his own proper store, of that which is emphatically his own.

for he is a liar, and the father thereof, i.e., the father of the liar. Linguistically it might mean, 'the father of the lie—of lying'; but the opening of the verse, 'You are of your father,' forbids this interpretation. Our Lord is showing that the Jews are the children of Satan, because they are murderers and liars.

45. *But if I say the truth*. In the Greek there is a strongly marked antithesis, "But I, because (ὅτι) I say the truth, you believe Me not." They believe Satan; they will not believe Christ. Yet in the life of our Lord they could find no ground of suspicion, or any reason for doubting His word.

46. *Which of you shall convince me of sin? i.e.*, can convict Me (iii. 20) (ἐλέγχει).

If (then) *I say the truth to you, why do you not believe me?* To this there is no answer except that they are of the devil (lovers of lies, haters of truth), and not, as they had boasted (v. 41), of God.

47 do you not believe me? He that is of God heareth the words of God. Therefore you hear them not, because you
48 are not of God. The Jews therefore answered, and said to him: Do not we say well that thou art a Samaritan,
49 and hast a devil? Jesus answered: I have not a devil: but I honour my Father, and you have dishonoured me.
50 But I seek not my own glory: there is one that seeketh
51 and judgeth. Amen, amen, I say unto you: If any man
52 keep my word, he shall not see death for ever. The Jews therefore said: Now we know that thou hast a devil. Abraham is dead, and the prophets; and thou sayest: If any man keep my word, he shall not taste death for ever.
53 Art thou greater than our father Abraham, who is dead?

47. *He that is of God heareth* (see ver. 43) *the words of God* (cf. Rom. viii. 14). Our Lord implies what, indeed, He had already asserted, that His words are the words of God. *Therefore* (cf. v. 16). This plain and open denial of their being sons of God appeared to the Jews to be an act of malicious frenzy.

48. *Do not we say well* (καλῶς: see iv. 17). There is strong emphasis on 'we.'

thou art a Samaritan, i.e., no true Jew, but a stupid enemy of God's people (see Eccli. l. 27, 28).

and hast a devil (cf. vii. 20). Our Lord with quiet earnestness refutes the charge, and, at the same time, warns them of the chastisement preparing for their malice.

49. *I have not a devil; but I honour my Father* (see v. 29, and v. 30). One possessed does not honour God. The Jews, on the other hand, do dishonour God by dishonouring Christ.

you have dishonoured (are dishonouring) *me:* see v. 23).

50. *But I seek not my own glory.* That is, not because I seek glory from you do I speak of your dishonouring Me (see v. 41); but because I wish to warn you that,

there is one that seeketh (v. 54; cf. v. 45) *and judgeth* (Deut. xviii. 19; cf. on v. 22, 30). Since, then, our Lord was not seeking to triumph in their ruin, He mercifully points out to them the path, not merely of avoiding God's judgment, but of reaching eternal life.

51. *If any man keep* (i.e., obey) *my word, he shall not* (οὐ μή = he shall certainly not) *see death for ever* (cf. iii. 16, iv. 13, 14, v. 24). The Jews, as before (vv. 32, 33), take as physical what was moral.

52. *Now we know* (i.e., now at length we perceive clearly) *that thou hast a devil* (i.e., art mad).

Abraham is dead. They are thinking only of physical death.

53. *Art thou greater than our father Abraham, who is dead* (ὅστις = one who died)?

and the prophets are dead. An anacoluthon = 'And art thou greater than the prophets, men who died?'

and the prophets are dead. Whom dost thou make thyself? Jesus answered: If I glorify myself, my glory is 54 nothing. It is my Father that glorifieth me, of whom you say that he is your God. And you have not known him, 55 but I know him. And if I shall say that I know him not, I shall be like to you, a liar. But I do know him, and do keep his word. Abraham your father rejoiced that he 56 might see my day: he saw it, and was glad. The Jews 57 therefore said to him: Thou art not yet fifty years old, and hast thou seen Abraham? Jesus said to them: 58 Amen, amen, I say to you, before Abraham was made, I am. They took up stones therefore to cast at him. But 59 Jesus hid himself and went out of the temple.

54. *If I glorify myself, my glory is nothing.* This is said as in v. 31.
It is my Father that glorifieth me (see i. 51, iii. 2, v. 20, 36, 37). The Father had glorified the Son by miracle, by direct testimony, by the teaching of Scripture. But that testimony of the Father had not been accepted by the Jews.

55. *You have not known* (better, 'recognised') *him* (cf. v. 37), *but I know him, i.e.*, by immediate and direct knowledge (οὐκ ἐγνώκατε ... οἶδα).

56. *Abraham your father.* They were not children of God, nor were they children of Abraham. For Abraham, whom they called father, *rejoiced* (exulted) *that he might see my day.* Abraham knew by faith that the Messiah would one day come, and exulted at the prospect of seeing that day. Nay, *he saw it* (for it was revealed to him, where he now is, in limbo), *and was glad.* The words cannot mean that Abraham saw only in promise—for such anticipation our Lord uses different language (see Matt. xiii. 17)—but that he saw in actuality. While, then, Abraham rejoiced at Christ's advent, they, who claim to be Abraham's children, hate and persecute Christ.

58. *Before Abraham was made* (= came into being, was born) *I am.* That is, Christ did not then come into being, but His existence is from before time, and is absolute, eternal, changeless (cf. Psa. lxxxix. 2). The Jews see clearly what our Lord means, and they at once prepare to stone Him as a blasphemer (Lev. xxiv. 16).

59. *They took up stones therefore to cast at him.* A stoning in the Temple was not an impossible event (2 Par. xxiv. 21; Matt. xxiii. 35; Josephus Antt., xvii. 9, 3). As there were no stones in the Temple itself, the Jews probably rushed for them into the Court of the Gentiles.
But Jesus hid himself. It is not necessary to suppose that our Lord made Himself invisible. He hid Himself, perhaps in the crowd, perhaps in one of the many passages or chambers of the Temple, and presently *went out of the temple.*

CHAPTER IX.

Jesus Cures a Man Born Blind.

(VERS. 1-38.)

AND Jesus passing by, saw a man who was blind from his birth; and his disciples asked him: Rabbi, who hath sinned, this man, or his parents, that he should be born blind? Jesus answered: Neither hath this man

In the following narrative we have the account of another symbolical miracle, one illustrative of the great truth that Christ is the 'Light of the world.' Hence our Lord heals the man's spiritual blindness (35-38) as well as his bodily blindness.

1. *And Jesus passing by, saw a man who was blind from his birth.* The narrative is closely connected with the preceding narrative, and the events flow on uninterruptedly. Jesus went out of the Temple, and passing by, saw a man who was blind from his birth. The Holy Name does not occur in the first verse of the original text, but has been repeated from viii. 59.

Rabbi, who hath sinned, this man, or his parents? That such inflictions as blindness, disease, &c., are punishments sometimes inflicted for sin, is quite certain; but it was a widespread Jewish opinion that all such calamities were punishments for personal sin, and that children were afflicted because of the sins of their parents. Besides, according to the Rabbis, evil impulse begins its dominion even from birth. We must suppose, therefore, that the disciples, impressed deeply by the greatness of the man's calamity, and with the current notions of the time running vaguely through their minds, put the question to our Lord. The very question is an incidental proof of their belief that our Lord knew all things. Our Lord answered, that the blindness was not the punishment of personal sin.

3. *But* (it happened) *that* (in order that) *the works of God* (*i.e.*, what God works) *should be made manifest in him.* The cause of the man's blindness was the natural working of the natural forces that work

sinned, nor his parents; but that the works of God should
be made manifest in him. I must work the works of him 4
that sent me, whilst it is day: the night cometh when
no man can work. As long as I am in the world 5
I am the light of the world. When he had said these 6
things, he spat on the ground, and made clay of the
spittle, and spread the clay upon his eyes. And said to 7

through all nature. God permits the ill results that occasionally spring
from those forces; but for a high moral purpose. Our Lord declares
the reasonableness of such results when they are viewed in connection
with that moral purpose. The actual case of the blind man is made an
instance in point. His calamity had been permitted in order that the
glory of God might be manifested by the miracle that was about to be
performed.

4. *I must work* (the better attested reading is, 'We must work') *the
works of him that sent me* (a weakly attested reading gives 'us'),
whilst it is day. Under the form of a general principle, applicable to
the Apostles in their association with Christ in the work of converting
the world, our Lord gives a reason why He is now about to heal the
man's bodily and spiritual blindness. He must accomplish, while in
the flesh on earth, the works which the Father had given Him to
accomplish, in the present visible mode and action, on earth. Verse
5, "as long as I am in the world," explains what is meant by 'day'
and 'night' of ver. 4, *i.e.*, the day of life, and the night of death
which brought Christ's mortal life to an end (cf. iii. 17, 19, vi. 14,
viii. 26). Hence our Lord is speaking of His visible mission on earth,
when, in a special way, He was the Light of the world; for, in fact, He
has always been the Light (i. 4, 5). The Greek runs literally, 'When I
am in the world, I am Light to the world.' That is, 'I cannot be in
the world unless at the same time enlightening the world.' The 'when'
also suggests a time when He would withdraw His visible presence
from the world.

6. *Made clay of the spittle*. Our Lord, although usually working
miracles by a word (cf. v. 8), sometimes added, as in the present
instance, some ceremony (cf. Mark vii. 33, viii. 23). St. John
does not inform us for what reason our Lord anointed the eyes of the
blind man, and we can therefore only conjecture. But we learn, at
any rate, how our Lord could have imparted to the sacramental signs
their spiritual efficacy.

7. *Go, wash in* (wash into, *i.e.*, wash away the clay into) *the pool
of Siloe* (Siloam). Or the εἰς may belong, not to νίψαι (wash), but to
ὕπαγε (go) = Go to the pool (see *v.* 11). The name of the pool still
survives in Birket Silwan, situated at the entrance of the Tyropœon
Valley, on the south-east of the hill of Sion. The pool is probably
that referred to in Isa. viii. 6; Neh. iii. 15.

which is interpreted, Sent. The term might be either a noun,

him : Go, wash in the pool of Siloe, which is interpreted, Sent. He went therefore, and washed, and he came seeing
8 The neighbours therefore, and they who had seen him before that he was a beggar, said : Is not this he that sat,
9 and begged? Some said : This is he. But others *said:*
10 No, but he is like him. But he said : I am he. They
11 said therefore to him : How were thy eyes opened? He answered : That man, that is called Jesus, made clay, and anointed my eyes, and said to me : Go to the pool of Siloe,
12 and wash. And I went, I washed, and I see. And they said to him : Where is he? He saith : I know not.
13 They bring him that had been blind to the Pharisees.
14 Now it was the sabbath when Jesus made the clay and

'ascending forth,' *i.e.*, of water, or a participial adjective, 'sent.' St. John shows that the name was providentially intended to be symbolical; and the prominence given to the pool in the Feast of Tabernacles (see on vii. 37) points to such symbolism. In the command, therefore, to wash in Siloe there is a symbolism of Him who was the Sent of the Father.

and he came (ἦλθε : perhaps, 'came home,' *v.* 8) *seeing*.

8. *They who had seen him before that* (ὅτι) *he was a beggar*. Better, 'because' he was a beggar, and had sat in public places begging.

9. *No, but he is like him*. The acquisition of sight altered his expression of face.

12. *Where is he?* The people were evidently perplexed about the violation of the Sabbath (vv. 13, 14) ; and as they could not themselves answer the question, they seek the authority of the leaders.

13. *To the Pharisees*. Not, however, to the Sanhedrin, for St. John never designates the Sanhedrin by the simple term, 'the Pharisees' (see vii. 32, 45; xi. 47, 56, xviii. 3).

14. *Now it was the sabbath*. The ground on which the charge would rest was plain : the healing involved a manifold breach of the Sabbath-law. The first of these was that Jesus had made clay. Next, it would be a question whether any remedy might be applied on the holy-day. Such could only be done in diseases of the internal organs (from the throat downwards) except when danger to life or the loss of an organ was involved. It was, indeed, declared lawful to apply, for example, wine to the outside of the eyelid, on the ground that this might be treated as washing ; but it was sinful to apply it to the inside of the eye. And as regards saliva, its application to the eye is expressly forbidden on the ground that it was evidently intended as a remedy (Eders. l.c., p. 334).

Our Lord worked seven specific miracles of healing on the Sabbath : (1) A man with an unclean spirit (Mark i. 23) ; (2) Simon's wife's

opened his eyes. Again therefore the Pharisees asked him, 15
how he had received his sight. But he said to them: He
put clay upon my eyes, and I washed, and I see. Some 16
therefore of the Pharisees said: This man is not of God,
who keepeth not the sabbath. But others said: How can
a man that is a sinner do such miracles? And there was
a division among them. They say therefore to the blind 17
man again: What sayest thou of him that hath opened
thy eyes? And he said: He is a prophet. The Jews 18
then did not believe concerning him, that he had been
blind and had received his sight, until they called the
parents of him that had received his sight. And asked 19
them, saying: Is this your son, who you say was born
blind? How then doth he now see? His parents answered 20
them and said: We know that this is our son, and that he
was born blind; but how he now seeth we know not: or 21
who hath opened his eyes we know not; ask himself: he is
of age, let him speak for himself. These things his parents 22

mother, *ibid. v.* 29); (3) a man with a withered hand (Matt. xii. 10);
(4) a woman with a spirit of infirmity (Luke xiii. 11, 14); (5) a dropsical
man (Luke xiv. 2, 3); (6) a paralytic at Bethesda (John v. 10); (7) man
born blind.

15. *Again therefore the Pharisees* (καὶ οἱ Φαρισαῖοι = the Pharisees
also). The statement looks back to the question put previously by the
crowd (*v.* 10). They had evidently not been satisfied with the
account given by those who had brought the man, and so made the
man himself repeat it. The shortness of the man's reply shows that he
is getting somewhat angry at the questioning.

16. *Some therefore . . . but others.* The undeniable truth of the
fact creates a great dilemma. Is their Sabbath-observance Divine, or
is the miracle Divine? They are puzzled to find an answer, and
therefore ask the man for his opinion. The man readily replied.

17. *He is a prophet, i.e.,* a man sent by God (cf. iii. 2). The
same conclusion had been drawn by Nicodemus, one of themselves;
there was force, therefore, in the inference. Only one course was now
open—to call in question the truth of the already-admitted fact. The
man's parents were summoned. They attested that their son had been
born blind; but, fearing the Jews, they prudently declined to make
any statement as to the manner in which he had recovered his sight,
and reasonably referred the Pharisees to the son himself. In *v.* 21
there is a strong emphasis on the pronouns—"*we* know not," "*he* is
of age."

22. *For the Jews had already agreed* (συνετέθειντο). Not necessarily

said, because they feared the Jews: for the Jews had already agreed among themselves, that if any man should confess him to be Christ, he should be put out of the
23 synagogue. Therefore did his parents say: He is of age,
24 ask him. They therefore called the man again that had been blind, and said to him: Give glory to God. We
25 know that this man is a sinner. He said therefore to them: If he be a sinner, I know not: one thing I know,
26 that whereas I was blind, now I see. They said then to him: What did he to thee? How did he open thy eyes?
27 He answered them: I have told you already, and you have heard: why would you hear it again? will you also
28 become his disciples? They reviled him therefore and said: Be thou his disciple; but we are the disciples of
29 Moses. We know that God spoke to Moses: but as to

by a formal decree of the Sanhedrin (see Luke xxii. 5; Acts xxiii. 20. The word occurs nowhere else in N.T.).

that (ἵνα) *if any man.* The particle represents what they had agreed upon as the purpose or intention of their agreement.

he should be put out of the synagogue (ἀποσυνάγωγος γένηται = he should become unsynagogued). Two, or perhaps three, kinds of excommunication are mentioned in Jewish writings. The first two were comparatively mild punishments, and took the form of an admonition or rebuke. The third, called the Cherem or ban, was the real casting out or unsynagoguing. The culprit became as a leper. He might buy the necessaries of life, but he was obliged to wear a culprit's dress, so that all might avoid him; for it was forbidden to eat or drink with him, to show him the road, or to hold intercourse with him.

23. *Therefore*: cf. v. 16.

24. *Give glory to God* (A.V. give God the praise). This is not an invitation to give praise to God for the cure, the truth of which the Pharisees do not wish to admit, but an adjuration to speak the truth, 'Give glory to God by speaking the truth' (cf. Jos. vii. 19). They desire the man to withdraw his profession of faith that Christ was a prophet (v. 17).

We (very emphatic—We, the leaders) *know that this man is a sinner.*

27. *I have told* (better, I told) *you already, and you have heard* (οὐκ ἠκούσατε—you did not hear). Better, interrogatively, 'I told you already, and did you not hear?'

28. *Be thou his disciple.* Better, 'Thou art that man's disciple.'

29. *We know that God spoke* (hath spoken: for the Mosaic revelation still remained) *to Moses.*

this man, we know not from whence he is. The man 30
answered, and said to them: Why, herein is a wonderful
thing that you know not from whence he is, and he hath
opened my eyes. Now we know that God doth not hear 31
sinners: but if a man be a server of God, and doth his
will, him he heareth. From the beginning of the world it 32
hath not been heard, that any man hath opened the eyes
of one born blind. Unless this man were of God he could 33
not do anything. They answered, and said to him: Thou 34
wast wholly born in sins, and dost thou teach us? And
they cast him out. Jesus heard that they had cast him 35
out: and when he had found him, he said to him: Dost
thou believe in the Son of God? He answered, and said: 36
Who is he, Lord, that I may believe in him? And Jesus 37
said to him: Thou hast both seen him; and it is he that
talketh with thee. And he said: I believe, Lord. And 38

30. *Why, herein is a wonderful thing.* Better, "Herein (=in this) certainly is *the* marvel, that you (the leaders of the people) should not know whence he is, and (=although) he hath opened my eyes." Moses by miracle had proved that he was sent by God; the Pharisees, therefore, believe in Moses' Divine mission: Jesus works miracles, and says He is sent by God; but the Pharisees know not whence He is!

31. *Now we (i.e.,* both you and I) *know that God doth not hear sinners.* It was a Rabbinic maxim, a maxim constantly repeated by them, that answers to prayer depended on a man's being pious. The maxim was an exaggeration and perversion of an undoubted Scriptural truth (Prov. xv. 29, xxviii. 9; Job xxvii. 8, 9; Isa. i. 15, lix. 2). But it was their own maxim, and the man urges it against them.

33. *He could not do anything, i.e.,* miraculous—anything like the wonder wrought in me. The Pharisees had nothing to answer. They turn on the man with bitter reproach. Would he presume to teach them?—he who was through and through a born reprobate ("wholly born in sins": cf. *v.* 2), as was proved by his being born blind.

34. *And they cast him out* (ἐξέβαλον αὐτὸν ἔξω), *i.e.,* out of the place of assembly; not excommunicated or unsynagogued him (cf. the different phrases in *v.* 22). But perhaps some form of excommunication is implied (*v.* 35).

36. *Who is he, Lord?* (=sir). As the man had already declared Jesus to be a prophet, he naturally believed He could point out the Messiah.

37. *Thou hast both seen him.* The Greek may be literally rendered, "Thou even (actually) seest (perfect in sense of present) Him, and He that speaketh with thee is He" (cf. iv. 26).

38. *Falling down he adored.* Although the verb προσκυνεῖν does

39 falling down he adored him. And Jesus said: For judgment I am come into this world; that they who see not
40 may see: and they who see, may become blind. And some of the Pharisees, who were with him, heard; and
41 they said unto him: Are we also blind? Jesus said to them: If you were blind, you should not have sin: But now you say: We see. Your sin remaineth.

not of itself necessarily imply supreme worship, yet St. John uses it solely of such supreme and Divine worship (iv. 20, 21, 22, 23, 24, xii. 20).

39. *For judgment* (κρίμα) *I am come* (came) *into this world*. As the man knelt at our Lord's feet in humble adoration (*v.* 38) our Lord, turning to the bystanders, explains the deep lesson of the miracle. The man had been blind both in mind and body; but in both he can now see. The Pharisees, although really blind of heart, had boasted that they could see (29, 34); but their pride involves them in still denser darkness. The term κρίμα, employed only in this place of the Gospel of St. John, occurs in the Apocalypse thrice (xvii. 1, xviii. 20, xx. 4), and in all three places it means a *sentence*, favourable or unfavourable. Outside the Apocalypse the term is used in the New Testament twenty-four times, so that it is easy to gather its meaning— a decree, a judgment which is formed or passed, a sentence.

that (ἵνα = in order that) *they who see not* (*i.e.*, those who are involved in the darkness of sin and ignorance) *may see* (of course, through their acceptance of grace and their obedience to the truth, i. 9, 12): *and they who see* (*i.e.*, wrap themselves up in the pride of self-sufficiency and boasted knowledge, as did the Pharisees), *may become blind* (*i.e.*, by God's decree and just sentence be buried in deeper darkness). Man's obstinacy is punished by withdrawal of grace. These results, on the one side salutary, on the other side condemnatory, of the Divine decree already passed, must not be confounded with the future judgment of eternal condemnation to be given by Christ (v. 22), from which judgment Christ desires to save all men (iii. 17); but such results are, in the case of the obstinate, true consequences, taking effect even in this life, that overtake those who believe not, and who are therefore "already judged" (iii. 18), and upon whom "the wrath of God abideth" (iii. 36). Compare, for the whole sentence, i. 4, 9, 12, iii. 14–21, 36, v. 22–24, viii. 21, 26. God's justice makes men eat the fruit of their own way.

40. *And some of the Pharisees.* Better, "And those of the Pharisees, who were with Him (probably for the purpose of malicious espionage), heard; (and, perceiving the spiritual drift of Christ's words) they said unto Him: But surely *we* also are not blind?"

41. *If you were blind* (*i.e.*, from simplicity and mere ignorance), *you should* (would) *not have sin: but now you say: We see* (are proudly self-reliant and boastful).

Your sin remaineth (abideth: cf. v. 38, vi. 27, 57).

CHAPTER X.

Our Lord's further Self-Manifestation.

(VERS. 1-21.)

AMEN, amen, I say to you: he that entereth not by the door into the sheepfold, but climbeth up

The continuation of our Lord's discourse is an allegory put in parabolic form—the nearest approach (cf. xv. 1-6) in St. John's Gospel to the parables of the Synoptics. In this allegory there are two points: (1) the door of the sheepfold; (2) the shepherd. In the first part (1-6) both are combined; in the second part (7-21) they are, for greater distinctness, treated separately. A parable is a short narrative of something in real life which shadows forth some ideal fact and is taken as a figure of that fact; but the figure is not applied to what it illustrates. The narrative is left, as a simple piece of narrative, to tell its own tale. An allegory, or extended metaphor, is an application or comparison of something real to an ideal fact; and the application of the figure is an essential part of the allegory. "A sower went forth to sow," is a parable; "I am the door," is an allegory. The following description, from 'The Land and the Book' (chap. xiv.), will help to an understanding of the allegory in St. John.

"Those low, flat buildings out on the sheltered side of the valley are sheepfolds. They are called mărăh, and, when the nights are cold, the flocks are shut up in them, but in ordinary weather they are merely kept within the yard. This is defended by a wide stone wall, crowned all around with sharp thorns . . .

"See, the flocks are returning home as the evening draws on . . . They are now converging to this single point from all quarters, like the separate squadrons of an army . . . They are so tame and so trained that they follow their keeper with the utmost docility. He leads them forth from the fold, or from their houses in the villages, just where he pleases. As there are many flocks in such a place as this, each one takes a different path, and it is his business to find pasture for them. It is necessary, therefore, that they should be taught to follow, and not

2 another way, the same is a thief and a robber. But he
that entereth in by the door, is the shepherd of the sheep.
3 To him the porter openeth ; and the sheep hear his voice :

to stray away into the unfenced fields of corn which lie so temptingly
on either side. Any one that thus wanders is sure to get into trouble.
The shepherd calls sharply from time to time to remind them of his
presence. They know his voice, and follow on ; but if a stranger call,
they stop short, lift up their heads in alarm, and, if it is repeated, they
turn and flee, because they know not the voice of a stranger. This is
not the fanciful costume of a parable; it is simple fact. I have made
the experiment repeatedly. The shepherd goes before, not merely to
point out the way, but to see that it is practicable and safe. He is
armed in order to defend his charge ; and in this he is very courageous.
Many adventures with wild beasts occur, for there are wolves in abundance, and leopards and panthers, exceeding fierce, prowl about these
wild wadies. They not infrequently attack the flock in the very presence of the shepherd, and he must be ready to do battle at a moment's
warning. I have listened with intense interest to their graphic descriptions of downright and desperate fights with these savage beasts.
And when the thief and the robber come (and come they do) the faithful
shepherd has often to put his life in his hand to defend his flock. I
have known more than one case in which he had literally to lay it down
in the contest. A poor faithful fellow last spring, between Tiberias and
Tabor, instead of fleeing, actually fought three Bedawin robbers until
he was hacked to pieces with their khanjars, and died among the sheep
he was defending.

"Some sheep always keep near the shepherd, and are his special
favourites. Each of them has a name, to which it answers joyfully;
and the kind shepherd is ever distributing to such choice portions
which he gathers for that purpose."

1. *Amen, amen, I say to you.* The address is continued to the
Pharisees of ix. 40, as is shown by a comparison of ix. 41 ('Jesus said
to them') with *v.* 1 ('I say to you') and *v.* 6 ('This proverb Jesus
spoke to them'); by the reference (*v.* 21) to the miracle just performed ; and by the fact that no discourse *begins* with the words
'Amen, amen,' except in answer to a question.

he that entereth not by the door. Since Christ is the door (*v.* 7),
the thief and robber is that self-made shepherd who has not been
legitimately appointed by Christ, but *climbeth up another way* (ἀλλα-
χόθεν = ἄλλοθεν : from another place). It occurs nowhere else in N. T.

2. *But he . . . is the shepherd.* No article: 'a shepherd'=a
shepherd indeed.

3. *To him the porter openeth.* A mere pictorial detail giving
greater life to the picture. When the various flocks are driven into a
large fold at night, they are given in charge to an under-shepherd, who,
of course, opens the door when each shepherd comes in the morning.
This detail gives vividness to the allegory, but must not be pressed as

and he calleth his own sheep by name, and leadeth them
out. And when he hath let out his own sheep, he goeth 4
before them : and the sheep follow him, because they know
his voice. But a stranger they follow not, but fly from 5
him, because they know not the voice of strangers. This 6
proverb Jesus spoke to them. But they understood not
what he spoke to them. Jesus therefore said to them 7
again : Amen, amen, I say to you, I am the door of the
sheep. All *others*, as many as have come, are thieves and 8
robbers : and the sheep heard them not. I am the door. 9
By me, if any man enter in, he shall be saved : and he

having any special and distinct application. In *vv*. 7, 8, no application is made of it.

4. *And when he hath let out* (ἐκβάλῃ = by taking hold of them and bringing them to the door) *his own sheep* (for several flocks may be together), *he goeth before them*.

5. *But a stranger* (not a thief or robber necessarily, but any one who is not their shepherd) *they follow not*. Better, 'they will certainly not follow, but will fly from him.'

6. *This proverb* (παροιμίαν). The term denotes either a wayside saying, or an out-of-the-way saying. Elsewhere in N. T. it appears only in xvi. 25, 29, and 2 Peter ii. 22.

But they understood not, i.e., did not perceive the drift.

7. *I am the door of the sheep.* Better, as the context is dealing with true and false shepherds, 'I am the door to the sheep.'

8. *All others, as many as have come*, (a probable reading adds, 'before Me') *are thieves and robbers*. The reference is not to any false Messiahs, for it is extremely doubtful whether there had been any such, but to the Pharisees and other blind leaders of the blind, against whom our Lord so frequently uttered such stern sayings. They were tyrannous (iii. 2, vii. 13, 49, ix. 22, 34) ; they crushed the people with intolerable burdens (Matt. xxiii. 4) ; they devoured the poor (Matt. xxiii. 14) ; they shut up the kingdom of heaven against men (Matt. xxiii. 13) ; and they left the people as sheep without a shepherd (Matt. ix. 36).

and (but) *the sheep heard them not*. That is, the true sheep did not follow them (cf. Matt. vii. 29).

9. *I am the door.* Emphatic repetition, quite in St. John's manner. Verse 9 repeats the thought of *v.* 7, and *v.* 10 the thought of *v.* 8. We must therefore take them as still referring to good and bad shepherds respectively.

By me (emphatic by position), *if any* (shepherd, not 'man': the words are simply ἐάν τις) *enter in, he shall be saved* (σωθήσεται = shall be delivered from danger, &c., by the protection afforded by the door): *and he shall go in and go out* (a Hebraism = shall act confidently ; or,

shall go in, and go out, and shall find pastures. The
thief cometh not, but for to steal and to kill and to destroy.
I am come that they may have life, and may have it more
abundantly. I am the good shepherd. The good shepherd giveth his life for his sheep. But the hireling, and he
that is not the shepherd, whose own the sheep are not,
seeth the wolf coming and leaveth the sheep and flieth:
and the wolf catcheth, and scattereth the sheep: and the
hireling flieth, because he is a hireling; and he hath no care
for the sheep. I am the good shepherd: and I know mine,
and mine know me. As the Father knoweth me, and I
know the Father: and I lay down my life for my sheep.
And other sheep I have, that are not of this fold; them

shall lead the sheep in and out, as in *v.* 3), *and shall find pastures*
(for this is the shepherd's work for the flock).

10. *The thief cometh not.* A thief has only one reason for his
coming, and that reason is a bad one (cf. *vv.* 1 and 8).

I am come (came). Christ now contrasts Himself with the false
shepherds, and by this fresh antithesis prepares the way for a transition
to the second part of the explanation of the allegory.

may have it more abundantly (καὶ περισσὸν ἔχωσιν = and have
abundance, or, have it overflowingly, abundantly). Cf. i. 16, vi. 52,
58.

11. *I am the good shepherd* (ὁ ποιμὴν ὁ καλός, i.e., *the* shepherd,
the only absolutely good one). In the prophets the Messiah was
foretold under the image of a shepherd of the people (Isa. xl. 11;
Ezech. xxxiv. 23, xxxvii. 24), and the definite article points to that
well-known description. The epithet 'good' may be taken in the
sense in which we speak of 'a good musician,' or 'a good poet.'

giveth his life (τίθησιν = layeth down, putteth down, payeth) *for*
(ὑπὲρ = for the good of) *his sheep.* The phrase 'to lay down his life'
is Johannean; in the Synoptics the phrase is 'to give his life.'

12. *But the hireling* (μισθωτός: the term elsewhere in N. T. only
in Mark i. 20). It denotes here one who is a mere mercenary, one
that "feeds himself." See Ezech. xxxiv.

seeth the wolf coming. By 'wolf' is understood every foe, or adverse
power: whatever seduces, persecutes, or leads into error any of the
sheep.

and the wolf catcheth (i.e., seizeth individual sheep), *and scattereth*
(the flock). The words, from 'scattereth' (*v.* 12) to 'because' (*v.* 13)
are doubtful. Moreover, *v.* 15 is connected with *v.* 14: "I know mine,
and mine know me, as the Father knoweth me, and I know the
Father."

16. *And other sheep I have.* This is said by anticipation and
prophetically (cf. Psa. ii. 8; Acts xviii. 10).

also I must bring, and they shall hear my voice, and there shall be one fold and one shepherd. Therefore doth the Father love me : because I lay down my life that I may take it again. No man taketh it away from me : but I lay it down of myself, and I have power to lay it down ; and I have power to take it up again. This commandment have I received of my Father. A dissension rose again among

that are not of this fold. These were the Gentiles, "the children of God, that were dispersed," and so in no fold (xi. 52). The emphasis, therefore, falls on 'fold,' not on 'this.' Hence there is only one fold.

there shall be one fold (ποίμνη = flock) *and one shepherd.* St. John tells (xxi. 15-17) how our Lord just before the Ascension appointed St. Peter to be the one visible shepherd of all the flock on earth, and committed to his care the whole flock : "Feed my lambs ; feed my sheep." Thus we have one shepherd, one flock, one fold—the visible unity of the Church, under one chief visible ruler.

17. *Therefore doth the Father love me.* Better, 'For this cause.' The full meaning is, 'Because I am the Good Shepherd, therefore the Father loveth Me, because, namely, I lay down My life' (cf. v. 16 and note on viii. 29).

that (in order that) *I may take it* (take it up) *again.* Our redemption was accomplished not only by the death, but also by the resurrection of Christ. By both Christ fought with, and triumphed over, sin and death, the two great evils brought upon mankind by the Fall (Rom. v. 8-21 ; 1 Cor. xv. 17-28). Although, therefore, Christ lays down His life, and for this obedience unto death the Father loves Him, yet He lays it down of His own free will, and with the intention of taking it up again for the triumph of His sheep.

18. *This commandment.* Christ as man did the Father's will in all things (viii. 28, 29). Therefore it is in obedience to the Father's command that He not only lays down His life, but also takes it up again. If, then, He died, it was not because the Jews had power, against His will, to take away His life, but because, in obedience to the Father, and the very perfection of the Sacred Humanity precluded all danger of disobedience, He laid it down and took it up again.

This commandment have I received. Better, 'I received,' *i.e.*, at the Incarnation.

The last discourses of our Lord had occasioned a controversy or dissension among the Jews. His enemies were eager for a declaration so clear that they could fasten upon it as a ground of accusation against Him. When, therefore, He appears at the Feast of the Dedication, they come crowding round Him—literally 'round' Him, and barring His way—and ask for a plain confession as to His office and Person. At first He declines to answer. He had already spoken with sufficient plainness, but they had not believed ; His works, too, had given unimpeachable witness that He was sent by the Father ; but perversity of

20, 21 the Jews for these words. And many of them said: He hath a devil, and is mad: why hear you him? Others said: These are not the words of one that hath a devil: Can a devil open the eyes of the blind?

The Feast of Dedication.

(VERS. 22-42).

22 And it was the feast of the dedication at Jerusalem;

will blinded the Jews. He then declares His oneness with the Father, for which declaration the Jews took up stones to stone Him. He justifies His declaration and shows that Jewish unbelief is without excuse. They attempt to seize Him, but He escapes.

At Bethany our Lord displays His Divine power by a stupendous miracle—the raising of Lazarus, who had been four days dead. The miracle is symbolical of our Lord's power as the Resurrection and the Life. It inflames the enmity of the Pharisees to intensest fierceness, and they inexorably resolve on His death.

22. *It was the feast of the dedication* (τὰ ἐγκαίνια = consecration: Vulgate, 'encaenia' = renovation). This feast was instituted by Judas Maccabaeus in B.C. 164 in commemoration of the purification and re-dedication of the Temple and altar after they had been desecrated by Antiochus Epiphanes (1 Mach. iv. 56-59). It was to be 'kept in its season from year to year for eight days, from the five and twentieth day of the month of Casleu (Chislev), with joy and gladness.' Casleu was the ninth month of the religious year, and corresponded to November-December. The feast, therefore, fell in the latter month, and about the time of the winter solstice.

There were many points of resemblance, undoubtedly designed, between this feast and the Feast of Tabernacles. Originally the people appeared at it 'with boughs, and green branches, and palms,' in express remembrance of what was done at the Feast of Tabernacles (2 Mach. x. 1-9). During the eight days of the feast the set of psalms known as the Hallel was chanted in the Temple as at Tabernacles. At a later date was introduced the custom of illuminating not only the Temple, but also every private house. The zealous set up a light for each person in the house, and added an equal number each succeeding night, so that in a house of ten persons there would be eighty lights burning on the last night of the feast. Hence it was sometimes called 'The Feast of Lights.' This illumination was symbolical. "As the once extinguished light was re-lit in the Temple, it grew day by day in brightness, till it shone out into the heathen darkness, that once had threatened to quench it. That Christ, who purified the Temple and was its True Light, should have spent the last anniversary season of His birth at that feast in the Sanctuary, shining into their darkness, seems most fitting" (Eders., l.c., p. 368).

and it was winter. And Jesus walked in the temple in 23
Solomon's porch. The Jews therefore came round about 24
him, and said to him: How long dost thou hold our souls
in suspense? if thou be the Christ tell us plainly. Jesus 25
answered them: I speak to you, and you believe not: the
works that I do in the name of my Father, they give
testimony of me. But you do not believe, because you 26
are not of my sheep. My sheep hear my voice: and I 27
know them, and they follow me. And I give them life 28
everlasting; and they shall not perish for ever, and no man
shall pluck them out of my hand. That which my Father 29
hath given me is greater than all: and no one can snatch

23. *Solomon's porch.* A covered porch in front of the Beautiful Gate, which formed the principal entrance into the Court of the Women.

25. *I speak to you.* Better, 'I told you, and you believe not.'

27. *My sheep hear my voice.* This verse explains what was said in v. 26, 'You are not of my sheep,' namely, because you will not hear My voice. He invites the Jews to become, by hearing and obeying, His sheep, and to share in that blessedness.

I know them, with the knowledge of approval and affection. *They follow me. And I give them life everlasting.* Observe the parallelism (27-28).

28. *They shall not perish for ever, and* (=for) *no man shall pluck* (seize, snatch: the same verb as in v. 12) *them out of my hand.* Those that are lost, are lost of their own free will, which Christ does not coerce; they cannot be lost through defect of Christ's protecting power.

29. *That which my Father hath given me is greater* (neuter) *than all* (*i.e.*, besides God). Our Lord, in this and the following verse, assigns the reason for the statement just made (v. 28). No enemy can snatch the sheep from Christ's hand, because the power given by the Father to Christ is supreme, invincible, omnipotent. The Vulgate reading, which is here followed, is the more difficult reading, and therefore the more probable. Another well-attested reading, but easier, and therefore a probably corrected reading, gives, 'My Father, who hath given (the sheep to Me) is greater than all.' The sense comes to the same. Our Lord's argument is this, 'No one can snatch the sheep from My hand, because the Father gave Me a power greater than all; and the power is greater than all, because *I and the Father are one*. 'One' is in the neuter; consequently it does not mean one Person, but, as also the very form of the argument shows, one power, one omnipotence. But if one power, therefore one nature or essence. This claim seemed blasphemous. *The Jews then* (therefore) *took up stones to stone him.*

30 *them* out of the hand of my Father. I and the Father are
31 one. The Jews then took up stones to stone him. Jesus
32 answered them: Many good works I have shewed you
from my Father; for which of those works do you stone
33 me? The Jews answered him: For a good work we stone
thee not, but for blasphemy; and because that thou, being
34 a man, makest thyself God. Jesus answered them: Is it
35 not written in your law: *I said, you are gods?* If he
called them gods, to whom the word of God was spoken,
36 and the scripture cannot be broken; do you say of him,
whom the Father hath sanctified and sent into the world:
Thou blasphemest, because I said, I am the Son of God?
37 If I do not the works of my Father, believe me not. But
38 if I do, though you will not believe me, believe the works:
that you may know and believe that the Father is in me,
39 and I in the Father. They sought therefore to take him;
40 and he escaped out of their hands. And he went again
beyond the Jordan into that place where John was baptiz-

32. *For which of those works do you* (present, in sense of immediate future = are you about to) *stone me?*

34. *Is it not written in your law?* Our Lord repels the charge of blasphemy, not by explaining away what He had said, but by an argumentum ad hominem. In Scripture (e.g., Psa. lxxxi. 6) the judges of the people, inasmuch as they were representatives of the Divine authority, are called 'gods.' Now, the judges did not receive their appointment from God directly and immediately, but only remotely; to them "the word of the Lord came" through the divinely established system of things. If, then, such judges could, without blasphemy, be called 'gods,' how was it blasphemy for Christ, who was consecrated by the Father to the Messianic office and came immediately from the Father, to call Himself the Son of God? The term 'law' is used for O.T. generally (xii. 34, xv. 25; Rom. iii. 19).

37. *If I do not the works of my Father* (explained v. 17, 18, 36).

38. *That you may know and believe* (γνῶτε καὶ γινώσκητε = that you may perceive and continually know) *that the Father is in me, and I in the Father* (cf. v. 30, 'I and the Father are one'). Not only by an argumentum ad hominem, but by direct proof, our Lord justifies His claim. In the eyes of the Jews, therefore, the blasphemy remained.

39. *They sought therefore* (or, again) *to take him; and he escaped* (ἐξῆλθεν: same verb as in viii. 59, which see).

40. *He went again beyond the Jordan.* That is, into Peræa.
into that place where John was baptizing first. That is, in Bethania (see on i. 28, and cf. iii. 23).

ing first: and there he abode. And many resorted to him, 41
and they said: John indeed did no sign: but all things 42
whatsoever John said of this man were true. And many
believed in him.

and there he abode. The stay could not have been a long one. It was only between three and four months to the Pasch when our Lord was put to death; and during the interval He went to Bethania, near Jerusalem (xi. 18), and abode for some time in Ephrem (xi. 54).

41. *John indeed did no sign.* That is, worked no miracle. But his life was miraculous, and his influence, in consequence, very great. Josephus indicates how great that influence was, when he records that some of the Jews thought "that the destruction of Herod's army (by Aretas) came from God, and that very justly, as a punishment of what he did against John, that was called the Baptist" (Ant. xviii. 5. 2). Since no one thought of attributing miracles to John, although John was so holy and so influential, we conclude that miracles were attributed to our Lord only because He had wrought them. It was this fact that impressed the Jews, *and they said* (kept saying) *John indeed did no sign. But all things whatsoever John said of this man were true.* The events of our Lord's public ministry were in harmony with what John had foretold. John had thus given the true prophetic sign appointed by God (Deut. xviii. **21**; Jer. xxviii. 9).

42. *And many believed in him.* The Greek adds 'there,' *i.e.*, in Perœa, where they were removed from the tyranny and overbearing influence of the leaders.

CHAPTER XI

The Raising of Lazarus.

(VERS. 1-54.)

NOW there was a certain man sick named Lazarus, of Bethania, of the town of Mary and of Martha her 2 sister. (And Mary was she that anointed the Lord with ointment and wiped his feet with her hair: whose brother

Our Lord was still in Peræa when a message was brought that Lazarus, whom He loved, was sick. But He waited for two days before starting for Bethania—indeed, until He knew, without the aid of messengers, that Lazarus was dead (6, 11, 12, 13). Like the other miracles recorded by St. John, the raising of Lazarus is symbolical. It typifies the great truth, 'I am the resurrection and the life: he that believeth in me although he be dead, shall live." But the miracle also marks a crisis in our Lord's own life. For in consequence of this miracle the Sanhedrin finally resolved to put Him to death, the High-priest declaring that Jesus must die, whether guilty or no, to remove all danger of resentment on the part of the Romans against the nation (47-51).

1. *Bethania* (see *v.* 18 and cf. i. 28). It was on the eastern slope of the Mount of Olives.

the town of Mary and of Martha. Better, perhaps, 'village.' St. John writes as if supposing that the sisters are already known to the reader. They must therefore be identified with the sisters, Martha and Mary, of Luke x. 38-42. Nothing is said in St. Luke of Lazarus. Many therefore conclude that he was much younger than his sisters. The name Lazarus is an abbreviated Greek form of Eleazar = whom God helps.

2. *And Mary was she that anointed* (ἡ ἀλείψασα) *the Lord with ointment and wiped his feet with her hair.* Does this look forward to the narrative that follows (xii. 3: cf. Matt. xxvi. 6-13; Mark xiv. 3-9), or does it look backward to the event narrated in Luke (vii. 36-38)? The answer is difficult. Yet St. John's usual manner of writing seems rather to imply that the participle recalls an event that had happened

Lazarus was sick.) His sisters therefore sent to him, saying: Lord, behold, he whom thou lovest is sick. And Jesus hearing it, said to them: This sickness is not unto death, but for the glory of God: that the Son of God may be glorified by it. Now Jesus loved Martha, and her sister

before the period referred to in the narrative in which the participle occurs. Thus the participle in vii. 50 (ὁ ἐλθὼν πρὸς αὐτόν) refers back to iii. 2 (cf. xix. 39), and the participle in xviii. 14 (ὁ συμβουλεύσας) to the narrative in xi. 49–51. But only one anointing had been recorded as having occurred before the present event in our Lord's life, viz., the anointing described in Luke vii. Hence St. John recalls that anointing, and supplies, what St. Luke had omitted, the name of the woman. We conclude, therefore, that the woman who was a sinner is identical with Mary the sister of Lazarus.

The reasons for identifying Mary of Bethania with Mary Magdalen are much slighter. St. Luke certainly gives no hint that 'Mary who is called Magdalen' (viii. 2) is the same person as the sinner of the immediately preceding narrative (vii. 36–50). It is noteworthy, too, that St. John introduces Mary Magdalen (xix. 25) in such a way that the very epithet 'Magdalen' seems chosen to distinguish her from the Mary of chapter xi. At any rate, although so careful in such matters he here gives no note of identification, but rather marks a distinction. The sister of Lazarus is always simply Mary (xi 1, 2, 5, 19, 20, 28, 31, 32, 45, xii. 3) and her village is Bethany; the other Mary is always Magdalen (xix. 25, xx. 1, 18), i.e., Mary of Magdala, in Genezareth. A similar mark of distinction is observable in St. Luke (cf. x. 39, 42 with viii. 2, xxiv. 10). There is, it is true, a strong Western tradition, from the time especially of St. Gregory the Great, that Mary of Bethany is the same as Magdalen (see Roman Breviary and Missal for 22nd of July); but the Fathers are not unanimous, and the tradition is not decisive. Under these circumstances we follow the presumptive evidence of St. John's language—identifying Mary of Bethany with the sinful woman, but distinguishing her from Mary Magdalen. Yet even the identification of Mary of Bethany with the sinful woman is very problematical; for, although St. John's language points in the direction of identification, St. Luke's narrative more naturally suggests distinction (cf. vii. 36–50 and x. 38–42).

3. *His sisters therefore, i.e.*, because he was sick. The request for help lay in the simple message that Lazarus was in danger.

4. *And Jesus hearing it, said to them.* The phrase 'to them' is an insertion.

This sickness is not unto (πρός) *death* (i.e., is not to result in death), *but for* (ὑπέρ = for the furtherance of) *the glory of God.* "Even that death itself was not unto death, but rather unto the working of a miracle" (St. Aug., Tract xlix. c. 6).

5. *Now Jesus loved* (ἠγάπα: a delicately chosen word, not the more emotional φιλεῖν of v. 3). This verse explains what follows.

6 Mary, and Lazarus. When he had heard therefore that
he was sick, he still remained in the same place two days:
7 then after that he said to his disciples: Let us go into
8 Judea again. The disciples say to him: Rabbi, the Jews
but now sought to stone thee: and goest thou thither
9 again? Jesus answered: Are there not twelve hours of
the day? If a man walk in the day, he stumbleth not,
10 because he seeth the light of this world: but if he walk in
the night he stumbleth, because the light is not in him.
11 These things he said: and after that he said to them:
Lazarus our friend sleepeth; but I go that I may awake
12 him out of sleep. His disciples therefore said: Lord, if

Because our Lord loved Lazarus, He 'therefore' remained two days in
Perea (v. 6), so as to make the miracle on behalf of Lazarus more
striking.

8. *The Jews but now sought* (were seeking) *to stone thee*: see x. 31.

9. *Are there not twelve hours of the day?* (see on i. 39). To the
anxiety of the disciples for His safety our Lord opposes His own
perfect assurance that His hour has not yet come. This is done in
figurative language. While the twelve hours of daylight lasted a man
might walk without dashing his foot against an obstacle, but when the
light is withdrawn, then he dashes his foot. Christ had received His
working day from the Father, and until that day had come to a close
the Jews had no power over Him, nor would Christ Himself waste
that day.

11. *Lazarus, our friend, sleepeth* (κεκοίμηται = has fallen asleep).
This was known to our Lord, not by message, but by immediate
knowledge.

The opening words of the sentence, 'These things he said: *and
after that* (better, this) he said,' mark a separation between the two
discourses, which are separated by a pause.

Lazarus was said, on account of the resurrection so soon to follow,
to be asleep. "To his sisters he was dead, to the Lord he was asleep.
He was dead to men, who could not raise him again; but the Lord
aroused him with as great ease from the tomb as one arouseth a sleeper
from his bed. Hence it was in reference to His own power that He
spoke of him as sleeping: for others also, who are dead, are frequently
spoken of in Scripture (*e.g.*, Matt. ix. 24, xxvii. 52; 1 Cor. xv. 6, 18,
20; 1 Thess. iv. 13, 14) as sleeping" (St. Aug., Tract xlix. c. 9).

The disciples, whose minds are filled with anxiety for our Lord's
safety, do not attend to the second part of the sentence, 'I go that I
may awake him,' but are absorbed in what corresponded so much to
their wishes, 'Lazarus sleepeth.' If Lazarus was asleep, the crisis of
his illness was over, and there was no need for Christ to enter Judea
(*v.* 12). *If he sleep, he shall do well* (σωθήσεται = he will be cured).

he sleep, he shall do well. But Jesus spoke of his death; 13
and they thought that he spoke of the repose of sleep.
Then therefore Jesus said to them plainly: Lazarus is 14
dead; and I am glad for your sakes, that I was not 15
there, that you may believe: but let us go to him. Thomas 16
therefore, who is called Didymus, said to his fellow-disciples: Let us also go, that we may die with him. Jesus 17
therefore came and found that he had been four days
already in the grave. (Now Bethania was near Jerusalem, 18
about fifteen furlongs off.) And many of the Jews were 19
come to Martha and Mary, to comfort them concerning
their brother. Martha therefore, as soon as she heard that 20
Jesus was come, went to meet him; but Mary sat at home.

14. *Lazarus is dead.* This plain declaration, coming after the statement, 'This sickness is not unto death' (v. 4), would cause painful surprise. Hence our Lord says that all had happened designedly for the sake of the disciples themselves.

16. *Didymus.* The Greek for the Aramaic Thomas, meaning 'twin.'

that we may die. He evidently believed that a return to Judea meant death (v. 8).

17. *Jesus therefore came.* That is, came into the neighbourhood of Bethany (v. 30), which was fifteen furlongs (less than two miles) from Jerusalem (v. 18: cf. vi. 19).

and found that he had been (ἔχοντα: cf. v. 5) *four days already in the grave* (μνημείῳ = sepulchre). According to custom, the funeral would take place on the day of death (v. 39; cf. Acts v. 6, 10). It is unnatural to suppose that Lazarus was already dead when our Lord sent the message of hope to the sisters (v. 4). The narrative obviously suggests that the death did not occur before the words of vv. 7-11 were spoken. Thus our Lord spent four days on the journey.

19. *Many of the Jews.* Probably people of position from the district and from Jerusalem itself. Since the narrative implies that Lazarus was buried not in a common cemetery, but in his own private sepulchre, in a cave (v. 38)—probably, according to custom, in a garden—his family must have been fairly well-to-do.

to comfort them. This would be in obedience to the Rabbinic injunction. Mourning for seven days seems to have been obligatory (Judith xvi. 29; Eccli. xxii. 13), but it really lasted for thirty days. There were three days of weeping, a special week of sorrow, and twenty days of less intense mourning.

20. *Martha therefore.* Martha appears to have been the eldest of the family, and to have had care of the household. The description of the sisters perfectly corresponds with that given in St. Luke (x. 38).

21 Martha therefore said to Jesus : Lord, if thou hadst been
22 here, my brother had not died. But now also I know that
whatsoever thou wilt ask of God, God will give it thee.
23 Jesus saith to her : Thy brother shall rise again. Martha
24 saith to him : I know that he shall rise again in the resur-
25 rection at the last day. Jesus said to her : I am the
resurrection and the life : he that believeth in me although
26 he be dead, shall live : and every one that liveth, and believeth in me, shall not die for ever. Believest thou this ?
27 She saith to him : Yea, Lord, I have believed that thou
art Christ the Son of the living God, who art come into
28 this world. And when she had said these things, she went,
and called her sister Mary secretly, saying : The master is

21. *If thou hadst been here.* This is what the two sisters must have frequently said to each other (cf. v. 32) from the time they had sent their message to our Lord (v. 3). But even death has not destroyed their hope ; for their belief in Christ's power can beg for the resurrection of the dead. The rumours of the raising of the widow's son at Naim had gone forth throughout all Judea (Luke vii. 17). Why should not Lazarus be raised? Martha makes the appeal (v. 22).

22. *God will give it thee.* She does not yet understand that Christ is God ; but she believes in His Divine mission (v. 27) and in His power to restore Lazarus "now also" (καὶ νῦν = even now).

25. *I am the resurrection and the life.* Not merely by supplication to the Father, but by His own power, Christ is the source of life. "Thou sayest my brother shall rise again at the last day : true, but by Him through whom he shall rise then, can he rise even now, for I am the Resurrection and the Life. The Resurrection because the Life" (St. Aug., Tract xlix. c. 14).

he that believeth in me, although he be dead (better, even though he die, *i.e.*, bodily), *shall live* (*i.e.*, shall come to the resurrection of life (v. 25, 29) I am the resurrection).

26. *And every one that liveth, and believeth in me, shall not die for ever* (*i.e.*, shall have eternal life, shall live in the spirit ; till the flesh also rise again, never more to die = I am the life : cf. vi. 39, 40).

Believest thou this? Martha's answer shows that she had not fully understood. But she makes a most emphatic act of faith in Christ as the Messiah, and in His power to do what as yet she only imperfectly understands.

27. *Yea* (ναί = very emphatic assertion), *Lord, I have believed* (perfect = I have believed and do believe) *that thou art Christ, the Son of the living God, who art come* (that cometh) *into this world* (= ὁ ἐρχόμενος = the Coming One = the Messiah : cf. vi. 14, i. 15).

28. *Secretly.* That is, to escape being overheard by the assembled Jews.

come and calleth for thee. She, as soon as she heard *this*, riseth quickly and cometh to him. For Jesus was not yet come into the town; but he was still in that place where Martha had met him. The Jews therefore who were with her in the house and comforted her, when they saw Mary that she rose up speedily and went out, followed her, saying: She goeth to the grave, to weep there. When Mary therefore was come where Jesus was, seeing him, she fell down at his feet, and saith to him: Lord, if thou hadst been here, my brother had not died. Jesus therefore, when he saw her weeping, and the Jews that were come with her, weeping, groaned in the spirit, and troubled him-

calleth for thee. "The evangelist has not said where, or when, or how the Lord called for Mary, namely, that in order to preserve the brevity of the narrative it may rather be understood from the words of Martha" (St. Aug., Tract xlix. c. 16).

30. *Where Martha had met* (ὑπήντησεν: aorist in relative sentence for pluperfect) *him :* see v. 20.

31. *The Jews therefore.* They followed Mary, thinking that she was again going to weep at the sepulchre of Lazarus. It was the custom to visit the grave, especially during the first three days. By this following of the Jews the great miracle had the presence of many witnesses.

to weep there. The verb κλαίω used here and in v. 33 means to weep audibly, to cry; whereas the verb δακρύω, used in v. 35, means to weep silently.

32. *When Mary therefore.* "When she came to Jesus she was forgetful of all around. She could only fall at His feet, and repeat the poor words with which she and her sister had these four weary days tried to cover the nakedness of their sorrow. For the rest it was far better to add nothing more, but simply to worship at His feet. It must have been a deeply touching scene : the outpouring of her sorrow, the absoluteness of her faith, the mute appeal of her tears. And the Jews who witnessed it were moved as she, and wept with her. What follows is difficult to understand. But if with a realization of Christ's condescension to, and union with humanity as its Healer, by taking upon Himself its diseases, we combine the statement formerly made about the resurrection (I am the Resurrection and the Life)—we may, in some way, not understand, but be able to gaze into the unfathomed depth of that fellow-suffering which was both vicarious and redemptive" (Eders. l.c., p. 435).

33. *Groaned* (ἐνεβριμήσατο) *in the spirit.* This verb is found five times in N. T., twice in St. John (here and v. 38), twice in St. Mark (i. 43, xiv. 5), and once in St. Matthew (ix. 30). Now, in Matthew and in Mark i. 43 it means to enjoin or to charge with stern

34 self, and said: Where have you laid him? They say to
35 him: Lord, come and see. And Jesus wept. The Jews
36 therefore said: Behold how he loved him. But some of
37 them said: Could not he that opened the eyes of the man
born blind, have caused that this man should not die?
38 Jesus therefore again groaning in himself, cometh to the
sepulchre: Now it was a cave; and a stone was laid over
39 it. Jesus saith: Take away the stone. Martha, the sister
of him that was dead, saith to him: Lord, by this time he

admonition; in Mark (xiv. 5) it is translated "to murmur at" = to be angry with. This is its classical sense—'to be very angry,' 'to be moved with indignation.' In this sense it is used by St. John. We notice, therefore, that our Lord was at once angry and sorrowful. Sorrowful for the death of Lazarus and the grief it caused (vv. 33, 35). But angry at what? St. John's references to 'the prince of this world,' against whose empire our Lord came on behalf of mankind (xii. 31, xiv. 30, xvi. 11), give us the idea that our Lord's anger was against Satan, who was a murderer from the beginning (viii. 44). The death of Lazarus, like the sin of Judas (xiii. 21), was Satan's handiwork, and as such 'troubled' our Lord.

and troubled himself. "For who could trouble Him save He Himself? Therefore, my brethren, first give heed to the power that did so, and then look for the meaning. Thou art troubled against thy will; Christ was troubled because He willed. In His own power it lay to be thus and thus affected or not. For the Word assumed soul and flesh, fitting on Himself our whole human nature in the oneness of His Person. . . . By this Word, wherein resided the supreme power, was infirmity made use of at the beck of His will; and in this way 'He troubled Himself'" (St. Aug., Tract xlix. c. 18).

34. *Where have you laid him?* "Thou knewest that he was dead, and art Thou ignorant of the place of his burial? . . . Similar in character was God's voice in Paradise after man had sinned: 'Adam, where art thou?'" (St. Aug., Tract xlix. c. 20).

35. *And Jesus wept* (see on v. 31). Thus He teaches us the lawfulness of moderate sorrow for the loss of friends and the charity of weeping with those that mourn (see v. 42).

37. *But some of them said.* There is no hint in the words that follow of unbelief, or scepticism, or irony, or malevolence; they are a most natural expression of simple wonder that He, who had worked so great a miracle on the man born blind, should now seem to weep helplessly over Lazarus.

39. *He is now of four days.* It was the common Jewish idea that corruption commenced on the fourth day, that the drop of gall which had fallen from the sword of the Angel and caused death, was then working its effect, and that, as the face changed, the soul took its final leave from the resting-place of the body (Eders l.c., p. 434).

stinketh, for he is now of four days. Jesus saith to her: 40
Did not I say to thee, that if thou believe, thou shalt see
the glory of God? They took therefore the stone away. 41
And Jesus lifting up his eyes said: Father, I give thee
thanks that thou hast heard me. And I knew that thou 42
hearest me always, but because of the people who stand
about have I said it; that they may believe that thou hast
sent me. When he had said these things, he cried with a 43
loud voice: Lazarus, come forth. And presently he that 44
had been dead came forth, bound feet and hands with
winding-bands, and his face was bound about with a
napkin. Jesus said to them: Loose him and let him
go. Many therefore of the Jews who were come to Mary 45

40. *Did not I say to thee?* For such had been the purport of His reply to the messenger (v. 4).

41. *Father, I give thee thanks.* The miracle has not yet been wrought; but our Lord *knew* that the Father *always* heard Him (v. 42). He returned thanks not for Himself, but for the bystanders. Salvation comes through faith in Christ (v. 40, vi. 40, viii. 24), and that faith is the Father's gift (vi. 44). The miracle, therefore, was a great grace, leading the bystanders to believe that Christ was the Son of God (v. 4), the Resurrection and the Life (vv. 25, 26), the Sent of the Father (v. 42), and one in power with the Father (x. 30). Not for the raising of Lazarus, then, but rather for the ordering and arranging of all the circumstances to so salutary a result, is thanksgiving made.

43. *Lazarus, come forth* (δεῦρο ἔξω). Literally, "Lazarus, hither, outside!"

44. *Bound feet and hands.* The body was dressed, and, at a later period, wrapped, if possible, in the worn cloths in which originally a roll of the law had been held.

winding-bands (κειρίαις). The word occurs only here in N. T.

his face (ὄψις). Used only here, vii. 24, and Apoc. i. 16.

napkin (σουδαρίῳ). Literally, 'sweat-cloth'—the Latin 'sudarium.'

Loose him. St. Augustine applying this passage says, "What is the coming forth but the open acknowledgment thou makest of thy state, in quitting, as it were, the old refuges of darkness? But the confession thou makest is effected by God, when He crieth with a loud voice; or, in other words, calleth thee in abounding grace. Accordingly, when the dead man had come forth, still bound; confessing, yet guilty still; that his sins also might be taken away, the Lord said to His servants: 'Loose him, and let him go.' What does He mean by such words? Whatsoever ye shall loose on earth shall be loosed in heaven" Tract xlix. c. 25).

45. *Many therefore of the Jews.* According to the Greek text, 'all

and Martha, and had seen the things that Jesus did, believed in him. But some of them went to the Pharisees, 47 and told them the things that Jesus had done. The chief priests therefore and the Pharisees gathered a council, and 48 said: What do we, for this man doth many miracles? If we let him alone so, all will believe in him, and the Romans will come, and take away our place and nation. 49 But one of them named Caiphas, being the high-priest that

of the Jews,' and they were many, who had witnessed the miracle, believed: πολλοὶ οὖν ἐκ τῶν Ἰουδαίων οἱ ἐλθόντες κ.τ.λ., (not τῶν ἐλθόντων κ.τ.λ.).

46. *But some of them.* This may mean 'some Jews,' viz., some of the Jews generally, who had not seen the miracle; or it may mean, 'some of those who had seen and believed.' In the first case, their going to the Pharisees was malicious; in the second case, the going was rather to speak in favour of our Lord (cf. v. 12-15).

The narrative of the miracle is evidently that of an eye-witness. Its truth cannot be denied except by those who, on principle, deny the possibility of all miracles. The other evangelists, who omit so much of what St. John has recorded, have omitted this and other miracles performed in Judea, because they confined themselves almost exclusively to our Lord's work in Galilee. St. John, on his side, omits the raisings narrated in the other gospels, because he, too, kept strictly to his own purpose.

47. *The chief priests.* The Sadducees, therefore, join the Pharisees in a general meeting of the Sanhedrin (council). They meet not to judge the claims of our Lord, not to test His doctrine and miracles, but simply to concert measures to remove Him out of the way for fear of political consequences if the populace should proclaim Him the Messiah-King.

48. *Take away our place and nation* (both our place and our nation). Probably = destroy the Holy City, and take away the people as captives.

49. *Caiphas.* According to Josephus, Ananos (Annas), the son of Seth, was appointed high-priest by Quirinus. This is the high-priest so well known in the N. T. (Luke iii. 2; John xviii. 13-24; Acts iv. 6). He was in office A.D. 6-15. But Valerius Gratus, setting him aside, appointed Ismael, the son of Phabi; and a year later (A.D. 16-17) appointed Eleasar, the son of Annas; and again in about a year, Simon, the son of Kamithos; and almost immediately afterwards appointed Joseph, surnamed Caiphas (Kajaph), who was high-priest from about A.D. 18 to 36. St. John (xviii. 13) tells us that Caiphas was son-in-law of Annas. We may thus readily understand that Annas still retained an extensive influence, and practically retained the power of the high-priesthood in his own hands. For, during this period (A.D. 6-36), the high-priesthood was almost exclusively in the family of

year, said to them: You know nothing: neither do you 50
consider that it is expedient for you that one man should
die for the people, and that the whole nation perish not.
And this he spoke not of himself: but being the high- 51
priest of that year, he prophesied that Jesus should die for
the nation. And not only for the nation, but to gather to- 52
gether in one the children of God, that were dispersed.
From that day therefore they devised to put him to death. 53
Wherefore Jesus walked no more openly among the Jews, 54
but he went into a country near the desert, unto a city
that is called Ephrem, and there he abode with his disciples. And the pasch of the Jews was at hand: and 55

Annas. Hence St. Luke (iii. 2) speaks of "the high-priests Annas and Caiphas" almost as if they were simultaneously in power. And in Acts (iv. 6) he shows the preponderating influence of the family in the Sanhedrin, "Annas, the high-priest, and Caiphas and John and Alexander, and as many as were of the kindred of the high-priest." The family was identified with the chief power.

being the high-priest that year. This does not mean that the office of high-priest was held only for a year, but that during the year in which these memorable events took place Caiphas was high-priest.

51. *He prophesied.* Of himself Caiphas simply quoted a well-known Jewish proverb, 'It is better one man should die than the community perish'; but as high-priest he became unconsciously, and in spite of himself, a prophet and the mouth-piece of God.

52. *The children of God;* see on x. 16. "This was the last prophecy in Israel; with the sentence of death on Israel's true high-priest died prophecy in Israel, died Israel's high-priesthood. It had spoken sentence upon itself" (Eders. l.c., p. 436).

53. *They devised.* The verb may mean either 'they resolved upon, decreed, His death,' or 'they considered *how* to put Him to death.' In the first case forty days were allowed for the production of witnesses for the defence.

54. *Ephrem* (Ephraim). The 'desert' or wilderness probably means the grassy mountain lands near Jerusalem; and Josephus mentions a small fort named Ephraim in the mountain district north of Judæa, which he couples with Bethel. Robinson identifies it with a village now called et-Taiyibeh, situated on a conspicuous conical hill commanding a view over the valley of the Jordan and the Dead Sea. It is four miles N.E. of Bethel, and about fourteen miles from Jerusalem (Hastings, B.D.).

55. *To purify themselves* That is, to undergo the prescribed purification in the Temple for any case of Levitical defilement. According to Numbers (ix. 6–10) one legally unclean, "by occasion of one that is dead," could not eat the Pasch, but had to wait till the fourteenth day

many from the country went up to Jerusalem before the
56 pasch, to purify themselves. They sought therefore for
Jesus; and they discoursed one with another, standing in
the temple: What think you, that he is not come to the
festival day? And the chief priests and the Pharisees had
given a commandmant, that if any man knew where he
was, he should tell, that they might apprehend him.

of the second month. Josephus speaks of several kinds of legal defilement, which forbade the defiled to eat the Pasch (Wars, vi. 9, 3). The purifications varied greatly (washings, sacrifices, &c.) according to the character of the legal uncleanness. Hence pilgrims set out in good time, according to their needs, before the feast.

56. *They sought therefore.* That is, the pilgrims sought, for their excitement was thoroughly aroused by the report of recent events.

What think you? Since the festival had not yet arrived, the people speculate as to whether Christ will come or no. He had not attended the previous Pasch (vi. 4, vii. 1), and the rulers openly expressed their determination to apprehend him (v. 56). The pilgrims, therefore, who were anxious to honour our Lord (xii. 12-13), kept asking (imperfect tense), 'What think you? (do you think) that He certainly will not come?'

CHAPTER XII.

The Supper at Bethany.

(VERS. 1-11.)

JESUS therefore six days before the pasch came to
Bethania, where Lazarus had been dead, whom Jesus
raised to life. And they made him a supper there:
and Martha served, but Lazarus was one of them that
were at table with him. Mary therefore took a pound of
ointment of right spikenard, of great price, and anointed
the feet of Jesus, and wiped his feet with her hair: and

1. *Jesus therefore*. The particle is resumptive of the history of
Christ from xi. 55.

six days before the pasch. It is difficult, if not impossible, to make
a certain and undoubted reckoning of the days. First of all, by the
term Pasch may be understood either the solemn day itself, or—since
the evening on which the Paschal lamb was slain and the Paschal meal
eaten was wont to be counted as belonging to the feast—the day before
the solemn day. Next, it is not quite clear whether we are to reckon
six days after the day of our Lord's arrival at Bethania, or whether the
day itself of arrival is one of the six: but see on xiii. 1.

came to Bethania. He did not come immediately from Ephraim
(xi. 54). Before going up to the last Pasch He made a journey through
Samaria and Galilee (Luke xvii. 11), then through Peræa (Luke xviii.
15; cf. Matt. xix. 1-13) and Jericho (Luke xix. 1) to Bethania (Luke
xix. 29; Mark x. 46, xi. 1).

2. *They made him a supper there*. St. John's words seem to imply
that the supper was a public one, given by the people of Bethany. It
took place in the house of Simon the Leper (Matt. xxvi. 6; Mark xiv. 3)
—that is, a man who had been a leper. Lazarus was one of the guests
and Martha helped in the service.

3. *Mary therefore*. Matthew and Mark, who narrate the incident
of the anointing, did not mention the name of Mary.

the house was filled with the odour of the ointment.
4 Then one of his disciples, Judas Iscariot, he that was
5 about to betray him, said: Why was not this ointment sold for three hundred pence, and given to the poor?
6 Now he said this, not because he cared for the poor; but because he was a thief, and having the purse, carried the
7 things that were put therein. Jesus therefore said: Let

a pound of ointment of right spikenard (μύρον νάρδου πιστικῆς): the same three words occur in Mark xiv. 3, who adds that it was in an alabaster box. In Matt. "an alabaster box of precious ointment," (xxvi. 7). Μύρον (from μύρρα, myrrh, or from μύρω, to trickle) was one of the more precious unguents. The English term spikenard is derived from the Vulgate of Mark xiv. 3, "nardi spicati," and refers to the head or spike of the nard. The word (Hebrew 'nerd' in Canticle of Canticles, Latin nardum, or nardus) bears a Sanskrit (some say Persian) name for a plant of the genus Valeriana which is found in India. The name is also used for any Indian perfume, *e.g.* attar of roses. Several conjectures have been made regarding the meaning of πιστικῆς: the most probable is 'pure,' 'unadulterated.' But a good case has been made out for the meaning 'potable.' A pound contained twelve ounces.

anointed the feet. She poured the ointment over our Lord's head and over His feet. St. John adds the account of the latter anointing, which was a more unusual form of anointing.

the house was filled. A vivid touch in the account of one who was present.

4. *One of his disciples.* Judas, in feigned sympathy with the poor, lamented the apparent waste, and by his lament influenced some others of the disciples to complain (Matt. xxvi. 8, 9; Mark xiv. 4, 5). St. John names the true author of the complaining, and lays bare the sordid motive actuating Judas.

5. *Three hundred pence.* About £10: see on vi. 7. In this valuation Judas did not exaggerate.

to the poor. Literally, 'to poor people,' without the article.

6. *The purse.* (γλωσσόκομον: in N. T. used only here and in xiii. 29). Originally the word denoted a case for carrying the mouthpiece of wind instruments; afterwards, in a more general sense, a casket, or purse.

carried (ἐβάσταζεν). This verb means 'to take up with the hands' (x. 31), then 'to bear, carry,' (xix. 17), 'to sustain' (Rom. xi. 18), 'to carry off' (xx. 15). It is here used in the sense of "carrying off," "pilfering." Judas was "a thief," and in the *habit* of pilfering (imperfect tense).

things (βαλλόμενα = offerings, gifts).

7. *That she may keep it.* (ἵνα τηρήσῃ, but some ancient authorities, τετήρηκεν = 'she has kept it'). St. John implies that all the ointment was used. This is confirmed by St. Mark's, "breaking the alabaster box" (xiv. 3), *i.e.* breaking the narrow neck of the vessel, in order

her alone, that she may keep it against the day of my
burial. For the poor you have always with you; but me 8
you have not always. A great multitude therefore of the 9
Jews knew that he was there: and they came, not for
Jesus's sake only, but that they might see Lazarus, whom
he had raised from the dead. But the chief priests 10
thought to kill Lazarus also: because many of the Jews 11
by reason of him went away, and believed in Jesus.

that the entire contents might be poured out. If the perfect tense be
the right reading, all is plain: "She did not sell it for the poor, but has
kept it against the day of my burial"; according to the common reading,
Judas exclaims at once against the waste, and wishes to stop it, but our
Lord interposing said, 'Let her alone, in order that she may now keep
it, and anoint me against the day of My burial.' "To understand
τηρήσῃ of the past—that she may have preserved it—is grammatically
wrong" (Meyer).

burial (ἐνταφιασμοῦ = entombment. Only here and in Mark xiv. 8).
Did Mary anoint our Lord in conscious preparation for His burial,
or was her act made such a preparation by our Lord's own destination?
More probably the latter. In any case, it *was* a preparation (cf.
Matt. xxvi. 12; Mark xiv. 8).

10. *Thought to kill* (ἐβουλεύσαντο). See on xi. 53.

11. *Went away.* Both verbs in the imperfect: 'Kept going away,
and believing.' In Matthew and Mark the narrative of the anointing
is given, not in its proper chronological order, but in its internal connection with the plotting of the chief priests, *two days before the Pasch*,
to apprehend our Lord. The plot is represented as plainly about to
succeed (Matt. xxvi. 2–4), and then there naturally follows an account
of the preparatory anointing for our Lord's burial. On the one side,
our Lord's enemies take their measures for putting Him to death, and
on the other side, Mary brings the ointment to prepare for His burial.

"At length the time of the end had come. Jesus was about to make
entry into Jerusalem as King: King of the Jews, as Heir of David's
royal line, with all of symbolic, typic, and prophetic import attaching
to it. Yet not as Israel after the flesh expected its Messiah was the
Son of David to make triumphal entrance; not in the proud triumph
of war-conquests, but in the 'meek' rule of peace.

"Although all the four evangelists relate Christ's entry into Jerusalem,
they seem to do so from different standpoints. The Synoptists accompany Him from Bethany, while St. John, in accordance with the
general scheme of his narrative, seems to follow from Jerusalem that
multitude which, on tidings of His approach, hastened to meet Him"
(Eders., l.c., p. 460). This explains why St. John omits all details
concerning the procuring of the ass's foal (Matt. xxi. 1–16; Mark xi.
1–11; Luke xix. 29–35). The words of St. Luke, 'When he was
come nigh to Bethphage and Bethania,' at first sight create a difficulty.

Our Lord's Triumphant Entry into Jerusalem.

(VERS. 12–36.)

12 And on the next day a great multitude, that was come to the festival day, when they had heard that Jesus was 13 coming to Jerusalem, took branches of palm-trees, and went forth to meet him, and cried : Hosanna, blessed is he that cometh in the name of the Lord, the king of 14 Israel. And Jesus found a young ass, and sat upon it, as 15 it is written : *Fear not, daughter of Sion : behold, thy king* 16 *cometh, sitting on an ass's colt.* These things his disciples did not know at the first : but when Jesus was glorified, then they remembered that these things were written of 17 him, and that they had done these things to him. The multitude therefore gave testimony, which was with him when he called Lazarus out of the grave, and raised him 18 from the dead. For which reason also the people came

But the difficulty vanishes when we remember that St. Luke says nothing whatever of the stay at Bethany, nothing of the Supper and anointing there, and that his words look back to our Lord's progress from Jericho, and mark His arrival at Bethany on the way to Jerusalem (Luke xix. 1, 28, 29). Cf. Matt. xx. 29, xxi. 1 ; Mark x. 46, xi. 1.

13. *And cried : Hosanna* (= 'Save now'). The words are taken from Psa. cxvii. 25, 26, and formed part of the responses by the people with which this psalm was chanted on some of the more solemn festivals ; they were also chanted by the people of Jerusalem, as they went to welcome the festive pilgrims on their arrival. Naturally, however, the people received our Lord with other joyful shouts also.

the king of Israel is in apposition with ' He that cometh.' Hence =' the King of Israel, who comes in the name of the Lord.'

15. *Fear not.* The passage is quoted *memoriter*, and according to sense, from Zach. ix. 9.

16. *These things.* The meaning is, ' His disciples at first (when it took place) did not understand the connection with the prophecy ; but afterwards they understood, and also that they themselves were fulfilling that prophecy in what they did—viz., in bringing the young ass, and placing Jesus upon it.

17. *The multitude therefore.* St. John explains the enthusiasm of the two crowds—the crowd from Bethany, and the crowd from Jerusalem. Those who had been by when our Lord raised Lazarus gave testimony (better, kept giving testimony) of the miracle, and so the people came out from Jerusalem to meet Him (*v.* 18).

to meet him: because they heard that he had done this
miracle. The Pharisees therefore said among themselves: 19
Do you see that we prevail nothing? behold, the whole
world is gone after him. Now there were certain gentiles 20
among them who came up to adore on the festival day.
These therefore came to Philip, who was of Bethsaida of 21
Galilee, and desired him, saying: Sir, we would see Jesus.
Philip cometh and telleth Andrew. Again Andrew and 22
Philip told Jesus. But Jesus answered them, saying: The 23
hour is come, that the son of man should be glorified.
Amen, amen, I say to you, unless the grain of wheat 24
falling into the ground die; itself remaineth alone. But 25
if it die, it bringeth forth much fruit. He that loveth his
life shall lose it: and he that hateth his life in this world,
keepeth it unto life eternal. If any man minister to me, 26
let him follow me: and where I am, there also shall my
minister be. If any man minister to me, him will my
Father honour. Now is my soul troubled. And what 27
shall I say? Father, save me from this hour. But for

when he called Lazarus (ὅτε). A less probable reading has ὅτι =
'*that* He called.'
 20. *Certain gentiles.* Literally Greeks.
who came up (were wont to come up). Evidently they were
proselytes.
 21. *To Philip* (see notes on i. 44, 45, and cf. i. 41, vi. 5, 7).
we would see Jesus. According to St. Mark (xi. 11) our Lord had
gone straight to the Temple, where also He taught on the following
days (Mark xi. 12, 15. Cf. Luke xix. 47; Matt. xxi. 12, 17, 18,
23). The scene, therefore, probably took place in the court of the
Temple.
 23. *The hour is come.* The desire of the Gentiles is already a
beginning of that which our Lord came to bring about by His death—
the conversion of the Gentiles (see x. 16, xi. 52). The fruitfulness of
His death is shown in a parable. The parable is a lesson to all.
glorified (see on vii. 39).
 26. *Where I am, i.e.,* in heaven (i. 18, iii. 13, xiv. 3).
 27. *Now is my soul troubled* (see on xi. 33 and cf. Matt. xxvi.
37, 38; Mark xiv. 33, 34). As in the garden, so here, our Lord felt a
sensitive shrinking from the coming cruelties of death. How intense
the suffering was is expressed in the exclamation, 'What shall I say?'
and in the prayer, 'Father, save me from this hour' (cf. Mark xiv.
36; Matt. xxvi. 39; Luke xxii. 42). The prayer should not be turned
into a question.

28 this cause I came unto this hour. Father, glorify thy
name. A voice therefore came from heaven : I have both
29 glorified it, and will glorify it again. The multitude therefore that stood and heard, said that it thundered. Others
30 said, An Angel spoke to him. Jesus answered and said :
This voice came not because of me, but for your sakes.
31 Now is the judgment of the world : now shall the prince
32 of this world be cast out. And I, if I be lifted up from
33 the earth, will draw all things to myself. (Now this he said,
34 signifying what death he should die.) The multitude
answered him : We have heard out of the law, that Christ
abideth for ever ; and how sayest thou : The son of man

Immediately upon the prayer of sorrow comes the act of resignation,
followed by the absolute prayer :—

28. *Father, glorify thy name*, *i.e.*, in the way Thou hast appointed,
through My sufferings and death (cf. xiv. 31).
I have both glorified it. In Greek simply 'I have both glorified,'
but the 'it' is naturally supplied from our Lord's prayer, 'Glorify thy
name.' The Father had been glorified in the whole of Christ's previous
work (*e.g.*, vi. 38, vii. 18, viii. 49), and would again be glorified by
Christ's death and resurrection. But the glory of the Father is also
the glory of the Son (v. 23, viii. 54, xi. 4).
As at the baptism and transfiguration of our Lord, so now a voice,
majestic and with a tone as of thunder, spoke those words. That
words were spoken is clear from the fact that St. John repeats them,
and that the "others" of *v.* 29 must have heard a speech. Not all,
however, caught the speech ; those that did not simply heard a sound
as of thunder. The verbs are in the perf. : "hath thundered," "hath
spoken."

30. *Not because of me* (for my sake), *but for your sakes*. The
Greek is same in both clauses (cf. xi. 42). = 'Not on my account
but on your account.' The disciples were to learn that the crucifixion
meant not defeat but victory ; and in being raised on the cross Christ
was being truly raised to His throne.

31. *Now is the judgment* (κρίσις) *of the world.* Our Lord speaks in
the prophetic present. As He looks on the Greeks who sought Him,
He considers them as the emblem of the harvest to spring from His
Passion. Judgment, therefore, had already come to this world, as it
lay in the power of the Evil One, since the Prince of it was cast out
from his present rule. And in place of it, Christ, being lifted up,
would draw all men (πάντας) to Himself (Eders. l.c., p. 476).

34. *Christ abideth.* The Jews so far understood what was a
common expression, that they saw our Lord referred to His death, or
departure from earth. But they had learned (*e.g.*, from Dan. vii. 13,
14 ; Isa. ix. 7) that the reign of the Messiah would last for ever.

must be lifted up? Who is this son of man? Jesus 35
therefore said to them: Yet a little while, the light is
among you. Walk whilst you have the light, that the
darkness overtake you not. And he that walketh in darkness knoweth not whither he goeth. Whilst you have the 36
light, believe in the light, that you may be the children of
light. These things Jesus spoke, and he went away, and
hid himself from them.

Retrospective Summary; Our Lord's Final Address.

(VERS. 37-50.)

And whereas he had done so many miracles before 37
them, they believed not in him: that the saying of Isaias 38
the prophet might be fulfilled, which he said: *Lord, who
hath believed our hearing? and to whom hath the arm of
the Lord been revealed?* Therefore they could not believe, 39

Christ, therefore, was not the Messiah, the Son of Man spoken of by
Daniel. Yet Christ was constantly calling Himself the Son of Man.
What does He mean? Our Lord will not now argue; He warns them.

35. *Yet a little while.* For meaning of passage, see on viii. 12, vii.
33, 34, xi. 9, 10.

that the darkness overtake (overcome) *you not.*

St. John, in a short epilogue, now sums up the painful contrast
between our Lord's labour of love and the hard unbelief of the Jews.
Whereas He had done so many miracles before them, they believed
not. Yet that wilful unbelief ought not to cause scandal, or to raise
doubts concerning the truth of Christ's Divine mission; for by their
unbelief the Jews were fulfilling ancient prophecy regarding the
Messiah.

37. *So many miracles.* St. John has recorded only seven. He
supposes the narratives of the other gospels to be known to the reader.

38. *That the saying.* Better, 'in order that.' The wilful blindness
of the Jews had been foreseen by God. But God permits evil only
because He can turn evil to good. He did so here; for He foretold
this Jewish blindness, and, in foretelling, made it serve the Divine
purpose as one of the proofs of Christ's Messianic character. The
words are taken from Isa. liii. 1, according to LXX. text.

our hearing = what they hear from us (cf. Rom. x. 16).

the arm of the Lord, i.e., the power of God shown in the work of
Christ.

39. *Therefore.* Better, 'for this cause,' *i.e.,* for the reason just
assigned (see on v. 16).

40 because Isaias said again : *He hath blinded their eyes, and hardened their heart, that they should not see with their eyes, not understand with their heart, and be converted, and I*
41 *should heal them :* These things said Isaias, when he saw
42 his glory and spoke of him. However many of the chief

they could not believe : see on ix. 39.

because, *i.e.*, namely, introducing the reason of unbelief more explicitly. The words which follow are quoted freely and according to sense from Isa. vi. 10. "There are some who mutter among themselves, and sometimes speak out when they can, and even break forth into turbulent debate, saying: What did the Jews do, or what fault was it of theirs, if it was a necessity that the saying of Isaias the prophet should be fulfilled? To whom our answer is, that the Lord, in His foreknowledge of the future, foretold by the prophet the unbelief of the Jews; He foretold it, but did not cause it. For God does not cause any one to sin simply because He knows already the future sins of men. For He foreknew sins that were theirs, not His own; sins that were referable to no one else, but to their own selves. The Jews therefore committed sin, with no compulsion to do so on His part, to whom sin is an object of displeasure; but He foretold their committing of it, because nothing is concealed from His knowledge. And accordingly, had they wished to do good instead of evil, they would not have been hindered.

"But the words that follow are still more pressing, and start a question of more profound import : for he goes on to say, "Therefore they could not believe, because Isaias said again, 'He hath blinded their eyes.'" But we shall give what answer we can. 'They could not believe,' because Isaias the prophet foretold it ; and the prophet foretold it because God foreknew that such would be the case. But if I am asked why they could not, I reply at once, because they would not ; for certainly their depraved will was foreseen by God. But the prophet, sayest thou, assigns another cause than that of their will. What cause does the prophet assign? That God 'hath blinded their eyes.' This also, I reply, their will deserved. For God thus blinds and hardens simply by letting alone and withdrawing His aid. If, then, we must be far from thinking that there is unrighteousness with God, this only can it be, that, when He giveth His aid, He acteth mercifully ; and, when He withholdeth it, He acteth righteously : for in all He doeth, He acteth not rashly, but in accordance with judgment " (St. Aug., Tract liii. c. 7).

41. *He saw his* (*i.e.*, Christ's) *glory.* The second half of the verse is better rendered,

and spoke of him. Isaias "saw the Lord," *i.e.*, the Supreme God. Therefore Christ is the Supreme God (see Isa. vi. 1, 9, 10).

42. *Because of the Pharisees they did not confess him* (see ix. 22). The Greek = "they were not confessing" (ὡμολόγουν : imperfect of continuous action).

men also believed in him: but because of the Pharisees they did not confess *him*, that they might not be cast out of the synagogue. For they loved the glory of men, more 43 than the glory of God. But Jesus cried, and said: He 44 that believeth in me, doth not believe in me, but in him that sent me. And he that seeth me, seeth him that sent 45 me. I am come a light into the world; that whosoever 46 believeth in me, may not remain in darkness. And if any 47 man hear my words, and keep them not: I do not judge him; for I came not to judge the world, but to save the world. He that despiseth me, and receiveth not my 48 words, hath one that judgeth him: the word that I have spoken, the same shall judge him in the last day. For I 49 have not spoken of myself, but the Father who sent me, he gave me commandment what I should say, and what I should speak. And I know that his commandment is life 50 everlasting. The things therefore that I speak; even as the Father said unto me, so do I speak.

43. *The glory of men*; see v. 44.

In contrast with all this want of faith, Jesus 'cried,' so as to be heard by all, His clear testimony and appeal to the Father. The Father had given Christ commandment, and in that commandment was life everlasting. Since our Lord had retired and hidden Himself (v. 36), we must not refer the speech that follows to any particular occasion, but regard it as a summary account of Christ's public teaching.

44. *Doth not believe* (cf. v. 30, vii. 16).
45. *Seeth him* (cf. v. 37, vi. 46, viii. 19).
46. *I am come a light.* The 'I' is very emphatic. (For meaning cf. viii. 12, ix. 5.)
47. *I do not judge* (cf. iii. 17).
48. *Hath one that judgeth* (cf. iii. 18, v. 45, viii. 50).
49. *Gave me commandment* (see on x. 18).

What I should say, and what I should speak. The two verbs are probably only a form of rhetorical emphasis. For the sense of the declaration cf. v. 19, 20, 24, 30.

CHAPTER XIII.

The Washing of the Feet.

(VERS. 1–30.)

BEFORE the festival day of the pasch, Jesus knowing that his hour was come, that he should pass out of

1. *Before the festival day of the pasch* (τῆς ἑορτῆς τοῦ πάσχα).

Here we are introduced to a great difficulty. The Paschal lamb was killed on the 14th day of the month Nisan in the afternoon, and eaten the same evening. Unleavened bread was eaten for seven days, *i.e.*, the feast of the unleavened bread lasted seven days, from the Paschal meal till the evening of the 21st Nisan. The first day (15th Nisan) and the seventh day (21st Nisan) were "holy and solemn," no work was allowed on those days "except those things that belong to eating" (Exod. xii. 1–20; see on ii. 13). In popular language the 14th Nisan was sometimes reckoned as the first day of the festival. Hence Josephus speaks of the feast as lasting eight days, and the first three evangelists speak of the 14th Nisan as the first day of the Azymes. Thus St. Mark, "on the first day of the unleavened bread, when they sacrificed the pasch" (xiv. 12), and St. Luke, "the day of the unleavened bread came, on which it was necessary that the pasch should be killed" (xxii. 7; cf. Matt. xxvi. 17). The three therefore agree in stating that the Last Supper took place on the 14th Nisan, and that our Lord and His disciples also ate the Paschal meal. St. John agrees; but, in more exact language, he speaks of the Paschal meal as being eaten before the feast of the Pasch. The "feast of the Pasch" is not the same as the Pasch (cf. ii. 23, vii. 14 with xviii. 28). All four evangelists therefore state that the Last Supper was eaten on the 14th Nisan, the legal time for the Paschal meal, and that our Lord suffered the following day. But now St. John seems to imply that when our Lord died the Jews had not yet eaten the Pasch. Thus they would not enter Pilate's hall "that they might not be defiled, but that they might eat the pasch" (xviii. 28). Again, the day of the crucifixion was "the parasceve (*i.e.*, preparation—day of preparation) of the pasch" (xix. 14; cf. xix. 31).

this world to the Father: having loved his own who were

How to account for this, several theories have been propounded.

(*a*) Some have thought that the Last Supper took place on the 13th Nisan, and did not include the Paschal meal. But this is excluded by the clear language of the Synoptics. The Last Supper took place on "the first day of the Azymes." Strictly speaking, this was the 15th Nisan, and only in popular speech was the 14th so called; but in no wise could the term be applied to the 13th Nisan. Besides, the evangelists assert that our Lord ate the Pasch on that last night. As He sat at table He said to the disciples, "With desire I have desired to eat this pasch with you before I suffer" (Luke xxii. 15; cf. Matt. xxvi. 17-21). Our Lord did truly eat the Pasch.

(*b*) Others have thought that our Lord anticipated the time usual among the Jews, in order to keep the feast with His disciples before He died. But this, again, is excluded by the clear language of the Synoptics. Our Lord partook of the feast "on the first day of the unleavened bread, when they sacrificed the pasch," "on which it was necessary that the Pasch should be killed" (Mark xiv. 12; Luke xxii. 7). Thus there was no anticipation of the legal time.

(*c*) Many have thought that the Jews, as well as our Lord, ate the Paschal meal on the night of the 14th Nisan, and that St. John's language may be so interpreted as not to imply that the Jews had not eaten the Pasch at the time of the crucifixion. We admit that some of St. John's statements may be so interpreted; but we feel that not all can be so interpreted without putting a force upon them. The statements are five in number—xiii. 1, 29, xviii. 28, xix. 14, 31. In xiii. 1 the reference is not to the Paschal meal, but to the Paschal feast, as already explained. The same remark applies to xiii. 29. But the other three statements seem to imply that the Jews had not yet eaten the Paschal meal. In xviii. 28 it is said, "They went not into the hall, that they might not be defiled, but that they might eat the pasch." It has been replied that this does not refer to the Pasch proper. First, because the Paschal meal was not eaten till evening, and before that time the defilement caused by entering a heathen house could have been removed. Next, to eat the Pasch may be understood in a large sense, viz., to partake of some of the Paschal sacrifices, particularly of the 'Chagigah,' a free-will offering made on the morning following the Paschal meal. Hence it is inferred that the reference was to something to be immediately partaken of, but not to the Paschal meal in the evening, when the defilement would have ceased. To this we answer, that although some defilements lasted only till evening, others were more serious and precluded the defiled from eating the Pasch, or required a longer purification (see on xi. 55). Now, it is quite gratuitous to assert that the defilement caused by entering a heathen house during the feast of unleavened bread lasted only till evening. The defilement of leaven was so peculiarly opposed to the character of the feast that, "whosoever shall eat anything leavened, from the first day until the seventh day, that soul shall perish out of Israel" (Exod. xii.

² in the world, he loved them unto the end. And when

15). Farther, there is no proof that the technical and peculiarly expressive phrase, 'to eat the Pasch,' means other than to eat the Paschal meal. The term Pasch may be used loosely, but 'to eat the Pasch' seems incapable of meaning anything but partaking of the meal that was exclusively and peculiarly Paschal.

In xix. 14 Pilate is said to have brought our Lord forth during the "parasceve of the pasch." Parasceve means day of preparation. It has therefore been said that it was really another term for Friday, the usual day of preparation for the Sabbath. Thus in Mark (xv. 42) we read, "Because it was the Parasceve, that is, the day before the Sabbath" (cf. Luke xxiii. 54). Hence St. John's words have been taken as meaning 'the Friday in Paschal week.' Although we do not deny the possibility of this rendering, we are dissatisfied with an interpretation which turns 'the preparation,' or, 'the day of preparation of the Pasch,' into 'Friday of Paschal week.' It is very much like turning the strong phrase, 'the day of the Lord,' into 'the Lord's day,' or a mere Sunday.

But xix. 31 has been quoted in confirmation, "Then the Jews, (because it was the parasceve) that the bodies might not remain upon the cross on the sabbath-day (for that was a great sabbath-day), besought Pilate that they might be taken away." Here it is urged that the ground of the request was the fact that the day was Friday, and that the Sabbath was near. Rather, we reply, the ground of the request was more urgent. The day was the day of preparation for the "holy and solemn" day—one of the two great days of the feast—in itself kept as a Sabbath, but doubly holy because also falling on a Sabbath. "For great was the day of that Sabbath," as the better-attested Greek reading gives it. Could such language be used of an ordinary Sabbath which happened to fall during the Paschal celebration? We think not. We conclude, therefore, that St. John, while stating, as the other evangelists state, that our Lord ate the Paschal meal on Thursday evening, the 14th Nisan, the proper legal day, and that He died on Friday, the 15th Nisan, yet states no less clearly that when Christ died the Jews had not yet eaten the Paschal meal. That the Jews, therefore, changed the day, we are constrained by the clear testimony of St. John to admit; but *why* they did so, there is no historical evidence to show. At a later period, indeed, the Jews, when the Paschal *feast* would legally fall on a Friday, have been accustomed to transfer it to the Saturday, to avoid two immediately successive Sabbaths. If this practice were as old as the time of our Lord, it would at once explain the matter; but the balance of evidence is against the supposition of such high antiquity. Some other reason, then, must have prompted the Jews; but what that reason was, must be left to conjecture.

We may now answer the question reserved from xii. 1. There it was question of six days "before the pasch," whereas in xiii. 1 it is question of the day "before the festival day of the pasch." St. John,

supper was done (the devil having now put into the heart
of Judas Iscariot the son of Simon, to betray him), knowing that the Father had given him all things into his
hands, and that he came from God, and goeth to God.
He riseth from supper, and layeth aside his garments, and
having taken a towel, girded himself. After that, he
putteth water into a basin, and began to wash the feet of
his disciples, and to wipe them with the towel, wherewith

as we have seen, distinguishes them. The Pasch is the 14th Nisan,
the festival day of the Pasch is the 15th Nisan. Six days before the
Pasch (Thursday) was a Friday. The day after was the Sabbath, and
the supper prepared for Him at Bethany was the special festive meal of
the Sabbath. The next day, the day of triumphal entry into Jerusalem,
was the first day of the week, now Sunday; and the following days
were spent teaching in the temple.

having loved his own who were in the world (*i.e.*, the Apostles
whom He would leave behind), *he loved them unto the end* (εἰς τέλος).
This evidently does not mean merely till the end of His mortal life,
but, as the Greek Fathers explain it, to the extreme of love. He is
about to give them extraordinary proofs of love. What the proofs
were, the narrative that follows will show.

2. *When supper was done.* The better Greek reading is δείπνου
γινομένου = 'during supper.' This is confirmed by a reference to
vv. 4 and 12. Therefore what immediately follows occurred before
the institution of the Blessed Eucharist, which was instituted "after
he had supped" (1 Cor. xi. 25). St. John makes no mention of that
institution, because it was universally known.

the devil having now put. A more accurate translation is, 'having
already put.' (Vulgate, 'cum jam misisset.') A grammatically possible
rendering of the sentence would be, "The devil having already put it
into the heart (*i.e.*, his own heart) in order that Judas should betray
Him." So too the Vulgate, "cum jam misisset in cor ut traderet eum
Judas." But there is no doubt that the heart of Judas is meant. The
thought of betrayal had suggested itself to Judas during the supper at
Bethany (xii. 4-6).

3. *Knowing that the Father.* St. John mentions all these things
in a vivid historic present, in order to impress us more deeply with a
sense of Christ's love in performing for the disciples what slaves usually
did for the guests.

4. *He riseth from supper.* Better, 'from the supper.' The article
probably implies that the reader will have in mind what supper is
meant.

his garments. Greek = His upper garment: what was worn over
the tunic. Hence 'His Tallith.'

5. *Into a basin.* Greek, 'into the basin,' which usually stood there
for such purposes.

6 he was girded. He cometh therefore to Simon Peter.
And Peter said to him: Lord, dost thou wash my feet?
7 Jesus answered, and said to him: What I do, thou knowest
8 not now, but thou shalt know hereafter. Peter said to
him: Thou shalt never wash my feet. Jesus answered
him: If I wash thee not, thou shalt have no part with me.
9 Simon Peter saith to him: Lord, not only my feet, but also
10 my hands and my head. Jesus saith to him: He that is
washed, needeth not but to wash his feet, but is clean
11 wholly. And you are clean, but not all. For he knew

6. *He cometh therefore.* This is immediately connected with, "He began to wash, and cometh therefore to Simon Peter." With Peter, then, the washing began; and this fact explains Peter's astonishment.

Lord, dost thou wash (present = art thou about to wash) *my feet?* If others had been already washed Peter's surprise would have been unnatural. The Apostles had been watching our Lord, but did not know what was coming; but as soon as Peter understood, from our Lord's coming to him first, what was intended, he was overwhelmed.

7. *Hereafter.* Not ὕστερον, which might refer to a remote future, but μετὰ ταῦτα = after these things, *i.e.*, as soon as I am finished. The explanation came immediately after the act (vv. 12-17).

8. *Thou shalt have no part.* Greek = 'thou hast no part.' A difficult passage. First, then, the loss that Peter would have suffered would have arisen directly from not having been washed by Christ. 'If I wash thee not, thou hast no part with me.' The loss, therefore, would not have been properly a punishment of disobedience, but a loss arising from the simple non-reception of what would have bestowed a great good. Thus a person who through ignorance does not receive baptism loses a good of incalculable preciousness, but the loss comes simply from the non-reception of baptism, and is not inflicted as a punishment of ignorance. So here, Peter's loss would have been not a punishment of disobedience, but 'if I wash thee not'—the missing of a rite conveying a great benefit.

Secondly, our Lord intended the rite to be efficacious of good to the Apostles; and what kind of good, is immediately explained (v. 10).

10. *He that is washed* (rather, 'bathed') *needeth not.* As one who has bathed need only remove the dust picked up by walking home, and then he is wholly clean, so the Apostles who had already been made pure in heart and soul, needed only to be cleansed from lesser things and then were wholly clean—needed only a spiritual consecration to follow now perfectly in the footsteps of their Divine Master, and so have share with Him, both in the Messianic work on earth and in glory hereafter.

but not all, i.e., not all of them, however, were pure in heart and soul.

11. *Therefore he said.* Better, 'for this cause' (see on v. 16).

who he was that would betray him; therefore he said: You are not all clean. Then after he had washed their feet, and taken his garments, being sat down again, he said to them: Know you what I have done to you? You call me Master, and Lord: and you say well, for so I am. If then I, being *your* Lord and Master, have washed your feet; you also ought to wash one another's feet. For I have given you an example, that as I have done to you, so you do also. Amen, amen, I say to you: The servant is not greater than his lord: neither is the apostle greater than he that sent him. If you know these things, you shall be blessed if you do them. I speak not of you all: I know whom I have chosen: but that the scripture may be fulfilled, *He that eateth bread with me, shall lift up his heel against me.* At present I tell you, before it come to pass: that when it shall come to pass, you may believe

13. *You call me Master and Lord.* "They were wont to call Him by the two highest names of Teacher and Lord, and these designations were rightly His. How much more, then, must His service of love, who was their Teacher and Lord, serve as example of what was due by each to his fellow-disciple and fellow-servant!" (Eders. l.c., p. 547).

18. *I know whom I have chosen.* Therefore He knew that Judas would betray Him. But that betrayal did not come upon our Lord as a surprise; for it had been foretold in Scripture, and the Scripture must needs be fulfilled (see on ix. 39, xii. 39). The quotation, which is cited freely from the original (Psa. xl. 10), gives the sense, but not the *ipsissima verba* of the original. It deviates from both the Hebrew and the LXX., and uses a phraseology agreeing with the Eucharistic language of chapter vi. (ὁ τρώγων μου τὸν ἄρτον: cf. vi. 54, 56, 57, 58). In the LXX. we find the more common verb ὁ ἐσθίων ἄρτους μου. This certainly gives colour to the opinion that Judas received the Blessed Eucharist.

He that eateth bread with me, shall lift up (lifted up, Heb. and LXX. = 'magnified') *his heel against me, i.e.,* to give a treacherous kick.

19. *At present I tell you.* Better, 'from henceforth' (ἀπ' ἄρτι), for this is the usual meaning in N. T. of the Greek phrase (xiv. 7; Matt. xxiii. 39, xxvi. 29; Apoc. xiv. 13). Our Lord now declares that from this time forward He will speak plainly of the matter, so that the Apostles also may see the fulfilment of prophecy in our Lord's betrayal.

that you may believe that I am he. See on viii. 24. Hence, what might have been scandal, is now a ground of faith; for by Judas's betrayal the Messianic prophecies were fulfilled in Christ.

²⁰ that I am he. Amen, amen, I say to you, he that receiveth whomsoever I send, receiveth me: and he that
²¹ receiveth me, receiveth him that sent me. When Jesus had said these things, he was troubled in spirit: and he testified, and said: Amen, amen, I say to you, one of you
²² shall betray me. The disciples therefore looked one upon
²³ another, doubting of whom he spoke. Now there was leaning on Jesus's bosom one of his disciples whom Jesus
²⁴ loved. Simon Peter therefore beckoned to him, and said
²⁵ to him: Who is it of whom he speaketh? He therefore leaning on the breast of Jesus saith to him: Lord, who is

20. *He that receiveth whomsoever I send.* These words seem abrupt. Perhaps our Lord did not speak all these things continuously, but from time to time, after He had sat down. Yet there is here a sequence and internal connection of thought. Our Lord had given the Apostles a command, with a promise of blessedness (*vv.* 16, 17). But the promise would not be fulfilled in all; there was a traitor amongst them (*v.* 18); Christ now mentioned the fact in order to save the faith of the others (*v.* 19). Let them therefore go forward in firmness of faith, for their mission was His mission—He and the Father would be its security.

Our Lord next recurs to the subject of Judas's treason and, not without anguish of heart, begins to testify with more definiteness (*v.* 21) what before He had only hinted at (*vv.* 10, 18).

21. *He was troubled in spirit* (see on xi. 33). Not Judas alone was the occasion of that trouble of spirit, but the whole of that dreary prospect of which Judas's treason was an item. The present 'trouble' is rather the beginning of that agony which grew so intense in the Garden of Gethsemani.

23. *Leaning on Jesus's bosom* (ἀνακείμενος . . . ἐν τῷ κόλπῳ). Better, 'on the lap.' "The custom was to lie with the left arm supported on the cushion and the feet stretched out behind, so that the right hand remained free for eating. The one who lay next reached, with the back of his head, to the *sinus* of the girdle of the first." (Meyer). St. John, then (for the evangelist refers here to himself), was reclining in front of our Lord, and had the back of his head almost in front of our Lord's breast.

24. *Beckoned.* St. Peter was, therefore, probably facing St. John, *i.e.,* on the opposite side of the table, and beckoned across.

and said to him (A. V., 'that he should ask'; but the best-supported Greek agrees with the Douay version). St. Peter asked by making an interrogative gesture.

25. *He therefore leaning on the breast of Jesus* (ἀναπεσὼν ἐκεῖνος οὕτως ἐπὶ τὸ στῆθος). A graphic representation continued from *v.* 23. With scarce a change of position, and while remaining as he

it? Jesus answered: He it is to whom I shall reach 26 bread dipped. And when he had dipped the bread, he gave it to Judas Iscariot, *the son* of Simon. And after the 27

was (οὕτως), John rests his head on our Lord's breast, and whispers the question.

26. *Bread dipped* (ψωμίον), A. V. 'a sop.' It means a bit, a morsel (*vv.* 27, 30). "The Paschal supper was proceeding. According to the rubric, after the 'washing,' the dishes were immediately to be brought on the table. Then the head of the company would dip some of the bitter herbs into the salt-water or vinegar, speak a blessing, and partake of them, then hand them to each in the company. Next, he would break one of the unleavened cakes, of which half was put aside for after supper. This is called the *Aphigomon*, or after-dish, and as we believe that 'the bread' of the Holy Eucharist was the Aphigomon, some particulars may here be of interest. The dish in which the broken cake (not the Aphigomon) lies is elevated, and these words are spoken: 'This is the bread of misery which our fathers ate in the land of Egypt. All that are hungry, come and eat; all that are needy, come, keep the Pasch.' After this the cup is elevated, and then the service proceeds somewhat lengthily, the cup being raised a second time and certain prayers spoken. This part of the service concludes with the two first psalms in the series called 'the Hallel,' when the cup is raised a third time, a prayer spoken, and the cup drunk. This ends the first part of the service. And now the Paschal meal begins.

To the whispered question of John, the Lord gave the sign that it was he to whom He would give 'the sop' ('bread dipped') when He had dipped it. Even this perhaps was not clear to John, since each one in turn received 'the sop.'

We have direct testimony that, about the time of Christ, 'the sop' which was handed round consisted of these things wrapped together: flesh of the Paschal Lamb, a piece of unleavened bread, and bitter herbs. This, we believe, was 'the sop' which Jesus, having dipped it for him in the dish, handed to Judas. But before He did so, probably while He dipped it in the dish, Judas, who could not but fear that his purpose might be known, reclining at Christ's left hand (John was on the right hand), whispered into the Master's ear, 'Is it I, Rabbi?' (see Matt. xxvi. 21-25). It must have been whispered, for no one at the table could have heard either the question of Judas or the affirmative answer of Christ." (See John xiii. 28.) Eders. l.c., pp. 549, 550.

27. *And after the morsel* (τότε, added in Greek, = at that moment) *satan* (not elsewhere mentioned by St. John) *entered into him*. Judas knew that Christ had detected his treachery, but he hardened his heart against Christ's merciful warning, and boldly took the offered morsel. At that moment of final hardening he was given up by Christ to the unhindered control of satanic suggestion. This fact our Lord's language now implies.

morsel, satan entered into him. And Jesus said to him:
28 That which thou dost, do quickly. Now no man at the
29 table knew to what purpose he said this unto him. For some thought, because Judas had the purse, that Jesus had said to him: Buy those things which we have need of for the festival day: or that he should give something to
30 the poor. He therefore having received the morsel, went out immediately. And it was night.

Our Lord's Manifestation to His Disciples.

(Vers. 31–38.)

31 When he therefore was gone out Jesus said: Now is the son of man glorified, and God is glorified in him.
32 If God be glorified in him, God also will glorify him

That which thou dost (present, for immediate future = that which thou art about to do), *do quickly* (literally, 'more quickly'). Permissive imperative. The meaning is, 'Since you have determined to betray Me, do it at once.'

28. *Now, no man knew.* Even St. John had not overheard Judas's question, nor had he fully understood the sign given by Jesus. (See on v. 26).

29. *For the festival day.* See on v. 1.

30. *And it was night.* A deeply tragic, and awe-inspiring ending. There is a shuddering horror in the suggestiveness of this brief note. From the Paschal meal, which had scarcely begun, Judas rushed out wildly into the night.

Judas's departure left our Lord, as it were, free to institute the Sacrament of His love, and to make a fuller revelation of His affection and care for the disciples. St. Matthew (xxvi.) and St. Mark (xiv.) expressly record the institution of the Eucharist after the events just narrated; St. Luke (xxii. 20) and St. Paul (1 Cor. xi. 25) state that the institution took place after the supper. The perfect harmony of these statements with the narrative of St. John, and their own internal coherency cannot be disarranged by the apparently adverse statement of St. Luke (xxii. 21). We must take St. Luke's statement as parenthetic, and not in strict sequence of time. (Cf. on xii. 11.)

31. *Now is the son of man glorified.* In view of its nearness our Lord speaks of the victory of His death as already won (cf. xii. 31-33), and because by death His life-work will be accomplished, He says, 'Now is the son of man glorified.'

and God is glorified, for the Father's work is completed in that of the Son (v. 17, 23, 30; xii. 28).

32. *If God be glorified in him.* Many authorities omit these words.

in himself: and immediately will he glorify him. Little 33
children, yet a little while I am with you. You shall
seek me, and as I said to the Jews: Whither I go,
you cannot come: so I say to you now. A new com- 34

They are best taken causally, 'Because God is glorified in Him, God
also (*i.e.*, in turn) will glorify Him in Himself.'

in himself. This may refer either to the Father, *i.e.* He will glorify
Christ by exalting Him to the Father's own glory in heaven (cf. xvii. 5;
Phil. ii. 11; Heb. i. 3); or it may mean, the Father will make Christ
in Himself glorious. This is preferable, for the better attested reading
is ἐν αὑτῷ not ἐν ἑαυτῷ.

and immediately (εὐθύς = straightway) *will he glorify him*, for
Christ's death is close at hand. Some, not improbably, see this immediate beginning of Christ's glory in the stupendous mystery of the
Blessed Eucharist, which was now instituted. Certainly, if our Lord
could say, 'And I, if I be lifted up from the earth, will draw all things
to myself,' referring to the triumph of the Cross, He could with equal
truth refer to the triumph of the Blessed Sacrament. The Blessed
Sacrament is the centre of Catholic worship and devotion; it is a mystery
of love inflaming our hearts with love of Christ. From the earliest days
of Christian history, Christian worship has been 'in the breaking of
bread'; emblems of the Eucharist are everywhere found in the catacombs, thus showing that the triumph of Christ found its most natural
expression in the triumph of the Eucharist. The words, then, 'And
immediately will he glorify him,' are a most appropriate introduction
to the institution of the Blessed Sacrament. That institution implied
Christ's near departure, and concluded with the farewell command,
'Do this for a commemoration of me' (Luke xxii. 19; 1 Cor. xi. 24).

33. *My little children* (τεκνία). This diminutive, found only in St.
John (and frequently in his First Epistle), is expressive of the tenderest
affection.

yet a little while. This means, according to our Lord's own interpretation, till the time of His death. Just after the Resurrection the
time of our Lord's previous converse with the Apostles was called the time
'while I was yet with you' (Luke xxiv. 44). Therefore the reference
is to a continuous visible presence, such as the Apostles had hitherto
enjoyed. An invisible presence was promised always (xiv. 18, 23);
and the break in the visible presence, 'Wither I go, you cannot come,'
was only temporary (xiv. 2-4), and even that for the good of the Apostles
themselves (xvi. 7). Similar words had been addressed to the Jews,
'Ye shall seek me . . . and where I am, thither you cannot come,'
but with a threatening addition: 'You shall seek me, *and shall not
find me*' (see on vii. 34).

34. *A new commandment . . . that you love one another as I have
loved you* (καθὼς ἠγάπησα). The aorist is used ('as I loved') because
our Lord is speaking as it were historically, considering Himself as
already at the end of His work (*v.* 1, 31). Our Lord, then, about to

mandment I give unto you: That you love one another, as I have loved you, that you also love one another.
35 By this shall all men know that you are my disciples,
36 if you have love one for another. Simon Peter saith to him: Lord, whither goest thou? Jesus answered: Whither I go, thou canst not follow me now, but thou
37 shalt follow hereafter. Peter saith to him: Why cannot I
38 follow thee now? I will lay down my life for thee. Jesus

leave the Apostles, gives them instruction for their guidance; and first 'a new commandment.' But in what sense new? for the command itself of love was very old (Lev. xix. 18; Matt. v. 43, xix. 19, xxii. 37-39). Two very different Greek adjectives are translated 'new' in the English Testament (Matt. ix. 17); the one is νέος, denoting the 'new' primarily in reference to *time* (= recent, young), the other is καινός, denoting the 'new' primarily in reference to *quality* (= fresh, unworn, that which as recently made is superior to what it succeeds). (See Thayer-Grimm's Lexicon.) St. John uses the latter adjective. Therefore the commandment is not merely of recent institution, but is intrinsically superior to the old commandment of love. The words that follow explain this superiority, 'That you love one another as I have loved you.' The term καθώς may mean, (1) in the same measure in which I have loved you ('according as,' *i.e.*, in the degree that); (2) according to the type of love that I have given ('according as' *i.e.* in accordance with, just as); (3) on account of My love, *because* I have loved you ('seeing that' *i.e.* agreeably to the fact that). Now, the first is impossible, for we are incapable of loving in the same degree and measure in which Christ loved. The second and third are not mutually exclusive; but the second, without excluding the third (1 John iv. 10), is more prominent in the teaching of St. John (see xv. 12, 13; 1 John iii. 16), and it goes beyond the 'Thou shalt love thy neighbour as thyself,' of the O. T. Besides, the motive power is greater, 'because Christ loved us,' *i.e.*, Christ's own living example is a powerful incentive not found in the O. T., to imitate the type of His disinterested love. This love is not only commanded, but is also the distinctive mark and test of Christ's perfect disciples (*v.* 35).

36. *Lord, whither goest thou?* St. Peter's thoughts are running on the statement of *v.* 33.

37. *Why cannot I follow thee now?* St. Peter has not understood our Lord's meaning. Thinking still of earth, and feeling that he is ready to sacrifice his very life for our Lord, he cannot imagine why our Lord has so spoken. Even if he had understood, Peter's 'hour' had not yet come.

38. *The cock shall not crow, till thou deny me thrice.* That is, 'before cock-crowing.' This was a definite note of time. Thus, 'You know not when the lord of the house cometh: at even, or at midnight, or at the cock crowing, or in the morning' (Mark xiii. 35). SS. Matthew

answered him: Wilt thou lay down thy life for me? Amen, amen, I say to thee, the cock shall not crow, till thou deny me thrice.

(xxvi. 34) and Luke (xxii. 34) quote our Lord in the same form as does St. John; but St. Mark (xiv. 30) records the prediction more minutely. According to St. Mark, the denials of St. Peter will take place before "cock crowing," but the prediction itself is given in more emphatic and antithetical language. "Before the cock crow *twice*" (not before two "cock crowings"), "thou shalt deny me *thrice*." At 'cock crow' the cock crows many times. St. Luke, like St. John, records the prophecy as delivered during the Supper, while SS. Matthew and Mark record it as delivered on the way to Gethsemani. But how natural it is that so startling an announcement, just made during the Supper, was returned to during the journey to the garden! Could Peter, with his impetuosity, really have remained silent? (cf. *v*. 36.)

CHAPTER XIV.

Our Lord's Manifestation to His Disciples

(*Continued*).

(VERS. 1–31.)

LET not your heart be troubled. You believe in God, believe also in me. In my Father's house

1. *Let not your heart be troubled.* Our Lord resumes His address, which had been interrupted by St. Peter's question (36–38). The announcement of His departure had filled them with sorrow and anxiety (xiii. 33; xvi. 6), and He urges them to lay aside all fear and apprehension.

You believe in God, believe also in me. In both clauses is found πιστεύετε. This may be taken indicatively in both, imperatively in both, or indicatively in the one and imperatively in the other. But in all cases the underlying thought is the same—belief in Christ is belief in God, and this belief is a firm ground of hope and courage.

2. *In my Father's house* (οἰκία). In Attic (and especially legal) usage οἶκος denotes one's household, one's entire property, οἰκία, the dwelling itself. But in the N. T. there is no scrupulous observance of this distinction.

many mansions, i.e., mansions for many. The language itself gives no suggestion here of the further truth of different degrees of blessedness. The term μονή, 'mansion' (=abiding place) occurs in N. T. only here and in *v.* 23.

that (ὅτι) *I go*. This is not the ὅτι recitativum after 'told,' as if the meaning were, 'If it were not so I would have told you that I go to prepare a place,' because Christ does tell them that He goes to prepare (*v.* 3). We must give ὅτι its meaning 'because,' 'There are many mansions; if it were not so I would have told you; but you may trust Me that there are many mansions, because I am going to prepare a place for you.' Elsewhere our Lord speaks of the heavenly kingdom as having been prepared for the blessed 'from the foundation of the world' (Matt. xxv. 34). Our Lord's preparation for the Apostles must

there are many mansions. If not, I would have told you, that I go to prepare a place for you. And if I shall go, 3 and prepare a place for you: I will come again, and will take you to myself, that where I am, you also may be. And whither I go you know, and the way you know. 4 Thomas saith to him: Lord, we know not whither thou 5 goest, and how can we know the way? Jesus saith to 6 him: I am the way, and the truth, and the life. No man cometh to the Father but by me. If you had known me, 7 you would without doubt have known my Father also; and from henceforth you shall know him, and you have seen him. Philip saith to him: Lord, show us the Father, 8

refer, therefore, to something He would do for them after His return to the Father, *e.g.*, the sending of the Paraclete (*vv.* 16, 26; xvi. 7).

3. *I will come again.* Literally, 'I am coming again' (the present, for certain future). Our Lord's departure does not mean permanent separation, rather it implies a return, because He is going to prepare for them. That return is primarily for individuals at their death (Matt. xxiv. 44; Mark xiii. 36, 37), and secondarily for the Church at Christ's Second Advent (1 Thess. iv. 15-17; 1 John ii. 28).

4. *And whither I go.* The Greek more commonly, 'And whither I go you know the way,' omitting the rest of the sentence. The 'way' is that designated in *v.* 6, and this way the Apostles certainly ought to have known (v. 40; vi. 40, 47).

6. *I am the way.* The pronoun is emphatic. Christ is the sole objective medium of redemption, the one mediator of redemption; neither is there salvation in any other (1 Tim. ii. 5, 6; Acts iv. 12).

and the truth, and the life. Christ is in Himself eternal truth and eternal life, absolute truth and absolute life, because He is God; and He is also the Truth and the Life, the Light and the Giver of Life to all mankind (see i. 4, 9, 12, 16, 18; v. 24, 25; xi. 25, 26).

7. *If you had known me.* The more critical Greek runs thus: "If you had recognized (emphatic = really recognized) Me you would have known My Father also; and (= but) henceforth you recognize Him, and have seen Him." The knowledge here spoken of is not an intuitive knowledge of the Divine Persons, for 'no man hath seen God at any time' (see on i. 18); but an indirect and notional knowledge. Our Lord, therefore, says that if the Apostles had really known Him, had recognised the full meaning of His statements (*e.g.*, v. 18, 19; viii. 58; x. 30, 38), they would have known the Father also in the same way in which they ought to have known Christ (cf. xii. 45). But now, after Christ's plain declaration, they recognize the Father, and have seen **Him** (*i.e.*, as manifested in the life and doctrine of Christ) (cf. vi. 46; viii. 19; v. 36, 37).

8. *Show us the Father* (δεῖξον: aorist imperative = only give us one

9 and it is enough for us. Jesus saith to him: So long a time have I been with you: and have you not known me? Philip, he that seeth me, seeth the Father also. How
10 sayest thou, show us the Father? Do you not believe, that I am in the Father, and the Father in me? The words that I speak to you, I speak not of myself. But the
11 Father who abideth in me, he doth the works. Believe you not that I am in the Father, and the Father in me?
12 Otherwise believe for the very works' sake. Amen, amen, I say to you, he that believeth in me, the works that I do, he also shall do, and greater than these shall he do.
13 Because I go to the Father: and whatsoever you shall ask the Father in my name, that will I do: that the Father

look at the Father). He desired some visible manifestation of the Father—a theophany.

9. *Have you not known me?* Better, 'hast thou not recognized Me?' (see *v.* 7).

10. *Do you not believe?* Better, 'dost thou not believe?'

I am in the Father, and the Father in me (cf. x. 38). This verse, and the verses that immediately follow, are a summary of our Lord's previous declarations. Between Him and the Father there is unity of word (see on vii. 16, viii. 26, xii. 49), and unity of work (see on v. 20, 30, 36; viii. 28, 29), and unity of nature (see on x. 30).

11. *Believe you not.* The verbs are now in the plural, and the address is no longer intended for Philip alone. Nor is there a question in the Greek, but an injunction, 'Believe Me that I am in the Father,' &c.

12. *Believe for the very works' sake* (cf. iii. 2, v. 36, vi. 27).

greater than these shall he do. Because I go to the Father. Greater than these shall he do, because I go to the Father. This is the better attested punctuation. The Apostles will do 'greater works' because Christ goes to the Father. These greater works are the triumph of the Church over Judaism and Paganism—a triumph that was gained because Christ, returning to the Father, sent the Paraclete, whose coming, in the providence of God, was conditional upon that return of Christ to the Father (see vii. 39, xvi. 7).

13. *Whatsoever you shall ask.* This clause also is dependent upon 'because' in the previous clause. 'Because I go to the Father, and will do whatsoever you ask.'

in my name. The name stands for the person (i. 12, ii. 23, iii. 18). To ask in the name of Christ is to ask in union with Him, in His spirit, and for the same end for which He came into the world.

that the Father may be glorified in the Son. Because the honour of the Father and the fulfilment of His will was the object of Christ's whole life (iv. 34, v. 30, vi. 38-40).

may be glorified in the Son. If you shall ask me anything 14
in my name, that I will do. If you love me keep my com- 15
mandments. And I will ask the Father, and he shall give 16
you another Paraclete, that he may abide with you for ever.
The Spirit of truth, whom the world cannot receive, 17
because it seeth him not, nor knoweth him : but you shall
know him ; because he shall abide with you, and shall be
in you. I will not leave you orphans : I will come to you. 18
Yet a little while : and the world seeth me no more. But 19

15. *Keep my commandments.* Not merely the commandments of the O. T., but Christ's own teaching (*e.g.*, xiii. 34). This observance prepares for the gift of the Paraclete (*v.* 16).

16. *I will ask . . . another Paraclete.* Christ here speaks as man, for as God He Himself sends the Paraclete (xvi. 7, xx. 22). The term παράκλητος (from παρακαλέω), like the simple word κλητός (= 'called,' *e.g.*, Rom. i. 1, 6, 7), is passive, and means (chiefly in a legal sense) one summoned to plead a cause, a counsel. It thus corresponds to the Latin word 'advocatus.' In N. T. it is used only by St. John (xiv. 16, 26; xv. 26; xvi. 7 of the Holy Ghost; and 1 John ii. 1 of our Lord). In the last reference the Vulgate translates by 'advocatus,' in the other passages it leaves the word untranslated. Since Christ is our Advocate, He speaks of the Holy Ghost as 'another Paraclete.' The Holy Ghost as Paraclete is 'the Spirit of Truth,' who gives testimony to our Lord (*vv.* 17, 26 ; xv. 26).

17. *Whom the world* (*i.e.*, unbelievers, i. 10) *cannot receive* until they have laid aside their unbelief; then they can receive, just as a lame man can walk when his lameness is removed (cf. 1 Cor. ii. 14).

because it seeth (contemplateth) *him not.* Rather, instead of contemplating, it turns away its eyes from Him (i. 5, iii. 20) ;

nor knoweth (recognizeth) *him.* The verbs that follow are also in the present tense. "But you recognize Him because He abideth with you, and is in you."

The particles (*vv.* 16, 17) are very expressive in the Greek. The Holy Ghost is by the side of (παρά) the Apostles to defend them, He is with (μετά) them for fellowship and consolation, He is in (ἐν) them for their strength and illumination.

18. *I will not leave you orphans.* An orphan is one who has lost his parents by death, not by mere absence. Christ, therefore, will return in life to His 'little children.'

I will come to you. Better, 'I am coming.' That is, first visibly, immediately after the resurrection, then invisibly and by continual spiritual fellowship.

19. *The world seeth me no more.* That is, neither bodily nor spiritually (cf. *v.* 17).

But you see me. Present, in sense of immediate future.

because I live. Christ has life in Himself (v. 26), and He takes up

20 you see me: because I live, and you shall live. In that day you shall know that I am in my Father, and you in
21 me, and I in you. He that hath my commandments, and keepeth them: he it is that loveth me. And he that loveth me, shall be loved of my Father: and I will love
22 him, and will manifest myself to him. Judas saith to him, not the Iscariot: Lord, how is it, that thou wilt manifest
23 thyself to us, and not to the world? Jesus answered, and

again the life even of His body (x. 17, 18). Therefore the Apostles shall see Him.

and you shall live. Christ will make the Apostles sharers in His own triumph over death, and bestow on them a new life here below and a deathless life hereafter (cf. xi. 25, 26).

20. *In that day you shall know.* The day referred to is the day of Pentecost, when the manifestation of Christ's triumphant power was begun and the new era of the Christian Church was solemnly opened (see on vii. 39, xiv. 12, and cf. xvi. 23, 26). Then, indeed, the Apostles would recognize still more clearly, in the greatness of the work accomplished within them (see *vv.* 10-12), Christ's union with the Father, by unity of nature, and their own union with Christ by grace (cf. xv. 5). "There is, therefore, a kind of inward manifestation of God, which is entirely unknown to the ungodly" (St. Aug., Tract lxxvi. c. 2).

21. *He that hath my commandments.* Cf. v. 38.

he it is. With exclusive emphasis; he and no one else.

shall be loved. To keep Christ's commandments is itself a gift of God's love. Reference is, therefore, made to a gift of love which is the reward of loving obedience — a deeper and more perfect love, leading to fuller and more perfect knowledge. "The triune God, Father, and Son, and Holy Spirit, come to us while we are coming to them: They come with help, we come with obedience; They come to enlighten, we to behold; They come to fill, we to contain: that our vision of Them may not be external, but inward; and Their abiding in us may not be transitory, but eternal" (St. Aug. l.c., c. 4).

22. *Judas . . . not the Iscariot.* Called 'Jude of James' (Luke vi. 16; Acts i. 13) and Thaddeus (Matt. x. 3; Mark iii. 18).

how is it? ($\tau\iota$ $\gamma\epsilon\gamma o\nu\epsilon\nu$) = how has it come to pass, what has happened (*i.e.*, what has determined Thee), that, &c. Looking for a glorious Messianic manifestation with a triumph over, and visible judgment upon, all enemies, Judas does not understand how Christ should not be manifested to the world. In reply to Judas's question, our Lord, as on other occasions (iii. 5-8, iv. 11-14, vi. 41-59, &c.), merely amplifies His teaching.

23. *We will come.* God is everywhere present by His essence, His power, and His clear vision of all things. In Him we live and move, and have our being. But He is said in a special manner to be present

said to him: If any one love me, he will keep my word, and my Father will love him, and we will come to him, and will make our abode with him: he that loveth me not, 24 keepeth not my words. And the word which you have heard is not mine; but the Father's who sent me. These 25 things have I spoken to you, abiding with you. But the 26 Paraclete, the Holy Ghost, whom the Father will send in my name, he will teach you all things, and bring all things

where He bestows unusual gifts or manifests Himself in an unusual way. Hence He was said emphatically to dwell in the temple. "That thy eyes may be open upon this house night and day: upon the house of which thou hast said: My name shall be there . . . that thou mayst hearken to the supplication of thy servant and of thy people Israel, whatsoever they shall pray for in this place" (3 Kings viii. 29, 30). He is said, therefore, to come and abide in a soul when He pours out upon it richer and more abundant gifts of His love and affectionate tenderness, when He turns a ready ear to its prayer, and, as in the temple of old, dwells within it.

24. *Is not mine* (see on vii. 16, and cf. xii. 44). The verb of the preceding clause is in the present, 'The word which you hear.'

25. *Abiding with you.* That is, while being visibly present.

26. *But the Paraclete* (v. 16), *whom the Father will send in my name* (v. 13). The Son, because He is begotten of the Father, is said to be unable to do anything of Himself but what He seeth the Father doing (v. 20); to have received from the Father 'to have life in himself' (v. 26); to judge according as He hears, for of Himself He cannot do anything (v. 30); and to have come in the name of the Father (v. 43). These expressions do not break up the Godhead, or separate the action of the Divine Persons; they reflect the distinction of the Persons and mark their relations: for the Son is begotten of the Father, and the Holy Ghost proceeds from the Father and the Son. "The whole Trinity, therefore, both speaketh and teacheth: but were it not also brought before us in its individual personality it would certainly altogether surpass the power of human weakness to take hold of it. For as it is altogether inseparable in itself, it could never be known as the Trinity were it always spoken of inseparably; for when we speak of the Father, and the Son, and the Holy Spirit, we certainly do not pronounce them simultaneously, and yet in themselves they cannot be else than simultaneous" (St. Aug., Tract lxxvii., c. 2). It must be borne in mind, then, that in the discourse that follows, the mission of the Holy Ghost is spoken of in language similar to that already used of the mission of the Son. But there is this difference—the Son is begotten of the Father alone, and is therefore said to be sent by the Father; the Holy Ghost proceeds from the Father and the Son, and He is therefore said to be sent either by the Father or by the Son, but by neither exclusively (cf. 16, 26, xv. 26, xvi. 7, 13-15).

27 to your mind, whatsoever I shall have said to you. Peace I leave with you, my peace I give unto you: not as the world giveth, do I give unto you. Let not your heart be
28 troubled, nor let it be afraid. You have heard that I said to you: I go away and I come unto you. If you loved me, you would indeed be glad, because I go to the Father:

Our Lord promises that the Paraclete, coming in His name, would instruct the Apostles in all revealed truth (xvi. 13), including truths not yet revealed by our Lord (xvi. 12), although He had revealed all that the Father had so far desired the Apostles to know (xv. 15), and in particular the Paraclete would reveal the future (xvi. 13: *e.g.*, the Apocalypse); but above all, He would bring to their recollection, and in its full meaning, whatsoever Christ had said to them. Therefore they need not now be anxious in asking many questions.

27. *Peace I leave with you.* At the end of this discourse our Lord now returns, with fuller meaning, to its beginning (*v.* 1); for He had made known His purpose more fully, and so had given them clearer assurance of peace. There seems to be an allusion to the Oriental custom of wishing peace at partings (3 John 14; Mark v. 34; Luke vii. 50; Jas. ii. 16). But our Lord, who, according to the prophets, was the true author of peace (Isa. ix. 6, 7; xxvi. 3, &c.), really bestows the peace He wishes, and gives it as a legacy to the disciples. It is *His*, the *peculiar* peace, spiritual and eternal, which proceeds from Him, and is the fruit of His death.

not as the world giveth. "He giveth His own peace, not after the world's way, but in a way worthy of Him by whom the world was made, that we should be of one heart with Himself, having our hearts run into one, that this one heart, set on what is above, may escape the corruption of earth" (St. Aug. l.c., c. 5).

28. *You have heard that I said.* Better, 'You heard' (see *vv.* 3, 18). *If you loved me, you would indeed be glad.* Better, 'You would have rejoiced.' "Their hearts might have become filled with trouble and fear, simply because of His going away from them, even though intending to return; lest, possibly, in the very interval of the Shepherd's absence, the wolf should make an onset on the flock. But as God, He abandoned not those from whom He departed as man; and Christ Himself is at once both man and God . . . Why, then, should their heart be troubled and afraid? . . . But that they might understand that it was only in respect of His human nature that He said, 'I go,' He went on to say, 'If you loved Me, you would indeed be glad, because I go to the Father; for the Father is greater than I.' For human nature is worthy of congratulation in being so assumed by the only-begotten Word as to be constituted immortal in heaven, and, earthy in its nature, to be so sublimated and exalted, that, in itself only dust, it should become incorruptible, and take its seat at the right hand of the Father" (St. Aug., Tract lxxviii.).

for the Father is greater than I. And now I have told you before it come to pass: that when it shall come to pass you may believe. I will not now speak many things with you. For the prince of this world cometh, and in me he hath not anything. But that the world may know that I love the Father: and as the Father hath given me commandment, so do I: Arise, let us go hence.

29. *You may believe.* Not with a new, but with an augmented faith, believe that He was indeed the Christ, the Son of the living God.

30. *The prince* (ruler) *of this world cometh* (is coming). He points to the devil as the ruler of sinners, whom He designates by the name of 'this world' (viii. 44; cf. 1 John iii. 8; 2 Pet. ii. 19). The devil had already instigated Judas; and probably again assailed our Lord Himself by temptation (see Luke iv. 13; xxii. 53), besides procuring His death.

in me he hath not anything. "For neither did He come with sin as God, nor had His flesh any hereditary taint of sin" (St. Aug., Tract lxxix. c. 2). Why then did Christ die? 'For the wages of sin is death'; and the devil 'had the empire of death' (Rom. vi. 23; Heb. ii. 14). Thus it would seem that Satan had power over Christ. But—

31. *That the world may know.* Christ explains the coming of Satan against Him. It was not because Satan had any power over Christ, but in order that Christ, by His obedience to the Father's commandment (see x. 18), might exhibit the perfect love He had for the Father, who sent Him to redeem mankind.

Arise, let us go hence. From xviii. 1 we learn that the discourse and prayer (xv.-xvii.) were uttered before our Lord crossed the brook Cedron to Gethsemani, and, in all probability, before He left the house. But the words of the text here clearly indicate that He left the 'upper chamber' in which the Last Supper had been taken.

CHAPTER XV.

Our Lord's Manifestation to His Disciples.

(*Continued.*)

(Vers. 1–27.)

1 I AM the true vine; and my Father is the husband-
2   man. Every branch in me, that beareth not fruit, he

In the discourse just finished our Lord had raised the thoughts of the Apostles to heaven, and had opened to their gaze a vision of Himself exalted in power, and using that power for their guidance and protection. In the discourse that follows He reveals to the Apostles what He will be to them here below on earth. By the outpouring of His Spirit upon them He will ever maintain with them an effective union, truly vital and most tender. By persecution they will be called to imitate Him. But let them not fear. He now warns them of this lest their faith should waver, and promises that His strength shall be with them—that strength which has already mastered the prince of this world and has overcome the world.

1. *I am the true vine.* In a beautiful allegory our Lord declares that He gives life and nourishment to all His disciples, to His whole Church, as a vine gives life and nourishment to its branches. The allegory gives us some idea of the wonderful mystery of the Church's internal unity within herself and union with Christ (see Rom. vi. 4–6, xii. 5; 1 Cor. xii. 12–14; Eph. i. 19–23, iv. 15, 16, v. 29–32; Col. ii. 19). In the Old Testament the vine was the symbol of Israel as the cherished congregation of God (Ps. lxxix 8–12; Is. v. 1–4; Jer. ii. 21, &c.). Under the Machabees it appeared on Jewish coins as the national emblem.

Christ calls Himself the true ($ἀληθινή$) vine, because He is the reality of the idea figuratively set forth in the natural vine, just as He is the 'true light' (i. 9), and 'the true bread from heaven' (vi. 32).

"This passage of the Gospel declares that the Mediator between God and men, the man Christ Jesus, is the Head of the Church, and that we are His members. For as the vine and its branches are of one nature, therefore, His own nature as God being different from ours, He

will take away: and every one that beareth fruit he will purge it, that it may bring forth more fruit. Now you are 3 clean by reason of the word which I have spoken to you. Abide in me: and I in you. As the branch cannot bear 4 fruit of itself, unless it abide in the vine, so neither can you, unless you abide in me. I am the vine; you the 5 branches: he that abideth in me, and I in him, the same beareth much fruit: for without me you can do nothing. If any one abide not in me: he shall be cast forth as a 6

became man, that in Him human nature might be the vine, and we who also are men might become branches thereof. Christ is the vine in the way in which He said, 'The Father is greater than I': but in the way in which He said, 'I and the Father are one,' He is also the husbandman. And yet not such a one as those whose whole service is confined to external labour; but such, that He also supplies the increase from within. 'For neither he that planteth is anything, nor he that watereth; but God that giveth the increase' (1 Cor. iii. 7) ... He says, 'Now you are clean by reason of the word which I have spoken to you' (v. 3). Here, you see, He is also the pruner of the branches—a work which belongs to the husbandman, and not to the vine" (St. Aug., Tract lxxx. cc. 1, 2).

2. *Every branch* (κλῆμα = vine-branch specifically; not the generic κλάδος) *in me, that beareth not fruit, he will take* (present tense = He takes it) *away*. A mere outward profession of the faith cannot make a vine-branch in Christ. By the vine-branches that bear not fruit we must therefore understand those that have been baptized in Christ, but are fruitless in good works (see Jas. ii. 20; and cf. Luke xiii. 7, "Cut it down therefore; why cumbereth it the ground?") *he will purge it* (= He pruneth it). He said, 'Now you are clean' (v. 3, cf. xiii. 10), but yet still further to be cleansed. "For, had they not been clean, they could not have borne fruit: and yet every one that beareth fruit is pruned, that he may bring forth more fruit. For who in this life is so clean as not to be in need of still further and further cleansing?" (St. Aug. l.c.)

3. *Now* (already) *you are clean by reason of* (because of) *the word*. The word is the whole word, the entire doctrine delivered to them by our Lord. It is the power of God (Rom. i. 16) to make sons of God (Jas. i. 18). Already had our Lord said that "they that hear shall live" (v. 25); because His words "are spirit and life" (vi. 64). (See note on vi. 64.)

5. *Without me you can do nothing*. If the branch abide not in the vine, and draw its life from the root, it can of itself bear no fruit whatever, little or much. 'Without me' is better rendered, 'because apart from Me.'

6. *He shall be cast forth*. According to the Greek the thought is more expressive. By the very fact of not abiding in Christ, a branch is

branch, and shall wither, and they shall gather him up, and cast him into the fire, and he burneth. If you abide in me, and my words abide in you, you shall ask whatever you will, and it shall be done unto you. In this is my Father glorified ; that you bring forth very much fruit, and become my disciples. As the Father hath loved me, I also have loved you. Abide in my love. If you keep my commandments, you shall abide in my love ; as I also have kept my Father's commandments, and do abide in his love. These things I have spoken to you, that my joy may be

already cast forth, and is withered (the verbs are in the past tense), and they (this is said indefinitely) gather them (αὐτά, i.e., the withered branches) up and cast into the fire, and they (the branches) burn.

7. *If you abide . . . you shall ask.* Better in the imperative, 'Ask whatever you will.' This must be understood in the sense of xiv. 13, 14. (Cf. 1 John v. 14.)

8. *In this is my Father glorified: that (ἵνα) you bring forth very much fruit.* The phrase 'in this' looks forward to what follows ; and ἵνα, as not infrequently in later Greek, has a weakened force, and is equivalent to 'namely.' The sense then is, 'In this is My Father glorified, namely, that you bring forth very much fruit, and become indeed My disciples.' Some, however, take 'in this' retrospectively, and give to ἵνα its full force : ' In this (i.e., in granting your request, v. 7) is My Father glorified. (And He grants your request) in order that you may bring forth much fruit.' The first interpretation is obviously preferable.

9. *As the Father hath loved.* The aorist is twice used, 'As the Father loved'; because our Lord has placed Himself in thought at the end of His life, and is, as it were, looking back upon it (see xiii. 1). The Father's love of Christ was a most effective one, showing Christ all things which the Father Himself doth (v. 20) ; so too Christ's love of the Apostles was an effective love—the very source of life to them (vv. 4-7). Therefore they are warned not to separate themselves from that love.

Abide in my love. Of this continuance of Christ's effective love towards them, the first condition is that they should keep His commandments, as He kept the Father's commandments and so retained the Father's love (see viii. 29, x. 17, 18).

"Here He certainly intended us to understand that fatherly love wherewith He was loved of the Father. For this was what He had just said, 'As the Father hath loved Me, I also have loved you'; and then to these He added the words, 'Abide in My love'; in that, doubtless, wherewith I have loved you. Accordingly, when He says also of the Father, 'I abide in' His love,' we are to understand it of that love which was borne Him by the Father" (St. Aug., Tract lxxxii.)

11. *These things* (vv. 9, 10) *I have spoken to you, that my joy*

in you, and your joy may be filled. This is my commandment, that you love one another, as I have loved you. Greater love than this no man hath, that a man lay down his life for his friends. You are my friends, if you do the things that I command you. I will not now call you servants: for the servant knoweth not what his lord doth. But I have called you friends: because all things whatsoever I have heard of my Father, I have made known to

may be in you, and your joy may be filled (fulfilled, made complete). The joy of Christ was His joyful alacrity and contentment in doing the Father's will (see iv. 34, v. 30, vi. 38, viii. 29, xiv. 31); and He desires the Apostles to feel the same joy in themselves. For it leads to the perfect joy of eternal life.

12. *This is my commandment*. Our Lord further explains how they are to abide in His love (v. 10, xiii. 34).
that (ἵνα = namely, that) *you love one another*. Moreover, His love for them should be the type and motive of their love for each other; and He explains the greatness of His love.

13. *Greater love than this no man hath, that* (ἵνα = namely, that) *a man lay down his life for his friends*. There is no contrast here between friends and enemies. The Apostles are the friends of Christ (v. 14), and our Lord tells them He is about to give them the greatest proof of friendship that any one can give a friend. For a man can give his friend no greater proof of love than to die for him.

14. *If you do the things that I command*. Perhaps better, 'that I am commanding.'

15. *I will not now* (οὐκέτι = no longer) *call you servants*. Certainly He had called them servants (xii. 26, xiii. 16), and the same term He will apply to them again (xv. 20); yet He here introduces the name of friend in such a way as to withdraw that of servant. He who serves is a servant; and the Apostles continued to serve Christ. St. Paul's constant description of himself is, 'servant of Jesus Christ.' The words, then, express our Lord's generosity and condescension. For whereas one cannot be even a good servant unless he do his master's commands, the Apostles, in doing the Lord's commandments, cease to be servants, and are admitted by Him to the close proximity of friendship and to a knowledge of all His secrets.

But I have called you friends: because all things whatsoever I have heard of my Father, I have made known to you. So it runs in the Greek. The past tense is employed because our Lord is speaking as if His work were already completed (see on v. 9). For the same reason, perhaps, He says He had made known all things, although, in point of time, He had yet many things to say to them (xvi. 12). But the words may also be taken in the sense explained in xiv. 26, *i.e.*, He had made known all things which the Father had so far desired them to know.

16 you. You have not chosen me: but I have chosen you; and have appointed you, that you should go, and should bring forth fruit, and your fruit should remain: that whatsoever you shall ask of the Father in my name, he may
17 give it you. These things I command you, that you love
18 one another. If the world hate you, know you that it hath
19 hated me before you. If you had been of the world; the world would love its own: but because you are not of the world, but I have chosen you out of the world, therefore

16. *You have not chosen me.* Again the past tense, 'You chose not Me, but I chose you.' He is speaking of their call to the apostolate; but the words bear a wider application. For such, too, is the general election of grace. If we maintain the priority of merit, grace is no more grace. But grace does not find merit; it effects merit. Therefore He says, 'You chose not Me,' because His mercy anticipated us (see Rom. xi. 5, 6). He makes the goodness of those whom He chooses.

and have appointed you, that (ἵνα = in order that) *you should go* (i.e., on your apostolic mission in the world), *and should bring forth fruit, and your fruit should remain.* The fruit is that of which He had just spoken (vv. 4, 5)—fruit, not only in themselves, but in the harvest of souls to be gathered for eternal life (see on iv. 36).

that (ἵνα = in order that) *whatsoever you shall ask.* This second ἵνα is co-ordinate with the first, and equally dependent on the principal verb 'appointed.' The Apostles were appointed also to pray, as they themselves understood (Acts vi. 4). Such prayer was intimately connected with the function of a true apostolate, and with its fruitful results (vv. 7, 8).

in my name: see on xiv. 13.

17. *These things.* Plural for singular (see i. 50).

I command (am commanding) *you, that* (ἵνα = namely, that) *you love one another.* In all things, therefore, our fruit is charity. "Appropriately does the good Master so frequently commend love, as the only thing needing to be commended, without which all other good things can be of no avail, and which cannot be possessed without bringing with it those other good things that make a man truly good" (St. Aug., Tract lxxxvii.).

18. *If the world hate you.* Our Lord prepares the Apostles for the trials of their ministry, by setting before them what He had Himself endured. Union with Christ implies repudiation by the world; and the Apostles must be ready to endure along with their Master the hatred of the world.

19. *If you had been* (were) *of the world, the world would love its own,* and would therefore love you (see on vii. 7): *but because you are not of the world ... therefore* (for this cause: see v. 16) *the world hateth you.*

the world hateth you. Remember my word that I said to 20
you: The servant is not greater than his master. If they
have persecuted me, they will also persecute you: if they
have kept my word, they will keep yours also. But all 21
these things they will do to you for my name's sake:
because they know not him that sent me. If I had not 22
come, and spoken to them, they would not have sin: but
now they have no excuse for their sin. He that hateth me, 23

20. *Remember my word.* That is, the warning of xiii. 16. The verbs that follow are in the past tense (see *vv.* 9, 15). "If they persecuted me. . . . kept my word." In this the Apostles should find strength and consolation, that their lives would be modelled on the pattern set by Christ; in both suffering and success they would reflect His life. For the phrase "Keep my word," see viii. 51, 52, 55, xiv. 15, 21, 23, 24. It is quite Johannean.

21. *All these things* (i.e., hatred and persecution) *they will do to you for my name's sake*. It is Christ Himself, His doctrine and spirit, that the world would hate and persecute in the Apostles. And the worldlings persecute Christ.

because they know not him that sent me. Our Lord frequently declared that the world knew not the Father (v. 37, vii. 28, xvi. 3, xvii. 25), yet He also declares that, 'he that hateth me, hateth my Father also' (*v.* 23). But who can hate one whom he knows not? Did the Jews not know God? Did they wish to hate the Father? If they did not wish, where was the sin? If they did wish, how could it be without their knowing Him? And does not our Lord Himself say, 'They have both seen and hated both me and my Father'? (*v.* 24). Yet, on the other hand, He said to them, 'Neither me do you know, nor my Father' (viii. 19). The explanation is found in what has already been asserted. The Father had really manifested Himself to the world, if only the world chose to see (v. 36-47). But, although gazing upon the Father's manifestation of Himself, they wilfully failed to recognise Him (v. 42-44, viii. 42). Thus they have seen, and do not see ; have known, and yet do not know. In the deep blindness that came, by their own wilfulness, upon them (xii. 37-40), they loved darkness rather than the light: for their works were evil (iii. 19, 20). Thus, in their moral blindness they hated the doctrine of Christ, and, in so hating, they hated the Father whom that doctrine revealed ; but instead of the truth regarding the Father, they clung to a figment of their own devising, and this figment they loved. So it happened that they hated the Father whom they did not truly know. And this hatred was a sin, for their blindness was wilful (*vv.* 22, 24).

22. *They would not have sin.* Reference is made, not to sin in general, but to their specific sin of unbelief, which, after the unparalleled miracles of Christ, was absolutely inexcusable. The phrase 'to have sin' is peculiar to St. John (ix. 41, xix. 11 ; 1 John i. 8).

24 hateth my Father also. If I had not done among them
the works that no other man hath done, they would not
have sin: but now they have both seen and hated both me
25 and my Father. But that the word may be fulfilled which
is written in their law: *they have hated me without cause.*
26 But when the Paraclete cometh, whom I will send you
from the Father, the Spirit of truth, who proceedeth
27 from the Father, he shall give testimony of me; and you
shall give testimony, because you are with me from the
beginning.

24. *But now they have both seen and hated.* The double καί is
better translated, 'though they have seen, yet they have hated (see
vi. 36; and, for doctrine, cf. xiv. 7).

25. *But that* (ἵνα = in order that) *the word may be fulfilled.* Even
in their unbelief the Jews are bearing prophetic testimony to Christ.
But on this point, and on the telic force of ἵνα, see xii. 38, 39; and
cf. xiii. 18.

written in their law. 'Law' is used for O.T. generally (see x. 34).
The words that follow are probably taken from Psa. lxviii. 5. (On the
Messianic character of this psalm, see on ii. 17.) The same words
occur in Psa. xxxiv. 19 also.

26. *But when the Paraclete cometh.* For meaning of this verse, see
on xiv. 16, 26.

from the Father (παρὰ τοῦ πατρός). These words denote, not the
eternal procession, but the temporal mission of the Holy Ghost (cf.
viii. 42).

who proceedeth from the Father (παρὰ τοῦ πατρὸς ἐκπορεύεται). It
is difficult to say whether these words are a mere repetition of the
previous idea of the temporal mission, or whether they refer to the
eternal procession of the Holy Ghost. The verb itself means to come
forth (see v. 29), and the particle is certainly used of the Son's eternal
generation from the Father (vi. 46, vii. 29). But, on the other hand,
although implying the eternal generation, it seems more directly to
denote the Son's coming into the world by the Incarnation (xvi. 27,
xvii. 8). In either case the substance of the thought is the same.
Temporal mission implies eternal procession of the person sent from
the person sending; and since the Holy Ghost is sent by Father and
Son (xiv. 16, 26), He proceeds from both.

27. *And you shall give testimony* (καὶ ὑμεῖς δὲ μαρτυρεῖτε = you also
are indeed witnesses) *because you are with me from the beginning* (i.e.,
of My public Messianic activity). 'Are' = have been and still are
(cf. 1 John iii. 8). As the hatred of 'the world' against Christ would
certainly continue, so should testimony to Him likewise continue.
This we take to be the connection (somewhat obscure) of vv. 26, 27
with what had gone before.

CHAPTER XVI.

Our Lord's Manifestation to His Disciples.

(*Continued.*)

(VERS. 1-33.)

THESE things have I spoken to you that you may not be scandalized. They will put you out of the synagogues: yea, the hour cometh, that whosoever killeth you, will think that he doth a service to God. And these things will they do to you, because they have not known the Father, nor me. But these things I have told you, that when the hour shall come, you may remember that I told you of them. But I told you not these things from the beginning, because I was with you. And now I go to him

1. *These things*, i.e., the persecutions of the world, and the coming of the Paraclete (xv. 18-27).
that you may not be scandalized (cf. xiii. 19, xiv. 29).
2. *They will put you out of the synagogues*. Better, 'the synagogue' (see ix. 22, xii. 42).
yea, the hour cometh (ἀλλ' ἔρχεται ὥρα). The meaning is, 'Excommunication is not all you will suffer; nay, there cometh an hour.'
that (ἵνα = namely, an hour when) *whosoever killeth you* (see xv. 8). Aorist participle (ἀποκτείνας) used of a single act characteristic of a class.
doth a service to God (λατρείαν προσφέρειν — offereth service, sacrifice).
3. *Because they have not known*. Better, 'did not recognise' (see on xv. 21).
4. *When the hour shall come*. Better, 'when their hour shall come' (v. 2; cf. Luke xxii. 53).
5. *But I told you not these things from the beginning*, i.e., when I first called you to the apostolate (see on vi. 65). In a general way He

that sent me, and none of you asketh me: Whither goest
6 thou? But because I have spoken these things to you
7 sorrow hath filled your heart. But I tell you the truth: it
is expedient to you that I go: for if I go not, the Paraclete
will not come to you: but if I go, I will send him to you.
8 And when he is come, he will convince the world of sin,
9 and of justice, and of judgment. Of sin: because they
10 believed not in me. And of justice: because I go to the

had foretold that persecution awaited them at the hands of unbelievers (Matt. v. 11, 12, x. 17 *seq.*); but never before so fully, so clearly, so definitely, and so connectedly. And that because He had been with them. But now it was necessary to tell them because He was going away.

And (εἰ = but) *now I go to him that sent me*. This ought to have consoled them (xiv. 2, 28); but they are absorbed in the sense of loss.

and none of you asketh me. As far as mere words go, St. Peter had asked this very question (xiii. 36), and St. Thomas had equivalently asked it (xiv. 5); but the purport of their question *then* was quite different from what it ought to be *now*, after our Lord's explanations. Their minds had been thrown into such confusion of personal sorrow that they thought chiefly of their own loss, and did not attend to the true purpose of Christ's going (*v*. 6).

7. *It is expedient*. That is, because the Father has so established the law which governs the connection of events one with another. According to that law, the departure of Christ will benefit the Apostles (for meaning, see on xiv. 13, 16, 26). Our Lord further declares what the work of the Paraclete will be, in relation to the world (9–11), in relation to the Apostles (12, 13), in relation to Christ Himself (14).

8. *He will convince* (*i.e.*, convict: see iii. 20) *the world of* (*i.e.*, concerning) *sin*, &c.

9. *Of sin: because they believed* (Greek believe) *not in me*. 'Because' (ὅτι), as is evident from *v*. 10, is explanatory merely, and in immediate dependence on 'He will convince.' It does not mean, 'He will convince the world that its unbelief is a sin,' but 'He will convict the world that it is in a state of sin, for they believe not in Me.' Besides ὅτι οὐ states a fact, and does not express a charge (cf. iii. 18). We have already explained how those that do not believe are already judged, and still in their antecedent state of sin, both original and actual (see iii. 18, 19, and cf. viii. 24, ix. 41). Of that universal state of sin, from which deliverance is obtained only through faith, the Holy Spirit, by the ministry of the Apostles, by their teaching and miracles, has plainly convicted the world (see Rom. cc. i.–v.).

10. *And of justice* (holiness): *because I go to the Father*. Our Lord's triumph over death and glorious ascension into heaven, with the promised manifestations of Divine power which were fulfilled after the

Father; and you shall see me no longer. And of judg- 11
ment: because the prince of this world is already judged.
I have yet many things to say to you: but you cannot 12
bear them now. But when he, the Spirit of truth, is come, 13
he will teach you all truth. For he shall not speak of
himself: but what things soever he shall hear, he shall
speak: and the things that are to come he shall shew
you. He shall glorify me; because he shall receive of 14
mine, and shall shew *it* to you. All things whatsoever the 15
Father hath, are mine. Therefore I said, he shall receive
of mine, and shew *it* to you. A little while, and now you 16

Ascension, show that Christ was the true Son of God, and 'seal' Him
(vi. 27) as the Sent of God. But the world called Christ a sinner, and
put Him to death as a malefactor (ix. 24, xviii. 30). Concerning this
also the world was convicted (see Acts ii. 22–36, iii. 12–19).

11. *And of judgment: because the prince of this world is already
judged.* The world is doomed to impending judgment, as it may learn
from the condemnation of its father (viii. 41, 44), who is already judged
and condemned (see explanation xii. 31).

12. *I have yet.* A general explanation of the verses that follow
(12–15) has already been given (see on xiv. 26). The relation of the
Holy Ghost to Christ is described in language similar to that describing
the relation of Christ to the Father. All that remains is to point out
some specific parallels.

13. *He shall not speak of himself* (*i.e.*, from Himself). (Cf. v.
19, viii. 28, vii. 16–18.)

what things soever he shall hear, he shall speak. The future tense
is used of the hearing, because it is connected here with a revelation
that had yet to be made (cf. v. 30, viii. 26, 40, xv. 15).

14. *He shall glorify me* (cf. xi. 4, xiii. 31, xvii. 1, 4, 6).

because he shall receive of mine. The Holy Spirit, who proceeds
eternally from the Son, is here said to receive His infinite knowledge
from the Son. But the future tense is used in reference to the temporal
manifestation of that knowledge (see on v. 20).

and shall shew (declare) *it to you*.

15. *All things whatsoever* (see x. 29, 30).

Therefore I said (for this cause, v. 16). Because the Son and the
Father are one, the Holy Ghost, 'who proceedeth from the Father'
(xv. 26), receiveth (here the present tense is used, λαμβάνει) of the
Son's, *i.e.*, proceeds from the Son also. The Father and the Son are
the one principle of the Holy Spirit.

16. *A little while, and now you shall not see me* (οὐκέτι θεωρεῖτε =
you behold Me no longer: see v. 10): *and again a little while, and
you shall see me* (ὄψεσθε). Change of verb implies a difference in the
kind of vision. The sight hereafter promised is not of the same

shall not see me : and again a little while, and you shall
see me : because I go to the Father. Then some of his
disciples said one to another : What is this that he saith
to us : A little while, and you shall not see me : and again
a little while, and you shall see me, and because I go to
the Father? They said therefore : What is this that he
saith, A little while? we know not what he speaketh. And
Jesus knew that they had a mind to ask him : and he
said to them : Of this do you inquire among yourselves,
because I said : A little while, and you shall not see me :
and again a little while, and you shall see me? Amen,
amen, I say to you, that you shall lament and weep, but
the world shall rejoice : and you shall be made sorrowful,
but your sorrow shall be turned into joy. A woman, when
she is in labour, hath sorrow, because her hour is come :
but when she hath brought forth the child, she remembereth
no more the anguish, for joy that a man is born into the
world. So also you now indeed have sorrow, but I will see
you again, and your heart shall rejoice ; and your joy no

character as their present beholding. Him, indeed, they should see,
but in quite different manner (cf. xiii. 33). The same distinction of
verbs is retained in the following verses (17, 19).

because I go to the Father. The best MSS. omit this clause. It has
apparently slipped in from the next verse.

17. *And because I go to the Father.* The Apostles are perplexed
at the seeming contradiction, ' You shall see me,' ' You shall not see
me,' and ' for (ὅτι) I go to the Father ' (v. 10).

19. *And Jesus knew.* That is, by reading intuitively their thoughts
(see on ii. 25). Hence the Apostles recognized the miraculous character
of that knowledge (v. 30).

among yourselves (μετ' ἀλλήλων = ' with one another '). Kindred
phrases used are πρὸς ἀλλήλους ' one to another ' (v. 17, iv. 33,
xix. 24) ; πρὸς ἑαυτούς = ' among themselves ' (xii. 19).

20. *Lament and weep* (said of outward manifestation) . . . *made
sorrowful* (said of inward feeling). Their sorrow at the death of Christ
would be like the piercing but transitory pangs of child-birth, and, like
them, give way to permanent joy—joy ushered in by the triumph of
Christ's resurrection (cf. xx. 20 ; Acts v. 41).

21. *A woman.* Lit. *the* woman, with definite article, because used
generically.

22. *Your joy no man shall take from you.* Compare the emphatic
statements of St. Paul, " In all things (tribulation, persecution, &c.)
we overcome because of him that hath loved us. For I am sure that

man shall take from you. And in that day you shall not ask 23
me anything. Amen, amen, I say to you: if you ask the
Father anything in my name, he will give it you. Hitherto 24
you have not asked anything in my name. Ask, and you
shall receive: that your joy may be full. These things I 25
have spoken to you in proverbs. The hour cometh, when
I will no more speak to you in proverbs, but will shew
you plainly of the Father. In that day you shall ask in 26

neither death, nor life, nor angels . . . nor any other creature shall be
able to separate us from the love of God, which is in Christ Jesus our
Lord" (Rom. viii. 37-39). "Knowing that he who raised up Jesus
will raise up us also with Jesus. . . . For which cause we faint not:
but though our outward man is corrupted, yet the inward man is
renewed day by day" (2 Cor. iv. 14-16). The hope which springs
from our Lord's triumph is to the disciples of Christ a perennial fount
of joy. *Spe gaudentes.* This joy cannot be wrested from us. We lose
it only by our own will.

23. *And in that day.* That is, not merely the forty days that
immediately followed the Resurrection, but the day of triumph which
included the Ascension, and the mission of the Holy Ghost (see on xiv.
19, 20).

you shall not ask me anything. The reference is to their mental
perplexity (*v.* 19). When the Paraclete came He would teach
them all truth (cf. *v.* 13, and see on xiv. 26). Hence the need of
asking such questions about our Lord as they had been asking would
be removed (xiv. 20).

if you ask (petition) *the Father* (cf. xiv. 13, 14). Some authorities
connect 'in my name,' not with 'ask' but with 'give': "In my name
He will give it you" (cf. xiv. 26). But the Vulgate punctuation is
preferable, being confirmed by *v.* 24.

24. *Hitherto you have not asked anything in my name.* Because
Christ Himself had not yet been fully revealed to them (*v.* 14; cf.
xiii. 19, 31, 32, xiv. 7, 13). But afterwards they were able to ask with
full knowledge of Christ, with perfect trust in His power and merits,
and according to His Spirit (see 23, 26).

Ask (present imperative — continue asking). We must be constant in
prayer.

that your joy may be full = be made complete: see on xv. 11.

25. *These things, i.e.,* the dark, obscure statements of *vv.* 16 *seq.*

in proverbs. Better, 'in allegories' (see on x. 6). It means enig-
matically, obscurely, as contrasted with the plain showing that was to
succeed.

The hour cometh. Better, 'there cometh an hour' (= a time: *vv.*
2, 21, 26, iv. 21, 23, v. 25).

will shew you plainly (= declare plainly: see *vv.* 13, 14, 15f.

26. *In that day.* At the time mentioned in *vv.* 23, 25.

my name: and I say not to you, that I will ask the Father
for you: for the Father himself loveth you, because you
have loved me, and have believed that I came out from
God. I came forth from the Father, and am come into
the world: again I leave the world, and I go to the Father.
His disciples say to him: Behold now thou speakest
plainly, and speakest no proverb. Now we know that
thou knowest all things, and thou needest not that any
man should ask thee. By this we believe that thou comest
forth from God. Jesus answered them: Do you now
believe? Behold the hour cometh, and it is now come,
that you shall be scattered every man to his own, and shall
leave me alone: and yet I am not alone, because the

I say not . . . that I will ask. Our Lord's merits, from which all our graces flow, are a perpetual intercession for us before the Father (1 John ii. 1, 2 : Heb. vii. 25 : Rom. viii. 34). Through those merits and effective intercession the cause of the Apostles had, so to speak, been already won, and the Father's affection for them had already been gained, so that, in our human way of speaking, it was no longer necessary for Christ to make petition on their behalf.

27. *Loveth* (φιλεῖ). The stronger verb, expressive of affectionate attachment (see on xi. 5). Contrast, 'God so loved (ἠγάπησεν) the world' (iii. 16).

I came out from God (Greek, 'from the Father'). For meaning of this and the following verse, see on xv. 26, and cf. vi. 46, vii. 29, viii. 42.

30. *Now we know.* They know because of Christ's reading their thoughts (see v. 19).

By this (i.e., herein: see iv. 37) *we believe* (i.e., more fully and firmly : see on xiv. 29).

31. *Do you now* (ἄρτι, not νῦν as in vv. 29, 30) *believe?* The word νῦν denotes a definite point of time, the immediate present, ἄρτι denotes properly time closely connected with present, 'just now.' In Attic Greek it marks something begun or finished just before the time of speaking, as with us 'just now' sometimes means 'just a moment ago.' Later it meant strictly present time, i.e., emphatically 'at this precise time.' From its root idea (ἄρω = to join, fit together) we might translate 'at this juncture.' The verse is interrogative only in form, for the question is merely suggestive: 'Do you just now believe? But how long will your firmness continue?'

32. *Behold the hour cometh* ('there cometh an hour': as in v. 25). *and it is* (now) *come* (ἐλήλυθεν : cf. νῦν ἐστιν of iv. 23). It 'has come,' so immediately at hand is it.

that (ἵνα = namely, that) *you shall be scattered every man to his own* (τὰ ἴδια = to his own place of sojourn : see on i. 11).

Father is with me. These things I have spoken to you, **33** that in me you may have peace. In the world you shall have distress: but have confidence, I have overcome the world.

and yet I am not alone: see on viii. 16, 29.

33. *These things.* Probably the last discourse after leaving the supper-room (xv. 1).

may have peace: see on xiv. 27 and cf. xiv. 1.

you shall have distress. Better, 'You have.' It has already begun.

I have overcome: see on xii. 31, xiii. 31.

CHAPTER XVII.

Our Lord's Prayer for His Disciples.

(VERS. 1–26.)

THESE things Jesus spoke, and lifting up his eyes to heaven, he said: Father, the hour is come, glorify 2 thy Son, that thy Son may glorify thee. As thou hast given him power over all flesh, that he may give eternal 3 life to all whom thou hast given him. Now this is eternal life: that they may know thee, the only true God, and

"We now enter most reverently what may be called the innermost sanctuary. For the first time we are allowed to listen to what was really 'the Lord's Prayer,' and, as we hear, we humbly worship. That prayer was the great preparation for His Agony, Cross, and Passion; and also, the outlook on the Crown beyond" (Eders. l.c., p. 565).

In the first part (*vv.* 1–5) Christ, as man, prays for Himself, but in connection with His work as our Great High-Priest; in the second part (*vv.* 6–26) the High-Priest prays for the Apostles, and for all the faithful.

1. *Lifting up his eyes to heaven*, in assured confidence of being heard (xvi. 33: cf. xi. 41 and contrast, 'would not so much as lift up his eyes towards heaven,' Luke xviii. 13).

the hour is come: see on ii. 4.

glorify thy Son: see on xiii. 31, 32.

2. *As* (καθώς=because: see on xiii. 34) *thou hast given him power over all flesh* (*i.e.*, all mankind: see i. 14), *that* (ἵνα=in order that) *he may give eternal life to all whom thou hast given him* (see on v. 21, vi. 37-40, 44). Our Lord prayed for the glory of triumph over sin and death in order that He might give life to all. Note in this verse the nominative absolute neuter (πᾶν ὃ δέδωκας), which is afterwards resolved into the plural masculine (δώσῃ αὐτοῖς).

3. *Now this is eternal life*: see on iii. 15, 18, v. 24.

Jesus Christ, whom thou hast sent. I have glorified thee 4
on the earth: I have finished the work which thou gavest
me to do: and now glorify thou me, O Father, with 5
thyself, with the glory which I had, before the world was,
with thee. I have manifested thy name to the men whom 6
thou hast given me out of the world. Thine they were,

that (ἵνα = namely, that) *they may know thee.* Rather, 'recognize'; it is more than bare knowledge (cf. viii. 55, x. 15, 27, and see on xv. 21).

the only true God. On the sense of 'true' see i. 9. The Father, with whom the Son and the Holy Ghost are one, is said to be the only true God, in contrast with the false gods of the heathen world.

whom thou hast sent (cf. vi. 29). Aorist is used, 'Whom Thou didst send.'

4. *I have glorified thee* (cf. xiii. 31, 32, vi. 37–40). Again the aorist, 'I glorified thee.' Our Lord is, as it were, looking back upon His finished work (see on xv. 9). In the Greek it runs thus: "I glorified Thee, having finished (*i.e.*, perfected) the work which Thou hast given Me to do" (see iii. 16, 17, iv. 23).

5. *With thyself*, *i.e.*, in heaven. Observe the parallelism: 'I have glorified Thee on earth, and now (*i.e.*, in turn) glorify Thou Me in heaven.'

with the glory which I had (imperf., denoting continual possession), *before the world was* (see i. 1), *with thee* (*i.e.*, in fellowship with Thee: παρὰ σοί). The human mind cannot reach, by its highest thought, an adequate idea of the exaltation of the sacred humanity of our Lord, hypostatically united to the Eternal Word, and glowing amid the essential glory of the Godhead (see on i. 14, 18). "Being in the form of God, (He) thought it not robbery to be equal with God: but emptied himself, taking the form of a servant, being made in the likeness of men. He humbled himself, becoming obedient unto death: even to the death of the cross. For which cause God also hath exalted him, and hath given him a name which is above all names: that in the name of Jesus every knee should bow, of those that are in heaven, on earth, and under the earth. And that every tongue should confess that the Lord Jesus Christ is in the glory of God the Father" (Phil. ii. 6–11).

6. *I have manifested.* Better, 'I manifested' (see v. 4). It means effectually manifested. This verse explains v. 4: "I have glorified thee by manifesting thy name."

thy name, *i.e.*, the Father Himself — making known to men His unapproachable glory (see on xiv. 13).

whom thou hast given me out of the world: see on vi. 37, 44, 66, xv. 19.

Thine they were. For, 'he that is of God heareth the words of God' (viii. 47: see on iii. 21).

and to me thou gavest them: and they have kept thy
7 word. Now they have known that all things which thou
8 hast given me are from thee: because the words which
thou gavest me, I have given to them: and they have
received them, and have known in very deed that I came
out from thee, and they have believed that thou didst send
9 me. I pray for them: I pray not for the world, but for
them whom thou hast given me: because they are thine:

and to me thou gavest them: cf. x. 29, xviii. 9.
they have kept thy word. Because the word of Christ was the Father's (see on vii. 16).

7. *Now they have known.* Better, 'have recognized,' come to know.' It denotes the progress of the Apostles in keeping the word of the Father. They now know that the Father was in Christ—in His teaching and life (see on v. 19, 20, 36, vii. 16, viii. 16, 28).

8. *The words which thou gavest me* (cf. vii. 16, viii. 26, 28, 40). The verbs that follow are in the past tense (see *v.* 4). *Received— known—believed.* (For the doctrine, cf. vi. 69, 70, xvi. 27).

Verses 6-8 are really the introduction to our Lord's prayer for the Apostles. The Apostles are presented to the Father by the High Priest as those very men whom the Father Himself had chosen out of the world, and had specially given to Him. They were really the Father's own. It was the Father's word which they kept; it was the Father whom they had come to know, because Christ communicated to them the words which the Father gave Him. For them, and for their special needs, He now intercedes. To Him as Messiah the whole world belongs; and to save that world He had come from the Father. But He is not now interceding for the world; He is interceding for those whom the Father had specially given Him, whom He Himself had so far guided and protected, and whom He was now, in accordance with the Father's providential designs, about to leave behind amid all the trials of the world.

9. *I pray for them.* More literally and emphatically, 'I for them am praying: not for the world am I (now) praying, but for those whom thou hast given me.' The present tense ought not to be turned into an absolute present, as if Christ said, 'I never pray for the world,' an interpretation which is opposed to *vv.* 18, 20, 21, and to the clear teaching of 1 John ii. 2 ('He is the propitiation for our sins; and not for ours only, but also for those of the whole world'), but it ought to be taken as a simple present, as translated above. The prayer was a special prayer, based on special grounds, and for reasons not common to all men.

because they are thine. The allegiance of the Apostles (*v.* 8) was one ground of petition; another, and a higher ground, is now touched upon. The Apostles belong to Father and Son equally. Therefore the Son prays; therefore the Father is moved to hear that prayer.

and all my things are thine, and thine are mine: and I 10
am glorified in them. And now I am not in the world, 11
and these are in the world, and I come to thee. Holy
Father, keep them in thy name, whom thou hast given me:
that they may be one, as we also are. While I was with 12
them, I kept them in thy name. Those whom thou gavest
me have I kept: and none of them is lost, but the son of

10. *All my things.* In this verse Christ expresses His perfect
equality with the Father. Hence their glory is one.
I am glorified in them, because they know, and will teach, that
Christ is in the glory of the Father (*vv.* 7, 8). But the glory of
Christ is equally the glory of the Father (see xi. 4, xiii. 31, and cf.
v. 23). Moreover, Christ is the vine, the Father is the husbandman,
the Apostles are the branches: but the beauty and fruitfulness of the
branches are the glory both of the vine and of the husbandman
(cf. 1 Thess. ii. 18, 20).

11. *And now.* This verse brings forward the peculiar ground of need.
I am not (οὐκέτι = no longer) *in the world.* Present, for immediate
future.
Holy Father. An epithet not employed elsewhere. It most
appropriately introduces the petition for the Apostles to be preserved
from contagion in the world (*vv.* 15, 17).
whom thou hast given. In Greek, 'Which thou hast given.'
That is, 'Keep them in thy name, which thou hast given me for
manifestation to them' (see *v.* 6).
that (in order that) *they may be one* (*i.e.*, in Thy faith, and Thy true
spirit), *as we also are* (*i.e.*, after the type of the closest possible unity).
The unity of grace reflects, though, of course, it can never equal, the in-
effable unity of the Divine nature. This unity is based on faith. Hence
the Apostles are kept in the name (*i.e.*, in the knowledge) of the Father.

12. *While I was with them"* (see *vv.* 4, 11). The A.V. adds
the (non-genuine) phrase, 'in the world.'
I kept them (imperf. of continual action).
Those whom. Again the better-attested Greek runs, I kept (ἐτήρουν)
them in Thy name, *which* Thou hast given Me, and I guarded' (ἐφύλαξα).
τηρέω expresses watchful care, φυλάσσω indicates safe custody and
often implies assault from without; the former verb may mark the
result of which the latter verb is the means. (See Thayer-Grimm's
Lexicon).
and none of them is lost. Better, 'Not one of them perished, but
the son of perishing' (perdition). "Son of perdition" is a Hebraism
(cf. 'children of light' xii. 36; see Matt. viii. 12 (children of the
Kingdom), ix. 15 (children of the bridegroom), xxiii. 15 (child of hell),
Luke x. 6 (son of peace), xvi. 8 (children of this world). The phrase
indicates a close affinity, resembling that between child and parent.
that the scripture = 'in order that the Scripture may be fulfilled'

13 perdition, that the scripture may be fulfilled. And now I come to thee: and these things I speak in the world, that
14 they may have my joy filled in themselves. I have given them thy word, and the world hath hated them, because they are not of the world; as I also am not of the world.
15 I pray not that thou shouldst take them out of the world,
16 but that thou shouldst keep them from evil. They are
17 not of the world: as I also am not of the world. Sanctify

(see on xiii. 18). According to St. Peter (Acts i. 16–20) references to Judas are found in Psa. xl. 10, lxviii. 26, cviii. 8. See on ii. 17, and cf. xv. 25).

13. *And now.* Better, 'but now,' introducing a contrast.

these things I speak. Since I am now about to leave this world, before I depart I offer up this prayer to obtain Thy protection for My disciples.

my joy filled in themselves: see on xv. 11. The joy arises from a sense of protection.

14. *The world hath hated them* (past tense: see v. 4). For sense of verse cf. xv. 18–20. Because the world hated them, therefore the Father, whose doctrine they have received, will love and protect them.

15. *Keep them from evil* (τοῦ πονηροῦ). Is the word masculine (from the evil one = the devil) or neuter (from evil)? St. John's Epistles seem to imply the former (1 John ii. 13, iii. 12, v. 18); but the Gospel uniformly describes 'the evil one' with more circumstantiality than is here shown, and in a very marked way (viii. 44, xii. 31, xiv. 30). In the Gospel St. John records our Lord's words, but in the Epistles he speaks in his own person. Now our Lord habitually designated the devil plainly (Matt. iv. 10, xii. 26–28; Mark iii. 26, iv. 15; Luke x. 18, xi. 18, &c.) Since, then, it is a question of our Lord's own language, not of St. John's, we interpret, "Keep them from all evil."

Having prayed that the Apostles may be preserved in the world (9–16) our Lord now further prays that they may be consecrated for the due discharge of their sublime office.

17. *Sanctify them in* (the) *truth.* The verb here used (ἁγιάζειν) was employed to denote our Lord's consecration and dedication to the Messianic office (x. 36). It is a question whether it here means to purify internally through knowledge of the truth (cf. viii. 32); or to consecrate to the service of the truth. Most probably the latter. Our Lord had already prayed for the preservation of the Apostles in the truth (11, 12), for in the truth they had already been sanctified (6–8). This fresh petition must therefore be understood, not of internal sanctification, but of consecration to the ministry of the truth. This is confirmed by the grounds of the petition (18, 19).

Thy word is truth (vv. 6, 8). The truth is the Father's own word.

them in truth. Thy word is truth. As thou hast sent ¹⁸
me into the world, I also have sent them into the world.
And for them do I sanctify myself: that they also may ¹⁹
be sanctified in truth. And not for them only do I pray, ²⁰
but for them also who through their word shall believe
in me: that they all may be one, as thou, Father in me, ²¹
and I in thee: that they also may be one in us: that
the world may believe that thou hast sent me. And the ²²
glory which thou hast given me, I have given to them:
that they may be one, as we also are one. I in them, ²³

18. *As thou hast sent.* Better. 'As Thou didst send Me into the world, so I also sent them into the world' (*v*. 4). In what sense the Apostles had already been sent may be gathered from iv. 28. As the mission of the Apostles resembled that of Christ, so ought they to receive a similar consecration (see x. 36). But there is another reason for the consecration of the Apostles. Christ's own personal offering for that purpose, which purpose the Father will not suffer to remain unattained (*v*. 19).

19. *For them do I sanctify myself.* The verb ἁγιάζειν is a sacred word for sacrifices in the O.T. It must have this meaning here. Christ voluntarily offers himself in sacrifice (x. 18) on behalf of (ὑπέρ) the Apostles (xv. 13, 14) in order that they may in truth (*i.e.*, really and truly) be consecrated, or be consecrated to truth (see *v*. 17). Christ's own death, voluntarily offered, is the crowning plea for the Apostles. Mention of the Apostolic mission naturally leads to prayer for those on whose behalf the Apostles are sent.

20. *And not for them only.* Better, 'but not for them only.' The limitation of *v*. 9, is now removed in a more general prayer.

shall believe in me" (see on x. 16, xi. 52). In Greek, "who believe" (see *v*. 4).

21. *That they all* (in order that all, both Apostles and faithful) *may be one*: see *v*. 10. In *v*. 23 the phrase is "May be made perfect in one."

That (in order that) *the world may believe.* The unity of the Church must therefore be also a visible unity, testifying before the face of the world to the Divine power, which alone can produce and preserve such unity (cf. xiii. 35).

22. *And the glory which thou hast given me.* The glory is Christ's eternal glory, given to Him by eternal generation, and overflowing upon the assumed human nature (*vv*. 1, 5, 24). But the Apostles had by grace been made the adopted sons of God, and joint-heirs with Christ (see on i. 12). Thus they are said to have received the glory given to Christ by the Father. The fruit of this glorious sonship should be unity.

23. *I in them*: see xiv. 23. The indwelling of Christ will thus be made manifest in visible unity, which at once proclaims the Divine mission and the Father's protecting care of the Church.

and thou in me: that they may be made perfect in one;
and the world may know that thou hast sent me, and
24 hast loved them, as thou hast also loved me. Father, I
will that where I am, they also whom thou hast given
me may be with me: that they may see my glory which
thou hast given me, because thou hast loved me before
25 the creation of the world. Just Father, the world hath
not known thee: but I have known thee: and these have
26 known, that thou hast sent me. And I have made known
thy name to them, and will make it known; that the love,
wherewith thou hast loved me, may be in them, and I in
them.

24. *Where I am, i.e.*, in heaven (i. 18, iii. 13.)
they also, a less probable reading has 'that which,' as in 11, 12.
because thou hast loved me (see on iii. 35, v. 20), *before the creation*
(literally foundation) *of the world:* see i. 3.
may see my glory: i.e., may behold in beatific vision the eternal
glory of My Godhead.
25. *Just Father.* A fresh appellation, introducing the ground of
a fresh appeal—an appeal to the justice of God, who rewards the
obedience of faith.
*the world hath not known thee, but I have known thee: and these
have known that thou has sent me.* Better: "The world indeed (καί)
knew thee not (xv. 21), but I knew thee: and these (*i.e.*, the Apostles)
knew that thou didst send me." Christ's own merits, the faith of the
Apostles, forming such a contrast with the unbelief of the world, are
urged as a reason for the granting of this prayer (*v.* 24). The
reason is developed in the following verse.
26. *I have made known thy name to them, and will make it known,
i.e.,* still more.
that (=in order that) *the love wherewith thou hast loved me* (ἣν
ἠγάπησάς με: double accusative) *may be in them:* see on xv. 9, 10.

CHAPTER XVIII.

The Betrayal and Capture.

(VERS. 1-12.)

WHEN Jesus had said these things, he went forth with his disciples over the brook Cedron, where

As some great cathedral may be represented in different pictures according as it is studied from different points of view, so the history of our Lord's life, and, in particular, the history of His Passion, may give us different views—different, but not contradictory—of the same inexhaustible facts. St. John, keeping to his general plan, in the following history of the Passion sets in high relief those elements which reflect our Lord's heavenly majesty, whereas the other evangelists lay greater stress, in accordance with their own plan, on those elements which set forth the intensity of His human suffering. St. John also omits what his readers had already learned from the history given by the Synoptics —our Lord's prayer in the garden, His agony, and the appearance of the angel.

1. *He went forth with his disciples over the brook Cedron* (τοῦ χειμάρρου τῶν Κέδρων: al. τοῦ Κεδρών, and τοῦ Κέδρον), *where there was a garden* (κῆπος). The word χείμαρρος (from χεῖμα winter, and ῥέω to flow) means literally 'flowing in winter,' a torrent. The better attested reading τῶν Κέδρων means 'of the cedars'; the reading τοῦ Κεδρών, which is well supported, means 'dark,' 'black,' and may refer either to the colour of the water (turbid), or to the gloom of the ravine, or to the dark hue of the cedars. Josephus mentions the φάραγξ (ravine, gully) of the Kedron (Antiq. ix. 7, 3), and speaks of the ravine itself as named Κεδρών ('black') (Wars, v. 2, 3). He describes it as lying on the east, between the city and the Mount of Olives. Of the evangelists St. John alone names it. The "garden" (termed "country-place" in Matt. xxvi. 36, and "farm" in Mark xiv. 32) was named (or the place in which it was situated was named) Gethsemani = oil-press.

"Passing out by the gate north of the temple, we descend into a

there was a garden, into which he entered with his disciples. And Judas also, who betrayed him, knew the place: because Jesus had often resorted thither together with his disciples. Judas therefore having received a band of soldiers, and servants from the chief priests and the Pharisees, cometh thither with lanterns and torches and weapons. Jesus therefore knowing all things that

lonely part of the valley of black Kidron, at that season swelled into a winter torrent. Crossing it, we turn somewhat to the left, where the road leads towards Olivet. Not many steps farther . . . we turn aside from the road to the right, and reach what tradition has since earliest times pointed out as 'Gethsemane.' It was a small property enclosed, 'a garden' in the eastern sense, where probably, amidst a variety of fruit-trees and flowering shrubs, was a quiet summer retreat, connected with, or near by, the 'olive-press.' The present Gethsemane is only some seventy steps square. But we love to think of this 'garden' as the place where Jesus 'often'—not merely on this occasion, but perhaps on previous visits to Jerusalem—gathered with His disciples. And as such it was known to Judas, and thither he led the armed band, when they found the 'upper-chamber' no longer occupied by Jesus and His disciples" (Eders., I. c. p. 569).

2. *Judas . . . who betrayed him* (pres. partic. = who was betraying Him).

3. *A band of soldiers* (τὴν σπεῖραν). The σπεῖρα is the Roman cohort, designated by the article as the well-known band, namely, because serving as the garrison of the fort Antonia. It is not necessary to suppose that the whole cohort, a tenth part of a legion, came; but a division ordered for the present service. The band was led, not by a centurion, but by a tribune (Chiliarch, *v.* 12), one of the six tribunes attached to each legion. This implies that our Lord's arrest was considered a serious, and even dangerous, step, as likely to cause a riot (Mark xiv. 2). But so serious a step would hardly be taken without consultation with the Procurator, Pontius Pilate. This explains Pilate's preparedness to sit in judgment early next morning (*vv.* 29-31).

servants from the chief priests and the Pharisees. These would be servants from the High-Priest's palace, and officers of justice appointed by the Sanhedrin.

lanterns (φανῶν: used only here in N.T. = torches) *and torches* (λαμπάδων = lamps). These were the ordinary equipment for night duty, to prevent any possible concealment.

and weapons (*i.e.*, swords and clubs, Matt. xxvi. 47; Mark xiv. 23).

4. *Knowing all things:* cf. ii. 25.

went forth. Not necessarily from the garden (*v.* 26), but from the spot where Judas, who had preceded the band, had saluted Him (Luke xxii. 47).

and said to them, i.e., to the Jewish ministers and leaders. The

should come upon him, went forth, and said to them: Whom seek ye? They answered him: Jesus of Nazareth. Jesus saith to them: I am he. And Judas also, who betrayed him, stood with them. As soon therefore as he had said to them: I am he: they went backward, and fell to the ground. Again therefore he asked them: Whom seek ye? And they said: Jesus of Nazareth. Jesus answered, I have told you, that I am he. If therefore you seek me, let these go their way. That the word might be fulfilled, which he said: Of them whom thou hast given me, I have not lost any one. Then Simon Peter having a sword, drew it; and struck the servant of the high-priest, and cut off his right ear. And the name

soldiers, as being only a guard to protect the emissaries of the Sanhedrin, would be in the rear.

5. *I am he.* More accurately, 'I am.'

Judas also, who betrayed him. With greater vividness, 'Judas . . . who was betraying Him, was standing.'

6. *They went backward.* The immediate effect of our Lord's answer was truly a miraculous result of Divine power. The Jewish representatives of the Sanhedrin, those whom our Lord had interrogated, drew back, and fell to the ground. Thus our Lord made known His power over His enemies, and the voluntariness of His surrender. "What will He do when He cometh to judge, who did this when giving Himself up to be judged? What will be His power when He cometh to reign, who had this power when He came to die?" (St. Aug., Tract cxii. c. 3). But His hour had come.

8. *Let these, i.e.,* the disciples, who had followed up, and were now near Christ.

9. *That the word, i.e.,* of xvii. 12. "The evangelist sees in this watchful care over His own the *initial* fulfilment of the words which the Lord had previously spoken concerning their safe preservation, not only in the sense of their outward preservation, but in that of their being guarded from such temptations as, in their then state, they could not have endured" (Eders., l.c. p. 576). "He commands His enemies, and they do what He bids them" (St. Aug. l.c.).

10. *Then Simon Peter.* Only St. John here names St. Peter and Malchus (a name of frequent occurrence), who was servant ($δοῦλος$ = slave) of the High-Priest. The 'servant' was probably about to rush upon our Lord. St. Luke also mentions the cutting off of the *right* ear, and adds the account of the miraculous healing. St. John omits our Lord's words as given in St. Matthew (xxvi. 52-54), but alone mentions the saying, 'The chalice which my Father hath given me, shall I not drink it?'—a saying which obviously refers to the prayer in the garden, of which prayer St. John has said nothing.

¹¹ of the servant was Malchus. Jesus therefore said to Peter: Put up thy sword into the scabbard. The chalice which my Father hath given me, shall I not drink it? ¹² Then the band and the tribune, and the servants of the Jews, took Jesus, and bound him.

St. Peter's Denials.

(VERS. 13-27.)

¹³ And they led him away to Annas first, for he was father-in-law to Caiphas, who was the high-priest of that ¹⁴ year. Now Caiphas was he who had given the counsel to the Jews, that it was expedient that one man should ¹⁵ die for the people. And Simon Peter followed Jesus, and so did another disciple. And that disciple was known to the high-priest, and went in with Jesus into the

12. *Took Jesus, and bound him.* Only St. John narrates that our Lord was bound in the garden itself. But Judas had given warning, 'Lay hold on him, and lead him away carefully' (Mark xiv. 44). As the band now closed in round our Lord, none of the Apostles dared to stay, but forsaking him they fled.

13. *To Annas first* (πρῶτον = at first). Of this circumstance, and of the subsequent private examination of our Lord concerning His disciples and His doctrine (v. 19), the Synoptics say nothing; of the public judicial trial before Caiphas St. John says nothing, but the πρῶτον here seems to show that he took for granted his readers would have that public trial in mind.

14. *Now Caiphas was he* (xi. 49-51). On account of the influence, and probably the known disposition of Annas, a preliminary examination before him was considered a safe step to take with a view to secure our Lord's condemnation.

15. *And Simon Peter followed* (descriptive imperfect: 'was following').

and so did another disciple. Some authorities give 'the other disciple.' The reference is to the evangelist himself. After the first panic caused by our Lord's capture (v. 12) Peter and John seem to have again taken courage; and the Synoptics imply that Peter was the first to rally, and to follow our Lord, though he still lingered 'afar off' (Matt. xxvi. 56-58; Mark xiv. 50, 53, 54; Luke xxii. 54). John seems to have entered the court of the High-Priest along with the guard, while Peter remained at the street door of the court till John had spoken to the portress and so procured his admission. The 'court of the High-Priest' was the quadrangular interior court of the High-

court of the high-priest. But Peter stood at the door 16
without. The other disciple therefore who was known to
the high-priest, went out, and spoke to the portress, and
brought in Peter. The maid therefore that was portress, 17
saith to Peter: Art not thou also one of this man's disciples? He saith: I am not. Now the servants and 18
ministers stood at a fire of coals, because it was cold, and
warmed themselves. And with them was Peter also
standing, warming himself. The high-priest therefore 19

Priest's official residence. It would thus seem that Annas lived in a
portion of his son-in-law's palace.

17. *He saith: I am not.* This is St. John's narrative of St. Peter's
first denial. Efforts are sometimes made to show that in the details of
St. Peter's three denials there are a number of minute discrepancies in
the four Gospels. The discrepancies are the creation of a criticism
which is wanting in historical imagination. No one will seriously
maintain that, in a court filled with our Lord's enemies, whose attention
was attracted by the presence of Peter, a Galilean follower of Christ,
the whole history of each denial is comprised in one short question and
an equally short answer. Rather, there were "reiterated expressions
of recognition, and reiterated and importunate denials on each occasion"
(Alford); and the evangelists have given us, this the words of one
questioner, and that the words of another questioner—for there were
really knots of questioners, and no doubt St. Peter moved about somewhat restlessly. (For the first denial, cf. Matt. xxvi. 69, 70 : Mark
xiv. 66-68 : Luke xxii. 55-57.) Each denial comprised a group of
connected incidents, which groups were separated from each other by a
clearly disconnecting interval of time. Thus, between the second denial
and the third there was an interval of about an hour (Luke xxii. 59).
The form of the portress' question, 'Art not thou *also* one of this
man's disciples?' implies great contempt of our Lord, and a knowledge on the part of the portress that John was a disciple.

18. *Now the servants.* This statement is connected with that of
v. 17; and marks the circumstances of Peter's first denial. Literally
the verse runs, 'Now the servants (δοῦλοι) and the officers (see on
v. 3) having made a fire of coals (ἀνθρακιάν), for it was cold, stood
and were warming themselves.' The soldiers, having brought the
prisoner in safely, had probably withdrawn.

19. *The high-priest therefore* (οὖν, resumptive of narrative from
vv. 13, 14, after the episode about St. Peter). Who is the High-Priest
here mentioned? Annas, or Caiphas? Many suppose it is the latter,
and in consequence they maintain that nothing passed before Annas,
who had immediately sent our Lord to Caiphas (v. 24). But this
interpretation violently forces upon the aorist of v. 24 the sense of the
pluperfect, giving it a meaning which it may bear, but only in *relative*
clauses; and it sets the whole verse in such an unnatural place that

asked Jesus of his disciples, and of his doctrine. Jesus answered him: I have spoken openly to the world: I have always taught in the synagogue, and in the temple, whither all the Jews resort; and in secret I have spoken nothing. Why askest thou me? ask them who have heard what I have spoken unto them: behold they know what things I have said. And when he had said these things, one of the servants standing by gave Jesus a blow, saying: Answerest thou the high-priest so? Jesus answered him: If I have spoken evil, give testimony of the evil: but if well, why strikest thou me? And Annas sent him bound to Caiphas the high-priest. And Simon

some authorities have transferred the verse to a place between vv. 13 and 14. We believe the High-Priest referred to is Annas. St. John is accustomed to speak of the High-Priests (v. 3, vii. 45, xi. 47, 56, xviii. 35, xix. 6, 15, 21. See on xi. 49, and cf. St. Luke iii. 2, 'the high-priests Annas and Caiphas'), and Annas, to whom our Lord was brought, is the High-Priest who conducts the first inquiry.

of his disciples and of his doctrine. Why did He gather disciples? Was He teaching false doctrine?

20. *I have spoken openly.* If the judge wished to act fairly and according to law, let him call witnesses, for Christ had spoken out publicly, and witnesses could not be wanting. 'I have always taught in synagogue (without article: see on vi. 60) . . . where all the Jews come together; and in secret I spoke nothing (*i.e.* no doctrine to be kept secret').

22. *One of the servants* (or officers: v. 3).

gave Jesus a blow (ῥάπισμα). The term itself may mean a stroke with a rod, a blow on the face, or a box on the ear (this last usually). In Acts xxiii. 2, St. Paul, for a supposed impudent speech to the High-Priest, was condemned to be struck on the mouth.

24. *And Annas.* Better, Annas therefore

sent him bound to Caiphas. By the private interrogation Annas had not succeeded in establishing anything against our Lord; he therefore sent Him to Caiphas for a more judicial trial.

25. *And Simon Peter was standing.* Peter is now, during the trial by Caiphas, in the same court where he stood during the examination by Annas (v. 18). This fact shows that both High-Priests were in the same palace.

Putting together the notices of the second denial (Matt. xxvi. 71, 72; Mark xiv. 68-70; Luke xxii. 58), we learn that Peter walked down the porch towards the outer court, and, as he went, first one maid met him, and then, as he returned from the outer court, the portress again accused him; and as he returned to join the group around the fire, first one man, and then the group itself, brought the same charge against

Peter was standing, and warming himself. They said therefore to him: Art not thou also one of his disciples? He denied it, and said: I am not. One of the servants of the high-priest (a kinsman to him whose ear Peter cut off) saith to him: Did I not see thee in the garden with him? Again therefore Peter denied: and immediately the cock crew.

Jesus and Pilate.

(VERS. 28-40.)

Then they led Jesus from Caiaphas to the governor's hall. And it was morning: and they went not into the hall,

him. To each separately, and to all together, he gave the same denial —but now with an oath. He was not molested for an hour. But then came a third denial (v. 26), for not only, as the Synoptics narrate, did the bystanders detect St. Peter's Galilean speech, but, as St. John adds, a servant of the High-Priest (v. 3), and kinsman of Malchus, declared that he had seen Peter with Christ in the garden. And now Peter denied with oaths and curses. Immediately upon his denial came the shrill crowing of a cock, and as Peter, no doubt startled in conscience, looked up, his eyes met the full gaze of Jesus—a gaze piercing him to the centre of his soul. And going out in sorrow, he wept bitterly.

The history of our Lord's trial before Caiaphas, and of all His maltreatment, is passed over by St. John as known to the reader (see Matt. xxvi. 57-68; Mark xiv. 55-65; Luke xxii. 63-71). St. John also passes over the meeting of the Sanhedrin, held in the early morning, when they "took counsel against Jesus, that they might put him to death."

28. *Then they led Jesus.* Better, 'they led therefore,' continuing from v. 24.

to the governor's hall (prætorium). "The residence of the Procurator of Judea was not at Jerusalem, but at Cæsarea. On special occasions, especially during the chief Jewish feasts, when, on account of the crowds of people that streamed into Jerusalem, particularly careful oversight was necessary, the Procurator went up to Jerusalem, and resided there in what had been the palace of Herod." (Schürer, div. I. vol ii. p. 48.)

And it was morning (πρωΐ) early in the morning: used particularly of the fourth watch of the night (three to six o'clock a.m.). A Roman court could be held immediately after sunrise, and Pilate might have expected them at an early hour, as he had given orders for the 'band' of soldiers on the previous night (v. 3).

might not be defiled: see on xiii. 1.

that they might not be defiled, but that they might eat the
29 pasch. Pilate therefore went out to them, and said:
30 What accusation bring you against this man? They
answered and said to him: If he were not a malefactor,
31 we would not have delivered him up to thee. Pilate
therefore said to them: Take him you, and judge him
according to your law. The Jews therefore said to him:
32 It is not lawful for us to put any man to death. That the
word of Jesus might be fulfilled which he said, signifying
33 what death he should die. Pilate therefore went into the

29. *Pilate therefore.* Pilate is suddenly introduced as one whose name is already familiar to the reader. With the customary Roman considerateness for the religious feelings of subject peoples, the Governor goes outside to the Jews.

What accusation? Pilate demands, as Roman law required, a formal indictment against the accused. The Jews had evidently expected an immediate sentence on our Lord. Pilate's interrogation found them quite unprepared with an answer; they reply with evasion.

30. *If he were not a malefactor.* A charge so vague was simply worthless as a legal accusation. Pilate, therefore, points out, in language somewhat suggestive of contemptuous irony, the absurdity of the proceeding.

31. *Take him you.* Under the Roman law the Jews had no authority to put our Lord to death. Pilate therefore insinuates that the Jews would be acting just as legally in putting our Lord to death themselves, as would Pilate in sentencing Him without legal trial. Matters are thus at a dead-lock; for Pilate is as powerless as the Jews.

32. *Signifying what death* ($ποίῳ\ θανάτῳ$ = by what manner of death) *he should die.* Our Lord had foretold His death by crucifixion at the hands of Gentiles (iii. 14, xii. 32; Matt. xx. 19; Mark x. 33; Luke xviii. 32). If our Lord had been sentenced by the Jews as a blasphemer and false prophet, He would, like St. Stephen, have been stoned (cf. viii. 59, x. 31), but not condemned to the Roman punishment of crucifixion, a punishment which was unusual amongst the Jews.

To escape from their dilemma the Jews had to formulate a capital charge. This they now did (Luke xxiii. 2). The charge contained three heads: (1) seditious disturbance, (2) prohibition of tribute to Cæsar, (3) His claim to be Christ, a King. The Jews were not so loyal to Roman rule that they should be so active in its defence, and Pilate saw clearly that they were inspired merely by hatred of our Lord (Matt. xxvii. 18; Mark xv. 10). But a charge of treason had been formally made, and Pilate dared not disregard it. He re-enters the prætorium, and summons our Lord before him.

33. *Art thou* (the pronoun is emphatic by position) *the king of the*

hall again, and called Jesus, and said to him: Art thou the king of the Jews? Jesus answered: Sayest thou this 34 thing of thyself, or have others told it thee of me? Pilate 35 answered: Am I a Jew? Thy own nation and the chief priests have delivered thee up to me: what hast thou done? Jesus answered: My kingdom is not of this world. 36 If my kingdom were of this world, my servants would certainly strive that I should not be delivered to the Jews: but now my kingdom is not from hence. Pilate therefore 37 said to him: Art thou a king then? Jesus answered: Thou sayest, that I am a king. For this was I born, and for this came I into the world: that I should give testimony to the truth. Every one that is of the truth, heareth my voice. Pilate saith to him: What is truth? And 38

Jews! There is certainly astonishment, and possibly an element of scorn in Pilate's question. Our Lord, by His counter-question, claims the right to know the author of the accusation, and to have the *status causæ* clearly set forth. Such a question could not fail to impress Pilate still more deeply as to the groundlessness of the accusation. To name the authors of the charge was to discredit the charge itself.

35. *Am I a Jew?* Pilate scornfully rejects the first part of our Lord's question. He was not a Jew, and had no personal knowledge of the thoughts that had been running through Jewish brains. But Jesus has been given up by His own nation, and especially by its leaders. What had He done? This surely called for explanation.

36. *My kingdom* (our Lord thus confesses that He is a King) *is not of this world.* Christ is King of a kingdom such that His claim to it involves no treason against any earthly power. His kingdom is not of this world at all. If it had been of this world, surely His servants (*i.e.*, officers, ministers: see *vv.* 3, 12, 18, 22) would have struck a blow for Him.

37. *Art thou a king then?* Better, 'So then, thou' (again strongly emphatic) 'art a king?' Pilate is perplexed and surprised; moreover, a vague feeling of dread is beginning to take possession of him (see xix. 8).

Thou sayest, i.e., thou speakest truly. A king I am indeed.

For this (*i.e.*, to this end) *was I born, and for this came I into the world.* The second clause is an emphatic repetition, under another form, of the idea contained in the first clause (see i. 9).

that is of the truth (cf. iii. 21; viii. 47).

38. *What is truth?* Pilate is somewhat irritated at the visionary character of Christ's kingdom—a kingdom of truth presents no very clear idea to his mind. But he does see that there is no treason in it; yet, instead of releasing our Lord at once, he unwisely seeks, in order

when he said this he went out again to the Jews, and saith
to them: I find no cause in him. But you have a custom
that I should release one unto you at the pasch: will you
therefore that I release unto you the king of the Jews?
Then cried they all again, saying: Not this man, but
Barabbas. Now Barabbas was a robber.

not to be unpopular, an indirect way out of the difficulty. And first of all, he sends our Lord to Herod, who, like Pilate, had come up to Jerusalem on account of the Feast. St. John omits this incident, supposing it to be familiar to the reader. Immediately after v. 38, then, is to be inserted the narrative of St. Luke (xxiii. 5-15); and this narrative supplemented by the details given in St. Matthew (xxvii. 12-14: cf. Mark xv. 3-5). The attempt to leave the responsibility of a decision with Herod had failed. Pilate now turned to another scheme, hoping to avoid the odium of the Jewish leaders by inducing the people to ask for our Lord's release. This also failed; for the people, instigated by their leaders, clamoured for the release of Barabbas. St. John says, "They cried out, therefore, *again* all of them." The "again" either looks to the fuller narrative of the Synoptics, or implies that the previous answers (vv. 30, 31) had been given with a great shout.

40. *Now Barabbas was a robber* ($\lambda\eta\sigma\tau\eta\varsigma$ = bandit, brigand). He had also been guilty of sedition and murder (Mark xv. 7). His very name, Bar-Abbas = son of Abba (father), adds a tragic suggestiveness to his choice by the Jews and our Lord's rejection by them (cf. Acts iii. 14).

CHAPTER XIX.

Jesus condemned by Pilate.

(Vers. 1–16.)

THEN therefore Pilate took Jesus, and scourged him. And the soldiers platting a crown of thorns, put it

Two schemes having fallen through, Pilate resolves on a third. He will commit a minor act of injustice to save himself from the commission of a greater; by cruelly scourging our Lord he may move the Jews to relent in their blood-thirsty pursuit of our Lord's life. That this was Pilate's intention in ordering the scourging is clear from a comparison of St. John's narrative with St. Luke's (xxiii. 22).

1. *Then therefore* (because his previous attempts had failed) *Pilate took Jesus and scourged him.* This scourging was not the more merciful one of the Jewish law, strictly limited to forty stripes, "lest thy brother depart shamefully torn before thy eyes" (Deut. xxv. 3), and in practice, to avoid all danger of exceeding, restricted to thirty-nine stripes, but an unmeasured scourging with the "horrible flagellum" (Horace, Sat. i. 3, 119) of the Romans—a punishment so severe that it was sometimes fatal. Of the scourging St. John uses the verb μαστιγόω, but St. Matthew (xxvii. 26) and St. Mark (xv. 15) use the verb φραγελλόω, a verb derived from the Latin 'flagellum.' The flagellum was made of cords or leathern thongs, with knots of hard wood or bone or bronze. With hands tied and back bent, our Lord would have been bound to a column in front of the prætorium. Then He was led back to the prætorium, was decked out as a mockery-king, and made the object of ribald jesting.

2. *Platting a crown of thorns.* That is, 'making a royal diadem out of thorns' (ἐξ ἀκανθῶν). What was the species of thorn it is impossible to determine; but certainly not, as the name would seem to suggest, the acanthus, for St. John (v. 5) calls the crown of thorns ἀκάνθινον στέφανον (as does St. Mark xv. 17), an adjective which means 'thorny,' and is never used with reference to the acanthus, as though denoting what is made of the acanthus. Besides, it would be

upon his head: and they put on him a purple garment.
3 And they came to him, and said: Hail, king of the Jews:
4 and they gave him blows. Pilate therefore went forth again, and saith to them: Behold I bring him forth unto you, that you may know that I find no cause in him.
5 (Jesus therefore came forth bearing the crown of thorns, and the purple garment.) And he saith to them: Behold
6 the Man. When the chief priests therefore and the servants had seen him, they cried out, saying: Crucify him, crucify him. Pilate saith to them: Take him you, and crucify
7 him; for I find no cause in him. The Jews answered him: We have a law; and according to the law he ought

necessary to read ἀκάνθων (from ἄκανθος = the acanthus) instead of ἀκανθῶν (from ἄκανθα = thorn, brier).

a purple garment. The term translated purple denotes a bright, rich colour, not necessarily purple. We know from St. Matthew (xxvii. 28) that the garment was a crimson military cloak - the sagum. Kings and emperors wore the sagum, only in their case it was longer and of a finer material.

3. *And they came to him,* or kept coming to Him, one by one, bending the knee in mock obeisance (see Matt. xxvii. 29). St. Matthew also adds that having spat upon Him, they kept hitting Him on the head with the reed, which they had before put as a sceptre into His hand.

gave him blows (ῥαπίσματα, as in xviii. 22). Pilate had ordered the scourging, and had permitted the contumelious treatment which followed, with a hope of awakening the compassion of the Jews.

5. *Behold the Man.* Better, 'Look you, (here is) the man.' One glance ought to have sufficed to disarm suspicion and to inspire pity. But the spectacle only goaded the Jewish leaders to greater frenzy.

6. *The chief-priests . . . and the servants* (= officers) *. . . cried out* (i.e., with a loud shout), *saying: Crucify! Crucify!* (see Greek, which omits pronoun). Their obstinate fury irritates Pilate, who now fairly loses his temper, and replies, "Take him you," i.e., 'if you will insist upon His crucifixion, crucify Him yourselves; I will not, for I find no cause in Him' (cf. xviii. 31). At this the Jews adroitly change their ground and put forward another argument, legally valid in form, and quite in conformity with Roman policy. According to Roman policy, Pilate is bound to respect the Jewish law. The leaders, therefore, urge that by the authority of their law Jesus ought to die as being a blasphemer.

7. *Because he made himself the Son of God.* The Jews had rightly understood those words in their deeper, fuller meaning as explained by our Lord Himself (see v. 18, viii. 58,, x. 33). Pilate had already been vaguely disturbed by our Lord's impressiveness (see on xviii. 37),

to die, because he made himself the Son of God. When **8**
Pilate therefore had heard this saying, he feared the more.
And he entered into the hall again, and he said to Jesus: **9**
Whence art thou? But Jesus gave him no answer. Pilate **10**
therefore saith to him: Speakest thou not to me? knowest
thou not that I have power to crucify thee, and I have
power to release thee? Jesus answered: Thou shouldest **11**
not have any power against me, unless it were given thee

and by the strange dream and vehement warning of his own wife (Matt. xxvii. 19). And now, hearing of our Lord's startling claim, "He feared the more," *i.e.*, to condemn Him to death.

9. *He entered into the hall again.* Pilate returned to the prætorium, taking our Lord with him for a private audience, or a further examination on account of the fresh charge.

Whence art thou? The question corresponds to the charge of claiming to be the Son of God (*v.* 7). Of course, Pilate did not comprehend the true meaning of the phrase 'Son of God,' but, as a pagan, he might understand that Christ claimed to be the offspring of a divinity. He therefore asks our Lord for a declaration on this point, whether He were of human or of Divine origin.

Jesus gave him no answer. To refuse an answer was like a legal admission of the charge. Jesus was the Son of God. But how could Pilate understand this, even if an answer had been given? Our Lord, too, had already answered sufficient to enable Pilate to give a just judgment. Such silence intensifies Pilate's eager feeling. By words now of hope, and now of fear, he urges Christ to reply. Would He not speak? Did He not know that Pilate had the power to release Him or to crucify Him? (In the best MSS. 'to release' comes first, and 'to crucify' second).

11. *Thou shouldest* (wouldest) *not*. Yes, Pilate had power; but neither from himself nor an absolute power. It came from, and was dependent upon, a Higher Will (ἄνωθεν, 'from above': see on iii. 31). It was a trust not to be abused. Pilate might abuse, and the abuse be permitted—to that permission Jesus voluntarily submitted.

unless it were given (ἦν δεδομένον). The neuter cannot agree with 'power,' which is feminine. The sense is not 'unless it (the power) were given,' but, quite impersonally. 'Thou wouldest not have power over Me unless it were given thee from above to have such power.'

Therefore (for this cause) *he that hath delivered me to thee, hath the greater sin.* The nexus is very obscure, and has been variously explained. A simple explanation is this: Since power is a trust from above, its abuse is a sin. That sin Pilate was committing. But Israel and its leaders, who had abused the power of the law of God to betray our Lord, well knew whence that power came and to Whom they were responsible for its exercise. Therefore they had the greater sin (see Eders., l.c. p. 599).

from above. Therefore he that hath delivered me to thee,
12 hath the greater sin. And from thenceforth Pilate sought
to release him. But the Jews cried out, saying: If thou
release this man, thou art not Cæsar's friend. For whoso-
13 ever maketh himself a king, speaketh against Cæsar. Now
when Pilate had heard these words, he brought Jesus forth;
and sat down in the judgment-seat, in the place that is
14 called Lithostrotos, and in Hebrew Gabbatha. And it was

12. *Thenceforth* (ἐκ τούτου: better, 'thereupon': see note on vi.
67) *Pilate sought* (ἐζήτει, impf., because the attempt, though made,
remained ineffectual) *to release him*. He therefore at once went outside (see v. 13), and evidently announced his intention of setting our
Lord free. But his courage failed before the frenzied outburst of the
Jews, who fiercely warned him that if he set Christ free he would himself be involved in the charge of treason. The threat of such a danger
altogether dismayed Pilate; the Jews hated him for the bloody stern-
ness of his administration; he was not in high favour at Rome, where
his patron Sejanus was declining steadily to execution; and he knew
that under Tiberius, now morbidly suspicious, a mere charge of treason
meant almost certain death. He therefore yielded, and proceeded to
pass formal sentence on our Lord.

13. *Judgment-seat.* The 'judgment-seat' (βῆμα) was a portable
tribunal which was taken about by a Roman magistrate, and placed
wherever he directed.

Lithostrotos, from λίθος and the verbal adjective στρωτός (= spread,
paved), means "paved with stones," but substantively a 'mosaic,' a
'pavement.' From its outlook over the city the place was also called,
in Aramaic, Gabbatha (= hill, eminence). This Hebrew (Aramaic)
name of a definite spot shows that the Greek Lithostrotos does not
denote the portable mosaic work which Roman generals sometimes
carried with them (Suetonius, 'Cæsar,' 46).

sat down in the judgment-seat (ἐκάθισεν). The verb καθίζειν is also
a transitive verb, and some take it transitively here, 'he brought Jesus
forth, and set him in the judgment-seat . . . and he saith to the Jews:
Behold your king.' This is a not altogether improbable rendering.
But the rendering 'he sat down' is far more probable. In the N. T.
the verb is usually intransitive; it is intransitive in all the other
passages where it is used by St. John (viii. 2, xii. 14; Apoc. iii. 21,
xx. 4); the context implies that Pilate was now about to pass formal
sentence on our Lord, and would naturally ascend the tribunal; for a
transitive meaning the insertion of the pronoun (ἐκάθισεν αὐτόν) would
obviously be expected.

14. *The paraseeve of the pasch, i.e.*, the day of preparation for the
Pasch (see on xiii. 1).

about the sixth hour. According to St. Mark's narrative, "It was
the third hour, and they crucified him. . . . And when the sixth hour

the parasceve of the pasch, about the sixth hour, and he was come there was darkness over the whole earth until the ninth hour" (xv. 25, 33). From this it is evident either that the two evangelists do not follow the same system of reckoning the hours (see on i. 39), or that a copyist's error has crept into one of the two Gospels. We cannot accept the very common hypothesis of a copyist's error. It is quite true that, if the ancient sign for the numeral three was Γ, and the sign for six was F, one might often be taken for the other; but it is hard to believe that the same error should have crept into so many independent authorities as to have infected almost all the best MSS. and the most ancient versions. Some ancient authorities, it is true, give 'the third hour' in the text of St. John; but in some instances this reading is demonstrably an attempt to bring the text of St. John into harmony with that of St. Mark. In these circumstances we do not feel warranted in accepting this very facile solution, which compels us to alter the text of St. John's Gospel. The difficulty, after all, is not a formidable one, and arises chiefly from our modern familiarity with clocks and watches, and a scientific precision in counting minutes and seconds. Ordinary people in ancient times designated the hours with a generous largeness of spirit, as ordinary people in Ireland still generously compute mileage. To reckon the hours of the day the Jews had only three fixed points—sunrise, mid-day, and sunset. The hours, as we before said, varied considerably in length. Twelve hours were reckoned between sunrise and sunset on the shortest day in winter, as well as on the longest day in summer. To name an hour a man had to guess vaguely at this or that twelfth part of the total sunlight. So necessarily indeterminate was the mode of reckoning the hours that witnesses were legally held not to disagree if one said the third hour and another said the fifth, because both hours were on the same side of mid-day; but the witnesses were held to disagree if one said the fifth hour and another said the seventh, because these hours were on different sides of mid-day. Outside the three fixed points all reckoning of hours was large and liberal. The language of both evangelists would thus correspond to any point from about 9.30 to 11.30 a.m.

This reckoning of the hours must not be confused with the limits of each day. Romans, as well as Jews, counted the hours from sunrise; but while Jews reckoned the day from sunset to sunset, Romans reckoned from midnight to midnight. Pliny says, "Ipsum diem alii aliter observavere. Babylonii inter duos solis exortus, Athenienses inter duos occasus, Umbri a meridie in meridiem, vulgus omne a luce ad tenebras, sacerdotes romani et qui diem finiere civilem, item Ægyptii et Hipparchus a media nocte in mediam" (Nat. Hist. ii. 79 [77]): see Knabenbauer, 'St. Mark,' pp. 414-418.

Behold your king. Pilate, irritated at being forced to act against his own conviction and his undefined sense of fear, utters these words in a spirit of angry scorn—scorn, not of our Lord, but of the Jews. The blow went home, as the fierce tumultuous shout of the Jews plainly showed.

saith to the Jews: Behold your king. But they cried out: Away with him, away with him, crucify him. Pilate saith to them: Shall I crucify your king? The chief priests [16] answered: We have no king but Cæsar. Then therefore he delivered him to them to be crucified. And they took Jesus, and led him forth.

Death and Burial.

(VERS. 17-42.)

[17] And bearing his own cross he went forth to that place

15. *But they.* Better, 'these therefore.'
Shall I crucify? Better, 'Your king shall I crucify?' Another touch of Pilate's bitter irony, which goaded the chief-priests to make an open declaration of national servitude.

We have no king but Cæsar. This was a base denial of the Theocracy, with all its prophetic promises and Messianic hopes. "With this cry Judaism was, in the person of its representatives, guilty of denial of God, of blasphemy, of apostasy" (Eders., l.c. p. 599). By it they purchased the death of Christ.

16. *Then therefore,* Pilate pronounced sentence on our Lord.
he delivered him to them to be crucified. St. Luke says, "delivered up to their will" (xxiii. 25).

And they took Jesus. Better, 'they therefore received Jesus' (cf. i. 11, xiv. 3, the only other places in this Gospel where the verb occurs).

and led him forth. This clause is of doubtful authority. If the subject of the verb 'took' is 'the chief-priests' of v. 15, still they acted through the Roman soldiery (v. 23).

17. *And* (Himself) *bearing his own cross.* St. John omits the incident of Simon of Cyrene, as being already well known.

he went forth. Arrayed again in His own garments, and bearing the cross, He went forth (outside the city) to the place of execution. "Jesus suffered without the gate" (Heb. xiii. 12.) Three kinds of cross were in use: the so-called St. Andrew's cross (✗, crux decussata), the cross in the form of a T (crux commissa), and the ordinary Latin cross (✚, crux immissa). Since the cross of our Lord bore at its head the board with the threefold inscription; it was most probably a Latin cross, which gave most facility for the affixing.

Ordinarily, the procession was headed by the centurion, or preceded by one who proclaimed the nature of the crime, and carried a white wooden board, on which it was written (see Eders., l.c., p. 602).

which is called Calvary (κρανίον = skull). This name cannot have been derived from the skulls which lay about, since such exposure would have been unlawful, and would have occasioned a deal of levitical

which is called Calvary, but in Hebrew Golgotha. Where 18
they crucified him, and with him two others, one on each

defilement, but must have been derived from the skull-like shape and
appearance of the place. It was "nigh to the city" (*v.* 20), and
became the place of Christ's burial (*vv.* 41, 42). By Christian
tradition, most ancient and unbroken, its site is fixed with certainty
within the walls of the modern city, and at the Church of the Holy
Sepulchre.

Conder accepts the statement of modern Jews who point out the site
at the cliff, north of the Damascus Gate, where is a cave now called
'Jeremiah's Grotto' ('Handbook to the Bible'). This identification,
like others which have been suggested, is purely fanciful. Christians
were not likely to forget the site of the most sacred spot on earth. So
clear was tradition on this point that, although the Scriptural text
assigned a spot *outside* the city, and would thus have misled a tradition
not founded on fact to choose a spot outside the later city walls, when
St. Helena, the mother of Constantine, sought for the site, Christians
unhesitatingly led her to that spot, *within* the walls of the later city,
where the cross and the nails were subsequently found buried, and
where the Church of the Holy Sepulchre has enshrined the memory
ever since. The 'via dolorosa,' unless a long circuit were made, would
thus be considerably less than a mile in length. "Since the Paschal
Supper Jesus had not tasted either food or drink. After the deep
emotion of that Feast, with all of holiest institution which it included ;
after the anticipated betrayal of Judas, and after the farewell to His
disciples, He had passed into Gethsemane. There had He agonized
in mortal conflict, till the great drops of blood forced themselves on His
brow. There had He been delivered up, while the disciples had fled.
To Annas, to Caiaphas, to Pilate, to Herod, and again to Pilate ; from
indignity to indignity, from torture to torture, had He been hurried all
that livelong night, all that morning. Unrefreshed by food or sleep,
while His pallid face bore the blood-marks from the crown of thorns,
His body was unable to bear the weight of the cross" (Eders., l.c.
p. 602).

At the city gate (Matt. xxvii. 32, "going out") His strength gave
way, and the soldiers laid hold on a man who was coming from the
opposite direction, returning from his labours in the fields (Mark xv. 21),
and him they forced to take our Lord's cross. But so weak has Jesus
become that, according to a not improbable translation of St. Mark,
He has almost to be carried by the soldiery (xv. 22, φέρουσιν).

18. *They crucified him.* "The punishment was invented to make
death as painful and as lingering as the power of human endurance.
First, the upright wood was planted in the ground. It was not high,
and probably the feet of the Sufferer were not above one or two feet
from the ground. Thus could the communications described in the
Gospels take place between Him and others ; thus, also, might His
sacred lips be moistened with the sponge attached to a small stalk of

side, and Jesus in the midst. And Pilate wrote a title also: and he put it upon the cross. And the writing was, JESUS OF NAZARETH THE KING OF THE JEWS. This title therefore many of the Jews did read: because the place where Jesus was crucified was nigh to the city: and it was written in Hebrew, in Greek, and in Latin. Then the chief priests of the Jews said to Pilate: Write not, the King of the Jews; but that he said: I am the king of

hyssop. Next, the transverse wood was placed on the ground, and the Sufferer laid on it, when His arms were extended, drawn up, and bound to it. Then (this not in Egypt, but in Carthage and in Rome) a strong sharp nail was driven, first into the right, then into the left hand. Next, the Sufferer was drawn up by means of ropes, perhaps ladders; the transverse either bound or nailed to the upright, and a rest or support for the body fastened on it. Lastly, the feet were extended, and either one nail hammered into each, or a larger piece of iron through the two. (The second seems to be a most awkward, if not an altogether impracticable operation.) And so might the Crucified hang for hours, even days, till consciousness at last failed.

"And so was He nailed to His cross, which was placed between, probably somewhat higher than, those of the two 'malefactors' (St. Luke, 'robbers,' or brigands, SS. Matt. and Mark) crucified with Him" (Eders., l.c. p. 604).

19. *Pilate wrote a title.* Technical Roman expression for a public inscription, particularly for the tablets, naming the criminal and his offence. It was intended to be set over the cross. Pilate, who was not present at the crucifixion (Mark xv. 43, 44), had worded the title maliciously, so as to deride the Jews and to avenge himself on them. It was written in three languages, so that it could be read by everybody, including foreigners. St. John doubtless gives us the exact wording of the title; the other evangelists record its substance.

20. *Many of the Jews did read.* Thousands came up for the Feast of the Pasch.

21. *Then the chief-priests.* Better, 'the chief-priests therefore.' They had brought the charge against our Lord that He had claimed the royal dignity; they had forced Pilate to condemn Him: and now they find themselves derided before thousands, with the words of their own charge. They hasten to Pilate, and beg him to alter the offensive title. But now secure against any charge of treason, he absolutely refuses to change a word. "When they found that Pilate would not yield to their remonstrances, some of them hastened to the place of crucifixion, and, mingling with the crowd, sought to incite their jeers, so as to prevent any deeper impression which the significant words of the inscription might have produced. The words, when taken in connection with what was known of Jesus, might have raised most dangerous questions" (Eders., l.c. pp. 605, 609).

the Jews. Pilate answered: What I have written, I have 22
written. The soldiers therefore when they had crucified 23
him, took his garments (and they made four parts, to every
soldier a part) and also his coat. Now the coat was without seam, woven from the top throughout. They said then 24
one to another: Let us not cut it, but let us cast lots for it
whose it shall be; that the scripture might be fulfilled,
saying: *They have parted my garments among them: and
upon my vesture they have cast lot.* And the soldiers indeed
did these things. Now there stood by the cross of Jesus, 25

23. *The soldiers therefore* (οὖν, resumptive of narrative from *v.* 18).
made four parts. A mark of accurate knowledge. Four soldiers (a quaternion) would be detailed for each cross. During a night-watch there would be four quaternions—one for each of the four watches of the night (Acts xii. 4). The garments of our Lord—head-dress, sandals, girdle, toga, cloak—would be made into four prizes of nearly equal value, and given by lot to each soldier (Matt. xxvii. 35; Mark xv. 24; Luke xxiii. 34).
also his coat (χιτών = inner garment, reaching from the neck to the knees or ankles). It was usually made of two pieces, but our Lord's was a single texture, woven from above (where it fastened) entirely throughout, without seam, similar to that of the High-Priest (see Josephus, *Ant.* iii. 7, 4).
24. *They have parted.* These words are taken from the LXX. version of the Messianic Psalm xxi. 19 (see on ii. 17).
25. *Now there stood.* The small group here named by St. John must not be confused with the group of *many* women who, after our Lord's death, stood afar off (Matt. xxvii. 55, 56; Mark xv. 40, 41; Luke xxiii. 49). In St. John's text 'Mary of Cleophas' is in apposition with 'His mother's sister.' The Syriac, Ethiopic, and Persian versions, as well as some critical authorities, do, indeed, make a distinction between them, and thus number four women instead of three; but the overwhelming mass of authority is in favour of numbering only three women.
his mother's sister, Mary of Cleophas. The name Cleophas, or Clopas, must not be identified with Cleopas, sometimes erroneously written Cleophas, of Luke xxiv. 18. Clopas is abbreviated from Cleopatros (Cleopater), as Antipas from Antipatros (Antipater), Lucas from Lucanus, and Silas from Silvanus. The phrase 'of Clopas' might mean daughter of, mother of, sister of, or wife of Clopas. Most probably the last (cf. Matt. i. 6). Eusebius mentions, on the authority of Hegesippus, that Clopas was brother of St. Joseph. In that case Mary of Clopas would have been our Lady's sister-in-law.
Mary Magdalen. Magdala, or Migdal-el, the present Mejdel, on the plain of Gennesaret (Genezareth), lay north of Tiberias. St. John

his mother, and his mother's sister, Mary of Cleophas,
26 and Mary Magdalen. When Jesus therefore had seen his
mother and the disciple standing, whom he loved, he saith
27 to his mother: Woman, behold thy son. After that, he
saith to the disciple: Behold thy mother. And from that
28 hour the disciple took her to his own. Afterwards Jesus
knowing that all things were now accomplished, that the
29 scripture might be fulfilled, said: I thirst. Now there was

supposes the reader to be acquainted with Mary of Magdala (see on xi. 2).

26. *Whom he loved.* This, of course, is St. John himself. "The consciousness of pre-eminent love on the part of the Lord, true, clear, and still glowing with all intensity and strength, in the heart of the old man, is inconceivable without the deepest humility" (Meyer).

The words that follow express the filial care and protection which our Lady (γύναι: see on ii. 4) was to expect from John, and which John was to exercise towards her.

27. *From that hour.* That is, John forthwith entered on his charge, and received our Lady into his own home (τὰ ἴδια). The necessity of entrusting such a charge to the disciple John is absolutely fatal to the theory that by the expression 'brethren of the Lord' is meant literally our Lord's (uterine) brothers. If our Lady had sons such a charge would have been not only superfluous, but most unnatural. To break the force of this argument it has been suggested, without any solid proof, that St. John was a relative, his mother, Salome, being 'His mother's sister' of *v*. 25.

28. *Afterwards* (μετὰ τοῦτο) That is, 'after this scene with Mary and John,' but not necessarily immediately afterwards.

all things were now (ἤδη = already) *accomplished.* Our Lord knowing that His death was now at hand (xiii. 1), and that by His obedience unto death He was fulfilling the commandment of the Father and the prophecies of Scripture, in order that nothing should be left unfulfilled, *said: I thirst.* Many understand the reference to be to Psalm lxviii. 22, 'And in my thirst they gave me vinegar to drink,' and the fulfilment is supposed to be marked in *v*. 29. But the drinking of vinegar in the psalm is the work of scorn and malice, an idea which is not appropriate here. The reference is to Psalm xxi. 16. 'My strength is dried up like a potsherd, and my tongue hath cleaved to my jaws.' This had already been fulfilled before our Lord spoke; and He spoke in order to declare that fulfilment (see ii. 17).

29. *Full of vinegar.* By vinegar is meant 'posca,' a thin, sour wine, from the skins of grapes already pressed. It was a common drink of labourers and soldiers. The vessel of posca, together with the sponge, and the stalk of hyssop, were in readiness for the sake of alleviating the burning thirst of the victims. Hyssop grows stalks from twelve to eighteen inches high; with such a stalk a sponge

a vessel set there full of vinegar. And they putting a sponge full of vinegar about hyssop, put it to his mouth. Jesus therefore when he had taken the vinegar, said: It is consummated. And bowing his head, he gave up the ghost. Then the Jews (because it was the paraseeve) that

moistened with posca could be raised to our Lord's lips, for the cross was not high. The *they* of this verse refers to the company of soldiers guarding our Lord.

30. *It is consummated.* The same verb which in verse 28 is translated 'accomplished.' He had fulfilled what He had said of Himself: 'The good shepherd giveth his life for his sheep' (x. 11); and, 'The son of man is come to give his life a redemption for many' (Matt. xx. 28). Hence we are admonished that we 'are bought with a great price' (1 Cor. vi. 20), 'not with corruptible things as gold or silver, but with the precious blood of Christ, as of a lamb unspotted and undefiled' (1 Peter i. 18, 19). For, 'we are sanctified by the oblation of the body of Jesus Christ once. . . . For by one oblation he hath perfected for ever them that are sanctified' (Heb. x. 10, 14). 'Christ died for all: that they also who live, may not now live to themselves, but unto him who died for them' (2 Cor. v. 15). He had also fulfilled what He had said, 'Now shall the prince of this world be cast out' (xii. 31); for, 'through his death he destroyed him who had the empire of death, that is to say, the devil' (Heb. ii. 14). He 'hath redeemed us from the curse of the law, being made a curse for us; for it is written: Cursed is every one that hangeth on a tree' (Gal. iii. 13). The old law was abolished, and its abolition was declared when 'the veil of the temple was rent in two from the top even to the bottom' (Matt. xxvii. 51). Therefore we have 'a confidence in the entering into the Holies by the blood of Christ: a new and living way, which he hath dedicated for us through the veil, that is to say, his flesh' (Heb. x. 19, 20). He hath thus opened for us a way into the true Holy of Holies above, so that we 'who some time were afar of, are made nigh by the blood of Christ' (Ephes. ii. 13).

bowing his head. "Then, because nothing now remained that still required to be done before He died, as if He, who had power to lay down His life and to take it up again (x. 18), had at length completed all for the completion of which He was waiting, 'bowing His head, He gave up the ghost.' Who can thus sleep when he pleases, as Jesus died when He pleased? Who is there that thus puts off his garment when he pleases, as He puts off His flesh at His pleasure? Who is there that thus departs when he pleases, as He departed this life at His pleasure? How great the power, to be hoped for or dreaded, that must be His as judge, if such was the power He exhibited as a dying man!" (St. Aug., Tract cxix. c. 6).

31. *The paraseeve.* That is, 'the day of preparation,

a great sabbath-day. Better, 'great was the day of that Sabbath.' It was the first festival day of the Pasch, one of the two 'holy and

the bodies might not remain upon the cross on the sabbath-
day (for that was a great sabbath day) besought Pilate that
their legs might be broken, and that they might be taken
32 away. The soldiers therefore came: and they broke the
legs of the first, and of the other that was crucified with
33 him. But after they were come to Jesus, when they saw
that he was already dead, they did not break his legs.
34 But one of the soldiers with a spear opened his side, and
35 immediately there came out blood and water. And he
that saw it hath given testimony: and his testimony is

solemn' days of the Feast (see on xiii. 1). It was doubly a Sabbath.
The legs were broken for the purpose of effecting death, and permitting
the removal of the condemned, "lest their continuing to hang on the
crosses should defile the great festal day by the horrible spectacle of
their day-long torments" (St. Aug., Tract cxxx. c. 1). One crucified
might hang lingering for days. But if the crucified had in the meantime died, the Sabbath, which was 'great,' *i.e.*, pre-eminently holy,
would be desecrated by the unburied bodies hanging on the cross—for,
according to the law, they should be buried on the day of death (Deut.
xxi. 22, 23).

32. *The soldiers therefore came.* The 'came' is merely pictorial—a
rhetorical amplification (cf. xi. 48, xxi. 12, 13).

34. *Opened his side.* Better, 'pierced His side' ($ἔνυξεν$ = a deep,
violent thrust). This was to make sure that He was dead. Which
side was pierced, the evangelist does not say.

immediately there came out blood and water. If St. John had
intended to give an account generally of a natural, physiological effect
of the lance-thrust, references to serum, watery lymph, placenta, the
pericardium, and broken hearts, might be tolerable, but irrespective of
the fact that we are not at liberty to substitute lymph ($ἰχώρ$) for 'water'
($ὕδωρ$), St. John manifestly describes the phenomenon as something
altogether marvellous, and as a prodigy so great that he specially
vouches for it, pledging his own veracity as an eye-witness, and
grounding on it an appeal for faith in the Divine mission and Messiahship of our Lord (*v.* 35). Hence he combines it with the fulfilment
of two Scriptural prophecies which point in the same direction (*vv.*
36, 37).

The miraculous outflow was symbolical of the two chief sacraments
of the Christian Church—the Eucharist and Baptism. Hence the
Church is said to have been formed from the side of Christ, the second
Adam, as Eve was formed from the side of the first Adam.

35. *He that saw.* Better, 'he that hath seen.' "The circum-
stantially solemn style fully corresponds to the quite extraordinary
importance which John attributes to the phenomenon" (Meyer). 'He
that hath seen hath given testimony (*v.* 34).'

true. And he knoweth that he saith true; that you also may believe. For these things were done that the scripture 36 might be fulfilled: *You shall not break a bone of him.* And 37 again another scripture saith: *They shall look on him whom they pierced.* After these things Joseph of Arimathea 38 (because he was a disciple of Jesus, but secretly for fear of the Jews) besought Pilate that he might take away the body of Jesus. And Pilate gave leave. He came therefore and took away the body of Jesus. And Nicodemus 39

and his testimony is true (ἀληθινή: emphatically placed first).
And he (ἐκεῖνος = the speaking subject himself, presented objectively: cf. ix. 37) *knoweth that he saith true* (ἀληθῆ = true things).
that you also may believe. St. John insists on the truth of the miracle in order that the reader may believe that Jesus is the Messiah who was foretold by the prophets, for in the fact just narrated two Messianic prophecies were fulfilled.

36. *These things were done* (ἐγένετο = came to pass).
You shall not break a bone of him. These words were said of the paschal lamb (Exod. xii. 46; Numb. ix. 12), but with reference to the true Lamb of God offered in sacrifice as our true Pasch, of which the paschal lamb was a type and prophecy (see i. 29, 36, and note on ii. 13). The more difficult it is to discover any symbolical meaning in this command with respect to the paschal lamb, so much the more clear does it appear that it was intended to be a prophecy of Christ. In Christ is found its significant purpose.

37. *They shall look on him whom they pierced.* These words are quoted according to sense from the Hebrew text of Zach. xii. 10 (cf. Apoc. i. 7). In the prophecy, according to the more probable reading, it is the Messiah who speaks, 'They shall look on me,' &c. To 'look on' (ὁράω εἰς) is a pregnant phrase, expressive of regard, sorrow, desire, hope, &c. It was a double prophecy, foretelling (1) the maltreatment of the Messiah, His 'piercing' by His own people; (2) the sentiments of sorrow and repentance that would follow in the hearts of men. St. John here notes only the first part of the prophecy, and its fulfilment; St. Luke's narrative contains a fulfilment of the second part (xxiii. 48).

38. *But after these things.* This is a mere indefinite sequence.
Arimathea. Joseph was a wealthy member of the Sanhedrin, a good and just man (Matt. xxvii. 57; Mark xv. 43; Luke xxiii. 50). The situation of Arimathea is not known. Perhaps Rama (Matt. ii. 18), about five miles north of Jerusalem (between Bethlehem and Hebron) = Ramathaim (1 Sam. i. 1). By Roman law the body of one executed was given to his friends for burial.

39. *Nicodemus ... who at first.* See on iii. 2. The 'at first' = the first time, is simply said with respect to the present public coming, and does not pre-suppose a frequent coming subsequently to the first visit.

also came, he who at first came to Jesus by night, bringing
a mixture of myrrh and aloes, about an hundred pound
40 *weight*. They took therefore the body of Jesus, and bound
it in linen cloths with the spices, as the manner of the Jews
41 is to bury. Now there was in the place where he was
crucified, a garden; and in the garden, a new sepulchre,
42 wherein no man yet had been laid. There therefore
because of the paraseeve of the Jews, they laid Jesus,
because the sepulchre was nigh at hand.

Nicodemus brought a hundred pound weight (the Roman pound of
nearly twelve ounces) of myrrh-resin and aloe wood. These fragrant
materials were pulverized and placed between the swathes or bandages
(ὀθόνια, *v.* 40) that were wrapped round the body, and all enclosed
in a large winding sheet (σινδών). "The surprising quantity is here
explained from the fact that superabundant reverence in its sorrowful
excitement does not easily satisfy itself (cf. xii. 3); we may also
assume that a portion of the spices was to be designed for the *couch* of
the body in the grave" (Meyer).

The nearness of the Sabbath, now almost commencing, and the
consequent need of haste, may have suggested the proposal of Joseph,
who offered his own tomb (Matt. xxvii. 60). A garden, nigh unto
Calvary, with a tomb hewn out of a rock and unused for any other
burial, might seem most worthy of the Messiah. "And so they laid
Him to rest in the niche of the rock-hewn new tomb. And as they
went out, they rolled, as was the custom, a 'great stone' to close the
entrance to the tomb, probably leaning against it for support, as was
the practice, a smaller stone. It would be where the one stone was
laid against the other, that on the next day, Sabbath though it was, the
Jewish authorities would have affixed the seal, so that the slightest
disturbance might become apparent" (Eders., l.c. p. 622).

CHAPTER XX.

The Triumph of the Resurrection.

(Vers. 1-31.)

AND on the first day of the week, Mary Magdalen cometh early, when it was yet dark, unto the sepulchre: and she saw the stone taken away from the sepulchre. She ran therefore, and cometh to Simon Peter, 2 and to the other disciple whom Jesus loved, and saith to

It is impossible, even by combining the details furnished by all the four evangelists, to reproduce a complete narrative of the Resurrection. Each evangelist has written independently, choosing out for himself just those details that suited his design, but passing in silence over the rest. From a passage in St. Paul we incidentally learn how much has been omitted from the history of the Resurrection by the evangelists (see 1 Cor. xv. 4-8).

Incident followed incident in rapid succession. The days that immediately followed our Lord's death were days of bewilderment for the disciples, days of grief and restless excitement. As soon as the Sabbath rest was over, what runnings to and fro! What trembling anxiety! What visits to the tomb! Incidents were crowded together in confused succession, and the key to their true sequence has been lost. We shall therefore be content with simply following the narrative of St. John.

1. *First day of the week* (μιᾷ τῶν σαββάτων). The word σάββατα denotes first, Sabbath, and then 'week.' The whole phrase means literally, 'day one of the week,' and corresponds exactly to the Rabbinical mode of designating the days of the week. We may compare it with our custom of saying, 'chapter one' for 'chapter the first.'

early (πρωΐ: see xviii. 28). She may have *then started* from her home. That she was not alone is implied in *v*. 2, "we know not."

2. *She ran therefore.* Because she had been excited by the spectacle

them: They have taken away the Lord out of the sepulchre, and we know not where they have laid him. Peter therefore went out, and that other disciple, and they came to the sepulchre. And they both ran together, and that other disciple did outrun Peter, and came first to the sepulchre. And when he stooped down, and saw the linen cloths lying: but yet he went not in. Then cometh Simon Peter, following him, and went into the sepulchre, and saw the linen cloths lying. And the napkin that had been about his head, not lying with the linen cloths, but apart, wrapt up into one place. Then that other disciple also went in, who came first to the sepulchre: and he saw and believed. For as yet they knew not the scripture, that he must rise again from the dead. The disciples therefore departed

of the opened tomb. She ran to Peter and to John; to Peter, because of his dignity and leadership, to John, because of his love for Christ.

They have taken away. The possibility of the Resurrection has not as yet suggested itself to her.

3. *Peter therefore went out.* The change of aorists and pictorial imperfects should be noted in this and the following verse. 'Peter therefore went out, and the other disciple, and they were coming towards the sepulchre. But they began to run together; and the other disciple ran on more quickly than Peter.' John's youth naturally made him more active; but a vague sense of dread withheld him from entering the sepulchre at once.

5. *When he stooped down* (παρακύψας), *i.e.*, bent his head forwards through the entrance in order to look within, and saw (βλέπει = seeth).

6. *And saw* (θεωρεῖ = contemplates). The cloths and napkins left behind in the grave, and wrapped up so carefully and put aside, were a proof that the body had not been carried off.

7. *Wrapt up.* This is in the singular, agreeing with 'napkin.' The napkin was wrapped up in one place apart, not lying along with the bandages. Hence St. John, standing at the entrance of the sepulchre, had not seen it (v. 5).

8. *And he saw* (εἶδε), *i.e.*, the significant facts just indicated.

and believed, not that the body had been removed, for the facts were all the other way, but that Christ had risen—for this is the leading object of all the narrative, and, from the unmistakable signs left in the sepulchre, must be taken as a matter of course. We notice how earnestly the eye-witness insists upon the fact of the empty grave and the other signs which brought conviction first to his own mind.

9. *For as yet they knew not.* Had they already known the meaning of Scripture, they would not have needed to inspect the empty grave before believing that Christ had risen—'*must* rise again.'

again to their home. But Mary stood at the sepulchre **11**
without, weeping. Now as she was weeping, she stooped
down, and looked into the sepulchre: and she saw two **12**
angels in white, sitting, one at the head, and one at the
feet, where the body of Jesus had been laid. They say to **13**
her: Woman, why weepest thou? She saith to them:
Because they have taken away my Lord: and I know not
where they have laid him. When she had thus said, she **14**
turned herself back, and saw Jesus standing; and she knew
not that it was Jesus. Jesus saith to her: Woman, why **15**
weepest thou? whom seekest thou? She thinking that it
was the gardener, saith to him: Sir, if thou hast taken
him hence, tell me where thou hast laid him: and I will
take him away. Jesus saith to her: Mary. She turning, **16**
saith to him: Rabboni (which is to say, Master). Jesus **17**

11. *But Mary.* She had followed the two Apostles, who had run
to the sepulchre, but had missed them as they returned.
She stooped down (see v. 5).
12. *In white* (ἐν λευκοῖς). Neuter plural, 'garments' being understood (cf. Apoc. iii. 4). The pure heavenly spirits, in keeping with
their nature of light, appear clothed in white. Yet Mary is so absorbed
in her deep feeling of sorrow that her listless gaze scarce recognizes the
angels.
14. *Turned herself back*, either because in her excessive grief her
eyes wandered about restlessly seeking our Lord, or becauses she vaguely
felt or heard some one present, or because of some Divine impulse.
16. *She turning.* She had therefore, after v. 14, again turned
towards the grave. Stunned by grief, she yet scarcely believed her
own eyes, and searched again and again through the empty grave.
Rabboni. A more respectful form than Rabbi. It means literally
perhaps, 'My Master'; but the pronominal force was gradually lost,
as in 'monsieur.'
17. *Jesus saith to her, Mary.* By His voice she had recognized our
Lord when He pronounced her name. For it was then only that He
wished to reveal His presence to her. "He spake her name in those
well-remembered accents that had first unbound her from sevenfold
demoniac power and called her into a new life (Luke viii. 2). It was
as another unbinding, another call into a new life. She had not known
His appearance, just as the others did not know Him at first, so unlike,
and yet so like, was the glorified body to that which they had known.
But she could not mistake the voice when it spake her name" (Eders.
l.c., p. 631).
Do not touch me (μὴ ἅπτου μου). Present imperative = do not
continue to cling to Me. The rendering, 'Do not touch Me,' would

saith to her: Do not touch me, for I am not yet ascended to my Father: but go to my brethren, and say to them: I ascend to my Father and to your Father, to my God 18 and your God. Mary Magdalen cometh and telleth the disciples: I have seen the Lord, and these things he said 19 to me. Now when it was late that same day, the first of

require the aorist. Magdalen was evidently labouring under the false impression that our Lord had returned from death in order to remain with the disciples, and perhaps now to restore the kingdom to Israel (cf. Acts i. 6). But it was not so. Christ had yet to ascend to the Father, and fulfil His promise to the disciples by sending the Paraclete (see xiv. 16-19, 28). Mary is therefore indirectly corrected of her error, and commissioned to bear the glad tidings to the Apostles that Christ's triumph is nearing its completion, and that their own period of sorrow is now over (see on xvi. 22).

To my Father and to your Father. Our Lord had said that He would no longer call the disciples 'servants' (see on xv. 15). In accordance with that gracious promise He now calls them 'brethren,' and children of the same Divine Father. "He saith not 'Our Father': in one sense, therefore, also is He mine, in another sense, yours; by nature mine, by grace yours. Nor did He say here, 'Our God': here, therefore, also is He in one sense mine, in another sense yours: my God, under whom I also am as man; your God, between whom and you I am Mediator" (St. Aug., Tract cxxi. c. 3). See notes on i. 12, 14.

19. *When it was late* (οὔσης οὖν ὀψίας). The word ὄψιος is really an adjective, but ἡ ὀψία (ὥρα being understood) is used as a substantive = evening. This may mean either from three to six o'clock, or from six o'clock to the beginning of night. It was used in both senses. Here it is used in the latter sense (see Thayer-Grimm's Lexicon). A more literal translation would be, 'When therefore it was evening on that day, the first of the week.' It need not have been very late, even though the two disciples who had been that day at Emmaus, had tarried there till 'towards evening' and 'the day was far spent' (Luke xxiv. 29). The day was said to turn 'towards evening' as soon as the sun had begun to decline after midday. When the Levite in Judges (xix. 9) was about to set out from Bethlehem, his father-in-law, wishing to detain him, said, 'The day is declining, and draweth toward evening.' Yet the sun did not set till the Levite, passing by Jerusalem, had arrived at Gabaa—a distance from Bethlehem of three hours' journey.

the doors were shut. Hence our Lord must have passed through them in virtue of the spiritual qualities of His glorified body. St. John calls attention to this phenomenon both here and in v. 26.

the disciples, i.e., 'the eleven, and those that were with them' (Luke xxiv. 33). Thomas alone of the Apostles was absent (v. 24). By the phrases 'the Eleven,' 'the Twelve,' is not meant the exact

the week, and the doors were shut, where the disciples were gathered together for fear of the Jews, Jesus came and stood in the midst, and said to them: Peace be to you. And when he had said this, he shewed them his hands, and his side. The disciples therefore were glad, when they saw the Lord. He said therefore to them again: Peace be to you. As the Father hath sent me, I also send you. When he had said this, he breathed on them; and he said to them: Receive ye the Holy Ghost: whose sins you shall forgive, they are forgiven them: and

number specified, but the Apostolic community. They bear the name of 'the Twelve,' although Judas has left them.

20. *He shewed them.* A glorified body does not cease to be a true human body, although it may supernaturally be able to rise superior to the ordinary conditions of matter. The 'shewing' is described more definitely by St. Luke (xxiv. 39): "Handle and see, for a spirit hath not flesh and bones as you see me to have." Our Lord's sudden appearance in their midst led the disciples to think it was the apparition of a spirit.

were glad: see on xvi. 22.

21. *As the Father hath sent me.* Christ had been sent with power and authority by the Father, and now He empowers the Apostles to carry on His work after Him. These words were addressed to 'the Eleven,' not to those that were with them (see Matt. xxviii. 16-20).

I also send you. The present tense here used is what is called the 'constant present,' and it denotes an action of indefinite duration. Cf. 'I am with you all days, even to the consummation of the world' (Matt. xxviii. 20). The office thus committed to the Apostles was therefore to be continued through those to whom the Apostles should afterwards entrust it.

22. *He breathed on them.* The verb here used (ἐνεφύσησε) is employed in Genesis (ii. 7) to describe the effective in-breathing of God by which man received a life-principle, raising him above all other living creatures on earth. What inward life-principle is now given to the Apostles is immediately explained.

Receive ye the Holy Ghost. The full and perfect communication of the Holy Ghost, with all its accompanying visible wonders, was reserved till the day of Pentecost (see on vii. 39); but here our Lord, by an expressive outward rite, inwardly bestows upon the Apostles the power of the Holy Spirit for a definite specific purpose. That specific purpose is plainly declared.

23. *Whose sins you shall forgive.* In this verse the verbs "*are forgiven*," "*are retained*," should be, according to the better attested reading, in the perfect tense. Literally, then, the verse runs thus: 'If you forgive any one's sins, they have been (=they are ipso facto) forgiven to them:

⁲⁴ whose *sins* you shall retain, they are retained. Now Thomas, one of the twelve, who is called Didymus, was ²⁵ not with them when Jesus came. The other disciples therefore said to him : We have seen the Lord. But he said to them : Except I shall see in his hands the print of the nails, and put my finger into the place of the nails, ²⁶ and put my hand into his side, I will not believe. And after eight days, again his disciples were within, and Thomas with them. Jesus cometh, the doors being shut,

if you retain any one's, they have been (= are ipso facto) retained.' This wonderful power of forgiving and retaining sin was an element in our Lord's own mission upon earth. Hence, when the Pharisees had judged our Lord guilty of blasphemy, because He had said to the palsied man, 'Thy sins are forgiven thee,' and when they had thought within themselves, 'Who can forgive sins, but God only?' our Lord worked a miracle to convince them 'that the son of man hath power on earth to forgive sins' (Mark ii. 1–12; Matt. ix. 2–8). And now our Lord, having appointed the Apostles to continue the mission given Him by the Father (v. 21), expressly declares that He communicates to them, as part of that mission, the power of forgiving and of retaining (*i.e.* of refusing to forgive) sins. This power, of course, is not an arbitrary power ; but just as the Jewish priests judged between leper and leper, and decided who might be admitted to social life, and who was still to be excluded, so the Christian priest judges whom he must absolve, and to whom he must refuse absolution. But as this judgment is not an arbitrary judgment, it requires previous confession as its just and solid basis.

24. *Thomas:* see xi. 16.

one of the twelve. The usual designation is still used, although the actual number has been reduced to eleven by the death of Judas.

25. *Except I shall see.* Thomas displays a critical tendency of mind, which will not accept the testimony of eye-witnesses as a sufficient ground of belief, and he imperatively demands the evidence of his own senses.

the print (τύπον) *of the nails.* Τύπος (from τύπτω) means the mark of a blow. Hence a figure, pattern, or type.

the place (τύπον) *of the nails.* This corresponds to the feeling, as 'the print,' or figure, corresponds to the sight. Very many ancient authorities read τύπον again here. But this reading seems to be a mere mechanical repetition, carelessly overlooking St. John's thought, and the strong evidence he wished to give—evidence both of sight and of touch—of our Lord's resurrection.

I will not (οὐ μή the strongest possible negative) *believe.*

26. *Again his disciples were within.* On Low Sunday, therefore, the disciples were again within, *i.e.*, in the house already referred to in

and stood in the midst, and said: Peace be to you. Then 27
he saith to Thomas: Put in thy finger hither, and see my
hands, and bring hither thy hand and put it into my side;
and be not faithless, but believing. Thomas answered, 28
and said to him: My Lord, and my God. Jesus saith to 29
him: Because thou hast seen me, Thomas, thou hast
believed: blessed are they that have not seen, and have
believed. Many other signs also did Jesus in the sight of 30

v. 19. As on the previous occasion, the doors were shut, and our Lord suddenly appeared in the midst of the disciples and saluted them with the customary salutation.

27. *Put in thy finger hither.* The invitation presupposes an immediate knowledge of the very words in which St. Thomas had questioned the fact of the resurrection (*v.* 25). Our Lord's display of Divine knowledge overwhelms the Apostle, who, immediately bursts out into an act of faith.

28. *My Lord* (= Master), *and my God.* That this exclamation is not a mere exclamation of surprise, is shown by the words, 'Thomas said to him.' It was St. Thomas's adoring act of faith in our Lord as his Risen Master and his God, and means 'Thou art my Lord and my God.' It is most unnatural to suppose that the Apostle, after the overwhelming confusion caused in him by our Lord's words, should, before making his act of faith, have proceeded critically to examine the Sacred Wounds. St. John's language rather implies a sudden outburst of triumphant faith, which followed immediately upon our Lord's address to Thomas.

29. *Blessed are they* (*i.e.*, more blessed) *that have not seen, and have believed* (μὴ ἰδόντες πιστεύσαντες)—Aorist participles used of an act which is the mark of a class (see on xvi. 2). Sufficient evidence for a reasonable act of faith had been given to St. Thomas by the testimony of the eye-witnesses. To demand the precise evidence of his own senses was an act of obstinate incredulity, and implied that every one might claim the right of demanding, before believing, some similar ocular demonstration. But having seen, St. Thomas went beyond sight. "He saw one thing, and believed another; for he saw [Christ] a man, and believed Him to be God." (St. Aug., Tract lxxix. c. 1).

In this sublime act of faith is expressed the doctrine with which the Gospel started (i. 14-18), and which, in various ways, has been constantly exhibited (*e. gr.* ii. 11, iii. 13, v. 18, vi. 70, vii. 29, viii. 58, x. 30, xi. 25, &c).

30. *Many other signs also.* This verse seems to have been intended as the original conclusion of St. John's Gospel, and the evangelist now looks back upon his writing as a finished whole, and speaks of it as "this book." There is thus no ground for restricting the miraculous signs here mentioned to the period after the resurrection. In this concluding summary St. John declares that our Lord did many more signs

31 his disciples, which are not written in this book. But these are written that you may believe that Jesus is the Christ the Son of God ; and that believing you may have life in his name.

than the evangelist has recorded—signs which were given to prove Christ's Messiahship and divine Sonship (v. 31. See xii. 37). The doctrine of the Sonship has been the theme of the whole Gospel, and not merely of the section which narrates the history of the resurrection ; and since the signs were worked "in the sight of his disciples," St. John, as one of the disciples, could have brought forward many more miracles which he had himself witnessed. The meaning of the verse, then, is this : 'Jesus did many more signs which I, as one of the original eye-witnesses, could describe, but I have mentioned enough to prove my point.'

31. *That* (*i.e.*, in order that) *you may believe*. In these words St. John declares what was the object he had in view when making his selection from the miraculous signs by which our Lord proved Himself to be " the Christ " (*i.e.*, the Messiah) the ' Son of God ' *i.e.*, in the Johannean sense). The "you" are the readers for whom St. John wrote his Gospel (see Introduction).

That believing (*i.e.*, through faith) *you may have life* · see on iii. 15, xvii. 3.

CHAPTER XXI.

The Miraculous Draught of Fishes.

(VERS. 1-14.)

AFTER this Jesus shewed himself again to the disciples at the sea of Tiberias. And he shewed *himself*

Writers frequently add a postscript. St. John has done the same here. We say 'St. John,' for there is absolutely no reason for separating this chapter from the rest of the Gospel. It has always formed an inseparable part of the Gospel ; no MS., no version, no Father has ever excluded it. All the external evidence is unanimous in testifying that this section is an integral portion of St. John's Gospel. Nowhere do we hear the faintest echo of doubt till the time of Grotius (d. 1645), who, judging solely by internal evidence, thought that the chapter was written as an appendix by the members of the Ephesian Church, after St. John's death. But there is complete identity of style between this chapter and the rest of the Gospel. All came from the same hand. (See Commentary).

In the supplement, the narrative, though centring in our Lord, directly regards the Church. In the first part (*vv*. 1-14) our Lord performs a symbolical miracle, which typifies the success of the Church as a fisher of men —as a fisher of souls in the wide and stormy sea of this life ; in the second part (*vv*. 15-23) our Lord, as the Good Shepherd, provides for the safe keeping of His flock by appointing St. Peter to its supreme visible headship. The mission and history of the Church are a continuation of the mission and history of Christ. Such a supplement, therefore, as St. John has here given us, is certainly most natural and appropriate. It forms a connecting link between the Gospels and the Acts of the Apostles. St. Luke, speaking in general terms, says that our Lord, after His resurrection, appeared to the Apostles and spoke of the Kingdom of God, *i.e.*, of the Church (Acts i. 3), but St. John, in his supplement, gives us an insight into the character of that 'speaking' about the Kingdom of God.

1. *After this*, *i.e.*, after these things (μετὰ ταῦτα). St. John's usual

2 *after this manner.* There were together Simon Peter, and Thomas, who is called Didymus, and Nathanael, who was of Cana in Galilee, and the sons of Zebedee, and two 3 others of his disciples. Simon Peter saith to them: I go a fishing. They say to him: We also come with thee. And they went forth and entered into the ship : and that 4 night they caught nothing. But when the morning was

indefinite note of time, and marking a transition (see iii. 22, v. 14, vi. 1, vii. 1, xix. 38). The things referred to are those contained in the last narrative immediately before the concluding summary of xx. 30, 31.

Jesus shewed himself (ἐφανέρωσεν ἑαυτόν). This reflexive form is peculiarly Johannean (cf. vii. 4, and contrast the passive form of Mark xvi. 12, 14—ἐφανερώθη).

again to the disciples. The 'again' points back to the two manifestations already made to the *general body* of the disciples (xx. 19, 26).

sea of Tiberias. St. John alone uses this name (cf. vi. 1). The scene has suddenly changed from Jerusalem to Galilee. Our Lord had commanded the disciples to retire thither (Matt. xxviii. 7 ; Mark xvi. 7), and St. Matthew describes their going (xxviii. 16), but St. John, in accordance with his usual practice, supposes the reader to know those details. The disciples had gone probably immediately after the Octave of Easter.

2. *Thomas, who is called Didymus.* This description is altogether in St. John's manner (cf. xi. 16, xx. 24).

Nathanael, who was of Cana in Galilee. St. John alone mentions Nathanael (see i. 45), and the added note is thoroughly Johannean.

two others of his disciples. The fact that they are unnamed would seem to imply a subordinate position – that they were disciples only in a wider sense, and not in the strict sense Apostles. If so, the mention last among the Apostles of the "sons of Zebedee" (*i.e.*, James and John), as well as the suppression of their names, will be quite in the manner of St. John's reserve about himself (see Introduction).

3. *I go a fishing.* The Apostles follow their ordinary employment until Christ has declared to them His further will in their regard.

they went forth. Possibly from the house where they were gathered together (v. 2. Cf. xx. 19, 26).

and that night. Either the failure was exceptional, or St. John marks the night as memorable (see on xi. 49, and cf. xviii. 13, xix. 31, xx. 19).

they caught nothing (ἐπίασαν). This verb, not used by any other evangelist, is characteristic in St. John (vii. 30, 32, 44, viii. 20, x. 39, xi. 57 ; Apoc. xix. 20). Outside St. John it is used only twice in all N.T.

4. *When the morning was come* (γενομένης). Better, perhaps, 'when day was now breaking' (γινομένης). As night was the most favourable time for fishing (cf. Luke v. 5), all reasonable hope of a productive catch would now be over.

come, Jesus stood on the shore: yet the disciples knew not that it was Jesus. Jesus therefore said to them: 5 Children, have you any meat? They answered him: No. He saith to them: Cast the net on the right side of the 6 ship; and you shall find. They cast therefore: and now they were not able to draw it, for the multitude of fishes. That disciple therefore whom Jesus loved, said to Peter: 7 It is the Lord. Simon Peter, when he heard that it was

Jesus stood on (ἔστη εἰς = came and stood on; see note on i. 12). The phrase is quite Johannean (cf. xx. 19, 26), and may denote the suddenness of Christ's appearance.

yet (μέντοι = nevertheless) *the disciples knew not* (comp. xx. 14). They did not recognise Him, either because 'their eyes were held' (cf. Luke xxiv. 16), or because He 'appeared in another shape' (cf. Mark xvi. 12). The particle μέντοι is used by no evangelist except St. John (iv. 27, vii. 13, xii. 42, xx. 5). Only twice besides in N.T.

5. *Jesus therefore, i.e.,* because they did not recognise Him.

Children. Not the affectionate τεκνία of xiii. 33, but παιδία, a common term of address to men in a state of service, or at work. Compare our English, 'Well, my lads, how are you doing?'

have you any meat? (προσφάγιον). Better, 'fish.' Our Lord, like some stranger wishing to buy fish, shouts out from the shore to the men in the approaching boat, 'Have you any fish?' The word προσφάγιον meant originally what was eaten with bread—a relish; but fish was so commonly used as a relish that the word came to mean fish.

6. *On the right side.* Possibly the net was already in the water, but on the other side of the boat.

They cast therefore. Fish frequently swim in shoals, and the Apostles probably thought that the stranger had observed a shoal passing near the right side of the boat.

not able to draw it (ἑλκύσαι = to draw up), *i.e.*, from the water, so as to tip the fish into the boat.

7. *It is the Lord.* Such a multitude of fishes so unexpectedly caught was, to the disciple whom Jesus loved, a sufficient indication of the Master's presence.

girt his coat (ἐπενδύτην) *about him.* The outer garment (the Tallith) was not girt with a belt. Therefore by ἐπενδύτης we cannot understand the outer garment (ἱμάτιον, or Tallith). Yet, as the name itself clearly indicates, the ἐπενδύτης was some sort of upper garment. Fishermen, and workmen generally, wore a linen blouse over the shirt, and sometimes over other articles of clothing. It has been described as a sleeveless garment reaching to the knees.

he was naked (γυμνός). The word is often used of one divested of his upper garments only; and in this sense it is used here.

cast himself. Very characteristic of St. Peter's loving impetuosity.

the Lord, girt his coat about him (for he was naked), and
5 cast himself into the sea. But the other disciples came
in the ship (for they were not far from the land, but as it
were two hundred cubits) dragging the net with fishes.
9 As soon then as they came to land, they saw hot coals
10 lying, and a fish laid thereon, and bread. Jesus saith to
them : Bring hither of the fishes which you have now
11 caught. Simon Peter went up, and drew the net to land,
full of great fishes, one hundred and fifty three. And

8. *Came in the ship.* Better, 'in the ship's boat' (πλοιαρίῳ). The
reason why they entered the small boat is immediately given.

two hundred cubits, i.e., about 100 yards. The phraseology (ὡς ἀπὸ
πηχῶν διακοσίων, is quite Johannean. (Cf. xi. 18 : ὡς ἀπὸ σταδίων
δεκαπέντε).

dragging (σύροντες) = dragging or hauling through the water.
Contrast v. 6.

9. *As soon then.* Better, 'when therefore they landed, they see.'

a fish . . . and bread. The Greek may mean either ' a fish and a loaf,
or—and this is more probable—' fish and bread.' The singular noun is
used collectively. The wording (ὀψάριον καὶ ἄρτον) is characteristically
Johannean (cf. vi. 11), and the term ὀψάριον (vi. 9, 11, xxi. 9, 10, 13)
occurs nowhere else in N.T.

11. *Simon Peter.* This circumstance in a miracle symbolising the fruitful activity of the Church, prepares us for the great commission which our
Lord immediately bestowed upon St. Peter, constituting him the Head
of the Church. In one of His parables He had said, 'The kingdom of
heaven is like to a net cast into the sea, and gathering together of all
kinds of fishes ' (Matt. xiii. 47). By a miracle He then gave point
and greater definiteness to the parable. " He said to Simon : ' Launch
out into the deep, and let down your nets for a draught.' And Simon
answering, said : ' Master, we have laboured all the night, and have
taken nothing ; but at thy word I will let down the net.' And when
they had done this, they enclosed a very great multitude of fishes . . .
and filled both the ships . . . And Jesus saith to Simon : ' Fear not ;
from henceforth thou shalt catch men ' " (Luke v. 3-11). We cannot
deny, then, what our Lord has made so plain—viz., that the miracle
typifies the abundant success of the Church, and that all this success
centres in Peter.

went up, i.e., went on board.

St. Augustine, comparing this miracle with that recorded by St.
Luke, speaks thus : " Jesus stood on the shore ; for the shore is the
limit of the sea, and signifies therefore the end of the world. The same
end of the world is shewn also by the act of Peter, in drawing the net
to land, that is, to the shore. And this the Lord has Himself eluci-
dated, when in a certain other place He drew His similitude from a

although there were so many, the net was not broken. Jesus saith to them : Come, and dine. And none of them 12 who were at meat, durst ask him : Who art thou? knowing that it was the Lord. And Jesus cometh and taketh 13

fishing-net let down into the sea : ' And they drew it,' He said, ' to the shore.' And in explanation of what that shore was He added, ' So shall it be at the end of the world ' (Matt. xiii. 47-49). That, however, was a parable in word, not one embodied in outward action ; and just as in the passage before us the Lord indicated by an outward action what character the Church would have in the end of the world, so by another fishing (Luke v. 3-11), He indicated its present character. . . On that previous occasion Jesus stood not, as here, on the shore, when He gave orders for the taking of the fish, but, ' entered into one of the ships, which was Simon's.' There also they put the fishes that were caught into the ships, and did not, as here, draw the net to the shore. On the former occasion the Church was prefigured as it exists in this world, and on this occasion, as it shall be in the end of the world : the one accordingly took place before, and the other subsequently to the resurrection of the Lord ; because there we were signified by Christ as ' called,' and here as raised from the dead.

" On that occasion the nets are not let down on the right side, that the good alone might not be signified ; but without any reference to either side, He says, ' Let down your nets for a draught,' that we may understand the good and bad as mingled together ; while on this occasion He says, ' Cast the net on the right side of the ship,' to signify those who stood on the right hand, the good alone. There the net was broken on account of the schisms that were meant to be signified ; but here, as there will be no more schisms in that supreme peace of the saints, the evangelist was entitled to say, ' And although there were so many, the net was not broken '; as if with reference to the previous time when it was broken. . . What is meant by the words, ' They were not able to draw it?' but this . . . that the Church possesses those right-hand ones after the close of this life in the sleep of peace, lying hid as it were in the deep, till the net reach the shore whither it is being drawn. . . . And last of all, in that former fishing the number of fishes is not expressed . . . while here there are none beyond calculation, but the definite number of a hundred and fifty-three "— (the definiteness of the number denoting ' the number ' of the elect) (St. Aug., Tract cxxii. 7).

12. *Come, and dine.* Better, ' Come, make your morning meal.'

who were at meat. Rather, ' of the disciples.' The Vulgate reads ' discumbentium,' but some Latin MSS. give ' discentium,' and some ' ex discipulis,' thus agreeing with the Greek μαθητῶν.

durst ask him . . . knowing. This seems to imply that, as far as mere external appearance went, the Apostles might have doubted whether He was the Lord, but that, convinced by manifest signs of His identity, they were filled with too much reverential awe to ask Him.

14 bread, and giveth them, and fish in like manner. This is
now the third time that Jesus was manifested to his
disciples, after he was risen from the dead.

The Charge to Peter.

(VERS. 15–23.)

15 When therefore they had dined, Jesus saith to Simon
Peter : Simon, *son* of John, lovest thou me more than

 14. *Now the third time.* St. John speaks of appearances made, not to individual persons, but to the group of disciples. Hence he does not refer to the narrative in xx. 11–17, but only to xx. 19–29.
 15. *When therefore they had dined :* see *v.* 12.
 Simon, son of John. (See on i. 42.) The full name is thrice mentioned, and thus is invested with "a certain solemnity of deeply-moved affection" (*vv.* 16, 17).
 lovest thou me? "He does not ask after his faith ; for this had not become wavering, but the love proceeding from the faith had not been sufficiently strong." (Meyer.)
 more than these (πλεῖον τούτων = πλεῖον ἢ οὗτοι) *i.e* , more than the other disciples love Me. Absolutely speaking it might be grammatically possible to translate 'Lovest thou Me more than thou lovest these?' and then to apply the pronoun 'these' to anything you please—to the boat and nets ; to the other disciples then assembled ; to the bread and fish. These interpretations have only to be stated in order to appear supremely ridiculous. The commentator Meyer says admirably : "Peter had given expression, in his whole behaviour down to his fall, to so pre-eminent a love for Jesus (let vi. 68, the washing of the feet, the sword-stroke, and xiii. 37 be borne in mind), and in virtue of the distinction, of which Jesus had deemed him worthy (i. 43), as well as by his post at the head of the Apostles (cf. Matt. xvi. 18), into which he was now for the first time to be introduced, so pre-eminent a love was to be *expected* from him, that there is sufficient reason for the πλεῖον τούτων."
 In *vv.* 15–17 the verb 'love' represents two different Greek verbs, ἀγαπάω and φιλέω, a distinction preserved in the Vulgate (diligo, amo). That the verbs are here used without any difference of meaning seems evident from *v.* 17. 'Peter was grieved, because He had said to him the third time, φιλεῖς με.' But our Lord had not said this the *third* time, except on the supposition that φιλεῖς is used in exactly the same sense as ἀγαπᾷς. The interchange of the verbs is only for euphony.
 thou knowest. St. Peter in reply "appeals to the Lord's knowledge of the heart, but leaves the πλεῖον τούτων unanswered, for which

these? He saith to him: Yea, Lord, thou knowest that I love thee. He saith to him: Feed my lambs. He saith to him again: Simon, *son* of John, lovest thou me? He saith to him: Yea, Lord, thou knowest that I love thee. He saith to him: Feed my lambs. He said to him the third time: Simon, son of John, lovest thou me? Peter was grieved, because he had said to him the third time, Lovest thou me? And he said to him: Lord, thou knowest all things: thou knowest that I love thee. He said to him: Feed my sheep. Amen, amen, I say to thee: when thou wast younger, thou didst gird thyself, and didst walk where thou wouldst. But when thou shalt

reason Jesus also, in tender forbearance, is silent as to that πλεῖον τούτων in the questions that follow—vivid originality of the narrative, marked by such delicacy of feeling." (Meyer.)

Feed (βόσκε = provide food for) *my lambs*. By using the term 'lambs' our Lord intensifies His appeal to St. Peter's care of the flock. The same verb (βόσκε) is used in v. 17.

16. *Feed* (ποίμαινε = shepherd) *my lambs*. The Vulgate follows the reading προβάτια, found in some most ancient Greek MSS., meaning 'little sheep.' But the better reading is πρόβατα = sheep. The phrase 'shepherd my sheep' is a phrase of intensest meaning, and includes all the elements of perfect rule, government, and protection (see on x. 1–18).

17. *Thou knowest all things*. Note St. Peter's act of faith in our Lord's omniscience.

18. *Amen, amen*. In words of solemn earnestness our Lord now connects with St. Peter's installation in the Primacy a prophecy of the martyrdom to which his vocation would bring him. All the firmness of his love for our Lord and for our Lord's flock would then be called for; and to strengthen him in that love our Lord had insisted, even to Peter's grief, on a three-fold confession. Could Peter ever forget those searching questions of the Master?

The prophecy is couched in symbolical language, which St. John, in quite his own way, has explained for us (cf. xii. 33, xviii. 32). As in all symbolism, so here, the substance of the thought must be looked for, without pressing every detail of the symbol (see on x. 3). Further, St. John, writing long after the death of St. Peter, presupposes the details as well-known. Let us see therefore how our Lord's symbolical language foretold by what manner of death (ποίῳ θανάτῳ) Peter should die.

when thou wast younger. This is said in reference, not to Peter's present age, but to the corresponding member of the symbol "when thou shalt be old."

thou didst gird thyself. As we have already seen (see on iii. 8, iv. 8)

be old, thou shalt stretch forth thy hands, and another shall gird thee, and lead thee whither thou wouldst not.
19 And this he said, signifying by what death he should glorify God. And when he had said this, he saith to him:
20 Follow me. Peter turning about, saw that disciple whom Jesus loved following, who also leaned on his breast at supper, and said: Lord, who is he that shall betray thee?
21 Him therefore when Peter had seen, he saith to Jesus:
22 Lord, and what *shall* this man *do?* Jesus saith to him: So I will have him to remain till I come, what is it to
23 thee? follow thou me. This saying therefore went abroad among the brethren, that that disciple should not die. And Jesus did not say to him: He should not die; but, So I will have him to remain till I come, what is it to thee?

our Lord's symbolism starts from a fact or object then present. The fact was St. Peter's impetuous girding of himself, and his plunge into the sea. With that fact our Lord connects a symbolic picture. As young men are self-reliant in their vigorous activity, but old men feebly stretch out their hands even to strangers, so Peter must serve Christ not only by the vigour of his Apostolic ministry, but also by suffering bondage from a hostile power, by being led to the place of execution, and by stretching forth his hands upon the cross.

19. *Follow me.* That is, Peter is to imitate his Master, even in the manner of his death. As our Lord spoke He began to move away, and Peter, taking the invitation too literally, began to follow after Him.

20. *Who also leaned:* see on xiii. 25.

21. *Lord.* The words run literally, 'Lord—and this man, what?' It was Peter's friendly interest in John which prompted the question. (See Introduction).

22. *So.* (ἐὰν = if). In the Vulgate 'sic' is printed instead of 'si.' Hence the 'so' of our English version. "If I will have him to remain." But what did the words mean? Our Lord did not explain; St. John has not explained; but he has corrected an erroneous interpretation which had been given by the brethren (*i.e.*, Christians). For the brethren thought, and St. John's great age seemed to justify them in thinking, "that that disciple should not die." But this was to go beyond the words of our Lord. Our Lord's statement was really not an answer to Peter, but the refusal of an answer; and that refusal was thrown into the form of an indefinite and purely hypothetical question. "If I will have him to remain (better, 'abide,' St. John's favourite word) as long as until I come (ἕως ἔρχομαι), what is it to thee?"

Epilogue.

(VERS. 24, 25.)

This is that disciple who giveth testimony of these 24
things, and hath written these things: and we know that
his testimony is true. But there are also many other 25
things which Jesus did: which if they were written every
one, the world itself, I think, would not be able to contain
the books that should be written.

24. *This is that disciple who giveth testimony* (οὗτός ἐστιν . . .
ὁ μαρτυρῶν). The phraseology is thoroughly Johannean (cf. i. 32,
xix. 35).
and hath written: γράψας = wrote.
these things, i.e., this supplementary chapter (xxi. 1–23).
we know (οἴδαμεν). A favourite Johannean word. It is employed
five times in six verses (1 John v. 15–20; and cf. 3 John 12). There
is thus no solid ground for doubting the Johannean authorship of the
epilogue, or, at any rate, of v. 24. As he had given a conclusion to
the book itself (xx. 31), so he here gives a conclusion to the supplement
—making it known as his own work (for this might have been doubted
by some), and attesting its truth.
25. *There are also.* This verse re-affirms the statement of xx. 30,
simply adding the hyperbolical statement that the world could not contain a full narrative of our Lord's life and doctrine if each detail were
written separately (ἐὰν γράφηται καθ' ἕν).